Library of
Davidson College

Library of
Davidson College

THE YOGI AND THE BEAR
Story of Indo-Soviet Relations

The Yogi and the Bear

Story of Indo-Soviet Relations

S. Nihal Singh

R

The Riverdale Company, Inc., Publishers
Maryland, U.S.A.

The Riverdale Company, Inc., Publishers
5506 Kenilworth Avenue
Riverdale, Maryland 20737
U.S.A.

First Published 1986
© S. Nihal Singh, 1986

Library of Congress Cataloging in Publication Data
85-62583

ISBN 0-913215-12-0

Printed in India by Allied Publishers Pvt. Ltd., New Delhi.

Acknowledgements

THIS book would not have been written but for the generous support and encouragement of the Carnegie Endowment for International Peace, in particular of its President, Thomas L. Hughes. Much of the research for the book was done during the two years (August 1982—July 1984) I spent with the Endowment in New York as a senior associate and the two trips to India I undertook in 1983 under its auspices. I had initiated work on the study in New Delhi early in 1980. Elisabeth Graffy, an undergraduate at Princeton, did yeoman's service during the summer of 1983 in digging out significant references in Soviet media to the Indo-Soviet relationship for the 1971-83 period. I have also benefited from the discussions I had with colleagues in the newspaper world in India and officials and ministers of past and present governments of India. I found the American academic community particularly rewarding to become acquainted with. Professor Leo E. Rose of the University of California at Berkeley was of special help in clarifying my ideas on the Moscow-New Delhi links while officials at the U.S. State Department shared their perspective on India and the Soviet Union with me with candour. I gratefully acknowledge the permission given me by *Asian Survey* to draw upon two of my articles, "Can the U.S. and India Be Real Friends?" and "Why India Goes to Moscow for Arms," published in the journal in September 1983 and July 1984 respectively. My thanks also go to Janet Y. Scheldt for her patience in deciphering my handwriting; her mastery of that wonderful boon, the word processor, must be the envy of every writer.

Introduction

THIS is an historical narrative of Indo-Soviet relations from Indian independence in 1947 to the present day, with a brief speculative look at the future. I chose the narrative, rather than the purely analytical, form to bring out the flavour of these relations, their dynamics and the political events and climate in India that have shaped them. The last element tends to get somewhat neglected in most accounts of the Moscow-New Delhi relationship. Yet, as the reader will discover for himself, domestic circumstances have played a major role in sustaining what has become the most important aspect of India's external policy.

It is, of course, an India-centred account although I have drawn upon my experiences as a foreign correspondent in Pakistan (in rather unique circumstances) and the Soviet Union, and on Pakistani, Chinese, Soviet and American sources, published and otherwise, to attempt to give all sides of the picture. The fact remains, however, that I have had greater access to, and understanding of, Indian policy-makers than those from the Soviet Union or other countries, particularly as political correspondent of *The Statesman*, later as editor of that newspaper, and, still later, as editor of *The Indian Express*.

The Soviet authorities, in their wisdom, did not permit me to revisit Moscow. I had applied for a visa in the fall of 1983 to the Soviet Embassy in Washington, D.C., and through the External Affairs Ministry in New Delhi. While based in Moscow for *The Statesman* in the late Sixties, I had not endeared myself to the Soviets by my sympathetic but critical dispatches. I had on one occasion been told by an official of the Press Department of the Soviet Foreign Ministry that I was "worse than *The New York Times* and the London *Times*." My dispatches in *The Statesman* did, indeed, present a striking contrast to the flow of sugary words that have traditionally emanated from committed Indian correspondents based in Moscow. Although major Indian newspapers reproduce at some length Western critiques of Soviet developments, the Soviet authorities perhaps felt that an Indian writing critical pieces out of Moscow had greater credibility at home and hence was doubly reprehensible.

Later, I blotted my copybook, in Soviet eyes, by advocating the vigorous pursuit of the China option while looking critically at aspects of the Indo-Soviet relationship in commentaries I wrote over the years for *The Statesman, The Indian Express* and the fortnightly news magazine *India Today*. The organ of the pro-Moscow Communist Party of India, *New Age*, once chose to question my patriotism in launching an attack on me.

I have, however, tried not to let the less than generous treatment I have received at the hands of the Soviet authorities colour my assessment of the Indo-Soviet relationship. It is for the reader to judge how far I have been successful. Some of my countrymen will not agree with my view that this relationship has reached a dangerous stage and needs a close, hard look.

Contents

Acknowledgements			v
Introduction			vii
Chapter One	:	THE NEHRU ERA	1
Chapter Two	:	CHINA	23
Chapter Three	:	AFTER NEHRU	42
Chapter Four	:	THE TREATY	60
Chapter Five	:	A WAR	83
Chapter Six	:	AFTER THE WAR	99
Chapter Seven	:	JANATA	123
Chapter Eight	:	AFGHANISTAN—I	150
Chapter Nine	:	AFGHANISTAN—II	180
Chapter Ten	:	TURMOIL	205
Chapter Eleven	:	PROSPECTS	225
Chapter Twelve	:	EPILOGUE	243
References			251
Index			319

Chapter One

THE NEHRU ERA

INDEPENDENCE came to India in August 1947. But when the British finally decided to give up the brightest jewel in their empire, it was on the basis of a compromise: partition of the subcontinent between a Hindu-majority India and a Muslim Pakistan, the latter consisting of an eastern and a western wing divided by 1,000 miles of Indian territory.

The Indian National Congress, the movement that led India to freedom, accepted the compromise reluctantly, over the objections of Mahatma Gandhi, the seer, saint and politician rolled into one. The Father of the Nation, as he came to be called, had transformed the Congress, a timid middle-class organization, into a mass movement.

Even while the Mahatma was leading his country to freedom, a brilliant Muslim lawyer, M.A. Jinnah, was galvanizing his co-religionists behind the demand for a separate nation, Pakistan. The mainspring of the demand was the fear that as a perennial minority, Muslims would never get full justice from the Hindu majority in an independent India.

Before the British came to India nearly two centuries earlier, large parts of what became British India were ruled by invaders from Afghanistan, Iran and further afield. The Mughals subdued the people, formed their own dynasties, proselytized the populace and built monuments to their faith.

Hinduism, more a way of life with a codified set of rules than a religion in the strict Christian or Islamic sense, proved resilient. It survived through the caste system and a complex set of religious and social mores. The arrival of the British found stored resentment among Hindus against the Mughal rulers and among some of them a harking back to the glories of Hindu kingdoms of yore.

The British, to be sure, exploited the Hindu-Muslim antagonism for their own ends to divide and rule. But protagonists on both sides, with their prejudices and the legacy of history, made the task of the

British easier. The Congress, it is true, had adopted a secular ideology and the Mahatma made the reconciliation of the two main communities an article of faith—he was to be assassinated for his philosophy by a Hindu in 1948.

When Jinnah gave his full backing to the demand for Pakistan and pursued it with single-minded purpose in his negotiations with the Congress and the British, it proved irresistible for a majority of the Muslims. Both the British and the Congress bowed to the demand. The subcontinent would be partitioned, with the Muslim-majority areas going to the new state. The Congress said it would stay secular and had in its ranks prominent Muslims as well as Sikhs and other minorities.

Lord Louis Mountbatten, a cousin of the British monarch, was installed in New Delhi on March 24, 1947 as the last Viceroy with a mandate to grant India independence by the "summer of 1948."[1] And he took the fateful decision to speed up the process on the ground that the country was becoming increasingly ungovernable. The date for independence, August 15, 1947, he picked "out of the blue," as it were, as he later confided to his *Boswells*, Collins and Lapierre.[2] But that proved to be an inauspicious day, by the reckoning of astrologers; the Constituent Assembly thus met on the night of August 14 and freedom came at midnight.[3]

A British civil servant, Sir Cyril Radcliffe, was asked hastily to demarcate the borders of the two new states. He did his job as conscientiously as anyone could under the impossible circumstances, based on "some rule of thumb."[4] But after the Radcliffe Award, as it came to be known, was out, there followed widespread carnage and modern history's greatest exchanges of populations. Millions of Hindus and Sikhs made their way to the Indian side while millions of Muslims travelled to areas that would comprise the new nation of Pakistan in the reverse direction. Murderous gangs on either side made short work of these caravans of uprooted humanity.

While the final act of the granting of independence to the two new dominions was a civilized affair, India and Pakistan were born in conflict and carnage. But even before the grant of independence by Britain, Jawaharalal Nehru functioned as Vice President of an "interim government."

Nehru was the designated political heir of Mahatma Gandhi. He was educated in the elite British institutions of Harrow and Cambridge and later travelled back to Britain and continental

Europe, once taking in the Soviet Union in November 1927. He became a convert to Fabian socialism and was greatly impressed by Lenin's legacy and aspects of the Soviet economic achievement. Nehru's education in Britain, and even more his later visits, were to leave an indelible impression, and his emotional attachment to Britain never wavered.

Nehru was a curious amalgam: a radical in the European tradition, as his biographer S. Gopal[5] describes him, deeply appreciative of *some* Soviet achievements, and a man passionately attached to maintaining India's independence. He searched for his roots in an effort to revive his country after centuries of colonial rule. But the methods he adopted were borrowed from the strategy of Soviet economic planning (through the five-year plans) tempered by British liberalism and a democratic setting.

In his first broadcast over All India Radio on September 7, 1946,[6] shortly after he had formed the "interim government," he greeted the people of the United States and then referred to "that other great nation of the modern world: the Soviet Union. . . . They are our neighbours in Asia and we shall have to undertake many common tasks and have much to do with each other." On China, he pronounced: "That mighty country with a mighty past, our neighbour, has been our friend through the ages and that friendship will endure and grow." Further, he declared:

> We propose as far as possible to keep away from the power politics of groups, aligned against one another, which have led in the past to world wars and which may again lead to disaster on an even vaster scale.

Indian independence, much less the above declaration, went unreported in *Pravda* or any other major Soviet newspaper. Stalin was the supreme ruler of the Soviet Union and Andrei Zhdanov the man who set the tone of Soviet attitude to the outer world from 1946 till his death in mysterious circumstances in July 1948. Zhdanov presided over the creation of Cominform in Warsaw in September 1947 and initiated the "two-camp" thesis.

In the spring of 1947 the Soviets adopted a hostile posture towards the Nehru Government and a conference of Moscow orientalists in June that year took a negative line on India and came out in favour of the left strategy. In July 1947, E. Zhukov, the Far East expert, condemned Indian nonalignment as a concept meant "to justify a policy of collaboration with English capitalism, a policy of establishing close contact between the Indian bourgeoisie and English capitalism."[7]

Mahatma Gandhi was described in the Soviet press as an enemy of the class struggle and mass revolution.[8] Volume I of "Most Modern History of the Countries of the Foreign East" called Gandhi a traitor to the national cause and Nehru's father Motilal a most unsavoury character.[9] *New Times* of October 12, 1949 suggested that "the vacancy left by Chiang Kai-shek is being offered to Nehru."

T.N. Kaul, a junior Foreign Service officer, went to open the Indian Embassy in Moscow in July 1947. The ambassador, Vijayalakshmi Pandit, arrived a month later. Nehru's gesture in sending his sister as the first ambassador to indicate the importance he attached to relations with the Soviet Union went unappreciated. Mrs. Pandit, a rather regal lady, was not allowed to visit the Central Asian republics or even Georgia and one of the few prominent Russians she could meet was Madame Kollantai, Lenin's first envoy to Sweden.[10] She told the Indian press with some bitterness after her return home in April 1949 that she had not met Stalin "even once."[11]

After the triumph of Communism in China, Beijing was as hostile to India as the Soviet Union, although New Delhi was the second non-Communist capital to recognize the new regime. The Chinese Communists, as the Soviets, viewed India as an appendage of Western imperialism. But Nehru took great care not to pay back his two Communist neighbours in the same coin because he was very conscious of the geopolitical realities—the proximity of the Soviet Union and China.

It was in part due to Soviet hostility, as also to Nehru's sentimental attachment to Britain, reinforced by Lord Mountbatten's persuasion, that led to India's remaining in the British Commonwealth, reversing the Congress party's unequivocal decision on severing the link. A special provision was made to allow India to retain its Commonwealth membership despite its adoption of a republican constitution in 1950. K.P.S. Menon, then India's Foreign Secretary, recalls Soviet Ambassador Novikov telling him after India's decision to remain in the Commonwealth, "Today is a sad day for India and the world."[12]

Enmity between India and Pakistan was becoming a central concern of Indian domestic and foreign policy. In 1947, the princely states under the British Raj in India were given the option of joining India or Pakistan. In an overwhelming number of cases, the choice was clear enough. Where individual rulers presented difficulties, like in the southern state of Hyderabad ruled by a fabulously wealthy Muslim Nizam in the heart of Hindu India, the solution was achieved through force in September 1948 without much problem.

But Kashmir, a Muslim-majority state in the north, was ruled by the Hindu Maharaja Hari Singh. It adjoined both India and Pakistan. There was not much love lost between him and Nehru and the Indian nationalist movement and he particularly detested the local symbol of this movement, Sheikh Abdullah. On the other hand, he did not want to join Pakistan but rather dreamed of an independent state of Kashmir. The Maharaja procrastinated.

The Pakistani leaders felt cheated because they believed that as a Muslim-majority state, it should rightly belong to them. They took the matter into their own hands and sent guerrillas to preempt Kashmir's option. The raiders stormed into the northwestern part of the state, pillaging and burning property on their way to the capital, Srinagar. Maharaja Hari Singh appealed to India for military assistance.

India had asked Lord Mountbatten to stay on for a time as free India's first Governor-General, although the original British understanding was that he would also be Pakistan's constitutional head to smooth over the two nation states' transition problems.[13] But Jinnah preferred to be his new nation's Governor-General.

India rushed military assistance to Kashmir after the state acceded to it. Despite Nehru's reservations, Mountbatten added a rider. Accession would be rendered permanent only after law and order had been restored and it had been confirmed as representing the will of Kashmir's people by a plebiscite.[14]

The guerrillas having been checkmated, Pakistan engaged more and more of its regular troops, and the two nations were at war.

After about two-thirds of the state had been freed of guerrillas and the Pakistan army, India agreed to a cease-fire. Mountbatten persuaded Nehru to refer the issue to the United Nations. But instead of a general reference to stop the fighting and conduct a plebiscite, India made a specific reference to Pakistan's aggression.[15] It was a decision Nehru and India were to come to regret.

India started with a romanticized version of Franklin D. Roosevelt's role in pleading for Indian independence with Winston

Churchill. And the Indian elite, which led the independence movement, was inspired by the concepts of liberty of America's founding fathers. Although the constitution of free India was patterned on the British parliamentary system, it borrowed ideas and ringing phrases from the American constitution.

But, unlike Nehru, most members of the Congress party were insular and wrapped up in Indian problems. Nehru, therefore, took it upon himself to educate his partymen and the country on foreign policy and his concept of India's place in the world. With independence, Nehru's world view became India's.

As early as 1935 he believed that "in India today the middle class intellectual is the most revolutionary force."[16] "My own picture of the future," he wrote in 1940, "is a federation which includes China and India, Burma and Ceylon, Afghanistan and possibly other countries."[17] Although he was somewhat bowled over by his first visit to the Soviet Union in 1927, he had over the years tempered his views. He wrote in 1944: "It [the Soviet Union] aims at having as many friendly and dependent or semi-dependent countries near its borders as possible."[18] And as far back as February 19, 1927, he was to advise the Congress Working Committee, "This [the prospect of gradual domination of Asia and Europe by the Soviet Union and China] does not mean that the Chinese Republic [after Communist victory] will be fashioned wholly on the lines laid down by Marx."[19]

Pan-Asianism was a major aspect of Nehru's philosophy and world view and he did not hide his unbounded admiration for China. It was no surprise, therefore, that his first major foray in foreign policy was to convene an Asian Relations Conference in New Delhi from March 23 to April 2, 1947. He claimed a pivotal role for India in Asia, suggesting that "she is the natural centre and focal point of the many forces at work in Asia."[20]

Nehru's nonalignment as a concept of state policy was born out of his fierce nationalism, his anticolonial and antiracial bent, and his pan-Asianism. The concept also grew out of India's backwardness and poverty and lack of military muscle. Beyond these limitations, Nehru saw India's role as a power to be reckoned with in the region and world. Indeed, Nehru confided to the lower House of Paliament in September 1954: "If you peep into the future and if nothing goes wrong—wars and the like—the obvious fourth country in the world [after the U.S., the Soviet Union, and China] is India."[21]

In the early years of Indian independence, Nehru's neutrality was tilted towards the West. This was inevitable because, apart from Nehru's own attachment to Britain, the manner of the transfer of power favoured the pro-West elite. The new Indian ministers occupied the slots of their British predecessors. The civil service, including that steel frame of British India, the Indian Civil Service, stayed in place. And the structure of administration and most of the laws remained unaltered.

By the beginning of 1949 Nehru had won general acclaim in the United States. He was a towering figure and an attractive spokesman for the developing world, and India was an obvious advertisement for a functioning democracy in a new nation. But events were already casting a shadow on the Indo-U.S. relationship.

After India took the Kashmir issue to the United Nations on January 1, 1948, it was shocked to discover that instead of pronouncing Pakistan the aggressor, which it was, the U.S. and Britain converted the situation into an Indo-Pakistani dispute and seemingly favoured Pakistan. The Indian assumption was that the U.S. attitude had been influenced by Britain, and the British view was in turn influenced by a strong pro-Pakistan lobby. Indeed, Kashmir became a festering sore in Indo-U.S. relations.

Soviet hostility to India continued to pose problems for Nehru. A spontaneous revolt against the feudal Nizam of Hyderabad and his policies in the Telengana region had been taken over by the local Communists. After Hyderabad's forced integration into India, the Communists' struggle became one between them and the new nation state. The Communist Party of India was then headed by a left leader, B.T. Ranadive, and the left line won support at the party's second Congress in Calcutta in March 1948, which coincided with the Youth Conference of the Asian Communist parties. At the CPI Congress, the Yugoslav leader Vladimir Dedijer gave forceful support to the Indian Communists' revolutionary mood. It is less important whether the Soviets used the Youth Conference to give a call to Asian Communist parties to take to the path of rebellion. Dedijer was following the prevailing Soviet line of left strategy and Ranadive was only too keen to grasp it to reinforce his own bent.[22] The Zhdanov line had, in any case, been unveiled in 1947.

By 1948 the postwar polarization of most of the world into hostile camps had taken place. Much of the Soviet attention was focused on Europe, but the unexpected rising fortunes of Mao in China in 1946-47 began to turn Moscow's interest to the Far East and India. Lenin's line of temporary collaboration with bourgeois democratic movements in the colonial and backward countries had prevailed against that of M.N. Roy, the Indian representative, at the Second Comintern Congress in 1920 and would soon be dusted off for use.[23]

But the first break for Nehru's policy of befriending the Communist neighbours was achieved in Beijing, rather than Moscow. The Korean war had broken out in 1950. Although Nehru initially supported the U.S. in condemning North Korea's aggression, an attitude which was widely criticized in India, he changed his stand. Nehru's objective became the evolving of a formula for peace, and he was soon to become a constant advocate of according China its rightful place in the United Nations and the world.

Zhou Enlai praised Nehru's role in 1951.[24] The Chinese attitude to India and nonalignment was changing. It did not take long for the Soviet Union to give signs of new stirrings in Moscow. In 1952, Moscow agreed to set up a Soviet pavilion at the International Industries Fair in Bombay. Stalin, who had not met a diplomat for two years, gave a parting interview to Indian Ambassador Radhakrishnan; his successor, K.P.S. Menon, was the last diplomat to see Stalin.

A significant change in the Soviet attitude to India took place in 1952. The Soviets had previously not participated in U.N. debates on Kashmir, but in the January debate they attacked the U.S. and Britain by charging them with seeking to convert Kashmir into their colony. Nehru's initial reaction was one of embarrassment because he did not want the question to be involved in the Cold War. In fact, he informed Washington and London that India had not sought Soviet support on Kashmir.[25]

The dimension of the Soviet change towards India was to become clear only after Stalin's death in 1953. In July that year Nehru's daughter, Indira Gandhi, spent nearly two months in the Soviet Union and was allowed to visit the Central Asian republics. In the eighteen months following Stalin's death, fourteen Indian delegations visited the Soviet Union. And in August 1954 Malenkov praised India's role in helping achieve the Korean armistice.[26]

The heyday of India's nonalignment spanned the 1950-56 period. Although the adversaries in Korea ultimately agreed to a formula for peace at least partly inspired by India, Nehru did not endear himself to Washington, despite its agreement to have India as chairman of the repatriation commission. The legacy of Korea was to last for years.

Nor was John Foster Dulles, closely associated with the Japanese Peace Treaty and later to become U.S. Secretary of State under President Eisenhower, particularly pleased with India's refusal to sign this treaty, a decision influenced by Nehru's pan-Asianism. One of India's objections was that Formosa was not being returned to China. India signed its own treaty with Japan in 1952, forswearing reparations.

The great divide between the two countries came in 1953-54, with the U.S. decision to arm Pakistan. While India was preoccupied with the difficult task of nation-building even as Nehru played a notable role on the world stage, the wartime *entente* between the Allies and the Communist powers had soured into a Cold War. Out of this was born the American policy of containment of Communism.

Dulles became the high priest of the policy of military alliances to contain Communism, but Indian political folklore assigns a disproportionate importance to him. Dulles' enlisting of Pakistan in the initial Middle East Defence Organization (MEDO) that led to the Central Treaty Organization (CENTO) and the Southeast Asia Treaty Organization (SEATO), after it became amply clear that India would have no part in them, brought Washington and New Delhi to a collision course.

The arming of Pakistan by the U.S. was unwelcome to India for several reasons. One of the objectives of Indian policy had been to try to keep both superpowers out of the subcontinent to the extent possible. The U.S. not only brought the Cold War to India's doorstep, as Nehru noted, but was also striving to negate India's natural preeminence on the subcontinent. In fact, Nehru said at one stage that the Baghdad Pact and the Manila treaty were tantamount to encircling India.[27] In New Delhi's view, Pakistan's interest in containing Communism arose entirely out of its desire to arm itself against India.

President Eisenhower tried to mollify Nehru by publicly assuring him that U.S. arms would not be used against India, an assurance Nehru answered more in sorrow than in anger. Indeed, from the summer of 1954 India's drift away from the U.S. and towards the Communist powers was noticeable.

Pakistan had a troubled beginning as a nation state. Unknown to Mountbatten, the new state's founder, Jinnah, was already dying of tuberculosis in 1947, his doctors giving him six or seven months to live.[28] He died in 1948. His lieutenant, Liaquat Ali Khan, who took over, was murdered in October 1951. Pakistan did not have the leadership underpinning to evolve a stable polity and take it through the crucial early phase of independence. The army finally acted by staging a coup.

Nehru had bemoaned in the Indian Parliament in March 1950 the fact that relations with Pakistan "completely overshadowed not only much of our domestic life but to some extent our foreign policy also."[29] But for Pakistan, India loomed even larger. The Kashmir adventure in 1947-48 merely reinforced the ruling elite's belief that India was out to undo the subcontinent's partition. According to G.W. Choudhury, a former member of the Pakistan Government, one of Pakistan's foreign policy objectives has always been to attain parity with India in politics and diplomacy, if not in military might.[30]

To buttress its security, Pakistan opted for a Western alignment, thereby foregoing for a time its intense desire to build close relations with the Muslim Middle East. Besides, since religion was the only cement uniting the two wings of Pakistan, the rulers decided to exaggerate their fear of India into a strident anti-Indian plank to bind East Pakistan to the dominant western wing.

Although Pakistan remained a drag on the pursuit of Indian objectives, Nehru's was essentially a global policy. He wished to convert Asia into a "zone of peace" and persuade a China less dependent upon the Soviet Union to become a *status quo* power. It was an effort to try to insulate Asia from the superpowers and also to achieve the goal of Asia being a nuclear-free area.[31]

Both the Soviet Union and China had their own reasons for changing their attitude towards India, although Nehru's moves over Korea and the Japanese Peace Treaty, among other actions, helped in their reassessment. Moscow's worsening relations with the West and the rise of a triumphant Mao, who would certainly prove to be a difficult pupil, were two reasons. Besides, the Soviets were mindful of U.S. penetration of their southern flank.

The Chinese leaders, on the other hand, wished to use Nehru's outstanding position in Asia and Africa to present a different face to the world. They also wished to secure Indian agreement on Tibet. The Chinese continued to have reservations about Nehru; their approach was hard-headed, though friendly, unlike Nehru's propensity to romanticize the relationship.

A striking result of the Sino-Indian detente was the Bandung conference of Afro-Asian nations, stage-managed by Nehru, in April

1955. Zhou undoubtedly stole the show at Bandung and showed Beijing's moderate and reasonable face. Nehru was well satisfied that he had helped in setting the stage for Zhou's triumph because his objective had been to bring China out of its isolation in the hope of tempering its external behaviour.[32] That Zhou had his own agenda is clear from the fact that he had quietly established cordial relations with Pakistan at Bandung. He assured Pakistan that there was no conceivable clash of interest between the two countries, but that this was not true of relations between India and China and a definite conflict of interest between them could be expected soon.[33]

China undertook military action in Tibet in October 1950 arousing anger in India. Perhaps misled by his nimble-minded ambassador in Beijing, K.M. Panikkar, about Chinese friendship and regard for India,[34] Nehru wrote to Zhou protesting against the action and pleading for Tibetan autonomy. Beijing's reply ten days later, on October 30, was angry, virtually snubbing Nehru, saying no interference in Tibet would be tolerated.[35]

The Chinese reply was deeply resented in India and Nehru's deputy, Sardar Vallabh Bhai Patel, wrote to him on November 7, 1950 accusing China of "perfidy"; the Chinese reply he described as a "gross discourtesy" and asked the Prime Minister to take urgent defence measures along the long Sino-Indian border against a "potential enemy."[36] Although after the Communist victory in China and the proclamation of the People's Republic in October 1949, India had firmed up relations with the border states of Nepal, Bhutan and Sikkim through treaties, Nehru was so single-minded in his resolve to befriend China that the misunderstanding over Tibet did not last long. Nor did the Chinese objection to the Indian outpost at Bara Hoti in the middle sector arouse more than suspicions.[37] Nehru did not answer Sardar Patel, but instead sent letters to others, with copies to Patel, on the need for understanding the new China.[38]

India had inherited from Britain special rights and privileges in Tibet which made it a buffer state within the Indian sphere of influence. Despite the general Indian regard for Buddhism and for the Dalai Lama, and Panikkar's suggestion during the Chinese civil war for establishing an independent Tibet,[39] Nehru had never seriously considered the idea. For one thing, it would have negated Nehru's policy towards China; for another, it would have brought about a confrontation with the northern neighbour for which India was militarily ill-prepared.

On April 29, 1954 India gave up its special rights in Tibet in an agreement signed with China. Of significance was the *Panch Sheel*, the five principles of peaceful coexistence, enshrined in the preamble to the agreement. The Chinese were initially reluctant to include the *Panch Sheel*, did not want it in the text of the agreement and did not agree to the automatic extension of the eight-year agreement.[40] The five principles were: mutual respect for each other's territorial integrity and sovereignty, mutual non-aggression, mutual non-interference in each other's internal affairs, equality and mutual benefits, and peaceful coexistence.[41]

India made great play of the *Panch Sheel*, but a question then raised, later to mock Nehru, was whether he should not have made Chinese acceptance of the Sino-Indian border the price for signing away the country's inherited rights in Tibet, untenable as they became. In retrospect, there seems to have been a failure of understanding in New Delhi. Nehru had publicly declared as early as 1950 that the McMahon Line represented the eastern boundary[42] and official Indian maps from 1954 showed the western sector as being delimited;[43] the Chinese were aware of the change. The middle sector, it was assumed by India, was demarcated by implication in the 1954 Tibet trade agreement which specified six border passes. Nehru convinced himself that to seek Chinese confirmation of the border would be to give them a handle to dispute it, disregarding the advice of his former seniormost civil servant in the External Affairs Ministry, G.S. Bajpai.[44]

It was a fateful mistake which would contribute to the border war of 1962. The truth was that although the McMahon Line was a generally recognized frontier in the East, the western sector had never been properly delimited, with the British having drawn up several claim lines over the years.[45] Although the People's Republic had never accepted the McMahon Line, the real dispute in this sector was over a very small area, and the Chinese acquiesced in the Indian move into Tawang. The western sector was another matter.

Nehru and his ambassador in Beijing did not grasp the significance of Zhou's remarks at the time of the signing of the Tibet agreement that questions "which were ripe for settlement" had been resolved.[46] But Nehru, during his visit to China in October 1954, did raise the question of some Chinese maps showing an incorrect boundary delineation, giving China 50,000 square miles of territory India claimed. Zhou did not raise his country's claims to the Aksai Chin in

Ladakh in the west, but merely said they were old Kuomintang maps his government had not had the time to revise. Zhou told Nehru in 1956 that China would recognize the McMahon Line.[47]

The Soviets' efforts to bring India firmly into the "peace camp" were accelerating. While Soviet academics were continuing to cavil at Indian developments, Nikita Khrushchev had evolved his own programme. Nehru was received with friendliness by the Chinese leaders in October 1954 and he had accepted a Soviet invitation to visit Moscow. After attending the Bandung conference in April 1955, he journeyed there in June.

The welcome and importance given to Nehru were unprecedented for a non-Communist leader. Perhaps there was an element of competition in the Soviets wanting to show India that they could be more exuberant than the Chinese in receiving the preeminent leader of the Third World. But there were good reasons for the Soviet leadership to try to draw India closer to Moscow.

Soviet ideological modifications had swiftly followed the Bandung conference. The signal came in the May 1955 issue of *Kommunist*.[48] Nehru's *Discovery of India* was published in a Russian language edition shortly before his visit and Soviet academics were brought into line in the summer of 1955.

The U.S.-Pakistan military alignment had taken shape posing a threat to Soviet interests on their southern flank and Moscow was already conscious of the difficulties Mao and the Chinese leadership would pose. T.N. Kaul, later to serve as Indian ambassador in Moscow, records that Khrushchev told Radhakrishnan, then Vice President of India, in 1956 that "in ten years' time the chief enemy [of the Soviet Union] would be China."[49] If one of Khrushchev's aims was to wean away India from China, as seems likely, Nehru was under no illusion on this score. In 1950, he had written to his ambassador to the United Nations, B.N. Rau, during the contretemps over Tibet that for entirely different reasons, neither the Soviet Union nor the Western powers would like India and China to come together.[50]

Although the Soviets had intervened in the U.N. debate on Kashmir for the first time in 1952, they had not pronounced on the merits of the dispute. The fact that there were divided counsels in Moscow on their approach is clear from a commentary by Petrunicheva on Kashmir during the time Sheikh Abdullah was the head of the provisional Kashmir government. She interpreted his acceptance of Indian troops to drive out Pakistani-supported tribesmen in return for the state's entry into India as a betrayal of the Kashmiri movement for national autonomy. The Soviets then apparently preferred an independent Kashmir.[51] This assessment was later to change with U.S. and British intervention in the dispute on Pakistan's side and Pakistan's adherence to U.S.-sponsored defence pacts.

Nehru's visit to Moscow had been preceded by a spectacular Soviet offer to build a steel mill at Bhilai in Madhya Pradesh with a one-million-ton capacity. An agreement to set up the mill was signed in February 1955. And now with the kind of welcome he received in the Soviet Union, Nehru was quite moved suggesting before his departure that he was leaving "a part of my heart behind."[52] Of greater significance was the joint statement he signed in Moscow precluding either country's participation in any coalition directed against the other.[53]

However, the event that was to transform the Indo-Soviet relationship occurred in November-December 1955 during the visit to India of Bulganin and Khrushchev. Nehru was still wary of getting too close to the Soviet Union and told his officials that he would only discuss Soviet assistance in training Indian technicians in heavy machine-building and drug manufacture and he rejected a proposal that the Soviet leaders be shown a draft of the Second Five-Year Plan to find out areas where they could help.[54]

But Nehru had not counted on Khrushchev's exuberance and the gift he and Bulganin were bringing with them. For the first time, Khrushchev announced his country's full support to the Indian stand on Kashmir[55] and Goa, one of the small Portuguese enclaves India was later to take over by force in December 1961. The B & K team received an emotional welcome wherever they went and Kashmir became a key linkage in Indo-Soviet relations. Indian receptivity to Soviet gestures was naturally enhanced by the U.S.-Pakistan alignment.

With India's relations with China seemingly friendly and those with the Soviet Union in a state approaching euphoria, Nehru's nonalignment had come of age. He now set out to conceptualize and formalize nonalignment together with President Nasser and President Tito. Nasser was then riding the crest of a wave of an anti-Western pan-Arabism. The Yugoslavs were very conscious of the link between the Soviet-Yugoslav rapprochement, which preceded the B

& K visit to India, and Moscow's new foreign policy[56] and wished to use the concept of nonalignment to buttress their independence.

The first nonaligned summit of twenty-five countries was held in Belgrade in 1961. Nehru by then was tiring of the clichés about imperialism whose legacy had brought the new nations together. Imperialism was very much on the way out and he sought to have the movement concentrate on issues of war and peace. In this approach, he came into direct conflict with that of President Soekarno of Indonesia and others, and the Soviets added their own sardonic rider to this first gathering of top nonaligned leaders by exploding a thermonuclear device in the atmosphere. The meeting decided to send two delegations to the two superpower capitals, Nehru going to Moscow. The results of his visit as that of his colleagues to Washington can only be described as disappointing.

Nehru was an early advocate of nuclear disarmament, but he was enough of a realist to recognize that only after the Soviet Union became a thermonuclear power could there be meaningful discussions between the two superpowers. India did not condemn the Soviet nuclear and thermonuclear explosions of 1949 and 1953. But in May 1954, Nehru opposed the Eisenhower Administration's proposal to impose international control over the world's nuclear energy resources for being less than fair to India and other countries.

Nehru's own commitment to disarmament was born out of his abhorrence of nuclear war and his belief that while harnessing the atom for peaceful purposes, India should never go in for nuclear weapons. But Nehru perhaps never fully grasped the implications of the U.S. doctrine of arms control or stability of the mutual deterrent. India initially effusively welcomed the Partial Test-Ban Treaty of 1963 and signed it.[57]

Meanwhile, at the Twentieth Congress of the Soviet Communist Party in February 1956, Khrushchev had cleared the decks for the vigorous pursuit of his new foreign policy goals. In a secret speech, he denounced Stalin, setting in train a chain of events in the Communist world. In public, he unveiled the important second plank: peaceful coexistence as the "fundamental principle" of Soviet diplomacy and the "parliamentary road" as a viable means of transition to socialism.[58]

Cominform was dissolved in April 1956, but the year was to prove a troubled one. On July 26 President Nasser nationalized the Suez Canal and an Anglo-French attack was launched on Egypt, with

Israeli participation, on October 29. Coinciding with the latter event was the Soviet military intervention in Hungary to suppress a popular uprising, fuelled in part by Khrushchev's de-Stalinization move.

Nehru sympathized with the Arab cause but was not hostile to the Jews. India recognized Israel in 1949. His approach to the Middle East came to be determined by both moral and political considerations. In the latter category were the substantial Muslim population in India, his regard for the seniormost Muslim in his Cabinet, the erudite Maulana Abul Kalam Azad, and the necessity of neutralizing Pakistan in the region.

Nehru reacted vigorously to the Anglo-French attack, condemning it in no uncertain terms, although he felt Nasser's original step was precipitate and had moved to try to resolve the dispute. After the cease-fire, he took a hand in bringing about a speedy settlement and again activated his peripatetic foreign policy advisor, Krishna Menon.[59] For Nehru, the Anglo-French attack was a clear case of Western imperialism and arrogance at work. But Nehru initially passed over the Hungarian events in silence, shocking his liberal constituency in the West in particular.

Perhaps stung by the Western criticism and the sharp protest of the respected Indian leader Jayaprakash Narayan, Nehru publicly expressed his sympathy for Hungarian national forces on November 5 and condemned Soviet conduct. Hungary, however, took second place to Egypt in the Indian Foreign Office.[60] Nehru's representative, Krishna Menon, had abstained from voting on a resolution condemning the Soviets for the use of force. He did so without New Delhi's authorization and although Nehru was unhappy, he stood by Menon. Pakistan then introduced a resolution calling for a police force and U.N.-supervised elections. With an eye on not setting a precedent for Kashmir, Menon voted against the part calling for elections.

But India later sponsored a resolution, despite Soviet objections, requesting the Hungarian government to receive observers. Moscow replied by having its ambassador in Delhi call on Nehru to discuss Kashmir, "an effort at gentle blackmail." Menon was directed to abstain on a resolution on Hungary being sponsored by the U.S., but Nehru vetoed India's non-participation. Moscow retorted later that month (January 1957) by abstaining on a Kashmir resolution—unacceptable to India—in the U.N. Security Council, reversing its stand a few days later.[61]

Nehru's admiration for the economic transformation of Soviet Central Asia and his own bent towards Fabian socialism were sharpened by India's widespread poverty and underdevelopment. At the same time, he was very conscious of the basic conservative nature of the Congress party, as also of many of the officials who would have to implement policy. In his own mind, he was unclear on how far to take economic radicalism.

Nehru had, however, from the beginning laid great stress on planned economic development. A Planning Commission was instituted in March 1950 and the outline of the First Five-Year Plan was published in July 1951. It was, in essence, a modest preparatory effort containing "the essential minimum of measures necessary to get some movement into a badly stagnant economy."[62] The plan gave only a general indication of priorities.

In 1951, the U.S. became the first country to offer technical assistance to India.[63] An agreement was signed providing American assistance for the anti-malaria programme and for village community development. An early major objective of Western aid was to reduce the chances of India being forced to adopt radical measures to tackle poverty.

But in the early 1950s, Nehru's mind was increasingly veering towards a form of controlled radicalism in economic planning to dramatize the development process, take the wind out of Communists' and socialists' sails[64] and build the economic superstructure so essential to the realization of India's great power ambitions.

The Avadi session of the Congress party on the outskirts of Madras proclaimed the goal of "a socialistic pattern of society" in January 1955. Nehru took steps to nationalize the Imperial Bank and life insurance and refined industrial policy through a resolution in 1956, with the "commanding heights of the economy" reserved for the public sector. The Second Five-Year Plan was framed with an accent on development of heavy and machine-making industry. It projected vast investments and a considerable measure of foreign assistance. The plan proclaimed the need for rapid expansion of the state sector and the goal of "greater equality of incomes and wealth." It began in 1956.

The joint communiqué issued at the end of the B & K visit in 1955 contained Soviet offers of machinery and help for oil exploration and hydro-electric projects[65]. The Bhilai agreement had dramatized Soviet commitment to Indian economic development. Although an Indo-Soviet trade agreement had been signed in 1953, it was only with the signing of the second such five-year agreement in 1958 that Indo-Soviet trade and Moscow's aid took a qualitative leap.

Under the 1958 agreement, all accounts were to be settled in Indian rupees and Soviet assistance was to be paid back in the form of exports of Indian goods. India was facing a balance of payments crisis in 1958, as it was to face often in later years, and the new barter arrangement gave a new dimension to the expansion of Soviet-aided projects and trade. Five Soviet aid agreements were signed between 1955 and 1959 and Indian exports to the Soviet Union jumped from $62.9 million in 1960 to $182.4 million in 1965.[66]

Soviet aid to the state sector provided an alternative source of development funds for India. Even more significantly, it stirred increasing Western assistance. Bhilai provoked Britain and West Germany to offer to build steel plants in India on more favourable terms. The U.S. promised $87 million a year in aid in 1954 compared to $4.5 million in 1951, and more than $100 million in 1959.[67]

America also took the initiative in forming an Aid India Consortium of Western nations in August 1958. But the U.S.'s most remarkable success was its primary role in bringing about the signing of the Indus Waters Treaty in September 1960 between India and Pakistan through the World Bank. This contentious issue of the equitable division of river waters between the two nations required a major American financial commitment and vigorous diplomacy. Between 1956 and 1975 India received more than $10 billion of U.S. assistance, half of it in PL480 foodgrain.[68]

Both the Soviet leaders and Nehru were conscious of the role of Soviet aid in inspiring the West into greater generosity. In fact, Khrushchev boasted to then Finance Minister Morarji Desai in Moscow in June 1960, "We help you in order that the Americans might give you more aid. They will give you more aid as soon as we give you aid."[69]

Strains in Indo-U.S. relations were to continue, however. Dulles had proclaimed nonalignment to be "immoral," and, provoked by anti-American statements of the B & K team in India in 1955, had lined up his country with Portugal on Goa, essentially a minor colonial issue. The arming of Pakistan remained a major issue while debates on Kashmir at the U.N. brought out what India considered to be a pro-Pakistan American approach.

The legacy of Korea still rankled in America and Nehru's approach to the Hungarian uprising led to Western charges of Indian double standards, a charge repeated on Nehru's ultimate, though reluctant, decision to resolve the Goa problem by force. Besides, Washington felt that the Indian brand of nonalignment was tilted against the West. And Nehru's roving envoy, Krishna Menon, with his pronounced anti-West bias, merely served to exacerbate relations.

India's initial approach to Indo-China was cautious and ambivalent. Two Indo-Chinese delegations had been invited to the 1947 Asian Relations Conference. Nehru's policy was determined by the Communist nature of the Vietnamese leadership, the French enclaves in India, the emergence of a Communist China and the fact that France and Britain were then India's main arms suppliers.

The internationalization of the Indo-Chinese conflict brought about a change, and Nehru appealed for a cease-fire on February 22, 1954. This was a vigorous phase of Indian diplomacy, with Krishna Menon very much to the fore. Although India was not a full-fledged participant in the Geneva conference on Indo-China, which took place from May 9 to July 21, 1954, its contribution was notable and widely acknowledged.

The end of the conference labours provoked France's Prime Minister, Pierre Mendes-France, to remark: "... This ten-power conference—nine at the table—and India."[70]

Nehru and his daughter Indira visited Hanoi in October 1954 lending the Ho Chi Minh government a measure of prestige. Sino-Indian enmity later came to be reflected in India's behaviour as Chairman of the International Control Commission for the Indo-China states.

There was a humanitarian aspect to American policies. The food aid was partly altruistic. Indeed, the U.S. can claim some credit for India's Green Revolution through its other assistance programmes, particularly in helping to set up eight agricultural universities in the 1950s. The major flow of aid was also guided by the philosophy of buttressing India, a democracy, in what Americans for a time saw as its race against China. For decades, India enjoyed a liberal constituency in the U.S. that helped the country's economic development. This constituency was often to be frustrated by India's seeming contradictions and eventually disintegrated.

U.S. relations with Pakistan were guided by other considerations, but with India proving recalcitrant, if not downright hostile, it was not unwelcome to a section of U.S. policy-makers to increase the costs of New Delhi's independent policies. This became particularly so with the American failure to befriend both India and Pakistan. The concept of military "parity" (in effect, a balance of forces decreed by the U.S.) was deeply resented by New Delhi because it was a denial of what India considered its preeminence.

India viewed U.S. policies as a form of Pax Americana intended to determine how strong or weak India and Pakistan should be. Besides, U.S. support for European colonial powers in Asia, as Nehru perceived it, went against India's grain.

To be sure, India's view of the United States was not entirely emotional. The U.S. was a primary source of economic assistance and technology, both desperately needed to relieve the backwardness and poverty of the people. At the same time, Nehru, as many Indian leaders, was wary of the U.S.'s "stifling embrace."[71] Nehru shared to an extent a British upper middle class disdain of American behaviour and attitudes. In May 1953, he wrote to his sister Vijayalakshmi, then Indian Ambassador in Washington, "It surprises me how immature in their political thinking the Americans are! They do not even learn from their own or other people's mistakes; more especially in their dealings with Asia, they show a lack of understanding which is surprising."[72]

The geopolitical and historical background of the two countries contributed to different outlooks. Indians have traditionally been less concerned about the evils of Soviet colonialism in East Europe than Americans while the evils of European colonialism in Asia are an evocative issue. But it is true that Indian spokesmen have been quicker to criticise the U.S. than the Soviet Union because of their belief that a closed society is more sensitive to public criticism than a democracy.[73] Soviet absorption of Central Asia and Siberia finds no echo in India or much of the developing world.

The years 1957 and 1958 represented a relative slackening in Indian activity in world affairs. Nehru was more preoccupied with domestic politics, particularly the questions posed by the second general elections and the states' reorganization. The first brought about the victory of the Communist party in Kerala, the first time in a free election held anywhere;[74] the second saw much turmoil and showed up Nehru's vacillation on a redivision of the country on the basis of linguistic provinces.

Dulles died in May 1959, and 1960 was the year "neutralism

became respectable," as *Time* magazine picturesquely put it.[75] The accession of John F. Kennedy to power in 1961 aroused hopes in India for better relations, in view of the new President's known sympathy for India. Already, in December 1959, President Eisenhower had visited India against the backdrop of rising Sino-Indian border tension, to be greeted with enthusiasm. He signalled a change in the U.S. approach to nonalignment, doubtless heartened by India's falling out with China.[76] The close and rather brief phase of Indo-U.S. military cooperation was to come later in disturbing circumstances. But the initial hopes in the Kennedy era proved illusory and Nehru's meetings with Kennedy in 1961 were disastrous.[77]

India's relations with Pakistan remained troubled and were not helped by the successful military coup in October 1948, in view of Nehru's antipathy to such regimes. Kashmir raised its head time and again in the United Nations to exacerbate relations, fuelled by Pakistan's efforts to unfreeze the situation. Nehru had gone back on India's commitment on holding a plebiscite after indications of the emerging Pakistan-U.S. military alignment on the ground that it changed the situation. India also said the Pakistanis had not kept their part of the bargain by leaving the one-third of the state occupied by them.

According to Gopal, there was a real chance of a solution of the problem on Pakistan's terms in 1953, which was thrown away by what Nehru described as Pakistan's "mere cleverness."[78] Indeed, Pakistan has from the beginning shown impatience in trying to secure Kashmir, first through the guerrillas it sent to the state in 1947-48; later through its misadventure of 1965. This impatience was born out of the feeling that the longer India retained two-thirds of the state, the more difficult it would be for Pakistan to secure it.

Over the years, Kashmir became the symbol of a larger problem of relations between the two countries and of the two-nation theory on which Pakistan was created against India's secularism and substantial Muslim minority. The state was progressively integrated into the Indian Union and the first use of the Soviet veto on Kashmir in the U.N. Security Council in September 1957[79] put a hammer lock on it.

Other measures to promote Indo-Pakistani amity did not fare much better. Nehru first made a proposal for a no-war pact, to reassure Pakistan on its security, in 1949. It was rejected by Prime

Minister Liaquat Ali Khan, as it was later by President Ayub Khan, primarily because of Pakistani fears that it would freeze the Kashmir issue.[80] President Ayub's proposal in 1959 for the subcontinent's joint defence, apparently a ploy to please the U.S., was turned down by Nehru, who asked, "Joint defence—against whom?"[81] The answer could only have embarrassed Ayub on what could be construed by Beijing as an anti-Chinese move.

India's decision to go ahead with constructing the Farakka barrage to save the fast-silting Calcutta port became another matter of dispute. Pakistani spokesmen's contention was that the barrage would adversely affect the water available to East Pakistan. The dispute concerns the dry season and over how to divide the water between East Pakistan and India.

Chapter Two

CHINA

CHINA cast an ominous shadow on India. In the Indian perception, there was a growing rigidity in Chinese domestic and external policies in 1958. Unrest in Tibet was growing, with the number of incursions across the border increasing. In any case, China decided to reveal its hand to India on January 23, 1959. In a letter to Nehru, Zhou Enlai for the first time disclosed Chinese border claims, contending in particular that the Aksai Chin area "has always been under Chinese jurisdiction."[1]

Did China decide in 1958 that "friendship with India had outlived its usefulness"? as suggested by Gopal.[2] Or had the Chinese revised their attitude to India as early as November-December 1956 by mistaking the popular acclaim the Dalai Lama received in India for the Government's encouragement of his asserting independence? as maintained by Dutt.[3] In fact, Nehru had prevailed upon the Dalai Lama to return to Tibet despite the fears he had privately expressed of future Chinese policy.[4]

A complex set of reasons influenced Chinese actions, as we shall see presently, but events in Tibet did play an important role in the attitude Beijing was later to adopt. The Khampa tribesmen's rebellion had begun in the northeastern parts of Tibet in 1956 and had spread to central and southern Tibet by early 1959. Thousands of refugees crossed over into India. Fighting broke out in Lhasa in March; the Dalai Lama threw in his lot with the rebels, proclaiming Tibetan independence.

The Dalai Lama fled to India with thousands of his followers in March and was promptly granted asylum; perhaps the Chinese themselves were interested in pushing him out.[5] On being granted asylum, the Khampa tribesmen were disarmed and the Dalai Lama and his men were asked not to indulge in political activity, an undertaking that was not entirely observed.

The Dalai Lama gave his story of what had happened and attacked

China. Beijing had complained in the past about Kalimpong in India being used as a base for instigating resistance in Tibet and now charged that the Lhasa rebellion was engineered from the "commanding centre" in Kalimpong.[6]

China's suppression of the Tibetan revolt sent shock waves through India, raising fears of Chinese intentions on the border. There was a great outpouring of sympathy for the Dalai Lama's plight and anti-Chinese demonstrations were held and insults meted out to Mao, provoking Chinese protests and ire.

In September, the Dalai Lama appealed to the United Nations. This caused intense anger in China, perhaps leading the Chinese leaders to believe that India was responsible for the troubles in Tibet and was directing the Dalai Lama to conduct anti-Chinese propaganda.[7]

A number of incidents along the Sino-Indian border took place in July-October 1959, the most serious of them at Kongka Pass in the western sector on October 21, leading to the death of nine Indian policemen and one Chinese soldier. The Chinese began building a road across the Aksai Chin in March 1956 and completed it in nineteen months. The Indian Government came to know of the road for the first time in September 1957 from Chinese press reports on the completion of the road, although it had received some earlier reports about Chinese road-building activity in the area. New Delhi viewed the road as a continuing Chinese encroachment on land claimed by India, which the Chinese were to tell India in January 1959, had never been delineated. This was later to lead India to adopt a "forward policy," in essence to try to check further Chinese advances by positioning pickets between the Chinese claim lines of 1956 and 1960.

The Longju incident on the McMahon Line in the east on August 25, in itself a minor one involving one Indian dead and one injured, was to be the spark of a major parliamentary involvement and a Soviet pronouncement. Indian newspapers reported the incident three days later and finally word on the Aksai Chin road leaked out. Nehru had told Parliament nothing about the boundary dispute, the road or Beijing's approach to the border question in the belief that he would thereby retain the freedom to negotiate with the Chinese. Now there was an uproar.

The predicament Nehru had placed himself in was tellingly revealed in the following exchange between him and a member in the Upper House of Parliament on August 31, 1959.[8]

D.P. Singh: May I know, Sir, why Parliament was not taken into confidence earlier with regard to this matter [border incursions and Chinese claims]?
Nehru: There was not much to take into confidence about, Sir .... Without our knowledge they [the Chinese] have made a road in that extreme corner and we have been dealing with it through correspondence. No particular occasion arose to bring the matter to the House, because we thought that we might make progress by correspondence and when the time was ripe for it we would inform Parliament.
Singh: In view of the fact that the Chinese claim that this admittedly Indian territory is within their frontier and that our protest was lodged as far back as July or August 1958, and in view of the fact that the Chinese claim is unjustified and no reply has been sent to the Indian Government, do not the Government of India contemplate ousting the Chinese from this Indian territory by force? Will not the Government of India at least consider the advisability of bombing the road built in our territory out of existence?
Nehru: No, Sir. The Government will not consider that course, because that is not the way the Government would like to function in such matters. In places like this, decisions can only be made by conferences, by agreement. Countries do not, and should not, go to war without proceeding in these other ways.
Singh: What are we to do when the Chinese Government does not even answer our protest sent as far back as August or so?

...

Nehru: .... We can only send further reminders.

An interesting outcome of the now publicized border clashes was a statement issued by Tass on September 9, over Chinese objections.[9] It deplored the incidents and suggested, "The Chinese and the Soviet peoples are linked by the unbreakable bonds of fraternal friendship based on the great principles of socialist internationalism. Friendly cooperation between the U.S.S.R. and India is successfully developing in keeping with the ideas of peaceful coexistence."
Nehru expressed his satisfaction, telling Parliament on September 25, 1959 that the Soviet Union was taking "a more or less dispassionate view of the situation."[10] The Chinese deeply resented

the statement which, they were to charge later, had revealed the Sino-Soviet rift to the world.[11]

The leftward swing in China's domestic and foreign policies became apparent in the latter half of 1957 after the failure of the *Hundred Flowers* movement. Mao's visit to Moscow in November 1957 did not yield further Soviet credits although earlier credits had probably been exhausted. India, on the other hand, was granted credits worth $375 million for the Third Plan in July 1959.[12]

Attempts to patch up differences were made at the Soviet Twenty-first Congress in January 1959, with agreement on Soviet assistance for a further seventy-eight Chinese projects, in addition to the forty-seven new projects to be helped under the agreement of August 1958. But the detente proved to be short-lived and the rupture in the military relationship came on June 20, 1959.[13]

There was a relaxation of international tension between the superpowers in 1959, symbolized by Khrushchev's visit to the U.S. and the "Camp David spirit." As a Soviet Government statement was later to charge, by provoking border clashes with India, the Chinese leaders "ultimately aimed at torpedoing the relaxation of international tension that had taken place.[14]

Ambassador K.P.S. Menon has recorded his conversation with Khrushchev on April 30, 1959 on the Sino-Indian differences over Tibet. Khrushchev suggested that the cause of "this misunderstanding" was perhaps because of Indian support for Tibet's independence [actually, India had then pleaded for autonomy] when the Chinese entered Tibet shortly after the Communist victory.[15] The tenor of his remarks left no doubt about Soviet sympathy for India over its differences with China.

Nehru and Zhou, meanwhile, had traded proposals on defusing the border tension but could come to no agreement. Perhaps primed by a visit to India Khrushchev was soon to make, Nehru invited Zhou, who came to a sombre Indian capital in April 1960. Zhou proposed that China recognize the McMahon Line in return for Indian acceptance of Chinese claims in eastern Ladakh. Given the state of Indian public opinion and the views of his Cabinet colleagues, Nehru had no room left for manoeuvre. The Nehru-Zhou meetings could only agree on officials of the two countries to sift the rival claims.[16] India published the reports of the two delegations in February 1961. According to the Indian case, China had by 1959 occupied 7,000 square miles of Indian territory. Over the next three years the Chinese occupied about 5,000 square miles more in Ladakh, going by Indian calculations.[17]

A Warsaw Treaty meeting in Moscow in February 1960 provided a stage for a Chinese-Soviet clash on the nature of imperialism. Khrushchev that very month undertook a tour of India and Indonesia, giving additional aid to both countries.[18] At the Third Congress of the Romanian Workers' Party in Bucharest in June 1960, Khrushchev brought up the Sino-Indian border dispute in his attack on China, apart from such questions as military cooperation, the Great Leap Forward and Defence Minister P'eng Teh-huai's dismissal.[19]

The Soviets withdrew all their 1,390 experts from China in August 1960 and ended contracts and projects affecting at least 125 projects. Sino-Soviet trade declined by over 50 per cent in 1961.[20]

The Moscow conference of eighty-one Communist parties in November 1960 gave the Communist world its first opportunity of assessing the Sino-Soviet rift. In 1958, Yugoslavia had assumed the role of the ideological middle man in Chinese criticism of the Soviet Union; from 1960-61 Albania served the same purpose for the Soviet Union. The Moscow Declaration represented a compromise platform of "the independent state of national democracy," but the effort to paper over the cracks could not succeed for long. Significantly, the Asian parties, except for India, leaned towards the Chinese.[21]

Events were meanwhile moving towards a seemingly predestined denouement. In May 1962, India renewed the proposal of November 1959 seeking withdrawal of both sides from Ladakh, with the Chinese being permitted to use the Aksai Chin road for civilian traffic. The Chinese again rejected the proposal and set up new check-posts. Fighting nearly broke out in July, with the Chinese surrounding an Indian post, but then transferred their military pressure to the east. In September 1962, the Chinese raised the question of the alignment of its western extremity and crossed the line, then proposed that the whole border be discussed. The Indians responded by first seeking vacation of the new intrusion.[22]

The stage was set for massive attacks on October 20 at various points across the McMahon Line and in Ladakh. The attack was well prepared over months and coincided with the Cuban crisis as the Soviet Union faced America eyeball to eyeball.[23] Indian defences crumbled and it was a military debacle for India. Indian forces were poorly equipped, unacclimatized to mountain conditions, and carried vintage bolt-action .303 rifles. There was a total failure of command, which was accompanied by panic in the civilian structure.

A variety of reasons contributed to the Indian humiliation on the battlefield. The Army was poorly led and riven by divisions provoked by the controversial personality of Defence Minister Krishna Menon. Nehru had brought him home after his extensive diplomatic forays. But the major failure was Nehru's; right till the end, he did not believe that the Chinese would launch the kind of attack they did. The "forward policy" was sufficiently provocative to give the Chinese an excuse for their massive attack. And Nehru, in a foolhardy statement made at the airport on October 12 before departing for Colombo, gave the Chinese an ideal *casus belli*. He said the Indian forces had been ordered to throw the Chinese out of NEFA (Northeast Frontier Agency).[24] The Chinese had succeeded brilliantly in achieving mastery on the battlefield and inflicting a stinging political humiliation on India. It was an example of "teaching India a lesson," an exercise they were to try to repeat many years later in Vietnam.

At the time of Indian independence in August 1947, Indian armed forces were almost totally British-equipped. This relationship with the former colonial power continued for some years.[25] Despite the Kashmir War in 1947-48 with Pakistan, the Indian armed forces remained largely neglected. The pacifism and nonalignment of Nehru meant that the modernization and strengthening of the armed forces was a low priority.

Between fiscal years 1951-52 and 1961-62 Indian defence spending never rose beyond 2 per cent of Gross National Product.[26] As of 1953, the Indian Army comprised between 325,000 and 350,000 personnel of all categories. The size and deployment of the Army remained fairly static till 1956 when its commitments were expanded to tame the rebellious Nagas in the northeast.[27]

There was a measure of antipathy between the Army, the dominant wing of the armed forces, and the new rulers. The bulk of the Army had remained loyal to the British during the country's fight for independence.[28] Interestingly, it was the fledgling Navy which mutinied against the British overlords in 1946, a step that hastened the departure of the war-exhausted British.

In any case, Nehru was loath to pour much money into modernizing the armed forces at the cost of economic development. During those years Army requests were granted to the extent of one-tenth of what was asked.²⁹ In 1962, the Indian Army had three commands embracing 550,000 personnel and the Navy one Majestic class aircraft carrier, two light cruisers, three destroyers, frigates and minesweepers of assorted classes and a fleet requirements unit. The Air Force was equipped with four squadrons of light bombers, one squadron of reconnaissance Canberras, six squadrons of transport aircraft and units of helicopters and trainers.³⁰

According to S. Dutt, the question of securing Soviet arms was considered by Nehru since the end of 1955.³¹ Worried by the incidents along the Sino-Indian border in the late Fifties, India made a request in 1960 for Soviet helicopters and supply-dropping planes. The Soviets reacted positively. This was the beginning of the Indo-Soviet military relationship, and purchases then totalled the modest figure of $31.5 million.³² In August 1962, the Soviet Union had agreed to set up a plant for the production of MIG-21, which China did not then possess.³³

The Soviet agreement of 1962 to let India manufacture the MIG-21 predated the war and was one of principle. Was there hesitation in Moscow because of its repercussions on its relations with China and did the Soviet leaders have doubts about Indian capacity to produce a supersonic fighter? Indian experts say no; the doubts rather were on the Indian side, with a committee under the industrialist J.R.D. Tata recommending in 1963 that India scrap the MIG project.³⁴

India going to the Soviet Union for supersonic fighters set alarm bells ringing in Washington and London. President Kennedy and British Prime Minister Harold Macmillan conferred together. The result was a counter-offer of the British Lightning at half its market price, $750,000 apiece, and its possible licenced production.³⁵

India's decision to remain loyal to the MIG agreement was partly determined by political factors. China was a major Indian preoccupation and the Russian agreement to let India produce the MIGs was a valuable symbol of Soviet support against China. Besides, there remained doubts over Western, particularly U.S., willingness to permit India to be a strong military power. Moscow seemed to be the only arms supplier sympathetic to India's philosophy of a self-sufficient military establishment.

The initial Indian approach to Moscow for arms was to counter U.S. policy towards the subcontinent as also symbolically to have the Soviet Union underwrite Indian defence against China. India's acerbic anti-West Defence Minister, Krishna Menon, used his considerable political clout to hasten the military relationship with Moscow. There also emerged another element of compulsion in going to Moscow. India's requests to secure F-104s were rebuffed by Washington.[36]

Nehru, shaken by the scale of the disaster and its implications for his policies, turned to the U.S. and Britain, among others, for military assistance, taking care to inform Moscow in advance.[37] The two countries' response was immediate. They rushed military aid to India worth $70 million. Nehru also sought, and received, air defence cover from America.[38]

The Chinese buttressed their military triumph with diplomacy, suggesting disengagement and withdrawal by India and China of their armed forces 20 km. "from the line of actual control." And on November 20 the Chinese announced a unilateral cease-fire and withdrawal.

Despite seeking Western arms, Nehru anxiously watched Soviet reaction. India had thought of obtaining Soviet arms for the first time in 1955, after the U.S.-Pakistan military alignment came into being. But it was in 1959, after growing tension along the Sino-Indian border, that Nehru approached Moscow for helicopters and transport planes for the border areas. Indian Ambassador K.P.S. Menon saw the first An-12 take off for India on the morning of March 13, 1961 from a Soviet military airfield and thanked Mikoyan for speeding up negotiations on "a number of An-12 and Il-14 planes."[39]

The signals on both sides were clear. The Soviets, on the one hand, were giving India planes, and helicopters,[40] for military use along the Sino-Indian border. New Delhi, on the other hand, was underpinning Soviet support for its China policy. A clearer signal came in August 1962 with the signing of the first agreement on the supply and manufacture of MIG-21s.

The first reaction to the border war from Moscow cast gloom on New Delhi. An editorial of October 25, 1962 in *Pravda*[41] supported the Chinese "three-point" proposal.[42] "The question of the Sino-Indian 'boundary,'" it said, "is a legacy of those times when British colonialists held sway on Indian territory, drawing and redrawing the map at their own will. The notorious McMahon Line which has never been recognized by China was foisted on the Chinese and Indian peoples. The imperialist quarters did their utmost to use border conflicts connected with the Line for provoking an armed clash."

Further, *Pravda* warned India that "in the struggle against the designs of imperialism, the Soviet side is entirely on the side of fraternal, great China."[43]

Nehru, however, did not give in to the public mood of disillusionment and waited, although he could hardly have been comforted by the reports of his ambassador in Moscow informing him towards the end of November about the Soviets' refusal to send MIGs, but they promised to give four helicopters and a few transport planes and set up the MIG factory in India.[44] Nehru did not have long to wait. *Pravda* of November 5 repudiated Chinese charges of Nehru being a representative of the big bourgeoisie and landlords serving imperialism by declaring, "The point is that these are clashes between two great countries, one of which is a socialist state, and the other a great force in the large group of young sovereign states taking an active part in the struggle against colonialism and for peace and international security." It described the Chinese and Indian peoples as brothers and friends, respectively, and urged an end to the fighting.[45]

The only conclusion one can draw from the distinct change in the Soviet line between October 25 and November 5 is that the first editorial tried to placate China when Khrushchev was facing his biggest international crisis; in fact, the Chinese had pledged support for the Soviet Union in the Cuban crisis in a statement on October 25.[46] Once Khrushchev backed down, the Soviets felt free to revert to a neutralism tilted towards India.

Six nonaligned states—Burma, Cambodia, Sri Lanka, Ghana, Indonesia and the United Arab Republic—got together to propose a solution to the problem. They proposed in December that China withdraw 20 km. in the western sector to enable the creation of a demilitarized zone and the McMahon Line be respected on both sides except for two small areas. Although disappointed with the Colombo proposals—the feeling in New Delhi was that Burma and Indonesia had let down India—Nehru finally accepted them after a "clarification" from Sri Lankan Prime Minister Sirimavo Bandaranaike; China accepted the proposal only in principle.

After a lull in Sino-Soviet polemics, they broke out again in September 1962. President Brezhnev's visit to Yugoslavia saw renewed Chinese attacks on Yugoslavia and Albania attacked Khrushchev, criticizing Soviet arms supplies to India. Chinese criticism of Soviet "capitulationism," later to be made public, and the Sino-Indian border war fuelled the new round of polemics. With the signing of the Test-Ban Treaty in July 1963 there was a definitive break between China and the Soviet Union, with totally overt polemics by both sides.[47]

With India in a weakened state after the 1962 debacle, the U.S. and Britain tried to twist its arm on Kashmir. President Kennedy was unsuccessful in getting Pakistan to make a gesture to India during the border war.[48] Americans were toying with the idea of India retaining Ladakh with an access route through the Kashmir valley, which would apparently go to Pakistan.[49] The talks, however, were foredoomed to failure because no government in power in New Delhi in the prevailing mood of defeat and humiliation could have made a substantial concession on Kashmir and survived.

While Kennedy's presidency raised hopes in India, it caused misgivings in Pakistan and fears that U.S. Democrats would promote India's importance. They gave a fillip to latent neutralist trends in the country. But the biggest shock for Pakistan was the supply of U.S. arms to India during the border war, over Pakistani objections and without it being consulted.[50] As President Ayub was to confirm later, he felt that the U.S. could have imposed a Kashmir solution on India as the price of its arms supply.[51]

As Sino-Indian relations deteriorated, Pakistan saw its opportunity to buttress its relationship with China. The Chinese had harboured suspicions about Ayub's policies in the Fifties. In Ayub's mind, friendship with China was a tactical alignment based on common interest in checkmating India.[52] Ayub, in fact, had made his first approach to Beijing on border demarcation towards the end of 1959.[53] The Chinese were then reluctant because it would have meant implicitly siding with Pakistan on Kashmir by giving legitimacy to the Pakistan-controlled part of the state bordering on China. In 1960, China had declined to discuss that part of the border with India.[54]

With Sino-Indian differences widening, Beijing revised its policy. The war prompted it to speed up border negotiations with India's neighbours, and Pakistan benefited by a speedy "complete agreement in principle" announced on December 26, 1962. The treaty was signed the following March, with the fig leaf of a proviso so that it was subject to the final determination of Kashmir's future. The initial agreement was announced while Indian and Pakistani negotiators were discussing Kashmir under U.S. prodding, leading to an Indian protest. The U.S. had unsuccessfully tried to delay announcement of the accord.

In the wake of the border agreement, Pakistan signed its first trade agreement with China for one year, with payments to be made in sterling.[55] In 1961, Pakistan had broken with the U.S. on the question of China's membership of the United Nations, abstaining on the vote for the first time. And during Foreign Minister Bhutto's visit to China in 1963, Liu Shaoqi told him, "We are now convinced that your participation in SEATO is only against India and not against China at all."[56] China and Pakistan signed an airline agreement in 1963.

Pakistan, however, had to proceed warily in promoting friendship with China so as not to tax the limits of tolerance of its main benefactor, the U.S. It was still a member of two U.S.-sponsored defence pacts and relied on the U.S. for arms and economic assistance. China had offered Pakistan a draft of a "friendship pact" in 1963 but the Foreign Ministry felt constrained to decline it in view of its membership of SEATO. The issue was revived in 1964 on the eve of Zhou's visit to Pakistan; Bhutto again declined the offer. It was during this visit that Zhou publicly offered support to Pakistan on Kashmir for the first time.[57]

India's defeat in the border war had serious consequences for Nehru and the country. He had to sacrifice Defence Minister Krishna Menon to placate the anger of his Congress party, and President Radhakrishnan's later harsh but just comment on the debacle was that it was compounded of credulity and ignorance.[58] India decided to double the defence budget in 1963. The defeat represented both a national humiliation and the crumbling of the central arch of Nehru's foreign policy: friendship with China.

What went wrong? On one plane Nehru was very conscious of the threat posed by China. As he was angrily to tell the Lower House of Parliament on November 27, 1959[59] when the country was greatly exercised over the border incidents:

> We realized—we knew that amount of history—that a strong China is normally an expansionist China. Throughout history, that has been the case. And we felt that the great push towards industrialization of that country, plus the amazing pace of its population increase, would together create a most dangerous situation. Taken also with the fact of China's somewhat inherent tendency to be expansive when she is strong, we realized the danger to India. .... If any person imagines that we have followed our China policy without realizing the consequences, he is mistaken.

Even more revealing is the advice Nehru gave to the noted journalist and writer, Frank Moraes, in 1952 before he left for China with a cultural delegation. Nehru told the group,[60] "Never forget that the basic challenge in Southeast Asia is between India and China. That challenge runs along the spine of Asia. Therefore, in your talks with the Chinese, keep it in mind. Never let the Chinese patronize you."

After his visit to China in 1954, Nehru privately confided to friends that his reception by Mao shocked and distressed him. He "had been almost made to feel as if he were being ushered into a presence, as someone coming from a tributary or vassal state of the Chinese empire."[61]

After the Chinese marched into Tibet in 1950, Nehru, as we have seen, made new treaties with Nepal, Bhutan and Sikkim. A committee on the border was formed and an extensive border roads programme was launched; work on the roads, however, proceeded slowly.

Nehru's approach to China was influenced by his broader foreign policy goals and by India's military weakness. On both these counts, he was willing to pocket the Chinese insult of October 1950, disregard Chinese objections in 1954 to the Indian post of Bara Hoti in the central sector and keep largely to himself Mao's patronizing ways. For his countrymen and the outer world, he presented an almost unblemished record of Sino-Indian friendship.

Nehru wished to prepare his country for a possible future conflict with Pakistan and had no desire to open a second front with China.[62] Apart from unilaterally making minor adjustments along the McMahon Line, steps taken along the border were, for the most part, discreet. In practice, his policy towards China approached appeasement doubly to reassure China of Indian bona fides, or, as Gopal prefers to put it, he sought the containment of China through friendship.[63]

When Zhou raised the question of the entire boundary in January 1959, Nehru felt betrayed, a betrayal that was later to be felt by all his countrymen. It appeared to Nehru, as to his people, that Zhou had deliberately lulled him on the border question to spring it upon him after the Aksai Chin road was built and in service and after the Chinese had occupied areas south of the road. At the very least, the Chinese had moved with great deliberation and were preparing to deal with India on the border question only from a position of strength, using Nehru to their advantage in the meantime.

Once the scale of dispute was known publicly, Nehru greatly reduced his freedom to strike a compromise. Apart from his initial mistake of failing to broach the entire border question with China in the early 1950s, from August 1959 he had both to temper the public anger and preempt it by striking an uncharacteristic shrill note.

Nehru tied his hands further by laying before Parliament in September 1959 the correspondence and exchange of notes between the two countries since 1964, promising to make public future exchanges; later exchanges thus became stymied by the public nature of the debate. Nehru had continued to make a distinction between the McMahon Line and the western sector until November 1959; he then took a more uncompromising attitude to the western sector as well.[64]

At the same time, Nehru did not fully share even with most of his Cabinet colleagues his remarkably clear view of the various factors involved in the relationship with China. This was almost certainly due to his belief—soon to be justified—that he would have had to take a much harder line. At any rate, Nehru never conceived of a large-scale Chinese attack. What was worse, the Army did not prepare for a general war along the border even with the limited and dated equipment it had.

This had tragic consequences. The "forward policy" could be viewed by China as a provocation while India remained woefully unprepared for a large-scale conflict. It gave China a tempting opportunity to humble India.

What prompted China to launch the kind of attack it did all along the Sino-Indian border? Few can take seriously the claim that it was "India's China war." Indira Gandhi believed that the border dispute "was the outcome of a more complex policy aimed at undermining India's stability and at obstructing her orderly progress."[65] An Indian commentator has speculated that "they [the Chinese] may have aimed at toppling the Nehru government or at pushing India into the Western camp in the hope of scoring a point vis-a-vis the Soviet Union in their ideological debate."[66]

The Soviets sent a confidential letter to all Communist countries towards the end of January 1963 saying, ".... Today capitalists are supplying arms to India because Chinese aggression forced them to do so."[67] The Chinese, on their part, said on November 2, 1963 that the Soviet stand on the Sino-Indian border dispute was "a complete betrayal of proletarian internationalism."[68]

There were basically three factors involved in the Chinese decision to "punish" India. An element of competition between India and China was inevitable after India's freedom and Nehru's adoption of a global policy and the Communist victory and the formation of a strong central government in China. This was accepted by both sides despite the public postures. While Nehru was irked by Zhou's arrogance and Mao's patronizing airs, Zhou himself was resentful of Nehru taking him under his wing to introduce him to Afro-Asia at the Bandung Conference.

The assessment of Michael Brecher, Nehru's biographer, is interesting. He spent several days with Nehru in 1956 and found that he was not oblivious to the inevitable long-run rivalry between Democratic India and Communist China for the leadership of Asia.[69]

The Chinese view is best summed up by Maxwell: "To Chou En-lai [Zhou Enlai] and his colleagues it must have seemed grotesque, however, that the Indian and national-bourgeois Nehru should aspire to be their sponsor [at Bandung]." But he wrongly asserts that irritation at Nehru's and India's assumption of a right to leadership in Asia did not influence Chinese policy.[70]

A second major factor was the enmeshing of the Sino-Indian dispute with the Sino-Soviet conflict, the latter being more nationalist in character than ideological, despite the garb in which it was clothed. The Chinese, from the beginning, resented the part India was playing in the Soviet Asian policy. The Chinese leaders, for instance, could not but have been upset by Khrushchev's proposal in July 1958 to invite India with the great powers for a conference on the Middle East, a proposal that met with a frosty Western response.

The Chinese, to be sure, had their own more serious differences with the Soviet leadership. They had never specifically endorsed the Soviet line of "peaceful coexistence," which, they felt, would work against their national interests. The Soviet refusal to deter the U.S. nuclear threat and assure China nuclear support during the Quemoy crisis in 1958 accelerated China's search for a nuclear option.[71]

In 1960, the Soviets terminated their aid programme to China, which was later to charge in a statement on September 1, 1963:[72] "Not only have you perfidiously and unilaterally scrapped the agreement on providing China with nuclear technical data but you have blatantly given more and more military aid to the Indian reactionaries, who are hostile to China and have made incessant armed provocations against it."

It was, indeed, not lost upon the Chinese that the greater Soviet capability to aid India had become possible because of the termination of Moscow's assistance to China. The rapid growth of Indo-Soviet relations in the 1950s took place against the background of a steady deterioration of Sino-Soviet relations. The *Tass* statement of September 9, 1959 was deeply resented by China and there is little doubt that the Chinese position on India hardened by Soviet intervention in India's behalf.

While the Sino-Soviet dispute had wider connotations and represented the imbalance in the relationship between a superpower and its fraternal ally, determined to achieve great power status, the Sino-Indian conflict became to an extent its focal point and fed it. The "Camp David spirit" was viewed by China as inimical to its national interest and the Soviet intimation to China in August 1962 that they intended to pursue negotiations with the U.S. on a Test Ban Treaty[73] could only have been construed in Beijing as a step against China's independent nuclear programme. The Chinese, meanwhile, had obtained an assurance from the U.S. at the Warsaw meeting on June 23, 1962 that Washington would not support a Nationalist Chinese attack on the mainland.[74] There was friction on the Sino-Soviet border as early as 1960.[75]

The Sino-Indian border conflict escalated in September 1962. Given the scale of Chinese military preparations and India's military weakness, the occasion must have presented to the Chinese leaders an opportunity both to humble the Soviet Union's new friend in Asia and "teach India a lesson."

The Chinese leaders were also clearly influenced by the internal situation in the country, the third factor in their decision to launch the attack on India. The Chinese began criticizing the concepts of peaceful coexistence and peaceful transition to socialism in the latter half of 1957; the *Hundred Flowers* movement was brought to a close in 1958 and an internal power struggle, with Defence Minister P'eng Teh-huai's ultimate dismissal and the disciplining of others, ended in a victory for the radicals. That relations with the Soviet Union were a central aspect of the Chinese turmoil is clear from subsequent Chinese charges of Soviet interference. By 1958 China was clearly veering away from a gradualist and moderate policy in domestic and external affairs.

Nehru tried to pick up the pieces of India's self-respect after the border defeat as best he could. Western enthusiasm to utilize Sino-Indian enmity to veer Nehru towards it was apparent. Joint air exercises were held in India in November 1963 with the U.S., Britain and Australia. But discussions on a longer-term military relationship with the U.S. did not proceed smoothly. In the American view, India's demands were extravagant while Indians gradually came to realize that the U.S. was interested in providing India with only a trip-wire force.

The West's new advantage in India was also sought to be utilized to secure Indian support for stationing a U.S. naval force in the Indian Ocean. Initial Indian reactions were apparently favourable enough for Ambassador Chester Bowles to report to Washington on December 19, 1963 that "given time, we believe concept of visits [by U.S. task group in the Indian Ocean] to Indian ports can be sold to Nehru and Indian leaders (Nehru has already blunted controversy over task group's presence in Indian Ocean high seas).'"[76] But Washington reported to its Embassy in New Delhi a week later that Ambassador B.K. Nehru had called at the State Department on December 26 to make a *volte face* on the U.S. deployment in the Indian Ocean.[77]

Nehru, however, had realized from the beginning of the border war that the Soviet approach to India would be crucial. On December 12, 1962 Khrushchev gave India outspoken support by deploring the fighting on the border, asserting Soviet neutrality on the Sino-Indian conflict and reaffirming friendship with both parties.[78]

There was an interruption of Soviet arms supplies during the border war. But by mid-1964 the total supply obtained since the Chinese invasion amounted to $140 million. Negotiations in 1963 and early 1964 led to Soviet agreement for delivery of An-12 cargo planes, air-to-air missiles and the establishment of a SA-2 anti-aircraft missile complex.[79] The Soviets, however, had refused to modify MIG fighters by adding all-weather and night capabilities to meet Indian requirements for an Indian interceptor at the Himalayan border.[80] Some time during the summer of 1964 the Russians had resolved their doubts about the MIG deal, having given up hopes of doing business with China.[81]

Plans for an Indo-U.S. military relationship of $100 million a year for five years came to nothing, despite Ambassador Chester Bowles' enthusiastic support. It was sabotaged by circumstances and a

Pakistan-inclined Pentagon.[82] Besides, Nehru had been shrewd enough to swing India back towards nonalignment because he believed that Indian and Western interests would clash again.[83]

There was, however, no getting away from the fact of India's diminished status in Asia and Africa. This was apparent at a preparatory meeting of the nonaligned conference held in Colombo early in 1964. Indian representatives adopted a slightly apologetic approach and gave an impression of half-heartedness and boredom with nonalignment.[84]

With China's presence at the Afro-Asian preparatory meeting at Djakarta, held a few weeks later in April, there was a change in the Indian attitude. Confrontation between India and China was in a low key but there was no air of apology about the Indian representatives' attitude. China, Indonesia and Pakistan acted together while India sprung upon the conference the issue of Soviet and Malaysian membership. India's main objective was to raise the question of the Soviet Union as also being an Asian power as a tactical ploy to get even with China and its friends. It was not made with any great conviction, probably because India itself had not formerly regarded the Soviet Union as such; the Soviets had not been invited to the first Afro-Asian conference in 1955.

Mikoyan made a ten-day visit to Djakarta in June 1964 to announce that the Soviet Union had given Indonesia new superior arms; Indonesia was then the largest recipient of Soviet arms in Asia.[85] Mikoyan beefed up Soviet support for Indonesia's prevailing policy of confrontation towards the new federation of Malaysia. The primary motive was to wrest the initiative from China.

This was the expansive phase in Indonesia's development. Perhaps influenced by the diminution in India's status, Brigadier General Hartono, head of the Indonesian Army's Logistics Service, announced on November 15, 1964 that Indonesia planned to trigger its first atom bomb in 1965. Eight months later, President Soekarno reiterated his country's resolve to make its own atom bomb "soon." It was a dream because Indonesian technological progress was far from the stage of exploding an atom bomb. The Indonesian perspective was to change with the abortive Communist coup on October 1, 1965 and the army's assertion of power over President Soekarno.

Nehru died eighteen months after the border war a disappointed man. He never quite recovered from the failure of his China policy. Yet despite his sad end, Nehru's projection and implementation of foreign policy during his seventeen years of rule were remarkable.

If Nehru's concept of India's role in the world was grandiose, the surprise is in how far he did succeed in achieving some of his objectives. Nehru gave India and the world the policy of nonalignment which, despite its elasticity, admirably served India's needs and has now become the badge of nearly every newly-independent nation.

Nehru's assiduous cultivation of India's two giant Communist neighbours was a wise policy and gave an essential basis to his nonalignment. Domestically, it stymied the Communist Party, which changed course from insurrection to cooperation. Indeed, the nonaligned policy, together with centralized planning, helped to harmonize the different and competing tendencies and consolidate central power. Nonalignment became an expression of Indian self-respect and dignity and bolstered his countrymen's fierce independence. Nehru laid the basis for industrial and technological growth, essential for achieving great power status. In defence, despite his early stepmotherly treatment of the Army, he, together with Krishna Menon, pioneered self-reliance for India. He gave enthusiastic support to the peaceful development of atomic energy. But the model of economic development he chose in India's setting could not achieve the objective of removing inequalities or banishing poverty.

Nehru failed singularly in his pan-Asianism although he helped bring China out and was to prove a farsighted prophet in forecasting the ultimate falling out of China and the Soviet Union, ironically at India's expense. Nor could Nehru succeed in his objective of keeping the superpowers out of the subcontinent.

Given the U.S. policy towards the subcontinent in the 1950s, Nehru was forced to involve the Soviet Union in India's affairs to a greater extent than he had wanted to.[86] Later, Moscow had to be used as a counterweight to China's hostility. Instead of minimizing the superpowers' role in the subcontinent, India had to opt for maximizing it to give the policy a form of "bi-alignment."

Nehru's objective of converting Asia into a nuclear-free "zone of peace" could not be achieved, especially in view of Chinese nuclear ambitions. He had also to learn the hard way that India's remarkable preeminence in world affairs could not be sustained after the border war without economic and military muscle.[87]

Perhaps the grand scale of Nehru's global policy was unrealistic, but in attempting to implement it, he brought about a far-reaching change in the roles of both the Soviet Union and China towards the Third World and helped the process of detente between the superpowers. To an extent, the world would have been different but for Nehru. Nehru set his sights high, inspiring his countrymen to pursue policies that remain the country's goal.

Chapter Three

AFTER NEHRU

NEHRU died in May 1964 and Khrushchev was ousted in October that year. China exploded its first atom bomb less than two weeks after Khrushchev's fall. The first two events, unconnected though they were, had portentous consequences for the Indian subcontinent. The third highlighted India's precarious strategic environment.

The last year of Nehru's rule was a transition phase. He was a broken man after the Sino-Indian border war and in January 1964 he suffered a stroke while attending a Congress session in Bhubaneshwar, Orissa. Despite his condition, he retained sufficient political astuteness to take two significant steps which would determine his succession.

Under the guise of the Kamaraj plan, named after K. Kamaraj, then chief minister of the southern state of Tamil Nadu, Nehru axed Morarji Desai, among others, in August 1963. The ostensible purpose of the plan was to relieve senior government leaders of their posts to enable them to revitalize the party. The real objective was to remove Desai from the line of succession because Nehru considered him too conservative and too rigid to be a good prime minister.[1]

Desai was a follower of Mahatma Gandhi and had acquired the reputation of being a strong man as chief minister of the undivided Bombay state before Nehru brought him to the Centre. He also tended to be self-righteous and was an enthusiastic supporter of prohibition as state policy. He was considerably to the right of Nehru in economic policy and did not necessarily regard private initiative in business and industry as evil.

Also axed under the plan was Lal Bahadur Shastri, a Nehru loyalist and essentially a party apparatchik.[2] But after his stroke, Nehru brought back Shastri into the cabinet as Minister without Portfolio to help him with affairs of state. This was widely read as a hint about his preference[3] although Nehru perhaps saw Shastri as an interim successor until his daughter Indira Gandhi was ready to take on the job.

Nehru's incapacity and his earlier loss of elan after the border debacle had increasingly led to a shift of power from the Centre to the states and to influential bosses in the party. The latter had their own agenda and met in the summer of 1963 in the southern temple city of Tirupati secretly to pick the next Congress party's president who, they felt, would be ideally placed to succeed Nehru. The consensus was in favour of Kamaraj, a strong man with a socialist outlook with enviable grassroot support. Kamaraj declined the offer. The party bosses then decided on Shastri because he was acceptable to them and was considered sufficiently pliable to enable them to exercise power from behind the scenes. Desai was ruled out for his rigidity.[4]

Desai objected to Shastri becoming the Congress president and said he would contest. Nehru did not want a divisive party election and Kamaraj had ultimately to take on the job. But in early 1964 Shastri was eminently placed to succeed Nehru. He had received the secret endorsement of the party bosses and Nehru had given him a nod by bringing him back in the cabinet. Although Desai threw his hat in the ring after Nehru's death, he was prevailed upon by the party bosses to agree to Shastri's unanimous selection to show the world, as they suggested, that the transition to the post-Nehru era could be smooth.

There could not have been a greater contrast to Nehru. Shastri was a diminutive man, five-feet-two, and entirely homespun. He had made his mark in party work by combining common sense with ruthlessness, when needed, while presenting a placid and amiable front to his partymen and the world, disarming criticism.

Shastri was almost totally inexperienced in international affairs and, as Mrs. Gandhi was to suggest later, "in the beginning, Shastri appeared unsure of himself."[5] He told James Reston of *The New York Times* in December 1965 that India was frankly not in a position to do anything in the realm of foreign affairs that might alienate it from the Soviet Union.[6] This was more an expression of his mood than reality.

Apart from the unflattering remarks people made about his physical and intellectual stature, compared to Nehru's, Shastri had a difficult legacy. Planned development had suffered a major setback after the border war, more money had to be provided for the spiralling defence budget, the economy was in bad shape and there remained the almost perennial problem of shortage of foreign exchange.

Shastri was essentially a centrist in his economic as well as political thinking. He was no socialist, even in the Nehru sense, and tended to be more prudent and conservative. At any rate, the economic crisis gave him no scope for bold planning. In domestic as in foreign policy, there was an inevitable scaling down of goals. As far as the economy was concerned, this was inevitable, given the problems and the emphasis of the Western aid donors on agriculture and less grandiose infrastructural facilities. Shastri himself was inclined to cater to the more immediate needs of the common man, an approach which made political sense.

There was little room for innovation in foreign policy, with the country facing two hostile neighbours, Pakistan and China, and Shastri's venture in foreign policy before the 1965 war was a holding operation. But he paid more attention to India's immediate smaller neighbours who had tended to get lost in Nehru's global view. He sent his foreign minister to Nepal, Afghanistan, Burma and Sri Lanka and himself visited Nepal.

Shastri had given Mrs. Gandhi the minor Information and Broadcasting portfolio to symbolize continuity with the Nehru era. She was then forty-six. She had been offered the foreign portfolio, for form's sake, which she declined. Later, he preempted her by giving it to the veteran cautious minister in Nehru's cabinet, Swaran Singh.

Conflict between Mrs. Gandhi and Shastri on economic policy developed as early as September 1964.[7] She made a point of highlighting the continuing relevance of Nehru's socialism, criticizing the movement away from it. This was a time of political confusion in the party. At the Durgapur session of the Congress in January 1965, Kamaraj, now Congress president, proclaimed the goal of "socialist society in our lifetime," but as a commentator was aptly to remark on the contradictory signals coming out of the session, "Is the party moving toward socialism or retracing its steps?"[8]

Kosygin flew to Delhi to attend Nehru's funeral and in the plane he asked Indian Ambassador Kaul travelling with him searching questions on the future direction of Indian policies. As Kaul was to record later, "Nehru's successor might also shift the emphasis in India's policy away from the Soviet Union. This is what the Soviet Union were concerned about and wanted to find out—especially in view of their deteriorating relations with China .... He [Kosygin] asked if there was likely to be a change in our stance towards China or our relations with America."⁹

Soviet policy towards India and the Third World was undergoing a change, but it was to be fully articulated only after Nehru's death and, to an even greater extent, after Khrushchev's fall. Ideologically, the Soviets were retreating from the more exuberant Khrushchev innovations in the face of a continuing Chinese assault.

Mrs. Gandhi later confessed to being "worried [about] what reaction it [Khrushchev's fall] would have on India, whether the Russians would change their policy" and hastily undertook a visit to Moscow on her own initiative. Kosygin "personally assured me that his policy would remain the same, that he had great respect for my father and that he intended to continue the same policy with Mr. Shastri."¹⁰ More specifically, Kosygin assured Mrs. Gandhi that Khrushchev's policy of helping India was not responsible for his fall.¹¹

Despite Kosygin's assurance, the new Soviet leadership frowned on Khrushchev's overcommitment to the Third World, and a reassessment had been in progress for some years of the simplistic economic themes of the late Fifties and early Sixties. Moscow reduced aid commitments to the bare minimum during 1961-62, a critical reevaluation began in late 1961 and the search for tangible gains took the form of a debate on profit versus dominant political motive. In working out a long-range policy, there was an increasing emphasis on the viability and performance of projects which would intermesh with the needs of Soviet economy, transcending the traditional approach to barter.¹²

World Marxist Review fired a first salvo at India in November 1964 by reprinting an article by G. Adhikari, former general secretary of the Communist Party of India. Adhikari's thesis was that India had taken the capitalist road, encouraged growth of monopoly capital which could now "impel the Government towards pro-imperialist and anti-democratic policies." Further, Adhikari suggested that reactionary forces were getting stronger in the Congress party while the progressive forces were weaker.

On January 19, 1965 *New Times* launched an attack on Morarji Desai, "who had done everything he could to defeat Nehru's socialist policies." Desai was not in Shastri's Government but the Soviets grew increasingly suspicious of India's lurch to the right in economic policies, as also of the military assistance it was receiving from the

U.S. The World Bank and the U.S. were, indeed, exercising considerable pressure on Shastri and the western assessment then was that he had given a pro-U.S. tilt to Indian policies. He did not share Nehru's more doctrinaire objections against private enterprise, was more under the sway of bureaucrats and played down India's differences with the U.S. on Vietnam so as not to annoy Washington.

An even more ominous development from India's point of view was what appeared at first as a subtle shift in Soviet policy towards Pakistan. In a 1964 debate on Kashmir in the U.N. Security Council, the Soviet delegate supported India but did not condemn Pakistan and acknowledged for the first time that there was a dispute between the two countries.

During his visit to Delhi to attend Nehru's funeral, Kosygin had raised the question of "greater autonomy" for Kashmir with Gulzari Lal Nanda, acting prime minister, only to beat a hasty retreat.[13] But the Soviets were not deterred. Anastas Mikoyan, stopping in Delhi on his way home from Indonesia in June 1964, had told Shastri that it was time to resolve disputes with Pakistan.[14] And when President Radhakrishnan visited Moscow in October 1964, the joint communiqué did not endorse the Indian position on Kashmir, a significant omission.

President Ayub Khan of Pakistan was following a policy of "triangular tightrope walking" in seeking to maintain good relations with the two superpowers and China at the same time.[15] Although Pakistan had declined Bulganin's offer of a steel plant in 1956 for fear of displeasing America,[16] it signed an oil agreement with Moscow in 1961 involving a five-year loan for oil exploration.

Pakistanis played down their membership of the two U.S.-sponsored pacts and recorded their dissent from U.S. policy in Vietnam in the SEATO council meeting in May 1965.[17] Although the latter move was more a gesture towards China, Ayub's overtures to Moscow had the aim of neutralizing Soviet support to India on Kashmir and sat well with his general drift away from pacts. Indeed, he was to suggest later that he did not know why Pakistan joined SEATO in the first place, although he took comfort from CENTO for providing the germ for the Regional Cooperation for Development (RCD), an economic grouping of Pakistan, Turkey and Iran.[18]

Ayub's new policy towards the Soviet Union bore fruit. Foreign Minister Bhutto paid a visit to Moscow in November 1965 and discussed, among other questions, the supply of Soviet arms to

India.[19] But the most significant development was Ayub's visit to Moscow in April that year. He made a considerable impression on the Soviet leadership.[20]

Ayub, meanwhile, had made headway in cementing relations with China, India providing the common binding factor for the two countries, although for Beijing the Soviet Union was the major factor. Ayub went to China in March 1965 to be told by Zhou Enlai, "If India commits aggression into Pakistan territory, China would definitely support Pakistan." And Mao reassured him, "We are with you and are not with Shastri."[21]

There was a break in Chinese hostility towards India after Nehru's death. Beijing played down its anti-Indian propaganda and Zhou made a proposal to Shastri in October 1964 proposing talks on the border dispute "at any time and at any place . . . with the Colombo proposals as the basis." Failing to receive a positive response from India, Zhou told the Third National People's Congress in December 1964, "But if India is determined not to have negotiations, no matter; we can wait . . ."[22]

The Chinese did not wait long before resuming attacks on India. After Shastri's visit to Moscow in May 1965, he was described by *Peking Review* of May 28, 1965 as a "rare anti-China cavalier as well as Washington's pet." The Chinese had, in any case, by then given up hopes of doing business with Khrushchev's successors, who were condemned by *People's Daily* of May 27, 1965 for "pursuing the Khrushchev line to form an anti-Chinese alliance with Nehru's successors."

Shastri was in no position to probe the Chinese offer, which seemed loaded; Beijing had not fully accepted the Colombo proposals when they were made. Besides, the country was in no mood to accept them as a basis for discussions and Shastri was too unsure of himself in international affairs to want to reopen a painful chapter in Sino-Indian history and was also perhaps fearful of the consequences it would have had on the Indo-Soviet relationship.

Zhou's offer coincided with the second nonaligned summit in Cairo in which Shastri's role was inglorious and tinged with an anti-Chinese slant. His odd proposal that a peace mission be sent to China to persuade Beijing to stop its nuclear programme met with a cold response.[23]

The Chinese had exploded their first atom bomb and there was genuine Indian concern over China's "nuclear blackmail." One proposal mooted at the time was that both superpowers jointly and publicly guarantee that China would not be allowed to use its nuclear stockpile to intimidate other Asian states. The proposal got nowhere because there were misgivings in the two superpower capitals and India was not prepared to pay the political price for a modified version of such a guarantee.

China's membership of the nuclear club ultimately persuaded Shastri to approve of a momentous decision, influenced more by the forceful personality and stature of Homi Bhabha, the father of India's nuclear programme, than his own inclination. Bhabha was able to convince Shastri that, confronted with the Chinese nuclear test, India must undertake an underground nuclear explosion.[24]

A secret Subterranean Nuclear Explosion Programme (SNEP) was sanctioned. But Bhabha died in a plane crash over Switzerland in January 1966, and SNEP died with him.[25] It was to be revived by Mrs. Gandhi years later.

Pakistan's signals to China were proliferating. In 1963, it voted for China's entry into the United Nations and two years later told the U.N. General Assembly that Taiwan was an integral part of China.[26] The two countries signed their first barter trade agreement in 1964, the year China gave Pakistan its first interest-free loan of $60 million.[27]

Ayub did some tightrope walking by undertaking a visit to the U.S. towards the end of 1965, largely to reassure President Johnson on his China policy. He was very conscious of the fact that good relations with the U.S. were important for sorely needed economic aid. On the testimony of Harold Wilson, then British prime minister, who confessed to being worried by Pakistan's "apparent flirtation with the Russians *and* the Chinese," Ayub's mission to Washington was a success. Meeting Ayub in London on his way to Washington, Wilson had a "very intimate talk with him and was much reassured—as was President Johnson a few days later."[28]

April 1965 saw border police clashes between India and Pakistan along the marshes of the Rann of Kutch. The Rann had remained undemarcated, Radcliffe having given no ruling, and Pakistan claimed the whole of it. The clashes soon involved the two countries' armed forces. Pakistan was apparently well prepared. It had an airport near the Rann and a network of roads along it which enabled it to bring up armour, including U.S.-supplied Patton tanks. Pakistani forces made gains in capturing territory.

General J.N. Chaudhuri, the Indian army chief, did not want to fight a prolonged battle in the swamp because he believed it was a diversionary Pakistani move.[29] A British-sponsored agreement brought about a cease-fire on June 30, 1965 and a tribunal upheld 2 to 1 Pakistan's claim to the northern half of the Rann. Even more distressing for India than the clashes was Moscow's attitude.

Moscow took a neutral position on the clashes, appealing to both countries to show restraint and settle the dispute among themselves.[30] China, on the other hand, supported Pakistan and condemned India for "provoking" the armed conflict.[31] It was the first instance in which Beijing had intervened in an Indo-Pakistani conflict on the subcontinent.

Shastri paid a visit to Moscow in May 1965 to be reassured by the Soviet leaders that the Soviet policy towards India had not changed. He was told that their attempt was to wean away Pakistan from China and loosen its links with military pacts. The resultant benefit, they said, would accrue more to India than to the Soviet Union.[32] Shastri's visit to Moscow coincided with the second Chinese nuclear test.

According to one observer on the scene, Shastri saw the logic of the argument.[33] "Shastri had always been of the view that it was easier to make up with Pakistan, the people of which were of the same stock as Indians, than with China."[34] At the end of the Shastri visit, there was no reference to Kashmir in the joint communiqué.

Buoyed by his diplomatic triumphs, Ayub cast an eye on India. The Pakistanis had made gains in the Rann of Kutch and Bhutto and other members of the Pakistani elite were egging Ayub on to confront India. "Little Shastri" was in power, and his diminutive stature and the economic difficulties he faced bolstered Pakistanis' confidence. The Indian defeat at the hands of the Chinese in 1962 was still relished in Pakistan.

As Bhutto was to relate later, "There was a time when militarily, in terms of the big push, in terms of armour, we were superior to India because of the military assistance we were getting [from the U.S.] and that was the position up to 1965."[35]

Pakistan indulged in the familiar ploy of sending infiltrators into Kashmir in civilian clothes, later to engage their troops in the state. India and Pakistan were again at war. Pakistani troops had crossed a small stretch of the international boundary in the Akhnur-Jammu sector on September 1, but the major thrust along the international border towards Lahore and Sialkot was made by Indian forces on September 6 to take the Pakistani pressure off the Chamb area in Kashmir.

This evoked a curious response from Britain. Prime Minister Harold Wilson condemned India's "aggression." Wilson was to confess later, "CRO [Commonwealth Relations Office] officials briefed me on the situation and inveigled me into issuing, on 6th September, a statement—justified as they said by cast-iron evidence—condemning India for an act of aggression. I was wrong... I had been taken for a ride by a pro-Pakistan faction in CRO..."[36] In April 1966 Wilson apologized to Mrs. Gandhi.[37]

The Soviets had listed Pakistan in a May Day slogan in 1965 for the first time, after Ayub's successful visit. And they had adopted a studied neutrality in the Rann of Kutch skirmishes. They did not wish to downgrade India but felt they had sufficient leverage on New Delhi to broaden their policy towards the subcontinent. Their major objective in Pakistan was two-fold: to use the growing anti-American and anti-pact trends there to weaken the hold of the West and try to detach Pakistan from a burgeoning relationship with China.

There were also other factors involved. The border war had proved that India's nonalignment was fragile and Moscow was getting increasingly worried by the strength of the rightist parties and "reactionaries," as it saw them. As Soviet Ambassador to Pakistan Smirnov was to explain in Karachi on May 18, 1982, the Soviets had "left the door open for friendly relations" even at the lowest point in the two countries' relationship. The Soviets' "significant attention" to Pakistan, he explained, arose out of its proximity to the Soviet border.[38]

At any rate, the Soviets adopted a neutral attitude towards the 1965 war, which lasted twenty-three days. They stressed the war's damaging repercussions on the two countries' economies, the proximity of the conflict to Soviet borders and dangers of the conflict escalating into a global war.

The last point was made with an eye on Chinese activities. Beijing gave vociferous support to Pakistan and condemned India. Foreign Minister Chen Yi stopped in Karachi for a five-hour talk with Bhutto on September 4 during the war. According to Choudhury, the Chinese sought two assurances from Ayub, that Pakistan not submit to any Kashmir solution favourable to India and that it resist American, Soviet or U.N. pressures for such a solution. Ayub gave them an assurance on these points.[39]

On September 8, the day Beijing Radio announced that its forces on the Indian border had been placed on alert, President Liu assured Ayub that China would respond to an Indian attack on East Pakistan. The same day a Chinese note accused India of putting up military structures on the Sikkim border and indulging in "frenzied provocative activities." India denied the allegation in a note on September 12.

Then arrived a Chinese ultimatum on September 16. India was told that unless it dismantled in three days all military facilities on the Chinese side of the Sikkim border, it must bear full responsibility for the grave consequences. It turned out to be a paper threat, but no one could be sure at that time that it was mere sabre-rattling, perhaps also intended to ensure that India did not move troops from the Chinese to the Pakistan border.[40] The Chinese were obviously fishing in the troubled Indian waters.[41]

The Soviets were indulging in vigorous diplomacy at the United Nations, and, for once, had the support of the United States. The two superpowers' interests in containing China were converging on the subcontinent. While Ayub sought to use the mechanism of the U.N. Security Council to reopen the Kashmir issue, the superpowers' interest was to end the fighting. India and Pakistan had to agree to the call for a cease-fire and the conflict ended after a Security Council session on September 22; the demand for the two countries to withdraw forces to the August 5 lines went unheeded. Ayub had slipped into China for one day of secret talks before accepting the cease-fire.[42]

"Little Shastri" had become a hero overnight in India as accounts of victories flooded the Indian press (reporting was inevitably partisan). A major Indian achievement was the capture of Haji Pir pass and Tithwal in Kashmir after bloody battles. The excited talk in Delhi during the 23-day war was the impending capture of the major Pakistani city of Lahore, which occupies an evocative niche in the North Indian psyche. General Chaudhuri later denied that that had been his objective.[43]

In military terms, the war was a stalemate, with Pakistan being in more difficult straits because of its greater need for arms imports than India to keep the war going. (The U.S. had embargoed arms to both countries during the war). But Pakistan was the loser because it had started the war to try to wrest Kashmir, an aim it did not achieve.

Nevertheless, it claimed a victory over India. (Reporting in the Pakistani press was even more partisan than in India's).

At the end of the conflict, the subcontinent's relations with outside powers presented an interesting pattern. Britain had ruled itself out as a peacemaker in view of Wilson's *faux pas*. Both sides became embittered by the U.S. because of stoppage of arms supplies, in addition to President Johnson's cancellation of visits by Ayub and Shastri earlier in the year. (The U.S. accused both sides of using American weapons in the conflict.[44]) China had of course come out blatantly on Pakistan's side in the conflict. The U.N. mechanism was ruled out because Pakistan feared it was too much under American influence and India did not want the Kashmir issue to be reopened.

That left only one country as a peacemaker, the Soviet Union. Moscow had maintained a posture of complete neutrality during the conflict and was now ready to capitalize on its enviable position through a bold strategy. It invited India and Pakistan to the Soviet Central Asian city of Tashkent to make peace, Kosygin offering to lend his good offices.

Both India and Pakistan were initially reluctant to accept the Soviet offer, the former because it feared a further loosening of Moscow's support on Kashmir, the latter because any agreement at Tashkent would merely highlight the folly of the Pakistani adventure. Ayub was also acutely conscious of Chinese hostility to the idea, but President Johnson pressured him to accept the Soviet offer.[45]

Would Mrs. Gandhi have gone to Tashkent if she had then been Prime Minister?[46] This question was subsequently to be raised in India. But neither of the two sides had any real alternative. The two superpowers were solidly behind the disengagement proposal. Although Shastri had made rash statements about not returning areas won in Kashmir,[47] Ayub had placed himself in an even more difficult position, having lost his gamble. The *Times* of London was wryly to remark on January 3, 1966, "How strange and intolerable it would have seemed to Curzon that the affairs of the subcontinent should be taken to Tashkent to be discussed under the patronage of a Russian!"

India linked an agreement at Tashkent with the two sides signing a no-war pact while Ayub unsuccessfully tried to wrest an Indian concession on Kashmir. Ayub had also to face the Bhutto problem. His foreign minister had gone to Tashkent determined to wreck the summit, and he received encouragement from the Chinese, who sent a threatening note to India on January 6. This was interpreted as an encouragement of the Bhutto line and a hint that he could break up the meeting if he wanted to. Bhutto wished to carve his political career out of the Tashkent meeting, knowing as he did that the results would lead to disillusionment in his country. Ironically, he had contributed to the Kashmir misadventure.[48]

In the event, neither side got what it wanted. There was no movement on Kashmir and India had to remain content with Pakistan accepting only the U.N. Charter on the question of not using force to resolve the Kashmir issue. On Pakistan's insistence, the disengagement agreement was called a declaration and Kosygin merely "witnessed" it. Pakistan did not want to have the Declaration registered as a U.N. document.

The agreement was by no means of a substantive nature nor could one have been expected. But it was a major diplomatic triumph for the Soviets. By common consent, Kosygin played a crucial part, exercising his country's clout by twisting arms when necessary.[49] There is little doubt that the Soviets told Ayub bluntly that he could not expect to win at the negotiating table what he could not on the battlefield. To India Kosygin held out the implicit threat that it could not bank on a Soviet veto on Kashmir in the Security Council if it didn't cooperate.

The Soviet achievement underscored many of Moscow's objectives. It was a remarkable demonstration of the Soviet Union's status and stake in Asia, particularly the subcontinent, giving it the mantle of the peacemaker. Moscow had humbled the Chinese by nipping their mischief in the bud. Tashkent also made Moscow a referee in Indo-Pakistani disputes; this though was later to prove to be a crown of thorns.

The Chinese, however, wished to make their point in relation to Pakistan. At the end of March 1966, Liu Shaoqi visited Pakistan to highlight the Beijing-Islamabad relationship. In June Zhou followed Liu to promise Pakistan military aid, including aircraft and spares.[50] The Chinese were plainly unhappy over Pakistan's acquiescence to the Tashkent Declaration, but began to give military aid shortly afterwards; Beijing feared Soviet penetration.

With arms supplies shut off by the U.S., its principal supplier, Pakistan was interested in Chinese arms. It received from Beijing 200 medium tanks, several squadrons of MIG-19s and some Il-28 bombers. There was, of course, the covert arms market, and

Washington winked at a deal West Germany made with Iran to sell ninety F-86s destined for Pakistan while the embargo was on.[51]

Even while striking up a more balanced posture towards the two major countries of the subcontinent, Moscow made a point of reiterating its continuing interest in India. In September 1964, the Soviets gave India military credits for forty-four MIG-21s, twenty helicopters and seventy PT-76 tanks, among other items. More significantly, they made technical and financial arrangements for MIG production and agreed to improve MIG capabilities for Indian requirements.[52] India's decision on the major arms deal with Moscow was made after repeated rebuffs from Western sources.[53] Indian inquiries for a suitable power plant for the HF-24 had led to interest in MIG-21 in 1962.[54]

The Sino-Indian border war had changed budgetary allocations for defence. There was widespread support and sympathy for the neglected Army. Defence allocations were doubled in 1963 to 4.5 per cent of G.N.P., primarily to expand and modernize the Army. But even after the 1965 war with Pakistan defence expenditure was maintained at around 3.5 per cent of G.N.P.[55]

While the U.S. embargoed arms to the subcontinent, Moscow did not stop arms supplies to India during the fighting. In fact, the Soviet Union agreed to give India submarines, destroyer escorts and patrol craft.[56] This was after the U.S. proved unresponsive to Indian requests for three destroyers.[57]

The U.S. approach to the subcontinent after the 1965 war was to reduce its commitments and let the Soviet Union fight the battles it wished to against China. The Sino-Pakistan military relationship that came into being brought the superpowers together on containing China, with one of them scaling down its vision of the subcontinent and the other extending it to include Pakistan. In the mid-Sixties, there were growing doubts in the U.S. Congress over the usefulness of military assistance as an instrument of foreign policy.

The 1965 war led to new Soviet-Chinese exchanges. China charged the Soviet Union with colluding with the U.S. to divide the world. The Chinese alleged that the Soviets had shown partiality towards India. The war, indeed, helped convince China that Khrushchev's successors were equally bad. The Soviets, for their part, gave up hope of a working arrangement with China. Soviet policy came to be guided by the fear of Chinese hegemony in Asia and concern over India coming under greater Western influence.

Violations on the Sino-Soviet border had become a continuing phenomenon since the early Sixties.

The Sino-Soviet split was the last straw for the deeply divided Communist Party of India. The left faction walked out of the CPI in April 1964 to create the Communist Party of India (Marxist). The causes of the split were largely indigenous, dating back to 1948 and the Ranadive-Andhra faction clash, but they were fuelled by the Twentieth Congress of the CPSU[58] and the split was, in the end, encouraged by the Soviets. Moscow had been surprised by the strength of the left faction in the CPI and was perhaps fearful of losing the party to the Chinese. The Soviets also wished to show other Communist parties the harm the Chinese were causing the world Communist movement.[59]

India's pro-Western economic policy in the mid-Sixties had a negative effect on Indo-Soviet trade. The volume declined two years thereafter even taking into account the Indian devaluation of June 1966.[60] Tashkent, meanwhile, had raised Moscow's prestige and the Soviet Union became a major power factor in South Asia. It had outflanked China and dramatized its also being an Asian power. The Chinese objective in buttressing relations with Pakistan grew out of their common interest in containing Indo-Soviet hegemony in South Asia, as they saw it.

In Pakistan, Bhutto's departure from the Ayub cabinet in the summer of 1966 made him a hero and he was soon to become a formidable cult figure in the student community of Lahore. President Ayub was very much on the defensive and had the unenviable task of trying to explain away Tashkent, which was ultimately to lead to his downfall.

The Tashkent Declaration was unpopular in India as well, but it became easier for the Government to sell it to the people by a fortuitous circumstance. Shastri died of a heart attack at Tashkent hours after he had signed the agreement on January 10.

Shastri's reign had lasted less than twenty months, and the Congress party bosses had again to contend with the succession problem. There was, for a brief while, a campaign to draft Kamaraj. He declined the offer; in any case, he would have made an unsuitable prime minister because the party's strong base remained in the Hindi heartland in the North and Kamaraj did not speak Hindi, the main northern language and the projected national language, or English. But he again emerged as the kingmaker.

The Syndicate, as the party bosses came to be known, was keen to prevent Morarji Desai from assuming the prime ministership, and it decided, with Kamaraj taking the lead, that Indira Gandhi was the one candidate who could defeat Desai. Unlike after Nehru's death, Desai refused to be fobbed off by the argument that there should be no contest. Nine days after Shastri's death, the Congress Parliamentary Party met to vote on his successor. Mrs. Gandhi won by 355 votes to 169 for Desai. She took over as prime minister on January 24.

Indira Gandhi had not made much of a mark as information minister in the Shastri regime and the Syndicate was determined to manipulate her; she was, in its view, a *goongi goodia* (dumb doll), a marionette to be manipulated. The choice of her cabinet was largely dictated by Kamaraj. Indeed, on assuming office, she seemed unsure of herself and came to rely increasingly on a "kitchen cabinet" composed of younger members who were political lightweights.

It would have been a difficult time for any prime minister. The next general elections were less than fourteen months away. The food crisis loomed large. The last year of the Third Five-Year Plan suffered from the effects of drought, the war with Pakistan and the interruption in American aid. Drought and industrial recession forced a postponement of the new Plan. In November 1966, a big agitation took place for banning cow slaughter, an evocative and explosive issue because cows are sacred to Hindus.

By the mid-Sixties, Western donors became increasingly critical of India's development strategy and took measures to change it through the lever of economic assistance. President Johnson has recorded that both India and Pakistan had used U.S. weapons, leading to doubts about the value of military and economic aid.[61] The day Mrs. Gandhi was sworn in, the U.S. Administration unveiled an aid budget whose general thrust was to reward those who followed an American assessment of priorities.

Mrs. Gandhi undertook a visit to the U.S. towards the end of March 1966. President Johnson was charming and told senators that they must help "this little lady."[62] The major problem confronting India was shortage of food and foreign exchange. Mrs. Gandhi was promised help on both these counts. She displayed tact over the Vietnam problem,[63] linking a halt to the bombing of Vietnam with a cease-fire in South Vietnam although this moderate position was also influenced by the China factor.

During her first months in office, Mrs. Gandhi confounded the left, which had greeted her election with enthusiasm. After her American visit, she "was accused of having turned too pro-American,"⁶⁴ as she herself confessed. But worse was to come. Her Government devalued the rupee by 57 per cent on June 5, 1966, falling in line with the World bank's advice. She later suggested that she took the decision because her ministers and the Planning Commission recommended it, not because the World Bank thought so, and that she "personally knew little about the whole thing."⁶⁵

In any event, the devaluation decision alienated her from Kamaraj, who opposed it, and the left. It was no secret that both the U.S. and the World Bank were exerting considerable pressure on India to change its economic strategy and couple devaluation with import liberalization. A substantial level of nonproject loans followed, but the aid increase evaporated after a year. Besides, President Johnson's decision to "short-tether" food aid in the 1965-67 drought years led to much bitterness in India.

Kosygin had journeyed to Delhi for the Shashtri funeral, as he had for his predecessor's, again with an eye on probing the likely shape of things to come. Mrs. Gandhi's election was welcomed by Moscow. *New Times* of February 2, 1966 said that she represented "that group in the Congress which has consistently striven towards social and economic renewal."

However, it did not take the Soviets long to revert to their doubts. On August 11, 1966 *New Times* referred to India's increasing dependence on American aid and "the growing strength of the capitalist monopolies with their close foreign ties." On September 21 *New Times* suggested that India was in an "exceptionally complex political situation" with the right "making more and more determined efforts to influence its policies." By October 9 *New Times* proclaimed the draft Fourth Five-Year Plan as being inadequate to ward off "increased dependence on the imperialist West" and to provide for "the needs of the masses of the people."

The Soviets at that time harboured the fear that the rightists in the Congress party would combine with the right-wing Sangh and Swatantra parties. The Jana Sangh was decribed as the "reactionary Hindu religious party" preaching "Indian domination-chauvinism and intolerance of religious minorities."⁶⁶ But the Soviets wanted to reform Mrs. Gandhi's Government, not topple it. A demonstration led by the Communist Party of India to demand her resignation did not find space in the Soviet press.

Mrs. Gandhi went to Moscow in July 1966 and modified India's position on Vietnam by merely calling for an immediate and unconditional halt to American bombing,[67] both to please her hosts and refurbish her leftist credentials. A tripartite summit with Tito and Nasser, held in Delhi in October, repeated this formulation. She recorded later, "This and my previous denunciations of bombing strained Indo-American relations."[68] In July 1966, the Pakistan air chief visited Moscow but the expected arms deal did not materialize. Mrs. Gandhi said after her own Moscow visit that there was no Soviet arms deal with Pakistan.[69]

The Tashkent meeting was held against the background of a succession of Chinese failures in foreign policy. The second Afro-Asian conference, on which they had set their hearts, evaporated; their unsuccessful intervention in the 1965 Indo-Pakistani war made them out to be paper tigers; and Beijing suffered a major setback in the Indonesian Communist Party's abortive coup attempt in October 1965.

To the Chinese, Tashkent represented a convergence of Soviet and American interests against China; indeed, Washington seemed to have recognized Soviet primacy on the subcontinent. "The policy of the new leaders of the CPSU [Communist Party of the Soviet Union]," said *Red Flag*, "is to unite with U.S. imperialists and the reactionaries of various countries in forging a counter-revolutionary ring of encirclement against China."[70]

By early 1966 the Chinese sought to spread dissent and disaffection in India, supported irredentist movements in Nagaland and the Mizo areas in the northeast and in Kashmir in the north, questioned India's treaty relations with the kingdoms of Bhutan and Sikkim and generally expressed a high degree of hostility. After launching the Cultural Revolution in mid-1966, the Chinese propagated with full force the relevance of the Maoist line to India. They called for the broadest possible front against the "reactionary Indian authorities" and saw the situation in early 1967 as being even riper for a Maoist revolution.

The Chinese could derive some wry satisfaction from the thought that their policy of strong support for Pakistan, now buttressed with military as well as economic aid, had made Moscow sing a different tune. The Soviets were now the most ardent advocates of Indo-Pakistani amity. Given Ayub's domestic compulsions and the legacy of the past, the "Tashkent spirit," as Moscow liked to characterize it, did not last long.

But the Soviets persevered, despite the limiting Chinese factor, in building a close relationship with Pakistan. (Pakistan was the only non-Communist country to escape abuse during the Cultural Revolution). Soviet advice to India remained constant: make up with Pakistan. Moscow was trying to repeat a policy the Americans had tried without success.

The Soviets were essentially following a three-track policy towards India after Nehru: befriend Pakistan; adopt a stern, even rude, approach to India; and at the same time continue to give military and economic assistance to New Delhi. A new trade agreement was signed in December 1966 on the Khrushchevian pattern of doubling the two countries' trade in five years.[71] At the Twenty-third Congress in 1966, Leonid Brezhnev proclaimed that Indo-Soviet relations were a "traditional friendship ... that has withstood the test of time."[72]

Unlike Shastri, Mrs. Gandhi shared her father's concept of India's global role. But she had to take into account the border war and the new Chinese policies and scuttle Nehru's pan-Asianism. The most dramatic change was in her style of conducting foreign policy. Till the end, Nehru kept a certain distance between himself and the Soviets. Mrs. Gandhi started from the premise that the Soviets were heavily involved in India and the subcontinent and used this involvement to buttress her power domestically and achieve the country's essential aims in foreign policy.

Moscow, it would seem, showed Mrs. Gandhi greater consideration than it had accorded Shastri, primarily because they associated her with Nehru's policies.[73] But their approach to the subcontinent did not change. Much as Mrs. Gandhi disliked the trend of Soviet-Pakistan relations, she had little option but to bide her time, particularly because she was bracing herself for the looming battle with the stalwarts in the Congress party.

Chapter Four

THE TREATY

IN 1967, the Congress party went into the general election without the comforting presence of Nehru. Given the scale of the economic problems and Mrs. Gandhi's hesistant beginning as Prime Minister, the results were little short of disastrous for the Congress. It lost majorities in nine of the sixteen states, surviving in power at the Centre with a reduced majority of barely forty.

Mrs. Gandhi's main theme in the election meetings was the need to obtain economic assistance from abroad "without strings" and the Congress election manifesto had called for "social control" of banks. The right-wing Jana Sangh declared itself against the policy of nonalignment as a "permanent creed," advocated "bilateral alliances" of convenience and suggested the "ultimate reunification of India and Pakistan."[1]

Mrs. Gandhi was attacked from the left and the right. Krishna Menon resigned from the Congress and contested the election as an independent candidate, with Communist support. After the Communists split in 1964, the parallel Communist Party of India (Marxist) was immediately dubbed pro-Beijing.

Both the Communist parties were breathing fire and brimstone. S.A. Dange of the CPI had led a demonstration to Parliament House the previous September, asking for the resignation of Mrs. Gandhi's government, and declared, "This is the last and final warning" to mend its policies.[2]

A CPI(M) spokesman said before the election that the Congress was "the main enemy of the people" and described his party's primary aim as one of defeating the Congress in as many constituencies as possible.[3] Morarji Desai was to charge later that Mrs. Gandhi had "selected some ex-Communists and persons who favoured her" as the party's candidates.[4]

The Congress reverses were laced with a significant message in the selective defeats of many of the party stalwarts. Kamaraj, Atulya

Ghosh of West Bengal and S.K. Patil of Bombay lost their seats in a seeming avalanche. Mrs. Gandhi was naturally not displeased with this development.

The party bosses were considerably less enthusiastic in confirming Mrs. Gandhi as Prime Minister than they had been in elevating her to the post in the first instance. She had proved less docile than they had been led to believe. But Kamaraj the kingmaker, having lost his kingdom, was in no position to challenge her. He and his colleagues decided on the next best option: to impose Desai on Mrs. Gandhi as Deputy Prime Minister to be the Syndicate's watchdog.

Mrs. Gandhi won no praise from the Soviets. *New Times* of March 29, 1967 said that her cabinet was "a coalition of the ruling party's centrist and rightist elements." *International Affairs* of April 1967 posed the question, "Given the present balance of forces in the Indian National Congress, is not the election victory a triumph for big monopoly capital?" The critical note was amplified by the fear of "potential departures from the established neutral course in foreign policy."

Moscow Radio warned on November 29, 1967 that India's "progressive gains, its independence and its foreign policy are threatened" and "the hand of reaction raised above its future must be stopped." Mrs. Gandhi could derive some comfort from the fact that the Soviets were not frontally attacking her.

The Chinese, in the thick of the Cultural Revolution, were lacing their animosity towards India with ideological fervour. Somewhat in the manner of school teachers taking backward pupils in hand, Beijing asked the CPI(M) to disregard Soviet advice to get together with the CPI. Their own advice was clear-cut: "relentless armed struggle" to "forcibly seize power."[5]

Beijing was further encouraged by a dramatic development on June 10, 1967. Peasants at Naxalbari and two adjoining villages in the Darjeeling district of West Bengal had risen in revolt. The Chinese line on India now became one of relying on peasants to establish base areas in the countryside and using it to encircle and finally capture the cities.

The Chinese had become sufficiently disillusioned with the Marxists—the CPI(M)—to abuse their leaders. The Marxists were in power through coalitions in the states of Kerala and West Bengal, although the latter government was to be dismissed by the Centre in November 1967, and accused China of "gross interference."[6]

According to Beijing, E.M.S. Namboodiripad, the Kerala Marxist leader, acted as "an apologist and protector of the imperialist agents of U.S. imperialism."[7]

On the other hand, despite President Ayub's fears that the Cultural Revolution might slow down his country's burgeoning relationship with China, Beijing went on building up links with Islamabad. In 1967, it increased the 1964 loan of $60 million to $67 million for food aid.[8] China had signed its first arms aid agreement with Pakistan in 1966 for $120 million. By 1968 it undertook to supply 100 T-59 tanks, 80 MIG-19s and 10 Ilyushin-28s. China also agreed to equip three Pakistani infantry divisions and build a munitions factory in East Pakistan.[9]

In April 1967, Mrs. Gandhi's own view of the world around her was that there had been a softening of the Chinese attitude, as far as Sino-Indian relations were concerned, but she did not believe the Cultural Revolution was the right time to initiate a phase of better relations. She hinted at informal approaches made to China.[10]

Mrs. Gandhi's reading of the Pakistan situation was that Ayub had to give in to pressures from Bhutto, who had been forced to leave the cabinet in the summer of 1966, to take up an anti-Indian stance. She felt that Bhutto believed that only an anti-Indian posture could keep Pakistan together, although his objective was also to resist the "tide" of Indian cultural and other influences; hence the Pakistani decision to ban Indian songs and films.

One way of improving relations with Pakistan, Mrs. Gandhi suggested, was to begin in the economic field. But she held out little hope, since Pakistanis preferred to buy coal from China at three times the price of Indian coal. And she added the rider that no Indian government could placate Pakistan on Kashmir, adding, "And what new solution can there be on Kashmir?"

Mrs. Gandhi blamed Britain, and only to a lesser extent the United States, for opposing India's "proper role" in the region. In her view, Britain first tried to build up Pakistan, failing which it successfully promoted friendly relations between Pakistan and China. She believed that Britain did not want relations between India and Pakistan to improve.

In Pakistan in 1967, the Kashmir problem was a symbol of Pakistanis' image of India.[11] It was also a yardstick to judge relations with third countries, an instrument for survival for the ruling elite and a foreign policy issue which emphasized Pakistan's approach to India.

India loomed large in Pakistan. Pakistanis believed that New Delhi's attitude to Muslims was basically antagonistic and only a strong Pakistan imbibed with the spirit of *jihad* (holy war) could keep India from subverting it militarily or culturally. Ayub's policy was based on these assumptions, and he used Kashmir to emphasize his country's separate nationhood.

Kashmir gave an edge to Ayub's desire to transform Pakistan into a West Asian country; East Pakistan's separate independence in the long run was taken for granted. For Ayub, the Regional Cooperation for Development was ultimately aimed at providing Pakistan with an economic base equal to India's and giving his country depth in defence.

In the Pakistan National Assembly in May, there were questions galore on India, on Pakistan's next step on Kashmir and on alleged Indians plans to go nuclear. A government spokesman amplified that there were "grounds for apprehension" that India might explode a nuclear device.[12]

The popular mood in Pakistan after the Middle East war of 1967 was that the country was living in a hostile world and could not rely on any of the big powers for support; even China's friendship was doubted by a minority. There was also the feeling that India had not accepted Pakistan. Most members of the National Assembly saw India as a mighty war machine equipped with nuclear potential. The U.S. was widely condemned for having "let down" Pakistan in the 1965 war.

By September 1967, significant sections of East Pakistanis had already decided that independence was the only way out for them, that otherwise they would always remain the ruled. It was univerally recognized that Ayub's successor would be the army commander in chief. The lessons East Pakistanis learnt from the 1965 war, when they felt they had been left defenceless, was that their defence did not lie in the western wing.[13]

President Ayub, meanwhile, had unveiled his political testament. The title of *Friends Not Masters* he took from a defiant speech he had made after a Washington-initiated postponement of the Aid to Pakistan consortium meeting in 1965. But his political account stopped short of the war, which had been a major error of policy and strategy.

Ayub proclaimed that his country was nonaligned despite its membership of two pacts. But he sought to distinguish it from India's policy of the Fifties, which he termed opportunistic, suggesting that his objective was "to conserve our resources and to cut our commitment." "Walking on a triangular tightrope," he explained, was necessitated by Pakistan sharing borders with three large countries. He sought friendship with two of them through a strategy of bilateral equations.[14]

There was a dramatic improvement in Pakistan's relations with the Soviet Union. Within two years of the first May Day slogan on Pakistan in May 1965, the slogan for India was changed, made identical to that of the former and brought down to just above Pakistan's. Slogans for all countries, except for Vietnam, were dropped on the 50th anniversary of the October Revolution.[15]

The Soviet Union signed a major aid agreement with Pakistan in September 1966 for setting up 15 broadcasting houses and 21 projects. By the end of 1967, Moscow had committed Rs.875 million of aid for Pakistan's Third Plan.[16] In 1967, Pakistan and the Soviet Union decided to "draft a plan on a further substantial increase in economic cooperation and trade" extending to 1975.

As India warily watched the success of Ayub's "triangular tightrope walking," its own relations with the Soviets had entered a rocky phase. As early as 1966, the CPSU Central Committee had sought to make a distinction between nonaligned countries "fighting for the social progress of their country" (the U.A.R., Algeria, Syria, Burma, Guinea and Mali) and others such as India.[17] And New Delhi had still to recover from the shock of sharing Moscow with a new bride, Pakistan. By 1968 Soviet patience with India was beginning to wear thin.

The denouement—Soviet arms for Pakistan—was not long in coming. In July 1966, the Pakistan air chief, Air Marshal Nur Khan, had gone to Moscow for arms, but the expected deal did not materialize. Before Ayub's second visit to Moscow in 1967, the confident Pakistani expectation was that they would receive some Russian arms.

Ayub's visit was significant, with the two countries reaching an identity of views on Vietnam and the Middle East. And during a speech at a Kremlin banquet on September 26, 1967 he pointedly referred to the "growing military imbalance" on the subcontinent, with the Kashmir problem unresolved.[18] In February 1968, it was reported that the Soviets had agreed to supply India more than 100 SU-7 fighter bombers.

The Pakistanis understandably demanded a token of Moscow's interest in their welfare in the shape of arms. The Soviets had supplied Pakistan twelve MI-6 helicopters and other equipment in the second half of 1967. To allay Indian fears, they concluded negotiations with India for delivery of about 100 SU-7 fighter bombers. The total Soviet military credits to India, including the new deal, were estimated at between $600 million and $700 million.[19]

This led to Pakistani protests to the Soviet Union and Kosygin went to Islamabad in April 1968 to reach an agreement in principle on the supply of arms while publicly making two major commitments: a steel mill and an atomic plant.[20] Foreign Minister Arshad Husain told the National Assembly on June 22, 1968 that the government was considering the question of arms supplies from the Soviet Union.[21] A few days later a military delegation led by the army chief, General Yahya Khan, left for Moscow to finalize the deal.

The fact that the Yahya delegation left Moscow the day before President Zakir Husain of India arrived on an official visit was not lost upon New Delhi. To drive the point home, President Podgorny's welcome speech bracketed India with Pakistan.[22] Zakir Husain warned the Soviets of the pressures their new policy would create on Mrs. Gandhi's government, but received less than full satisfaction. The Soviets tried to set Indian fears at rest, without success.

In January 1968, Kosygin had paid an important visit to New Delhi to warn at a dinner that the "alternative to this [peaceful settlement of problems between India and Pakistan] is only war."[23] His real purpose was to give assurances of Soviet support to India against the background of the deepening political crisis in the country, the intensification of the Vietnam war and the intended British withdrawal from Asia by 1971.[24]

Apart from pressing upon Mrs. Gandhi his theme that there could be no stability in South Asia without a "modus vivendi in the Indo-Pakistan subcontinent,"[25] Kosygin made no secret of his distress over the poor performance of Soviet-aided projects. He decided to send teams of experts to study the problem and suggest remedies. Kosygin had two long meetings with Mrs. Gandhi, with only Russian interpreters present.

The Soviet teams' visits culminated in the arrival of S. Skatchkov in December. He expressed concern over underutilization of plants and slow completion of other projects to suggest that unless public sector plants gave dividends for investment, there was something wrong with their organization and scale of production.[26] The Soviets agreed to buy Indian products from Soviet-aided projects to pull India out of difficulties, although the offer to buy 54,000 railway wagons came to nothing in view of disputes over price and specifications.[27]

India had begun to run up a favourable trade balance with the Soviet Union in the mid-Sixties. By late Sixties the Soviets were making plain their concern over the imbalance to visiting Indian delegations.[28] *Pravda* of May 9, 1968 took S.K. Patil, identified with the right lobby in the Congress party, to task for questioning Soviet motives in ordering rolled steel and railway wagons from India. It stressed that the orders were meant to help India's sluggish economy while pointing to the need for increasing Soviet exports to India.

Soviet criticism of India was muted before the Kosygin visit and a broadcast quoting *New Times* on January 24, 1968 said Indo-Soviet friendship had passed the "acid test of time." Moscow Radio had helpfully suggested the previous day that in the difficult year through which India had passed, progressives "value even more every step that strengthens Soviet-Indian friendship." In the event, the Skatchkov visit at the end of the year left a bad taste in the mouth because of his gruff and imperious manner.[29]

Indian Ambassador Kewal Singh had met Kosygin in April 1968 on the eve of the latter's visit to Pakistan and handed him a letter from Mrs. Gandhi. Kosygin's subsequent visit to New Delhi on his way back to Moscow surprised Pakistanis. The Pakistani announcement the next month that the U.S. intelligence base near Peshawar would not be extended won expected Soviet plaudits.[30]

The *Hindustan Standard* of Calcutta broke the story of the Soviet arms deal with Pakistan on July 8. There were ample Indian warnings about the consequences of military assistance to Pakistan, from Prime Minister Gandhi down. Mrs. Gandhi had written to Kosygin in April 1968 again to warn him about arms for Pakistan. Although the Soviets had taken Indian feelings into account, they had underestimated their intensity.

Mrs. Gandhi helped restrain Indian displeasure, but the biggest ever anti-Soviet demonstration, organized by the Jana Sangh, was held in New Delhi on July 24 and had to be dispersed with tear gas and *lathi* charges.[31] The Prime Minister and her ministers made it clear that Indo-Soviet relations had suffered in the process. The Russians were somewhat shaken by the growing anti-Soviet climate in India. The popular reaction was that the Soviets had betrayed India.

The Russians obviously felt India had no choice but to acquiesce in the Soviet policy of supplying arms to Pakistan.[32] It faced an unfriendly Pakistan and China and the Americans seemed in no mood to help, having relegated the subcontinent to the back burner after the 1965 war. The fact that India was not entirely helpless was indicated by Mrs. Gandhi. In two carefully timed statements—in September 1968 and January 1969—she made peace overtures to China.[33]

After the anti-Soviet demonstrations and the high level of public and official displeasure, Indian officials had made it clear to the Soviets that despite their protestations, Indo-Soviet relations could never be as they were if they continued to arm Pakistan.

Private discussions were held at various levels. The Soviets asserted that India was the most important country in Asia and no other nation was in the same category. To prove their point, Soviet officials said India could have a treaty with Moscow, if it wanted one. The suggestion was first made at a junior level.[34]

Discussions on the treaty were held in a desultory fashion from the second half of 1968. On the Indian side, the negotiations were largely conducted by Foreign Secretary T.N. Kaul and Ambassador D.P. Dhar, Prime Minister Indira Gandhi's trusted political aide. Indeed, it seems likely that Dhar's appointment to Moscow in the first place, in January 1969, was made by Mrs. Gandhi with an eye on the treaty.[35]

Mrs. Gandhi's primary aim in taking up the Russians on their offer of a treaty was to break the new compact between Pakistan and the Soviet Union. Her domestic compulsions had not become as urgent as they did after President Zakir Husain's death in early May 1969.

Mrs. Gandhi had written to Kosygin on July 10, 1968 on the dangers of giving arms to Pakistan. In his prompt reply Kosygin referred to the close Indo-Soviet relations, suggesting that even if Pakistan received arms, it was in the larger interests of the region. After Tashkent, Kosygin had emerged as the dominant voice in shaping Soviet foreign policy. Perhaps he also felt that he was responsible for forcing the Tashkent Declaration on Ayub, thus weakening his position domestically.

Kosygin and his colleagues were impressed by Ayub and, even more, by the content he gave to his country's nonalignment. Kosygin had convinced himself and the Kremlin leadership that the only sensible course to follow in South Asia lay in a more balanced approach to the two main countries to keep China at bay and assert the Soviet Union's dominance. The logic of this approach demanded that the Soviets give Pakistan some arms.

The crisis for the Soviets in Czechoslovakia, meanwhile, was building up. Soviet and other Warsaw pact troops marched into Czechoslovakia in August 1968 to subdue a people who, Moscow felt, were dangerously close to subverting the Socialist Commonwealth. Brezhnev unveiled his doctrine of limited sovereignty for the Communist world.

There was popular sympathy for the Czechs in India and demands were made even in Mrs. Gandhi's party to condemn the Soviet action. But India expressed only mild "regret" and abstained in the Security Council vote. Despite the tensions between India and the Soviet Union, New Delhi felt it had little option but to stop short of opposing Moscow in the United Nations; the Indian action was, in a measure, repayment for the vetoes Moscow had exercised in the past on India's behalf.

Against this background, Soviet Deputy Foreign Minister Firyubin's talks in New Delhi in September 1968 with Minister of State B.R. Bhagat were barely civil. Firyubin said Soviet arms to Pakistan were already paying dividends. He was evasive on support for Kashmir and asked if Beijing and New Delhi were coming together.[36]

Bhagat countered with an inquiry on reported moves for a Sino-Soviet rapprochement and also raised the question of Soviet maps on the Sino-Indian border following the Chinese version and the anti-Indian propaganda conducted over Radio Peace and Progress in Moscow. Firyubin did not offer satisfaction on any of these points.

In the first years of office, Mrs. Gandhi was still feeling her way while gradually preparing herself for battle to assert her authority. The crisis this was bound to create was suddenly brought forward by the death of President Zakir Husain. The Indian presidency is a largely ceremonial office, but Mrs. Gandhi feared—not entirely without reason—that the party bosses' choice of a presidential candidate would be the thin end of the wedge, and that if she wanted to exercise authority, she had to have her own man.

The political temperature in India was high in May 1969. Government leaders realized that the Congress had lost West Bengal for a time to the Communist front and would find it difficult to get back Punjab from the opposition.[37] Kashmir was in the throes of internal problems and an agitation was raging over the issue of a separate Telengana in the South. One intensely debated issue was whether the Congress would obtain a majority at the Centre in the 1972 general elections.[38]

On May 26, 1969 Mrs. Gandhi suggested[39] that the "President is the President of the nation"—a retort to the Congress bosses' view, widely reported at the time, that the candidate for presidency must be a Congressman. She said there was no indication of a friendlier approach from the Chinese, despite Indian overtures, and there was no proposal to exchange ambassadors. (The two countries' embassies were in the care of charges d'affaires since the 1962 war). She said the U.S. Secretary of State, William Rogers, was affable but cautious during his recent visit to New Delhi. On Pakistan she averred that "things have not got worse." Indo-Pakistani attempts at better relations were to be stalemated in July.

Events were moving towards a climax. A meeting of the All-India Congress Committee (AICC), the party's plenary body, was called in July in the salubrious southern city of Bangalore. It provided the setting for the confrontation between Mrs. Gandhi and the party bosses.

Mrs. Gandhi lost over the issue of the Congress candidate for presidency, but she had, as part of her strategy, proposed a vague radical economic programme at a party committee meeting.[40] The bosses' ability to have their candidate, Sanjiva Reddy, accepted by the party was a slap in Mrs. Gandhi's face.

It was clear that Mrs. Gandhi would stand up and fight. And fight she did, relieving Morarji Desai of the Finance portfolio and floating a radical economic package, including the nationalization of 14 major banks. But after some hestitation, she did file the nomination paper of Sanjiva Reddy, the Congress candidate for presidency. She was not quite ready to reveal her hand.[41]

There were indications during the July meeting of the AICC that Mrs. Gandhi was seeking to distance herself from Foreign Minister Dinesh Singh, a close associate during the early phase of her Prime Ministership.[42] He was a member of the so-called "kitchen cabinet." He was absent from the crucial AICC meeting and was not summoned home in a hurry from the U.N. General Assembly session in New York.

In August, Mrs. Gandhi repudiated Sanjiva Reddy's candidature and was obviously supporting the Vice President, V.V. Giri, for the office. Giri had already won the support of the two Communist parties.[43] There were organized rallies outside her residence, fighting speeches, and an attempt to identify Mrs. Gandhi with the poor. Her party opponents charged that there was danger of Communist infiltration in the Congress, that she, in fact, was under Communist influence. The party president, S. Nijalingappa, went to the extent of calling a press conference to assure her that she would not be toppled.[44]

The future pattern was set after the victory of Mrs. Gandhi's candidate, Giri, on August 16, 1969. There was increasing cooperation between the Congress and the two Communist parties. Mrs. Gandhi's cabinet ministers took to sharing tea trays with Communist members of Parliament in the lobbies. And some Communist members were asserting that they could help the Prime Minister's "progressive policies and measures." Even some of the left Congress members were having doubts. "They talk of the price the Russians will demand for CPI's support for Mrs. Gandhi's government in the changed context," I then reported.[45]

The Communists held victory celebrations. But they were disappointed that the split in the Congress had not yet come about, the Congress Working Committee having worked out a patchwork peace. The Communists were impatient to play an important role in the Centre's affairs.[46]

The formal split in the Congress occurred just before Mrs. Gandhi's 52nd birthday in November and an opposition Congress party was formed. The Congress majority of 48 in the Lower House was wiped out. The CPI had 24 members and there were 59 independents.[47] Towards the end of October, the Marxist-dominated government in Kerala fell, and the Marxists charged that the CPI was responsible for the manoeuvre for the benefit of Mrs. Gandhi's Congress.[48]

Kosygin visited New Delhi in May 1969 for Zakir Husain's funeral. It was a last-minute decision made on the persistent pleas of Foreign Secretary Kaul that lower level representation would be misunderstood in India.[49] While it was clear that the Russians were surprised by the intensity of the Indian reaction to Soviet arms for Pakistan, Moscow's attitude represented no change.[50] Such arms, it was suggested, were a microscopic proportion of what India received.

Soviet arms to Pakistan, Kosygin argued, were meant to reduce Chinese influence there and induce Pakistan to be friendly to India.

One aspect of the talks that caused much heartburn in the Indian External Affairs Ministry was the fact that Mrs. Gandhi had closed door meetings with Kosygin, with only Soviet interpreters present.[51] From what Mrs. Gandhi chose to reveal to her officials, the Soviets tried to assuage Indian feelings by offering more arms while sticking to their line. It is not farfetched to assume that the secret Kosygin-Gandhi talks concerned the treaty.

The Soviets were still greatly concerned with the strength of Indian right-wing parties, the economic direction the country was taking and difficulties experienced by Soviet-aided projects. On the Indian side, the issue of Soviet arms for Pakistan loomed large, but there were other irritants. Russian maps still delineated the Sino-Indian border according to Chinese claims and Radio Peace and Progress continued to fulminate against Indian leaders Moscow considered "reactionary."

The Soviets were put out by the belated support India gave Moscow on the Sino-Soviet border dispute.[52] Indeed, if there were any doubts, the Kosygin visit made it amply clear that the Soviets were obsessed with China and a Soviet objective was to build a strong and stable India as a counterweight to China.[53]

Kosygin made a significant speech at the Red Fort in New Delhi on May 6, 1969. He said, "The Soviet Union has always had complete understanding for the Indian people's peace-loving aspirations and their desire to live in peace with their neighbours, since without this it is impossible to resolve big and crucial tasks in the area of economic and social progress."[54]

That the discussions on the treaty had entered a delicate stage was clear from a letter I received from Ambassador Dhar in Moscow. It was dated May 22, 1969. It broached the following "suggestion": "While we should be clearly aware of our national interests, it is important again in our national interests that the present stage of our relations with the Soviet Union or its possible development should not be subjected to fortuitous comment and never, under any circumstances, to calumny. As an example, you and I know that Firubin [Firyubin] had nothing to do with the question of Soviet arms aid to Pakistan, yet he was described as the main architect of this proposal."

Dhar was objecting to a report appearing in *The Statesman* on

Indo-Soviet talks. An obvious problem for those discussing in secret the treaty was how to tone down public and press comments on the Soviets.[55] Serious discussions on the treaty began after the Sino-Soviet border incidents in the Ussuri in March 1969. The Soviets were suffering from a feeling of isolation.

Apart from the Kosygin visit in May, an important foreign visitor to New Delhi was President Nixon, who stopped over in the Indian capital in August for barely twenty-four hours in the course of his Asian tour. Nixon assured Mrs. Gandhi that the U.S. would remain a Pacific power, but he would ensure that there would be no more Vietnams although he would give support for fighting internal subversion. Nixon said he was opposed to the Indian proposal for the two superpowers guaranteeing Asian states' security.

The Indian side drew the somewhat optimistic conclusion from the Nixon visit that future U.S. policy would help, rather than hinder, possible Indian initiatives in the region. But the exchange of views was useful in pinpointing some U.S. policies. These were: no U.S. interest in involving itself in Indo-Pakistani disputes, the U.S. would not flood Pakistan with weapons, China would not be "isolated" and Nixon had no desire to help the Soviet Union's anti-Chinese policies and hence was not interested in underwriting Asian nations' security with the Soviet Union.[56]

While the Russians' Chinese compulsions, and the prospect of a U.S.-Chinese rapprochement, were responsible for their pushing the treaty with India, Mrs. Gandhi's domestic problems were making it a more attractive proposition. With the impending split in the Congress and the fact that Mrs. Gandhi would have to survive on Communist support, there was obvious benefit in securing the enthusiastic backing of the CPI's mentors in Moscow.

Important discussions were held in Moscow in July 1969, and with Ambassador Dhar in Moscow and Foreign Secretary Kaul in New Delhi functioning as essential links between the two leaderships, a treaty was drafted by P.N. Haksar, the Prime Minister's principal secretary.[57]

It was this draft Foreign Minister Dinesh Singh took with him to Moscow in September 1969. But before his departure, Mrs. Gandhi held a meeting with Kosygin in New Delhi. He stopped in the Indian capital on his way to Hanoi to attend Ho Chi Minh's funeral. India was represented in Hanoi by Foreign Minister Dinesh Singh.

The Kosygin-Gandhi meetings took place with only Soviet

interpreters present.[58] There were, of course, good reasons for the secrecy because the two leaders were discussing the draft of the treaty which was being finalized. According to Dinesh Singh, "The treaty was agreed to between me and [Soviet Foreign Minister] Gromyko when I went to Moscow. Swaran Singh [later to take over as foreign minister] finalized it [in June 1971]. As agreed to by me, it was compatible with nonalignment. But it was later amended to give it a deeper [Soviet] defence commitment"[59] Whether the ultimate treaty was stronger or weaker than the original document is a matter of controversy, as we shall see.

Although the draft of the treaty was accepted by both sides during Dinesh Singh's visit to Moscow in September 1969, the Indian Foreign Minister told Gromyko that he would not sign it for the present. Gromyko proved fully cooperative and said he would understand if Mrs. Gandhi wanted to delay signing it because it was "not convenient."[60]

The reasons for Mrs. Gandhi's hesitation in signing the treaty were no secret to the Russians. They were lending her vociferous support in her new economic and political programmes. After their fears of "right-wing reaction" gaining the upper hand in India, they were greatly relieved by, and supportive of, Mrs. Gandhi's radical rhetoric—*after* her victory over the Syndicate.

The measure of Soviet understanding of Mrs. Gandhi's position can be gleaned from an *Izvestia* commentary on September 20, 1969 shortly after Dinesh Singh's visit. It referred to the "complicated...domestic political situation" in India; the positions of the "reactionaries," it averred, were "still rather strong, and the forces of progress will have to go through difficult trials in the struggle."

With Mrs. Gandhi still to complete the takeover of the Congress and venture on the dangerous waters of a truncated Congress, a bombshell like the Indo-Soviet treaty would have blown her totally off course.[61] Despite the rhetoric, a majority of Congressmen had a visceral dislike of Communism.

If Mrs. Gandhi needed any proof, it came immediately after the party split. She appointed three ex-Communists as new members of her truncated party's working committee. There was an uproar in her party. The new members were charged by their fellow partymen with being "embassy men" frequenting the corridors of Communist embassies in New Delhi. Foreign Minister Dinesh Singh was among those disappointed and organized a deputation of five persons to see Mrs. Gandhi. Her motive seemed to be to test her supporters' reaction to a possible alignment with the CPI in fighting an early general election.[62]

The spillover of the power game played by Mrs. Gandhi into the field of foreign policy caused a search for new gimmicks as part of the efforts for projecting a radical image.[63] Dinesh Singh seemed to have convinced himself that the Indian consulate general in Hanoi should be elevated to a full-fledged embassy, contrary to the declared policy on divided countries. A decision was taken to upgrade the State Trading Corporation office in East Berlin to a trade commission.

There was still some hesitation in giving full diplomatic recognition to East Germany, in view of the substantial trade and aid relationship with West Germany. Dinesh Singh gave a radio talk in October, largely to explain away India's discomfiture in an Islamic conference in Rabat, Morocco, and blamed "imperialism" and "imperialist countries" nine times.[64]

Even while implementing these changes and voicing radical slogans, Dinesh Singh's heart was not in foreign policy. The domestic political crisis led him to buttress his position in his home state of Uttar Pradesh in September.[65] In November, he was leading the anti-Communist brigade in Mrs. Gandhi's new Congress party. And in December he was being looked upon with suspicion by Mrs. Gandhi's supporters.[66]

Dinesh Singh's replacement as Foreign Minister by Swaran Singh early in 1970 had nothing to do with foreign policy, despite U.S. allergy to the former.[67] Dinesh was trying to build a base in Uttar Pradesh, traditionally a major power factor in Indian politics. And Mrs. Gandhi felt it was time to cut him down to size.

Questions of the country's security and Chinese nuclear capabilities were very much in Mrs. Gandhi's mind in her second term. Her concern was heightened by a whole range of developments, apart from the limitations imposed on India by the Chinese nuclear capability. There was first the British announcement in 1968 of their military withdrawal from east of Suez by 1971. Second, President Nixon's Guam doctrine foreshadowed American withdrawal from Vietnam and refusal to fight land wars in Asia in the future. Third, there were growing indications of a possible U.S.-Chinese rapprochement. Fourth, there were dangers India saw in the Nuclear Nonproliferation Treaty.

After the serious border clashes in the Ussuri, the Soviets took note anew of India's nuclear worries. An analysis in *Komsomolskaya Pravda*[68] in August 1969 decried Chinese nuclear blackmail against India and other Asian states and implicitly offered the Soviet Union as an alternative security guarantee. The Soviets had achieved rough nuclear parity with the U.S. even as their relations with China had dipped to a new low, with border clashes occurring between Xinjiang and Kazakhstan.

India feared that the Nuclear Nonproliferation Treaty, which was being negotiated by the superpowers, offered it no security. In May 1967 it announced that *all* signatory powers to the NPT come to the aid of any non-nuclear power threatened by a nuclear nation. The way the NPT was drafted seemed a challenge to India, which it elected to call.[69] Despite strong Soviet pressure, India refused to sign the NPT. Moscow's efforts were directed at persuading Asian states that they could obtain security without nuclear weapons. In India's case, the Soviets feared that an Indian bomb could lead to a Pakistani bomb, bringing about a high degree of instability on their southern borders.

At the end of August 1966, Lee Kuan Yew, Singapore's Prime Minister, suggested on the eve of his first state visit to India that New Delhi could make a significant contribution towards enforcing a Monroe Doctrine for Asia in the "second decade", ten years from then.[70] Kosygin, during his visit to New Delhi early in 1969, had reportedly expressed interest in the Indian idea of an "Eastern Locarno Pact," an agreement among Asian countries to respect one another's sovereignty and territorial integrity with no obligation to come to anyone's help in an emergency.[71]

Mrs. Gandhi did some "loud thinking" of her own during a visit to Canberra in May 1968, suggesting that "it should be possible to allay their [Asian nations'] anxiety by providing international guarantees for the neutrality and independence of this troubled region."[72] According to one amplification, she talked "specifically of the need to cultivate a tripod Indian-Australian-Japanese framework within which the smaller countries of Southeast Asia can achieve greater cohesion and progress."[73] Other newspaper accounts of Mrs. Gandhi's idea spoke of a joint guarantee of the great powers for protecting the sovereignty, independence and territorial integrity of the countries of South and Southeast Asia.[74]

Mrs. Gandhi herself was far less specific and did not refer to her proposal in reporting to Parliament on her Southeast Asian tour. Successive reports of the External Affairs Ministry watered down the concept of a guarantee to a convention until it was dissolved in generalities. During a visit to Japan in June 1969 Mrs. Gandhi had, however, scouted the idea of an Indian-Japanese arrangement expanded to include Southeast Asia, with great power endorsement.[75] One reaction it evoked was that it was Soviet-inspired. But Mrs. Gandhi was hedging her bets; she suggested during the same month that if a vacuum should be created in Asia by the British pullout of forces, it could be filled by the countries of the region without foreign intervention, or "the U.N. could guarantee the security of the countries affected."[76]

It was against the background of this concern over security of Asian nations as they looked to an uncertain future that Brezhnev told the international Communist conference in Moscow in June 1969: "We are of the opinion that the course of events is also putting on the agenda the task of creating a system of collective security in Asia."[77] He linked the proposal to detente in Europe and the threat from China, as perceived by Moscow.

There was no amplification of Brezhnev's intriguing proposal, but those looking for substance were referred to an *Izvestia* commentary of May 29, 1969 by V. Matveyev suggesting that India, Pakistan, Afghanistan, Burma, Cambodia and Singapore could be likely candidates for membership of such a system because they were oriented against the imperialists.

A teaser was added to the Brezhnev proposal by remarks made by Kosygin on May 30, 1969 during a visit to Pakistan. He said "the Soviet Union would like to see Pakistan, Afghanistan, India and other states of this region developing mutual relations of friendship and constructive cooperation. The Soviet Union will do its utmost to facilitate this."[78]

Five days before Brezhnev spoke of the need for collective security, *Pravda* suggested on June 2 that the Soviet Union was "doing everything" to promote cooperation among India, Pakistan and Afghanistan, which was needed "both in the field of economics and in the struggle for the preservation of universal peace."

The fact that Kosygin's economic plan for the region was an old idea first broached at the Tashkent conference in 1966 was clear from an article Bhutto wrote in April 1968. He said, "An overland link through Pakistan would give India access to the frontiers of the Soviet Union and undermine the strategic importance of this country."[79]

Yahya Khan's own reaction to the Kosygin proposal was initially evasive until on June 10, the day he was still prevaricating, a Pakistan Foreign Office spokesman shot it down, saying it had "little economic advantage for Pakistan," which would not attend the conference, proposed to be hosted by Afghanistan, as long as disputes with India remained unresolved.[80] This upset the Russians because they felt that having earlier privately agreed to the economic proposal, Yahya had gone back on his word.[81]

Mrs. Gandhi's reaction to the proposal was clear-cut. She welcomed the Kosygin plan, telling a meeting of the Congress Parliamentary Party in New Delhi on June 16 that it had "always been India's policy to promote regional cooperation, especially in trade and economic relations."[82] The conference was never held because of Pakistan's refusal to attend it.

With little of substance to go on, Brezhnev's Asian Collective Security idea provoked intense speculation around the world and was quickly dubbed "Moscow's anti-China pact."[83] It was, in any case, so perceived by most Asian nations and by China. *Peking Review* called it "Soviet revisionism's tattered flag for an anti-China military alliance." China, it suggested, was the victim of this "sinister" plan picked up by the Soviets "from the garbage heap of the notorious warmonger Dulles." In its view, India and Japan were to serve as the linchpins of the proposed security system in which the revisionists and imperialists were collaborating.[84]

Brezhnev was later to amplify his proposal. He suggested in March 1972 that it was aimed at renunciation of the use of force between states; respect for nations' sovereignty and existing frontiers; noninterference in the internal affairs of other states and cooperation in economic and other fields.[85]

Yet even in the early days of the proposal it was clear that to describe it merely as an anti-China pact was to place too narrow a construction on it although the China element was an important factor. The very vagueness of the proposal was intended to take into account the difficulties in implementing such a grand scheme. Indeed, between June 1969 and January 1973 the Soviets talked of obstacles to its implementation, suggesting only in 1973 that the "first phase of the struggle for Asian security" had been completed.[86]

Brezhnev was seeking to serve several Soviet objectives in springing the ACS on the world. He was laying out a Soviet agenda for post-Vietnam Asia and claiming for Moscow the primary role in ordering peace and affairs in the region. He was staking out the Soviet Union's status as a global power, having achieved rough strategic parity with the United States, and a special role by virtue of its new power and the fact that it was an Eurasian nation.

The last point was emphasized in a revealing commentary by A. Dzasokhov in *International Affairs* in May 1980. He said: "Being a country a large part of whose territory lies in Asia, the Soviet Union has always sought to prevent the process of international detente, which gathered momentum in the 1970s, from bypassing the Asian continent."

Since Moscow viewed China as a major obstacle to its interests and to peace in Asia, the strategic implications of the ACS could not be spelled out and would, in any case, pose serious problems even otherwise. Indeed, to counter the anti-Chinese connotations the proposal evoked in Asia, Gromyko specifically brought all states within its ambit at the twenty-fifth session of the United Nations General Assembly.

For countries like India, the Brezhnev proposal offered a goal different from the Nixon-Kissinger idea of a "generation of peace" and an Asian order based on cooperation among the U.S., the Soviet Union, China and Japan. The ACS at least offered the major Asian powers an incentive for maintaining stability in the region.

In view of China's own construction on the ACS, Asian reaction to it could only be cool, although it aroused great interest in Moscow's Asia policy in Singapore and Malaysia in particular. Having been freed from its exclusive relationship with Indonesia in Southeast Asia as the dominant arms supplier after the abortive Communist coup and the pro-Western orientation of Soekarno's successors, Moscow had consciously set about improving relations with nations in China's backyard in the late Sixties.

Pakistan had no hesitation in ultimately coming up with its response. An official Foreign Office spokesman said that "Pakistan has no intention of getting involved in any arrangement which may cast doubts on Sino-Pakistan relations."[87] And to rub in the point, Air Marshal Nur Khan, during a visit to China in July 1969, implicitly rejected the concept of the ACS by suggesting that his country would never abandon its relationship with China.[88]

With secret negotiations on the Indo-Soviet treaty in progress, India did not wish to give a rebuff to the ACS proposal. In fact, after agreeing to the draft treaty in Moscow, which remained unsigned Dinesh Singh said on his return to New Delhi that India welcomed "the proposal of the Soviet Union on the creation of a system of collective security in Asia," suggesting that "the essence of the Soviet plan is the development of cooperation among the Asian countries for the purpose of strengthening peace."[89] India quickly backtracked from this position and Dinesh Singh himself was to suggest in December that India did not believe in the notion of big powers acting as the guardian of security for India and its neighbours.[90]

Mrs. Gandhi was quite clear from the beginning that she did not want to lock herself into an anti-China position through the ACS. In an interview to *Il Giorno*, published on October 2, 1969, she described an alliance of Asian countries as "useless" because an alliance of one group would cause an immediate reaction by another, with consequent increase in tension.

Japan did not reject the ACS, but first asked for the return of the four northern islands and was not prepared to repudiate its security treaty with the U.S. Moscow tried to use the Nixon "shocks" of 1971 and 1972 to woo Japan, but the Chinese cut the ground from under the Soviets by speeding up their rapprochement with Tokyo. Diplomatic relations between the two countries were consummated in September 1972.

In view of the generally unenthusiastic response from most Asian countries to the ACS—balancing their relations between the two main Communist powers, North Vietnam and North Korea studiously avoided the whole subject—Moscow let the concept rest for a time. It would pick it up and promote it vigorously in fairer political winds.

There was a spurt of violence in West Bengal, with the Naxalites[91] launching a terrorist campaign; nearly forty-five policemen were killed in the state during the year. Direct rule from New Delhi had to be imposed on the state in 1970 and it was not until later in the year that the Naxalites were largely controlled.

An official Indian assessment[92] of the dissident Nagas in the Northeast in September 1969 was that the back of the rebellion had been broken, with the Naga underground strength estimated at between 8,000 and 10,000. A total of 1,500 Nagas had gone to China for training and weapons; not all had returned and some had been intercepted on the way. It was an arduous 380-mile trail from the Yunnan border and the Nagas were harassed on the way by the Burmese.

India had found it impossible to seal the border; rather, the aim was to control the movement of Nagas. The rebels usually brought with them rifles, light machine guns and plastic mines. The Indian impression was that the Chinese had been disappointed that their help had not produced results and New Delhi projected a falling off of Beijing's interest.

In the other trouble spot in the region, the Mizo problem had been brought under control, with a little under half of the population living in regrouped villages. There were an estimated 500 to 600 Mizos in East Pakistan, being used by the Pakistan authorities to embarrass India. In New Delhi's view, the Pakistanis might force the dissident Mizos back into India, in view of the depredations they were causing there.

There had, indeed, been a thaw in Sino-Indian relations beginning in the fall of 1969. China stopped supporting the Naxalites and propagating their exploits in India. And on May 1, 1970, Mao sought out the Indian chargé d'affaires to make laudatory references to India.

The "Mao smile," as it came to be dubbed in India, led to a series of meetings between Indian and Chinese diplomats in Moscow and Cairo. They were in the nature of probing missions on both sides and went on into the early months of 1970. The fact that the Mao smile preceded the unveiling of the Brezhnev plan became an additional factor for India to ensure that it did not arouse Chinese suspicions by endorsing it.

Mrs. Gandhi decided in December 1970 to seek early elections in the hope of changing the minority nature of her government. She probably figured that things would have been much worse a year later; prices of goods were sharply going up, unemployment was rising, there were snowballing demands for wage increases and the 1971 crop prospects did not seem too encouraging. She surprised her opponents and the world by winning a landslide victory, obtaining 359 seats in the Lower House of 521. A slogan she used to telling effect was *garibi hatao* (banish poverty). The results greatly strengthened her position and obviated the need for Communist or other opposition support for survival.

Events in Pakistan, meanwhile, had been taking an ominous turn. In later years, Ayub had given the army a back seat after appeasing it with pay increases and choice plots of land in the new capital of Islamabad. He ruled through civil servants and "basic democrats," who received money and privileges and provided the regime with support in the villages.

The edifice crumbled the moment it was seriously challenged, as it was in five months of turmoil in East Pakistan towards the end of 1968. The Tashkent Declaration in 1966 had seriously weakened Ayub and the Kashmir war of 1965 had led to a further alienation of East Pakistanis from the federal government. Bhutto was building his constituency in West Pakistan at Ayub's expense.

In January 1969, the Soviets were plainly anxious over Pakistan developments. Moscow's main contacts in Pakistan were with the army leaders and they feared the acquisition of strength by pro-Beijing forces. When Ayub realized that the army would act only on its own terms to prevent the break-up of the country, he handed over power to Yahya Khan in March. *Pravda* promptly offered support to Yahya on April 1.

Yahya ordered the country's first free elections, which were held on December 17, 1970, in the smug belief that the results would be inconclusive and would leave him in the real seat of power.[93] He was in for a nasty surprise. In East Pakistan, Sheikh Mujibur Rahman's Awami League, fighting on a six-point programme of regional autonomy, swept the polls, winning 167 of the 169 seats. In the western wing, Bhutto's People's Party emerged as the dominant force with 88 out of 144 seats.

The results were unpalatable to both the army and Bhutto because, if they were to be honoured, Mujib should hold power over the whole country, the eastern wing being the more populous. Yahya first postponed the session of the new assembly on the strength of Bhutto's announcement that he would not attend it, leading to riots in East Pakistan, especially in Dhaka. He then conducted eleven days of talks with Mujib, Bhutto providing the army his support for his own purposes.

The talks were in the nature of a smokescreen to enable the army to move troops to the eastern wing. India had banned Pakistani overflights over its territory following the hijacking of an Indian Airlines plane to Lahore in January 1971 and its destruction there. The ban meant that Pakistan needed more time to send reinforcements. The army cracked down on East Pakistan on March 25.

Despite discussions on the Indo-Soviet treaty, the Soviets continued to pursue their objectives in Pakistan. Swaran Singh, now Defence Minister and a man known to weigh his words, told Parliament on April 9, 1969 that there had been a change in Soviet policy towards India since Tashkent. He said India was not solely dependent on Soviet arms supplies, but warned members not to underrate Soviet friendship.[94]

Two Soviet statements caused much disquiet in India, both of them made in Pakistan. In mid-March 1969, the deputy chief of the Soviet navy was reported to have said, "A powerful Pakistan navy would be a powerful precondition for peace in this part of the Indian Ocean." The same month Soviet Defence Minister Grechko reportedly said that Pakistan was being supplied Soviet arms in order to fight its enemy, a statement that figured in Indian Parliament on April 10.[95]

In 1969, the Soviets were willing to help Pakistan build a naval base, primarily for submarines, at Gwadar, fifty miles east of the Pakistan-Iran border.[96] New Delhi's assumption was that this was due to India's refusal to give the Soviets base facilities. The Pakistan project was ultimately dropped.[97]

One consequence of the understanding on the Indo-Soviet treaty in September 1969 was a Soviet commitment not to make new arms agreements with Pakistan. Yahya Khan received no encouragement during his Moscow visit in 1970 and President Giri, who undertook a state visit to the Soviet Union in September that year, was told of the Soviet decision.[98]

Chapter Five

A WAR

THE year 1969 was notable for many reasons. Beginning in 1969, Moscow resumed and intensified East-West detente. The Sino-Soviet clashes in the Ussuri in March had coincided with another Berlin crisis, leading the Soviets to warn of "collusion" between China and West Europe, particularly West Germany. China, on its part, was fearful of an attack by the Soviet Union after the unveiling of the Brezhnev Doctrine, with Soviet denials of preemptive attack merely serving as a spur to Chinese fears. And President Nixon, during his visit to Pakistan in August 1969, gave Yahya Khan a "God-sent gift": a private mission to sound out China on a new era of rapprochement with the U.S.[1]

The Pakistan army's crackdown in East Pakistan on March 25, 1971 was savage in the extreme. Sheikh Mujibur Rahman was arrested in the early hours of the morning of March 27 and incarcerated in West Pakistan. The scale and degree of repression triggered a massive refugee influx into India from mid-April. By May 21 nearly 3.5 million refugees had entered India, more than 80 per cent of them being Hindus.[2]

India's initial reaction to East Pakistan developments had been cautious, partly because it was involved in elections and the formation of Mrs. Gandhi's new government. As the refugee influx went on cascading, the country's economic burden became a major issue, with the international community eventually picking up only one-fourth of the cost.

The East Pakistan developments were even more unwelcome to India on political grounds. They were happening in the immediate vicinity of the volatile state of West Bengal, with a strong Marxist Communist party, and the Bengalis' cousins were being butchered across the border. In the hill states in the northeast, Naga and Mizo rebels were receiving Chinese assistance and Beijing had set up guerrilla-training camps for them in the Chittagong hill area of East

Pakistan. The Naxalites in West Bengal, though subdued, had not been vanquished. In the states of Tripura and Meghalaya, the tribal-nontribal ratio was being distorted by the massive refugee influx. And the Marxists were not above exploiting the relatively better conditions of the refugees, who received food and doles in camps, compared to the indigenous poor to fan anti-Centre sentiments.

New Delhi feared that the more prolonged the killings in East Pakistan, the greater the danger of an extremist leadership taking over to make the centrist leadership of Sheikh Mujibur Rahman irrelevant.[3] Such a development, combined with a Marxist and extremist leadership in West Bengal and the dissident Nagas and Mizos, could inflame the region.

To confirm Mrs. Gandhi's worst fears, the Marxists in West Bengal acknowledged that the "people's war" in East Pakistan would be long. In mid-June, the CPI(M) Politburo passed a resolution opposing Indian military intervention in East Pakistan which, it said, would transform a "people's war" into an Indo-Pakistani one. It urged the immediate recognition of the Bangladesh government in exile and asked New Delhi to give military assistance to all resistance forces.[4]

The Marxists, had, indeed, been quick to expand ties with the pro-Beijing wing of the Pakistan Communist Party and Maulana Bhashani's National Awami Party. The Naxalites teamed up with extremist factions and helped equip them with arms. Given the situation, there was little the government in New Delhi could do to end these clandestine activities.

There were no illusions in New Delhi about the immediate outcome of the contest in East Pakistan. By April 23, the Pakistan army was already gaining control of the major towns and was undertaking a thrust along the western portions of East Pakistan to deny the guerrillas a friendly base along India's borders.[5] A Pakistani victory in the towns held out the prospect of a prolonged guerrilla war, which would radicalize the region, and the crushing economic and political burden of the indefinite stay of refugees, numbering in millions.

Mrs. Gandhi took three steps to retain some control over fast-moving events. She had Parliament pass a resolution on East Bengal (a formulation that was to be used until the recognition of Bangladesh) expressing India's sympathy and support for the people there. She permitted the establishment of a Bangladesh government in exile in India and approved the setting up of camps for training East Pakistan guerrilla fighters.

In spite of the agreed draft of the Indo-Soviet treaty, Moscow had sought to maintain a public posture of balanced relations with the two major countries of the subcontinent, at least till late 1970. A Soviet nuclear agreement was signed in May 1970 in Karachi and the steel mill agreement was finally concluded during Yahya's Moscow visit in June. Moscow had, in fact, been generally supportive of the Yahya regime although it had some good words for Mujib after the results of the Pakistan elections had been announced.[6]

Privately, Moscow had been urging India not to take precipitate action on the new East Pakistan crisis.[7] As India waited anxiously to see the unravelling of the Soviet position, President Podgorny wrote to Yahya on behalf of the Supreme Soviet on April 2 appealing "for the adoption of the most urgent measures to stop the bloodshed and repression against the population of East Pakistan and for turning to methods of a peaceful political settlement."[8]

Yahya answered Podgorny with some acerbity on April 6 saying that no country could allow "anti-national and unpatriotic elements to destroy the country." Kosygin's letter to Yahya of April 12, however, assured him that the Soviet Union did not intend to take sides in the dispute.[9]

Although the Podgorny letter had pleased New Delhi, particularly because it spoke of the "repression" of the East Pakistanis, the tenor of subsequent Soviet press comment, striking a neutral tone, distressed India. A dichotomy in the Soviet and Indian approaches to the East Pakistan crisis was clear from the beginning and was not to disappear until at least October 1971, despite the treaty that had been signed in the meantime.

The Soviets gave overriding importance to maintaining Pakistan's unity because they were fearful of the consequences of a breakup for the stability of the subcontinent, particularly in view of China's capacity for mischief, and wished to retain the influence in Pakistan they had been painfully building up. India initially did not want to see the breakup of Pakistan, but placed the problem in the context of the Pakistanis having brought the tragedy on themselves and was firm in refusing to let Yahya resolve the crisis at India's expense.

Although the Indian Army had begun making contingency plans for a new war with Pakistan in the summer of 1971, Mrs. Gandhi hoped to bring the crisis to an end without Indian intervention. Her strategy was to bring overwhelming international pressure to bear on the Yahya regime to force him to negotiate with Mujib and his Awami League on the basis of acceptable political concessions. Indeed, her advisors were divided on the benefits an independent East Pakistan state would bring to India. She was disheartened by the response of not only the U.S., as we shall see, but also of the Soviet Union.

Henry Kissinger has confessed that the Nixon Administration's policy on the subcontinent was "to avoid adding another complication to our agenda."[10] This, coupled with the fact that Nixon and Kissinger were "profoundly grateful"[11] to Pakistan for being the channel to China, ensured that the Administration would view the subcontinental crisis through the spectacles of a strategic relationship it hoped to build with China.

Perhaps an element of personal pique with India also coloured Nixon's views. He had told Yahya in the White House in October 1980: "Nobody has occupied the White House who is friendlier to Pakistan than me."[12] And in the summer of 1970 Nixon approved the sale of military equipment to Pakistan, including modern planes, as a "one-time exception" to the embargo on weapon sales to the subcontinent following the 1965 war.

The Nixon Administration had already been battered by the passions aroused by the Vietnam war. As Americans read accounts of the scale of the East Pakistan tragedy and saw it on their television screens, they had another issue with which to attack the Administration. But Nixon and Kissinger refused to pass public judgement on the Yahya regime, contending that private diplomacy was a more useful instrument. On May 27, a U.S. statement calling for "restraint" by both India and Pakistan was not viewed by New Delhi as a helpful development. On May 24, Mrs. Gandhi had made a statement to Parliament holding out the threat of Indian intervention in East Pakistan.[13]

The last week of May was an important period in determining India's strategy. There was growing disenchantment with the willingness of the U.S. or the West generally to exert the pressure that was needed to bring Yahya Khan and the Awami League to the conference table, and the Soviet Union remained obsessed with the unity of Pakistan. Mrs. Gandhi refined her objectives while deciding to try to bring Moscow to view the situation from India's point of view. These were: the return of all refugees to East Pakistan; transfer of power by Islamabad to the Awami League and increased pressure to be applied to the Pakistan Army in the eastern wing. The questions of the Awami League assuming power within a Pakistan federation or outside it and Indian military intervention were left open.

Swaran Singh was dispatched to Moscow in June to finalize the Indo-Soviet treaty. According to an Indian participant in the talks, "Swaran Singh was careful to drop all references to Warsaw Pact implications and a reference to nonalignment was inserted. We brought in cultural relations, etc., including football, to dilute the treaty."[14] The operative part of the treaty was Article IX.

Left to herself, Mrs. Gandhi would have signed the original draft of the treaty in September 1969. But the split in the party, reducing her government to minority status, made such a treaty a risky venture, in view of opposition attacks it would have invited of abandoning India's nonalignment policy. Mrs. Gandhi's compulsions then were to detach Moscow from its new arms relationship with Pakistan and ensure the underpinning she needed from the pro-Moscow CPI in Parliament.

The 1971 events gave a new dimension to the treaty because India desperately needed Soviet diplomatic and strategic support in the event of war with Pakistan leading to the independence of its eastern wing. Besides, Mrs. Gandhi was now in an unassailable position in Parliament and the climate of the 1971 events would make selling the treaty to the country far easier. The revised treaty, however, was allowed to rest for a while to await the unfolding of events in East Pakistan and in the major world capitals.

April was the month of ping-pong diplomacy. Unknown to the world and most of the U.S. government establishment, Kissinger was preparing for his secret mission to China through Pakistan's good offices. He visited New Delhi in July, partly, he suggests, "to prepare India circumspectly for news of my visit to China."[15] He asked Mrs. Gandhi how much time she thought there was "and she replied that it was unmanageable now and that they are 'just holding it together by sheer willpower.'"[16]

Foreign Secretary Kaul, on the other hand, has made it clear that "Kissinger did not give any hint of his forthcoming secret visit to Peking [Beijing]."[17] In fact, Kaul records that Kissinger told him during a private meeting, "But, under no circumstances, shall we cooperate with China, directly or indirectly, in any move which is directed against India, and any military move by China against India would retard our political relationship with China."[18] However, according to Kaul, "G. Parthasarathy [Parthasarathi, a senior Indian diplomat] had been told about it [the possibility of a secret Kissinger visit to China] in Geneva by Edgar Snow on July 7 and mentioned it to us the next day when he arrived in Delhi."[19]

Kissinger went on to Pakistan from India and from there to his secret *rendez vous* with Zhou Enlai in Beijing. After his return home, he gave Indian Ambassador L.K. Jha a direct warning, "If war broke out between India and Pakistan, and China became involved on Pakistan's side, 'we would be unable to help you against China.'"[20]

This chilling warning led to two sets of decisions in New Delhi, one tactical and the other strategic. More direct supervision began to be exercised of the Bangladesh government in exile, now moved to Calcutta, and the Mukti Bahini and other guerrilla forces, Indian army personnel were permitted to participate in cross-border raids and more camps were set up to train guerrillas by the Indian Army. The objective of these decisions was to put greater pressure on the Pakistan army to force Yahya Khan to accept a realistic political settlement. Regular Indian Army forces were moved to the East Pakistan border in May and June.

The strategic decision was to send D.P. Dhar to Moscow on August 2 to finalize the details for signing the treaty and invite Foreign Minister Gromyko to New Delhi to sign it. The Soviets were surprised, if not taken aback,[21] by the speed with which India wished to formalize the treaty. But Gromyko came post-haste and signed the treaty with Foreign Minister Swaran Singh on August 9.

The dramatic announcement of Kissinger's secret visit to Beijing and President Nixon's slated visit in 1972 had immediate connotations for the Indian mind. A Sino-Pakistan alignment against India had suddenly become a global one, with the U.S. having entered the adversaries' circle. This momentous development, coupled with a Soviet refusal fully to share Indian objectives in East Pakistan, led to an acute feeling of isolation among the Indian elite. As Mrs. Gandhi herself suggested, the treaty, when it came, served as "a morale booster at a time we were very much in need of it."[22]

It was, of course, more than that. Article VIII precluded either country from entering into military alliances directed against the other party.[23] But the operative part of the treaty was Article IX, according to which, both sides will "abstain from providing any assistance to any third party that engages in armed conflict with the other party. In the event of either party being subjected to attack or threat thereof, the high contracting parties shall immediately enter into mutual consultations in order to remove such a threat and to take effective measures to ensure peace and security of their countries."

In the context of the events of 1971, the Indian side stressed the security aspect of the treaty, with the Soviets underplaying it. The Soviet embassy in New Delhi ran an advertisement in *The Indian Express* on September 4 declaring that the treaty had nothing to do with the Asian Collective Security idea. In its view, the treaty gave "judicial concretization to a manifold relationship" and contributed to "peace and stability and progressive social changes in Asia."

Gromyko declared at the signing ceremony that "the significance of the Treaty cannot be overestimated."[24] The joint communiqué for the first time called for the withdrawal of U.S. forces from Vietnam and settlement of the problem on the basis of the seven-point proposal of South Vietnam's Provisional Revolutionary Government,[25] something in the nature of an immediate trade-off for the Soviets. The Indian side was unhappy with some phrases insisted on by the Soviets in relation to East Pakistan in drafting the communiqué, but went along with them to obtain the treaty.[26] An Indian aim had been achieved by Article IX foreclosing Soviet arms supplies to Pakistan.

The treaty was generally welcomed by the various political parties, with reservations. A.B. Vajpayee of the Jana Sangh told Parliament, "If this treaty paves the way for having a real friend, we will perforce welcome it."[27] The Bharatiya Kranti Dal of Charan Singh, the leader of Jat peasant-proprietors, gave the treaty only limited support while the southern DMK party, a tactical ally of Mrs. Gandhi, urged the reduction of the treaty's duration from twenty years to five. C. Rajagopalachari, leader of the right-wing Swatantra party, welcomed the treaty.[28] But Morarji Desai expressed doubts over the wisdom of signing it and charged that Mrs. Gandhi's cabinet had not been consulted in advance.[29]

It soon became apparent that India and the Soviet Union had different objectives and expectations out of the treaty.[30] For the Soviet Union, the treaty served a larger strategic objective, in relation to China in particular, and perhaps as a first step towards the Asian collective security concept.[31] At any rate, Moscow felt that by allaying Indian anxieties over being isolated, it would be in a better position to exert pressure on Mrs. Gandhi.

The Soviets reportedly expressed their unhappiness to D.P. Dhar early in August when he suggested that India might have to use force to resolve the East Pakistan problem if a political solution failed to materialize in a few months. And Moscow made it plain that it was against Indian recognition of Bangladesh, a move which would have been tantamount to declaring war on Pakistan.[32]

For India, the treaty served the strategic purpose of deterring Chinese or American intervention in a possible Indo-Pakistani war. Further, it provided an insurance of Soviet diplomatic support in the United Nations if the issue reached the world forum. Since the majority in India expected full Soviet support for the Indian position on East Pakistan after the signing of the treaty, it was both disappointed and distressed.

Although Kissinger was to suggest later that the treaty came as a "bombshell," it does not seem to have created a stir at the time in the White House.[33] According to Kaul, the bombshell version was very different from what Kissinger had told him in New Delhi and Washington.[34]

Kissinger records, "I left New Delhi [in July] with the conviction that India was bent on a showdown with Pakistan. It was only waiting for the right moment. The opportunity to settle scores with a rival that had isolated itself by its own shortsightedness was simply too tempting."[35] Although Kissinger does not say so, he returned from Islamabad convinced that Yahya "would not be amenable to U.S. suggestions for political accommodation."[36]

During this secret Beijing trip, Zhou Enlai had "insisted that China would not be indifferent if India attacked Pakistan."[37] At any rate, Kissinger continued to view the crisis through his geopolitical spectacles and sought to pressure the Soviet Union to influence India. He quotes Soviet Ambassador Dobrynin as telling him on July 19, "Moscow supported India's political goals but was strongly discouraging military adventures." The ambassador's response on August 17 was that "the Soviet Union was urging a peaceful solution."[38] Further, during a meeting Nixon had with Gromyko, the latter proved "noncommittal."[39] Kissinger interpreted Soviet responses as being evasive and dishonest, despite the fact that they accurately reflected what Moscow was telling New Delhi.

India had sent a number of missions to various parts of the world to mobilize international opinion with the message that the East Pakistani refugees, ultimately to number some 10 million, were an "indirect aggression" against India and that the crisis was not an Indo-Pakistani dispute. The attempt was to explain the background to the crisis and allay anxieties in the developing world in particular, sensive as it was to the prospect of any new nation's disintegration.

India's resistance to accepting Secretary General U. Thant's offer of "good offices" to India and Pakistan in October stemmed from the fear of converting the issue into an Indo-Pakistani dispute. India also opposed the proposal of having a U.N. presence in the Indian refugee camps, not merely because of the fear that it would monitor Indian aid to the Mukti Bahini guerrillas but chiefly because New Delhi sought to avoid a U.N. involvement, in view of the legacy of the Kashmir dispute.

Strains between India and the U.S. were exacerbated by the revelation on June 21 that, although the U.S. had suspended military arms sales to Pakistan in early April, some shipments were continuing. The shipments involved, worth some $5 million, were hardly substantial,[40] but served further to heighten Indian suspicions.

In August, Americans began contacts with some members of the Bangladesh government in exile, specially with the "foreign minister," Khondakar Mustaque, through its consulate general in Calcutta. America's "one semi-serious effort"[41] at mediation was ended in October because of India's suspicions that the U.S.—and Yahya's—objective was to split the Awami League. In any case, no one in the U.S. Administration, including Kissinger at that time, had placed any real hopes on a settlement through this method.[42] In fact, in August, Yahya had announced that Mujib would shortly stand trial on a treason charge and he had disqualified 79 of the 167 elected Awami league members of the assembly.

After the signing of the Indo-Soviet treaty, Mrs. Gandhi wrote to Zhou Enlai to assure him that it was not aimed at any country.[43] Zhou made a statement saying that he was "satisfied" with the assurances of Soviet and Indian leaders that the treaty was not directed against his country.[44]

The first note the Chinese took of the March 25 crackdown was in a New China News Agency report on April 4 viewing it as suppression of "secessionist elements." *People's Daily* ran an editorial on April 11 criticizing Indian interference in Pakistan's domestic affairs, without making any substantive comment on East Pakistan developments.

Zhou wrote a letter to Yahya the same day pledging Chinese

support to "Pakistani people."[45] In the middle of April China is reported to have informed Pakistan that while it would support Pakistan politically, it would not intervene militarily in another Indo-Pakistani war. Leo Rose quotes a Bangladesh source to suggest that this exchange of correspondence between Chinese and Pakistani leaders was in India's hands at least by July. Besides, China reportedly delayed meeting Pakistani military requests, supplying only some small arms before the 1971 war.[46]

Bhutto was dispatched to Beijing with Air Marshal Rahim Khan and General Gul Hasan on November 7 to seek Chinese arms and a revision of its policy. But Zhou made it clear that he would not intervene directly in the conflict. Bhutto, however, made a statement on his return home saying China had assured Pakistan support in the event of an Indian attack, a version reiterated by Yahya in a television interview. This caused anxiety in New Delhi.

Did India concoct a U.S.-China threat merely to further its propaganda themes? In making contingency plans, the Indian Army had given thought to a possible Chinese intervention and hence favoured a winter operation because the Sino-Indian passes would be under snow. Even assuming that India possessed copies of the secret Chinese-Pakistani correspondence, it was never quite certain that China would not intervene.

Bhutto's statement on his return from China merely added to Indian worries. There were, of course, material factors which would seem to negate any impulse China might have had to intervene. It had only recently emerged from the debilitating Cultural Revolution and had lived through the trauma of the alleged coup attempt of September 1971 by Mao's successor, Lin Biao, leading to the temporary grounding of the air force.

India, meanwhile, was losing hope in U.S. willingness to bring about a political settlement it could live with. From India's point of view, two developments would have been worse than war. Islamabad's success in the suppression of East Pakistanis, it was felt, would inevitably lead to a prolonged guerrilla war and the ultimate victory of extremists. The second option, the internationalization of the issue through the U.N., was equally unwelcome because New Delhi believed it would then have to live through another interminable dispute with Pakistan, this time on its eastern border.

By about the middle of September Mrs. Gandhi seems to have made up her mind that a war was perhaps inevitable. She undertook a visit to Moscow on September 27 to lay her cards on the table. She made it clear to Soviet leaders why she found the existing options unacceptable and said she was determined to use force if necessary to safeguard her country's interests. Mrs. Gandhi's major purpose in undertaking the visit was to leave no doubt in Soviet minds that India would fight, if forced to.[47]

The Pakistan Foreign Secretary had gone to Moscow in August to inquire about the Indo-Soviet treaty to meet a "stiff Soviet attitude."[48] Early in September Kosygin described Yahya's policies in East Pakistan "indefensible." But the ambivalence in the Soviet attitude to the crisis remained till October. In the second half of September, for instance, the Soviet Union voted for two Arab resolutions supporting Pakistan at an Interparliamentary Union conference in Paris.[49].

Mrs. Gandhi undertook a tour of several Western countries, including Washington, towards the end of October "to give the West a last chance to save the peace on the subcontinent."[50] In Europe, she received "tea and sympathy," but not much else. Mrs. Gandhi's message was that Pakistan had got unstuck and could not be stuck together again. She said India could not bear the burden of refugees indefinitely and if denied world understanding and effective pressure on Yahya, New Delhi would resolve the problem to the best of its capacity. For India, mere avoidance of war was no solution.[51]

Mrs. Gandhi's meeting with Nixon was not a happy one. Nixon and Kissinger viewed the crisis through the Chinese prism. Nixon offered to assume full responsibility for refugee support, said Yahya was prepared to withdraw troops from the East Pakistan border if India later did the same and that he would meet any bona fide Awami League representative, but not Mujib.[52]

India viewed Yahya's moves as a delaying tactic "to reestablish his control over East Pakistan, so that he could force a solution down the throats of the East Bengalis,"[53] and "we would be having another Vietnam on our hands."[54] Nixon was later to charge Mrs. Gandhi with duplicity.[55] While Mrs. Gandhi was hardly sanguine about the results of her Washington visit, her effort was to find out if the U.S. Administration was willing and able to persuade Yahya to see the light, failing which war was inevitable.

On her return home, Mrs. Gandhi called for the unilateral withdrawal of Pakistani forces from the East Pakistan border and authorized Indian forces to cross the border to counter Pakistani artillery shelling. Indian military action in East Pakistan began in late November. It was steadily escalating pressure to force Yahya to deal with Mujib.

Kissinger has made it amply clear that the Nixon Administration's approach to the East Pakistan crisis was determined by two factors: Pakistan was China's friend and hence should be supported and the U.S. should do everything to avoid giving the Chinese the impression that it was ganging up with the Soviet Union against Pakistan. Kissinger had his first secret meeting with Huang Hua, China's ambassador to the U.N., on November 23 to discuss the subcontinent.

The State Department had asked Ambassador Jha in August for assurances that India would not change the West Pakistan border. Since this involved the disputed Kashmir state, part of which was under Pakistan's control, no official assurance on this account could be given. Jha in turn unsuccessfully asked for assurances that Pakistan would vacate those areas of Indian Kashmir its forces occupied.[56] But Kissinger chose to interpret the ambassador's response as India harbouring designs on West Pakistan.

Moscow realized after Mrs. Gandhi's September visit that she meant business and informed India in October that it was sending Firyubin to New Delhi for "consultations" under Article IX of the treaty. Indeed, Firyubin arrived two days before Mrs. Gandhi's departure for West Europe and Washington. Two days after Firyubin's departure—"the two sides reached full accord in the assessment of the existing situation"—Air Marshal Kutakhov reached New Delhi. During his visit to Moscow on August 2 to finalize the treaty, D.P. Dhar had made persistent requests for speeding up Soviet supplies for the Indian air force; these were not related to the treaty but were part of the continuing military supplies.[57]

Soviet supplies were considerably speeded up in the winter. Three shiploads were sent in November and an emergency airlift of specialized equipment was arranged directly from Moscow and from Egypt.[58] The Soviet Union was now fully and publicly supporting India in the East Pakistan crisis.

Facing growing Indian military pressure on the East Pakistan border, Yahya Khan made the worst possible move from his point of view. On December 3 Pakistan attacked eight airfields in northern and western India and made limited strikes across the West Pakistan-

India border, thus providing New Delhi with an ideal provocation for Indian troops to move openly into East Pakistan. Kissinger had the previous day received Yahya's letter invoking a 1959 U.S.-Pakistan bilateral agreement to seek American help.[59] There was, however, no American profit in a direct military intervention in the subcontinent.

India set up a joint command with the Mukti Bahini on December 6, the day it recognized Bangladesh. The Indian aim was speedily to complete its military operation in East Pakistan and Moscow expressed some concern over the Indian army's seemingly slow progress.[60] Moscow sent Vasily Kuznetsov, first deputy foreign minister, to New Delhi to coordinate policy while D.P. Dhar proceeded to Moscow on December 12 for the same purpose.

Moscow's concern was justified in that it was facing Chinese onslaughts in the U.N. Security Council and had to use its veto three times to ward off resolutions which were unfavourable to India.[61] Besides, the Soviet Union was also facing increasing pressure from Washington, with Nixon sending a letter to Brezhnev on December 6, and Kissinger hinting at the calling off of the Nixon visit to Moscow in 1972.

Kissinger was closely aligning his strategy with both China and Pakistan and ultimately brought the issue to the U.N. General Assembly, with the Indo-Soviet isolation recorded by the 104 to 11 vote, with even Yugoslavia and Egypt opposing India. The outcome in East Pakistan was a foregone conclusion, but Kissinger had convinced himself that India's objective was to dismember West Pakistan, despite Indian public and private assurances to the contrary.

Kissinger's anti-Indian tilt was quickly to become part of the political folklore, with columnist Jack Anderson revealing part of discussions held at the December 3 meeting of the Washington Special Action Group. Kissinger told the meeting, "I am getting hell every half hour from the President that we are not being tough enough on India.... He does not believe we are carrying out his wishes. He wants to tilt in favour of Pakistan."[62]

Bush called India an aggressor at the United Nations on instructions[63] and Kissinger received the seeming proof he needed to confirm his suspicions. A secret intelligence report was received in Washington suggesting that "Prime Minister Gandhi was determined to reduce even West Pakistan to impotence."[64] Kissinger misinterpreted a Chinese assurance of support for Pakistan as their willingness to intervene militarily in the subcontinent even at a late stage.[65]

Nixon ordered a task force of eight ships led by the nuclear-powered *Enterprise* into the Bay of Bengal, ostensibly to evacuate Americans but in reality to dissuade India from attacking West Pakistan and "in case the Soviet Union pressured China."[66] Kissinger believes it was this show of force which made the Soviet Union pressure India to desist in West Pakistan.[67] All evidence would seem to indicate that neither India nor the Soviet Union wanted to dismember West Pakistan, which would have created problems for both. Besides, the U.N. General Assembly vote was indication enough to India that it would be entirely isolated, should it proceed on such a venture.

Admiral Elmo Zumwalt, then chief of naval operations, has recorded, "My hunch is that the gesture [to order the task force] was untimely and futile."[68] Besides, a Brookings Institution study has revealed, "It is important to emphasize that Soviet and Indian support for a cease-fire was *not* the result of the military pressure generated by Task Force 74."[69] The task force did not reach the Bay of Bengal till December 15,[70] the day before Pakistani troops surrendered in the East Pakistan capital. The original December 10 offer of a Pakistani cease-fire in the east was held up for five days until Kissinger had sorted out the problem of West Pakistan, according to his light.

During the war the Soviets had twenty warships—thirteen surface ships and seven submarines—in the Indian Ocean. They sent four of these after the U.S. dispatched the task force, a move that was not lost upon India.[71] In the event, the Indian military operation in East Pakistan was completed with speed and efficiency.

For India, it was a significant victory, and it was, undoubtedly, for most Indians Mrs. Gandhi's finest hour. The map of the subcontinent had been reordered and there were as a consequence three major conglomerations of Muslims: 65 million in Bangladesh, 55 million in Pakistan and 50 million in India. Pakistan had been humbled and reduced to a nation of 55 million.[72] Its capacity to challenge India was no longer credible.

For the Soviet Union, the result of the Bangladesh war was also a triumph, although its hands were forced by Mrs. Gandhi. It had demonstrated its ability to help a friend despite mounting pressure from the other superpower, with China in the opposite camp.

Kissinger has drawn the conclusion that Soviet support of India was "in part to deliver a blow to our system of alliances, in even greater measure to demonstrate Chinese impotence."⁷³

Ironically, the Soviet share in the Indian victory in Bangladesh came at a price. It made India less dependent on the Soviets while Moscow's need for India as a counterweight to China had increased, rather than diminished. But Moscow had India's gratitude—a notoriously ephemeral article in relations between states—and the treaty, to run for twenty years in the first instance. It had in the process to give up its balanced policy towards the two major countries of the subcontinent.

Brezhnev pronounced that the treaty was a "brilliant illustration of the community of interests between the two countries."⁷⁴ Commenting on the 10th anniversary of the treaty in *International Affairs*, B. Levchenko took credit for what the treaty had achieved in 1971. "In these complicated conditions [of 1971]," he wrote in the September issue, "the Soviet-Indian Treaty of Peace, Friendship and Cooperation acted as a deterrent to the external anti-Indian forces, and was instrumental in restoring peace and stability on the subcontinent."

K.P.S. Menon records that when India signed the treaty Sir Olaf Caroe, the distinguished British civil servant who had in the Fifties inspired American interest in Pakistan as an essential part of West Asia's defence, warned him, "You are supping with the devil and I do not think you have a long enough spoon."⁷⁵

Mrs. Gandhi believed that she did have a long enough spoon. She was willing to sign the original draft of the treaty in 1969, without the compulsion of the 1971 events. As her one-time advisor, T.N. Kaul, has explained, "The prime objective [of the treaty] was to strengthen relations with a reliable friend such as the Soviet Union whose reliability had been proved in times of need. But this does not debar either country from developing friendly relations with third countries. The treaty was and is a long-term arrangement and not something done for tactical reasons. It is valid for twenty years."⁷⁶

Mrs. Gandhi's original motivation was to detach the Soviet Union from Pakistan, as far as an arms relationship was concerned, a long-term problem in her view. The arms issue for India did not merely represent the quantum of weapons supplied to Pakistan but was also a question of Moscow following the old U.S. policy of maintaining parity between the two countries. Even more importantly, it called into question Moscow's reliability as India's friend, supportive of its interests in the region and the world. The significance of the 1971 events was that India's need of Moscow in these roles was reduced even though Kaul and others continued to sing the old tune.

Unlike the treaty the Soviets signed with the United Arab Republic in May 1971, the Indo-Soviet treaty does not have an ideological content and does not provide for linkages between the Congress party and the CPSU. But the price India paid was to tarnish its nonalignment, leading many in the developing and developed world to assume a pro-Soviet orientation in Indian policies. Muammar al-Qaddafi of Libya, for instance, drew the conclusion in December 1971 that "India is not fully free and not neutral after signing a treaty with the eastern camp."[77] Mrs. Gandhi, as we shall see, would prove to be highly flexible in interpreting the treaty.

There is little doubt that Moscow views the Indo-Soviet treaty and other similar treaties as part of its concept of Asian Collective Security. They are not an aberration.[78] Dinesh Singh believes that there is this linkage in the Soviet mind.[79] *New Times* of September 1971 approvingly quoted a pro-Communist Indian newspaper's view that the treaty could become "the first step towards establishment of a collective security system." And *Pravda* had suggested on March 31, 1971, "For its part the Soviet Union invites those countries which accept [its] approach to conclude appropriate bilateral and multilateral treaties among themselves."[80]

A central question the treaty posed was to cast doubt on India's role as a leader of the nonaligned, hobbled as it became by its new commitment. For Mrs. Gandhi, the country's interests—with which she increasingly aligned her own—took precedence. Given the circumstances of 1969 and 1971, she felt she had no option to the treaty in the international configuration of forces. The pro-Soviet tilt in her case came in 1969.

Chapter Six

AFTER THE WAR

YEARS after the Bangladesh operation of 1971, Mrs. Gandhi suggested, ".... All things considered, I think it was a significant victory, not only a military victory but also a political and diplomatic one."[1] In the glow of victory, her aim was to achieve "durable peace" on the subcontinent, but first she sent signals to the two superpowers that, despite the Indo-Soviet treaty, she would chart her own course.

Talking to C.L. Sulzberger of *The New York Times* shortly after the war, Mrs. Gandhi said, "We are unable to display gratitude in any tangible sense for anything."[2] As for the United States, she assumed that Washington's policy towards India changed when "U.S. policy towards China changed."[3] Even earlier, on December 31, 1971, she emphasized the importance of friendly Indo-U.S. relations, taking into account the "new realities" on the subcontinent.[4]

In his 1972 foreign policy message to the U.S. Congress, President Nixon called for a "serious dialogue" with India while accepting its enhanced status. But the underlying contradictions and differences between the two countries were apparent enough. Nixon did not revise his formulation of a year earlier that the two superpowers and China had legitimate interests in the subcontinent, rejecting the Indian argument that only South Asian nations should have such interests. Nixon now pointedly made the state of Indo-U.S. relations conditional upon India's relations with the Soviet Union and its neighbours.[5]

During his historic visit to China in February 1972, President Nixon was further to exacerbate Indian feelings. The joint communiqué signed at Shanghai on February 27, 1972 called for the withdrawal of Indian and Pakistani forces to their own territories and on either side of the cease-fire line in Kashmir and recorded Chinese support for "the people of Jammu and Kashmir in their struggle for the right of self-determination."[6] This provoked Mrs. Gandhi to remark that "some mischief against India" was "in the offing."[7] At the very least, the communiqué signified a parallel U.S.-Chinese interest in the affairs of the subcontinent.

The Soviets received a trade-off for the Indo-Soviet treaty through the Indian decision early in 1972 to raise its representation in Hanoi to the level of an embassy. Mrs. Gandhi had specifically ruled out a Tashkent-style conference to resolve Indo-Pakistani problems, but Moscow was keen to retain a measure of influence it had built up in Pakistan since 1968, in addition to capitalizing on the Indian victory in its relations with India and Bangladesh.

President Podgorny sent a warm congratulatory message to Bhutto on his assumption of the presidency of his truncated country. In the first week of February 1972, the Soviets had warned New Delhi that a long stalemate with Pakistan would not be good for India or the Soviet Union.[8] India occupied more than 5,000 square miles of territory it had won in the war and held some 90,000 prisoners of war who had surrendered in Dhaka to the joint Indian-Bangladesh command.

In March 1972, Bhutto journeyed to Moscow after visiting Beijing, to be urged by Kosygin to "display a realistic approach to this important matter [of prisoners of war]."[9] Further, Kosygin told him, "We consider the relaxation of tension on the subcontinent would permit all its countries to proceed along the path of building a lasting peace and creating an atmosphere of mutual trust in their region... What is hampering progress? Clearly, the absence of agreements on talks between India, Bangladesh and Pakistan.... [W]ithout a minimum of trust it is hard to hope for a solution of existing problems"[10]

China's veto of Bangladesh's admission to the United Nations, an action supportive of Pakistan, gave Moscow an opportunity to twit Beijing by deriding its claim to be the "only loyal, true, and effective friend and protector of oppressed peoples."[11] China's intransigence, *Pravda* suggested on September 1, 1972, was based on "a view of introducing its own 'system' in South Asia. Peking [Beijing] has embarked on confrontation with the national liberation movement of the Bangladesh people." Besides, Moscow said that China's actions on the subcontinent were a way of torpedoing the Asian Collective Security concept.

That Moscow's thoughts were increasingly returning to the promotion of the ACS was clear from Kosygin's revival of the idea on March 12, 1972 in welcoming the Afghan Prime Minister to Moscow.

Brezhnev, as we have seen, further amplified the idea a few days later. And Radio Moscow said on October 11, 1972 that the ACS would create "a sturdy dyke in Asia against feeble imperialist attempts to restore a colonial or semi-colonial system."

In August 1973 Brezhnev said that the ACS gave no participant "unilateral advantage." But in the summer of 1973 the Soviets were expressing concern and went to the extent of countering the charge that, unlike in Europe, Asian conditions "have not ripened." The important point, they said, was to secure an agreement on principles.[12]

The major Soviet thrust towards India in the immediate post-Bangladesh war years was on economic and trade relations. By 1971-72 India's trade with Eastern Europe had jumped from 0.5 per cent in 1950-51 to 20 per cent in exports, and from a negligible amount to 11 per cent in imports.[13] Since much of the machinery and technical skills were now available in India, there was increasing Soviet pressure for new forms of partnership. Since the mid-Sixties, the Soviets had moved away from endorsing a Third World imitation of their own experience of the 1930s to less aid for individual projects and an increasing emphasis on interlocking economic activities.

In September 1972, just over a year after the signing of the Indo-Soviet treaty, an agreement was reached to set up a commission whose main function was to dovetail the two countries' economic plans. D.P. Dhar's role in relation to the treaty and in the commission's formation led to speculation that India would join the Council of Mutual Economic Assistance (Comecon).[14] The importance of the commission can be gauged from the fact that three Gosplan (Soviet Planning Commission) teams prepared reports on steel, metallurgy and consumer goods for submission to their Indian counterparts. The exercise involved hard bargaining.

K.B. Lall, a key Indian official in dealing with the Soviets in the trade and arms fields, has suggested that the need for the joint commission mechanism arose because Indo-Soviet trade had gone far beyond the ken of the commerce and industries ministries. It was thus found necessary to restructure trade and bring in the planning machinery of the two countries. According to Lall, while the Soviets looked at trade from the political perspective, it was economic in nature for India.[15]

The Soviet economic offensive culminated in Brezhnev's visit to New Delhi in November 1973. The Brezhnev-Gandhi declaration envisaged the by now traditional doubling of trade in five years. But there were other important agreements: on production cooperation and between Gosplan and the Indian Planning Commission on establishment of a joint study group in planning. Besides, a long-term, fifteen-year trade agreement was signed.

On the political plane, the Soviets took two significant steps. One was to encourage Indo-Iraqi cooperation; the other finally to support Indian claims on the Sino-Indian border. Moscow had signed a friendship treaty with Iraq in 1972, and the Iraqi naval chief, Brig. Abdu Al-Deri, paid a nine-day visit to India in August 1973. In early 1974, India had at least 30 instructors in Iraq training pilots for MIGs.[16]

The delineation of the Sino-Indian border in Soviet maps had been a contentious issue between New Delhi and Moscow for years. The Soviets had been either evasive or vaguely sympathetic, but had refrained from expressing full support. In 1972, the journal *Problemi Dalnego Vostoka* (Problems of the Far East) extended support for the Indian position on the border with China for the first time in print.[17] Soviet maps were changed only in 1978 with the McMahon Line shown as a firm border, but Aksai Chin was still shown as part of China.[18] Russian nervousness over Indian moves for a rapprochement with China in the late Sixties was both explicit and implicit. They now perhaps wanted to make a thaw in Sino-Indian relations more difficult to achieve through their belated support.

Significantly, Mrs. Gandhi made her point by paying the Soviets a left-handed compliment. She declared in November 1973, "... Over all these years, the Soviets have never exerted pressure to bear on us.... We consider it very important... because India follows its own way of development..."[19] The message was clear enough, although the Soviets chose to take it at face value, for the record.

As the power that had contributed to the Indian success in the creation of Bangladesh, the Soviet Union moved quickly to cement relations with the new state. The Soviet Union was the first country outside the subcontinent Sheikh Mujibur Rahman visited after being installed as executive head of Bangladesh. Moscow agreed to give Bangladesh fifty railway locomotives and offered to clear Dhaka and Chittagong ports of mines; the latter move had obvious strategic implications. But the Soviets kept their aid commitments to a minimal and prudent level.[20]

Mrs. Gandhi ruminated on November 25, 1972, "There seemed to have been a softening of the [Chinese] attitude after the Cultural Revolution. Then came Bangladesh and we were back where we were."[21] China's use of its first veto at the U.N. to keep Bangladesh out was to support Pakistan and to keep up pressure on India on the release of Pakistani prisoners of war.

China had no illusions about the unpopularity of its action in the U.N. or Pakistan's own contribution to the tragedy of East Pakistan. *People's Daily* of January 31, 1972 declared, "The Pakistan Government had made blunders and terrible blunders indeed in the past in handling the question of East Pakistan." Although Beijing's statements were liberally peppered with attacks on Indian "expansionists," its main thrust was against the Soviet Union.

Huang Hua told the U.N. Security Council in August 1972:

> Today they [the Soviets] push their "secure boundaries" to the Indian Ocean and Mediterranean and the next day they can press them further.... It is known to all what they have done to some of their "allies".... If certain people on the South Asian subcontinent still have some sense of national confidence, why can't they take the initiative to unite the South Asian subcontinent first and to facilitate a reasonable settlement of the relevant issues, and why should they allow themselves to be led by the nose?[22]

Perhaps stung by Soviet barbs on Beijing's opposition to Bangladesh's admission, Huang Hua explained his country's position further to the U.N. General Assembly session in late November 1972:

> We are not fundamentally opposed to the admission of "Bangladesh" into the United Nations. China has always cherished profound friendly sentiments for the people of East Bengal. We hope that the "Bangladesh" authorities will make their own decisions independently and meet with the Pakistan leaders at an early date so as to reach a reasonable settlement of the issues between Pakistan and "Bangladesh," thus demonstrating that it is a truly independent state. However, China cannot agree to the admission of "Bangladesh" under the present circumstances, that is, before the important U.N. resolutions are implemented by the parties concerned and a reasonable settlement of the issues between India and Pakistan

and between Pakistan and "Bangladesh" is reached.[23]

In September 1968, the Kashmir-Xinjiang road was opened through the Mitka pass and another road was opened between Xinjiang and Kashmir in February 1971 cutting through the Karakoram pass. China constituted an important market for Pakistani cotton and jute, and in 1970 China had given Pakistan a credit of $200 million, $10 million of it in hard currency.[24]

By 1970 Chinese tanks were 25 per cent of the total Pakistani tank force and the aircraft supplied by China represented 33 per cent of the Pakistan Air Force's 270 planes, 65 per cent of all interceptor bombers and 90 per cent of its front-line modern fighter planes. After the 1971 war, China became Pakistan's main arms supplier and rehabilitated Pakistan's army with the most modern weapons it had.

With the loss of East Pakistan, there was a decline in Pakistani exports to China. Beijing converted four loans into grants and deferred payment of the 1970 loan, waving some $140 million repayment. The Chinese terms of aid were, indeed, generous. Yahya Khan said in November 1971, before the war, "We get some things free and pay for others. But Chinese terms are so easy—twenty-five-year credit, interest-free. Last year when I was in Peking [Beijing] I negotiated $200 million worth of economic aid for our five-year plan with no interest."[25]

The military relationship with China was obviously important for Pakistan, in view of the U.S. embargo on arms to the subcontinent. The chief of staff of the Pakistan army, General Tikka Khan, went to China in 1973 and a return visit was undertaken the next year by the deputy chief of staff of the People's Liberation Army, Chang Tsai-chien.

Bhutto went to China in early 1972, to be received with less than full honours.[26] The joint communiqué condemned "India's naked aggression" and pledged "firm support to Pakistan." But Beijing turned down Bhutto's proposal for a military alliance between the two countries as a counterweight to the Indo-Soviet treaty.[27] China did not want to be locked into an anti-Indian position, despite the major economic and military support it was giving Pakistan. This was also revealed by Chinese condemnations of India generally staying clear of personal attacks on Mrs. Gandhi. In a sense, the Chinese leaders' attitude was parallel to Mrs. Gandhi's; one of her main reasons for adopting a gingerly and negative attitude to the

Soviet Asian Collective Security concept was to keep the door open to a settlement with China.

A demoralized and defeated Pakistan army had handed over power to Bhutto, who became President and Chief Martial Law Administrator on December 20, 1971. Before signing off, Yahya Khan had asked Bhutto if he could execute Sheikh Mujibur Rahman, still in prison in Pakistan, by predating an order, a suggestion the new ruler did not accept.[28] Although Bhutto had now achieved his life's ambition, it was at the cost of half his country. And he faced the formidable task of giving back his countrymen their self-respect to take his reduced nation to a new purpose and direction.

The brilliance and panache Bhutto brought to his new tasks could not have been matched by any other Pakistani leader. Domestically, he generally followed Mrs. Gandhi's populist policies and gestures of 1969 by identifying himself with the poor and underprivileged, his own feudal background notwithstanding, and sought to build as wide a coalition as he could.

To consolidate his hold, Bhutto needed to keep the army reasonably happy and secure India's tolerance of his policies. He sought to give a new direction to his country's foreign policy by emphasizing the Islamic link, particularly with countries of the Middle East, apart from buttressing the China relationship and engaging in a dialogue with the two superpowers.

The Pakistan army remained a major power factor,[29] despite its reduced status, and needed to be appeased. Bhutto offered the army a symbol, by elevating Tikka Khan to the post of chief of staff, thus legitimizing the army's controversial and deplorable role in the East Pakistan crackdown, and expanded the armed forces in spite of the fact that the "new" Pakistan was less than half as big as the old. Pakistan spent forty per cent more on defence in 1973-74 than united Pakistan had in 1970-71.[30]

India was more than willing to help Bhutto on its terms. Capitalizing on her victory in Bangladesh, Mrs. Gandhi won a big vote of confidence in the state assembly elections in the spring of 1972. New Delhi believed that the creation of Bangladesh offered it a new and unique opportunity to reorder relations among the countries of the subcontinent and between South Asia and the external powers. The new order would be based on the fact of Indian dominance.

"Durable peace" became the new catch phrase of Indian policy as New Delhi set about promoting the concept of bilateralism in India's relations with neighbours, thereby implying that problems would be resolved by the countries themselves without third party intervention. There was loud thinking in New Delhi on the long-term prospect of a tripartite security arrangement with Pakistan and Bangladesh,[31] an ironic twist to Ayub's proposal for joint defence with India back in the Fifties.

But Pakistan had not recognized Bangladesh, and since the Pakistani forces in East Pakistan had technically surrendered to the joint Indian-Bangladesh command, Dhaka's agreement was essential to the resolution of the problem. In view of the carnage Pakistani troops had indulged in, Mujib and his followers were adamant that at least some of the erring soldiers must be tried in Dhaka. Both India and Bangladesh insisted that Pakistan should first recognize Bangladesh before the question of repatriating P.O.W.s and their trial could be resolved. Bhutto sought to convert the weak hand he held into his strength by suggesting that his position would be undermined if P.O.W.s did not come home and if he could not first meet Mujib.

Against this backdrop, Mrs. Gandhi and Bhutto met in June 1972 at the northern Indian hill resort of Simla, the summer capital of British India and the scene of historic talks on Indian independence in the Forties between British negotiators and nationalist leaders. The Indian aim was ambitious: to bury the past and turn over a new leaf in Indo-Pakistani relations. To achieve this, it was necessary to bring to an end the Kashmir problem, apart from the fact that Pakistan should recognize Bangladesh.

Bhutto said his home base was too fragile to permit him to settle the Kashmir problem for all time. In the end, he received a generous settlement, getting back most of Pakistani territory captured by India in the war. India's gain was that Pakistan had accepted bilateral and peaceful resolution of all problems, including Kashmir, and it was able to convert the old cease-fire line in Kashmir into a new "line of control," which Pakistan promised to respect without prejudice to its stand. In the process, India gained about 400 sq. km. of territory, including key passes, which it formerly had to give back to Pakistan at Tashkent after the 1965 war.[32]

The Simla Agreement, as it came to be known, proclaimed the goal of "durable peace" for the subcontinent, and the two leaders promised to meet again "... to discuss further... a final settlement to Jammu and Kashmir."[33] Bhutto had done well for the leader of a defeated country. India was satisfied because it believed that it had made an investment in the future. It was, indeed, a landmark in Indo-Pakistani relations.

The agreement was welcomed by both the Soviet Union and the West. *Izvestia* said on July 4, 1972 that the summit meeting had shown that the path of peace and friendship was a realistic one for the countries of the subcontinent to follow. On August 31, 1972 the Soviet government newspaper was even more enthusiastic, hailing the agreement as having important significance for the relaxation of tension in Asia and the assertion of the principles of peaceful coexistence.

Western reaction can be gauged from *The Guardian* of London of July 4, 1972. Describing the agreement as "a fresh breeze from Simla," it said: "Simla, considered coolly, seems to be the best possible start—one that in its constructive statesmanship puts many other long-running world crises to shame."

The question of P.O.W.s remained unresolved. India and Pakistan could agree on the new "line of control" in Kashmir only by December 7. Withdrawals were completed on December 20, except for a few snow-bound areas in Kashmir. A few days later Bhutto said the line of control should not be construed as an international boundary and Pakistan's stand on Kashmir remained unchanged.[34] He was at least partly guarding his domestic flank.

Simla failed to live up to expectations, despite the Indian investment it called for, as we shall see. But the events of 1971 had another major impact; they helped in the militarization of the Indian Ocean leading to an intense superpower rivalry. The first major U.S. deployment in the Indian Ocean was made in December 1963 to demonstrate American support for India against China after the Sino-Indian border war and to familiarize the Navy with the area. The first Soviet display of its flag came shortly after Kosygin's visit to India in the spring of 1968. A goodwill visit to India was made in March by the commander in chief of the Soviet Pacific Fleet, Admiral Amel'ko, and four Soviet warships. A guided missile destroyer returned to Vladivostok while other ships continued the visit to ports in Somalia, Pakistan and the Persian Gulf before returning home in July.[35] The 1967 Arab-Israeli war had closed the Suez Canal.

The Soviets were disappointed over India's refusal to give them base facilities and concentrated their attention for a time on possible

Pakistani facilities. In mid-1969, the Soviets were reported to have a task force in the Indian Ocean of one or two very powerful cruisers capable of firing long-range rockets, supported by destroyers and perhaps submarines. The U.S. presence in the ocean was estimated by India at one communication ship, a nuclear submarine and guided missile destroyers based at Bahrain.[36] Taking the combined total of warships and merchant vessels, the Soviet presence in the ocean reached a peak in 1970.[37] In the Bangladesh war of 1971, the Soviets sent additional ships to the Indian Ocean to shadow the U.S. task force, led by *Enterprise*, into the Indian waters. They expanded their presence after the war.

Ironically, it was shortly before the Indo-Pakistani war that Sri Lanka and Tanzania proposed for the first time at the U.N. General Assembly in October 1971 that the Indian Ocean be declared a "zone of peace." Both the U.S. and the Soviet Union opposed the proposal because neither wished to accept restrictions on the free movement of its shipping. The "zone of peace" concept became a hardy perennial at the United Nations and nonaligned forums even as events were making the ocean a focus of superpower competition.

Soviet interest in a presence in the Indian Ocean was manifested after it had built up a substantial presence in the Mediterranean to emphasize its regional role and in the hope of influencing events in the Middle East. According to Soviet naval publications, the primary reason for maintaining a squadron in the Indian Ocean was to try to keep U.S. ballistic missile submarines beyond the range of industrial areas in the Ukraine.[38] Deputy Defence Minister Admiral Sergei Gorshkov has put it in the following words: "The U.S. nuclear-powered submarines, which appeared in the 1960s and carry ballistic missiles, are on permanent alert in the oceans and ready to strike at Soviet territory from various points."[39]

The need to counter the U.S. threat, an argument used in reverse by the Americans to justify their build-up, is only one of the factors responsible for the Soviet presence in the Indian Ocean. Soviet compulsions in building a blue-water navy and patrolling the Indian Ocean arise out of its desire to enhance its superpower status and to make its presence felt in an area it considers important. It is, in other words, an instrument of foreign policy intended to influence events in the littoral countries.

After the 1971 war, Americans were less concerned with maintaining a balance on the subcontinent and viewed Pakistan in relation to its value to the northwest littoral. Bhutto had, in fact, revived his country's interest in CENTO and Pakistan participated in naval exercises with the alliance in 1972 for the first time in a decade even as it left SEATO, which served little purpose for Pakistan after the loss of the eastern wing.

The 1973 Middle East war and the Arab oil embargo were to have a major role in the expansion of U.S. forces in the Indian Ocean although the issue became involved in a bureaucratic wrangle within the U.S. Administration. Defence Secretary Robert McNamara, increasingly consumed in the Vietnam war, finally rejected the base proposal on Diego Garcia on October 27, 1967. Despite the reluctance of a section of the Administration and the U.S. Congress to see a dramatic expansion of American forces in the Indian Ocean, the Navy was steadily but surely achieving its goal. McNamara left as Defence Secretary the next year, to be succeeded by Clark Clifford. The base proposal was repackaged as an "austere communications facility" and accepted.[40]

Much of the controversy centred round expansion of the communication facilities on the British island of Diego Garcia, 1,600 km. from the tip of southern India. An announcement in the British House of Commons on February 6, 1974 said an agreement had been reached with the U.S. on establishing support installations on the island for warships and aircraft. For the Nixon Administration, the western littoral had acquired prime importance, and it took to exaggerating threats to American interests to get money out of a reluctant Congress.

The expansion of the Diego Garcia base led to widespread protests in India, which feared that it would give America additional capacity to interfere in the affairs of the littoral countries.[41] In November 1974, Pakistan hosted the biggest naval exercises in the Indian Ocean to date with its CENTO partners, Iran, Turkey, Britain and the U.S., provoking Defence Minister Swaran Singh to declare: "The fact that CENTO—a product of the cold war—should be reactivated when they talked of detente and relaxation of tensions, could not but cause deep concern."[42]

India was among the most enthusiastic supporters of the "zone of peace" idea, but differences among the littoral countries were obvious from the beginning. Pakistan was plainly unenthusiastic because the absence of the U.S. Navy implied potential Indian dominance. China, which together with Pakistan supported the Diego Garcia base, favoured the "zone of peace" concept but wished the U.S. Navy to stay in the Indian Ocean as long as the Soviets were there.

Indian objectives in the Indian Ocean were spelled out by Minister of State Surendra Pal Singh in the Lok Sabha on August 16, 1974. They were to defend India's territorial integrity and freedom of navigation and to maintain the ocean as an area of peace, free of nuclear weapons. At the same time the Minister expressed his country's helplessness: "All we can do is to raise a hue and cry in world forums, and this we have done on every conceivable occasion."[43]

Earlier, Surendra Pal Singh had made a point of declaring, "The Soviet Union has not sought, nor have we given, any base facilities."[44] On December 12, 1974 the Deputy External Affairs Minister sought to deflect criticism in the Lok Sabha by suggesting, "I can only say that a military base is certainly different from a naval presence. Further, this is the way through which Russian ships have to go..."

American interest in the Indian Ocean was spelled out frankly in a Congressional hearing in 1974. J. Owen Zurhellen, Jr., deputy director of the U.S. Arms Control and Disarmament Agency, stated: "So our initial reason for deploying naval ships into the Indian Ocean was not because the Soviet Navy was there or was coming in; it was more in the direction, I feel, that we have interests in that area and these interests require us to be able, when the situation demands, to have our ships there."[45]

During Mrs. Gandhi's visit to Moscow in September 1971, the Soviets had merely agreed "to study" the proposal that the Indian Ocean be declared a zone of peace and "to solve it together with other powers on an equal basis."[46] The Soviet reservations were clear enough in the communiqué issued in New Delhi in November 1973 after the Brezhnev-Gandhi talks. In June 1976, the Soviets said they were ready "to participate" with other concerned countries to make the Indian Ocean a zone of peace and supported the desire of the people of the region to prevent the ocean "from becoming an arena for the setting up of foreign military bases." However, they added the usual rider: "in conformity with generally recognized rules of international law."[47]

New interest in the Indian Navy was, meanwhile, burgeoning. Traditionally, the Navy was the most neglected of India's three services. The legacy the British left was totally army-centred. Besides, India's main adversary remained Pakistan, despite the border war with China, and India's decision-makers, preponderantly hailing from the North, had little empathy with the demands of the Navy, the most expensive service to equip, when money was scarce.

The Navy's growth began in 1966 after the Indo-Pakistani war of the previous year.[48] It was based on a wider perspective of its role from coastal defence to safeguarding sea lanes, interdiction of hostile shipping and protection of economic installations.[49] After drawing a blank in the West, India negotiated with the Soviet Union for four new 2,300-ton F-class submarines, patrol boats, including Osa and Komar missile-firing classes, and other rocket-firing types.[50]

Although the acquisition of an aircraft carrier had proved a controversial decision,[51] the Navy continued to gather parliamentary support for a wider role. It won its spurs in the 1971 war with Pakistan by bottling the Pakistani Navy in Karachi and cutting off the escape route, in the Bay of Bengal, for Pakistani soldiers beleaguered in East Pakistan. The Indian naval actions around Karachi surprised, if not annoyed, the Soviets because armament essentially meant for defence was used offensively by the Indian navy.[52]

The steady acquisition of Soviet ships, in addition to the Leander-class frigates India had been making under a British licence, meant that the Navy became the most dependent of the Indian services on Soviet suppliers. The Indian submarine fleet, for instance, was entirely Soviet-equipped. Indeed, in recent years, the first major breach in the Soviet-supported service was the 1981 agreement with West Germany for the supply of two Type 1500 submarines and for assembling two more of them in Bombay.[53]

The deal with West Germany was not without raising a controversy. But the issue was settled in favour of the West because the Navy was very conscious of its preponderant reliance on the Soviets. Besides, the Navy wanted a quieter submarine, and the Soviets did not have anything suitable to offer, presumably because they were concentrating on nuclear-powered submarines.[54] There was no Soviet competition for equipping the lone aircraft carrier *Vikrant* with British Harrier jump jets and advanced Sea King helicopters.

Initially, Indian anti-aircraft guns were from Sweden, trucks from West Germany, light vehicles from Japan, mortars, missiles and helicopters from France, lightweight fighters, medium transport aircraft, carbines, tanks and frigates from Britain, and recoilless guns, VHF equipment and aircraft accessories from the U.S.[55]

Transfer of technology for any major weapon system or other acquisition is an article of faith with India. But the Indo-Soviet relationship had been far from trouble-free on this score. The Soviets proved hard bargainers and had often been parsimonious in giving spares and all stages of technology.[56] After the 1971 Indo-Pakistani war, the Soviets resisted Indian requests for a deep penetration aircraft, causing heartburn in New Delhi.[57]

There have been complaints about inadequacies in Soviet equipment—the performance of SU-7 bombers, for instance—and price of spares and their ready availability.[58] A Soviet aircraft costs roughly half its Western equivalent,[59] but the Soviets tend to compensate themselves somewhat by overpricing spares, the most lucrative field for aircraft manufacturers the world over. They have also been in the habit of withholding spares. Besides, the Soviets' penchant for secrecy is well known.

The sturdiness and relative simplicity of Soviet weapons emerged as a plus factor for the Indian Army in particular. Indeed, members of an initially British-trained Army which had adopted Soviet weapons with reluctance and out of necessity became their strongest advocates.[60]

According to former Defence and Foreign Minister Y.B. Chavan, the Soviets attached great importance to personal relationships with a country's leaders.[61] They seemed to have found a man after their own heart in Defence Minister Venkataraman. He had been telling the Soviets that the Indo-Soviet relationship superseded other factors, and they believed him.[62]

Indian officials in New Delhi have believed that the Indo-Soviet relationship is a cold-blooded one in which both sides understood each other. The Russians wanted to sell India military hardware for strategic and economic reasons.[63] Despite Western purchases, the Indian armed forces came to be basically and heavily equipped by the Soviets.[64]

Herself no ideologue, Mrs. Gandhi had led the country in the war with Pakistan encumbered with considerable ideological baggage. She had won the intra-party struggle in 1969 by inaugurating a populist phase in politics. Mrs. Gandhi had used refined techniques of propaganda and her storm troopers had attacked the concept of a free press, the right to property, the independence of civil servants and the judiciary. Instead of a "socialistic pattern of society" proclaimed by her father, she talked of "people's socialism."

Mrs. Gandhi had won the 1971 elections handsomely on the banish poverty slogan, with her party and the CPI cooperating at the state and local levels. India's victory over Pakistan in Bangladesh boosted her prestige at home and abroad, and in March 1972 the Congress captured 71.36 per cent of assembly seats in 16 states. But the euphoria induced by victory did not last long[65] and there were ominous signs on the horizon.

India was facing increasing economic difficulties even while radical changes were being made to the Fifth Plan. D.P. Dhar was given the planning portfolio, and the plan's objective of social justice was watered down and economic self-reliance emphasized. Guided by political, rather than economic, factors, the plan projected a growth rate of 5.5 per cent.[66] In 1972, drought necessitated food imports again, and there was chronic scarcity of resources.

A number of factors had combined to make the immediate post-1971 war years the worst in the country's history.[67] There were the economic costs of maintaining 10 million Bangladesh refugees and of the war. To add to Mrs. Gandhi's problems, a succession of monsoon failures added up to poor harvests and were topped by the quadrupling of oil prices. India's Gross Domestic Product, which had grown by 3.7 per cent in the 1960-70 period, declined to 1.2 per cent between 1970 and 1974.[68]

Disturbing signs were already appearing on the political landscape in 1972. The opposition had not been wiped out, despite Mrs. Gandhi's impressive victories. The left in the Congress was restive and two of its spokesmen charged the government in Parliament with failure to implement anti-monopoly legislation effectively.[69] A Congress party candidate was defeated in a parliamentary by-election in October 1972. There were an intra-party revolt in Orissa, language riots in Assam, an agitation on job reservations in Andhra and student unrest in large parts of the country.

By mid-1974 the opposition parties were in deep gloom and were expressing scepticism and dismay over the functioning of parliamentary democracy.[70] Part of the reason for this gloom was the Congress party's ability to return to power in Uttar Pradesh assembly elections in February 1974, despite the level of economic distress. A major students' revolt in Gujarat, something of a spontaneous explosion of feeling, had led to the dissolution of the state assembly, despite the Congress party enjoying a comfortable majority. The students' tendency was to paint all politicians black, but their movement collapsed under the weight of its own unexpected victory.

Jayaprakash Narayan took the torch of the Gujarat revolt across the country to his home state of Bihar. He highlighted two issues: corruption and the authoritarian tendencies of Mrs. Gandhi's government. He succeeded in doing what the opposition parties had failed to achieve: fire people's imagination. Most of the opposition parties climbed on to his bandwagon, the Jana Sangh being the most enthusiastic of the lot.

By January 1975, the major opposition parties, barring the CPI, had come to the end of the road in terms of their tolerance of Mrs. Gandhi's style of government.[71] But Mrs. Gandhi seemed to view her falling popularity and the growing alienation of the people from the government as a momentary phenomenon flowing from the acute economic difficulties. Her emphasis turned to "Save Democracy" and "Defeat Fascists," the latter being her description of the Narayan movement. The CPI and Mrs. Gandhi held a common view of this growing phenomenon, but she believed that she was aligning herself with the pro-Moscow Communists on her terms. In June 1975, *New Times* helpfully called Narayan a "notorious reactionary."[72]

By December 1974, the CPI was accusing Narayan of the desire to subvert parliamentary democracy to bring about chaos, leading to a rightist dictatorship. The party could hardly wait to cash in on the "unprecedented situation" in the country, displaying an almost boyish enthusiasm to attain shared power. The CPI believed that the country was heading towards a confrontation and its tactic was to support "left and democratic" forces in the Congress, nurse "progressives" and involve them in mass movements.[73]

Despite some efforts made by Mrs. Gandhi to build relations with the U.S. on a new basis, the American role during the Bangladesh war and the Indian political climate were hardly conducive to forging better relations. Attacks on America and the Central Intelligence Agency (CIA) were the rule, rather than the exception, in Indian politicians' repertoire. A statement made by Swaran Singh towards the end of 1972, calling for "friendly and cooperative relations," was promptly interpreted by many Americans as an exercise in seeking economic assistance. *The New York Times* commented on December 6 that "the sober second thoughts reflected in Mr. Singh's friendly overture may have been induced by a serious crop failure in India, which requires the Indians to seek grain imports that only the United States could provide."

In early 1973, Mrs. Gandhi criticized the heavy American bombing of North Vietnam and asked whether "this sort of war or the savage bombing" would have been tolerated for so long had the victims been European.[74]

This invited a rebuke from a State Department spokesman, who said it was "inadmissible" to suggest that the bombings "were motivated out of any racial considerations."[75] Not long afterwards Washington modified its embargo on "non-lethal" equipment and spare parts, leading Swaran Singh to declare that American arms to Pakistan "will once again pose a grave threat to India's security."[76] Bhutto had dismissed Indian protests as a "quite uncalled for storm in a teacup"[77] while President Nixon had told a press conference in March, "India's superiority is so enormous that the possibility of Pakistan being a threat is absurd."[78]

Efforts to improve relations with the U.S. continued somewhat fitfully. Swaran Singh met President Ford in September 1974 and claimed to be satisfied with the meeting, calling it "positive and helpful."[79] Henry Kissinger made his long-delayed visit to India in October 1974. It was a limited exercise to wipe the slate clean of the 1971 events. He took a relaxed attitude to the Indo-Soviet treaty and recognized India's leadership role in South Asia and the world because of "its size and position." A joint communiqué at the end of the visit said "there should be no intervention by outside powers in the affairs of South Asia, nor should they attempt to gain positions of special privilege in the region."[80]

The severity of the economic crisis was forcing Mrs. Gandhi to abandon her populist and doctrinaire policies to shift towards pragmatism in economic and industrial policies. By mid-1974 she had reversed a hasty and ill-conceived decision to bring food distribution under state control and made changes in industrial licensing policy. The 1974-75 budget raised new taxes, increased railway fares and impounded wage increases. Dhar left the cabinet.

A major problem was the quadrupling of oil prices, representing a $900 million increase in the cost of imported oil in 1974-75, in addition to other higher costs down the line.[81] Despite being badly hurt, India did not criticize the oil-producing nations. Instead, Mrs. Gandhi undertook a vigorous oil diplomacy in 1974 to sign several pacts with the countries of the Middle East. At the heart of this diplomacy was the Indian relationship with Iran.

The Shah of Iran was emerging as an American regional

policeman. The Americans were grateful to him for not having joined the Arab oil boycott of Israel and he had shown his mettle by sending troops to Oman in support of the Sultan and had helped Somalia in its war with Ethiopia. In 1971, the Shah seized the three Gulf islands of Abu Musa and the Tumbs. Fortified by his new wealth flowing from the quadrupling of oil prices, the Shah had sketched out a formidable agenda. He had the most ambitious nuclear power programme in the region and wished to build up the most powerful regional armed forces through a massive arms purchase programme. In 1974, Iran's military budget had jumped to $5,694 million, from $961 million in 1970.[82]

The Shah's dream of acquiring the status of Britain and France in the global hierarchy of powers by 1990 did raise some eyebrows in the U.S. Administration, but President Nixon was happy to give him all the arms he wanted. Although the Nixon doctrine was partially jettisoned by the beginning of 1974, the Shah fitted neatly into the American scheme of things. Iran seemed the ideal loyalist middle power and could also serve an American objective of buttressing Pakistan and perhaps participating in an informal American-Iranian-Pakistani condominium in the Arabian Sea.

Iran was a traditional friend and ally of Pakistan, siding with it in Indo-Pakistani disputes and helping Islamabad, on occasion by deflecting arms. The Shah was as interested in maintaining peace along his country's border with Pakistan as the Pakistani leaders. At the end of Bhutto's visit to Teheran on May 14, 1973, a joint communiqué said the two countries "would resolutely stand by each other in all matters bearing on their national independence and territorial integrity."[83] For Pakistani leaders, Iran provided an essential reassurance of security against the threat they perceived from India.

The Iranian armament programme had, indeed, caused concern in New Delhi. On July 20, 1973, Defence Minister Jagjivan Ram told Indian correspondents in London that it would have an impact on India. While the British view was that the military build-up in Iran presented no threat to India, Jagjivan Ram felt that Iran would not be able to fill Britain's past role in the Persian Gulf.[84]

The oil crisis and the horrendous economic implications it had for India merely buttressed Indian efforts to seek a rapprochement with Iran. Part of the exercise involved convincing the Shah that India was equally interested in preserving Pakistan's integrity. For his part, the

Shah was conscious of India's enhanced status. An oil pact was signed in February 1974 giving India a credit of $500 million.[85] Mrs. Gandhi went to Teheran in April the same year, with the Shah coming to New Delhi in October.

The Shah's October visit implied an increasing commitment by the two countries to building up a new kind of relationship. The Shah reportedly expressed his disenchantment with the Pakistan leadership in view of its close relations with the Arabs. The terms of Iranian loans to India were softened, a joint shipping line was agreed upon, as also the massive Kudremukh iron ore project to be financed by Iran.[86]

India made a major political concession in withdrawing its objections to Iran's growing military presence in the Persian Gulf and the Indian Ocean and supported "the formation of an economic interrelationship in the northern part of the Indian Ocean region." While the Shah mentioned the countries he had in mind as being Iran, Pakistan, India, Bangladesh, Burma, Thailand, Malaysia, Singapore and, eventually, the Indochinese countries as well as Australia, he did not spell out his concept.[87] At any rate, India had always been in favour of regional economic cooperation. The Shah's proposal drew a less than enthusiastic response from Pakistan.

Bhutto had taken his country out of SEATO and the British Commonwealth and emphasized bilaterism in relations with outside powers while drawing closer to the Muslim world. He recognized North Vietnam and decided to open diplomatic relations with North Korea. He de-emphasized Kashmir because there was little to be gained in that direction. Indeed, both India and Pakistan had other concerns than to harp on their differences. The prisoners of war issue, however, remained to be resolved.

Bhutto had a new constitution passed by the National Assembly in the spring of 1973 and assumed the prime ministership under it. He had still not recognized Bangladesh although the National Assembly had authorized him to do so in July 1973 at a moment of his choosing. He had also succeeded in getting most of the Muslim countries and China to refrain from recognizing the new nation. An agreement was signed in August 1973 among India, Pakistan and Bangladesh on the P.O.W.s and related issues.

The Pakistan Prime Minister neatly solved the problem of recognition by hosting an Islamic summit conference in February 1974 and getting Mujib to come to Lahore. The final act of reconciliation was thus staged in a Muslim setting from which India was automatically excluded. But Bhutto had his domestic problems. He never fully lifted the emergency imposed on the country in December 1971 and he ruthlessly undermined the opposition-ruled Baluchistan and North-West Frontier Province governments to replace them with his own rule. He organized a secret police, including the Federal Security Force, but the army opposed the arming of People's Guards under his People's Party.

Pakistan's projection towards the Muslim world gave Bhutto rich dividends, particularly after the oil crisis burst on the world scene. Although China remained Pakistan's main arms supplier, he was able to tap Arab money, particularly from Saudi Arabia, to purchase weapons in West Europe. By mid-1976, the Arab countries and Iran had given loans worth $973 million to Pakistan.[88] The Middle East also provided him with a useful outlet for excess armed forces officers, who were sent on deputation to several Arab countries. In 1973-74, Bhutto unsuccessfully tried to have the American arms embargo lifted by offering Nixon the use of the Gwadar base,[89] an offer he repeated to Ford in January 1975 in exchange for the lifting of the arms embargo.[90]

Mujib had given Bangladesh a new constitution in 1972 and won a big victory in the March 1973 elections. Almost all the Bangladesh refugees had returned home from India by the end of January 1972 and Indian troops left the new nation in March. India and Bangladesh had negotiated a twenty-five-year friendship treaty, closely patterned on the Indo-Soviet treaty, during Mujib's visit to New Delhi in February.[91] It was announced after Mujib's return from his trip to Moscow. By May 1972 India had given Bangladesh a little under $50 million in aid.[92] India gifted to Bangladesh three twin Otter aircraft and two light helicopters.[93]

Mujib sought to run his country through his Awami League on the model of India's Congress party and friendship with India was one of his main tenets. He faced a Herculean task, with his impoverished country devastated by the Pakistan army's crackdown and the war, and to make his job even more difficult, Pakistani troops had systematically eliminated Bengali intellectuals, indeed anyone they thought could play a leadership role.

The problems would have daunted a more capable administrator than Mujib proved to be. He had charisma and was loved by his people but had little talent for administration. Murmurs of protest were growing, and although India had wisely withdrawn its troops quickly, friction with New Delhi was increasing. In view of Mujib's identification with India, his opponents fastened on New Delhi to attack him, exaggerating reports of smuggling along the porous Indian-Bangladesh border to charge that India was taking away more than it was giving.

The Soviets maintained a considerable presence in Bangladesh. Aeroflot had been quick to start a service to Dhaka and the Soviets had given Mujib MIG-19s and transport planes and some helicopters.[94] The most notable Soviet presence, however, was of a twenty-unit fleet in the Bay of Bengal to clear mines and salvage ships at Chittagong and Cox's Bazar. The Soviets stayed two years to complete their job, overstaying their welcome.

Both Bangladesh and India seemed to look askance at the Soviets' extended stay. Although Rear Admiral Sergei Zuyenko denied that the Soviets were setting up a base,[95] there were enough indications to suggest a Soviet interest in acquiring access rights, and India reportedly advised Bangladesh to turn down Moscow's request.[96] Bhutto declared in March 1973 that the Soviets had "set up a base more or less in Chittagong... Bangladesh is the backdoor of China."[97] At any rate, the Soviets left without completing work at Chalna. According to Admiral Zuyenko, "The Bangladesh authorities say that they will be able to handle everything else that remains to be done in Chalna by themselves."[98] A few weeks later, a consortium under the U.N. relief operations was employed to complete the job.

Mujib, meanwhile, was facing increasing problems in governing his country, with dissent and economic difficulties growing. In a desperate measure, he decided to abrogate the constitution, disbanded all parties except his own and took over as President in early 1975. His weaknesses in administration and fondness for operating through family members and cronies could only be accentuated under the new dispensation.

The China factor had stimulated the Soviet quest for detente with the West in the early Seventies. The Soviets set their hearts on two immediate goals: universal acceptance of the post-war European borders and arms limitation agreements with the U.S. Two processes were set in motion, the first through the Helsinki conference and the second through the Strategic Arms Limitation Talks (SALT) with American negotiators. These efforts were crowned with success in

Helsinki in 1975 and in the agreement reached with the U.S. on SALT-1 in 1972.

President Nixon's dramatic visit to Beijing in early 1972 and his subsequent trip to Moscow implied a measure of competition between the two Communist powers in seeking detente with the U.S., a competition Washington was delighted to encourage. Both China and the Soviet Union encouraged North Vietnam to sign a peace agreement with the U.S. in 1973, and this competitive detente served further to exacerbate Sino-Soviet relations.

The Soviet Union was experiencing a surfeit of self-confidence in the wake of its universally recognized superpower status, denoted not only by its nuclear parity with the U.S. but, more recently, by its ability to deploy a blue-water navy in the world's oceans. Facing an impending defeat in Vietnam, America, on the other hand, was following a generally restrained military policy in the Third World in the Seventies.

The Chinese believed that the vigorous Soviet efforts to achieve detente with West Europe, also by encouraging Willy Brandt's Ostpolitik, and flexing of muscles in the Third World would harm their interests. Soviet divisions east of the Urals had risen from thirty-two to forty-four in 1971-72, more than a quarter of Soviet army formations.[99] The Chinese now buttressed their own relations with West Europe. Diplomatic relations with France were in existence since 1964, but Beijing moved to establish diplomatic relations with West Germany in October 1972, exchanged ambassadors with London the same year and welcomed President Pompidou to China in September 1973.

China also spread out the welcome mat for conservative West European leaders. This provoked the Soviets to accuse China of "forming a bloc with ultra-reactionaries... the right wing of the imperialist bourgeoisie," and "seeking to strengthen contacts with any political leaders in the West who display or may display willingness to cooperate with the Maoists on the basis of anti-Sovietism."[100]

Substantial Soviet arms began flowing into Uganda in early 1972 and a Soviet-Somali friendship treaty was signed in July 1974, but it was the Angolan civil war of 1975-76 that saw a dramatic rivalry between Moscow and Beijing. By July 1975 the Soviets made a major commitment to the Popular Movement for the Liberation of Angola (MPLA) to provoke the U.S. to give covert aid to the National

Front for the Liberation of Angola (FNLA) and the National Union for the Total Independence of Angola (UNITA). This was followed by direct South African support of UNITA and the introduction of Cuban troops by the Soviets.

The mood in the U.S., particularly after the fall of Saigon to the North Vietnamese in the spring of 1975, was against military escalation in Africa. As a consequence, South Africa withdrew from Angola and the MPLA, supported by the Soviet Union and Cuba, achieved a victory. The U.S. responded by giving military assistance to key African countries and Kissinger warned during a visit to Lusaka in April 1976 about pursuit of "hegemonical aspirations or bloc policies" by outside powers since "any attempt by one will inevitably be countered by the other."[101] More significantly, the Soviet adventure in Angola had jolted American public opinion and would play a major role in its view of detente.

To the delight of the Chinese, the Soviets did not have an uninterrupted run of successes. Their most serious setback was the decision of Egypt's President Sadat to expel Soviet personnel in 1972; the Soviet-Egyptian treaty was abrogated in March 1976. But Moscow proved agile in switching friends, abandoning Somalia for Ethiopia in an effort to acquire influence in the more important country in an area peripheral to the Middle East.

The Soviets supplied about $1 billion of arms to Ethiopia and airlifted 10,000 to 12,000 Cuban troops between November 1977 and January 1978 to prevent the disintegration of the empire, now under a new garb, and reverse the trend in the Ogaden war between Ethiopia and Somalia.[102] The formula ultimately agreed upon by Moscow and Washington was withdrawal of Somali forces from Ogaden and Soviet guarantee of Somalia's territorial integrity.

Somalia abrogated the friendship treaty, expelled Soviet personnel and cancelled the Soviet use of the naval base at Berbera in November 1977. The Sudan terminated the services of Soviet military experts in May 1977.

Brezhnev sent a message to the 1973 Algiers summit meeting of the nonaligned suggesting that the Communist countries were the "natural allies" of the nonaligned. Cuba, which enthusiastically promoted this approach, took new interest in the nonaligned movement in the early Seventies. But Cuba's own role in its military cooperation with the Soviet Union later raised a major debate among the nonaligned. It was a subject of discussion at the nonaligned foreign ministers' meeting in 1978 in Belgrade, with India performing something of a tightrope act.[103]

Beijing, meanwhile, kept hammering away at its major themes. The policy of detente and the Helsinki agreement, it suggested, were attempts of some Western nations to "free themselves from this Soviet peril at the expense of the security of other countries."[104] The arms control agreements between the U.S. and the Soviet Union, it said, was a camouflage for further arms expansion and war. Moscow engaged in disarmament and arms control discussion "to disarm the people of other countries, psychologically and materially," to submit them to "pressure and manipulation."

Mao's death in September 1976 induced the Soviets to show significant restraint in their criticism of China in the hope of improving relations. But this restraint was not matched by China, which showed hardly any change in its policy. The Soviets waited until mid-April 1977 to revert to their old policy by launching a major attack on China in *New Times*.[105]

The Gang of Four—Mao's wife and three others representing the radical faction—were ousted in October 1976. A Sino-Japanese treaty, including the controversial "hegemony" clause (Beijing's shorthand for Soviet policies), was signed in August 1978, to be welcomed by India. In December 1978 it was announced that the U.S. would recognize the Beijing government on January 1, 1979 and full diplomatic relations were effected shortly thereafter. Chinese concern over the Soviet threat, as perceived in Beijing, can be gauged from Deng Xiaoping's interview with *Time* magazine of February 5, 1979 seeking a U.S.-China-Japan alliance against the Soviet Union. Inevitably, the new strategic relationship Beijing sought with the U.S. exacerbated Sino-Soviet rivalry and caused anxiety in New Delhi.

The Soviets had completed a four-lane highway through the mountains of northern Afghanistan in July 1970. In July 1973, Mohammad Daoud carried out a successful coup against his cousin, the king, and revived the Afghanistan-Pakistan dispute on Pakhtoonistan. Afghanistan had never accepted the legitimacy of the Durand Line as the border between the two countries. But Daoud began to cause the Soviets concern as he moved away from pro-Soviet policies in 1975. The Russians responded by exerting strong pressures on the two Communist factions in Afghanistan—the Khalq and the Parcham—to merge. Moscow did not seem to have a direct hand in the Communist putsch of April 1978, but Afghanistan thereby explicitly came within the Soviet orbit.

Chapter Seven

JANATA

WHEN China exploded its first nuclear bomb in October 1964, nearly 100 members of the Indian Parliament had signed a petition urging the government to go in for nuclear weapons.[1] And when China launched a satellite in 1970—"the equivalent of the United States' 1957 Sputnik shock," as an astute American observer has put it[2]—it greatly strengthened the pro-bomb lobby in India, leading to speculation that Mrs. Gandhi could derive maximum political advantage "if it [an Indian bomb] can happen before the next general election."[3]

India's response, as we have seen, was largely a diplomatic one to seek some form of joint superpower nuclear guarantees. These proved unavailable on acceptable terms and were made irrelevant by the burgeoning U.S.-Chinese rapprochement. The Indo-Soviet treaty of August 1971 provided an implicit nuclear umbrella for India, but was unsatisfactory, dependent as it was on the dynamics of the emerging triangular Washington-Moscow-Beijing strategic relationship. The American decision to send the nuclear-powered, and reportedly nuclear-armed,[4] *Enterprise* into Indian waters during the Bangladesh war starkly brought home to the Indian leadership the country's nuclear vulnerability.

The Indian explosion of an underground nuclear device at Pokharan in the Rajasthan desert on May 18, 1974 evoked a predictable response at home. It led to an unmistakable air of excitement and was a shot in the arm for Mrs. Gandhi's government whose sagging morale was much in need of uplift. There was a chorus of praise from the entire political spectrum, including the pro-Moscow CPI.[5]

Mrs. Gandhi emphasized India's peaceful intentions and Defence Minister Jagjivan Ram indicated that the decision to explode the nuclear device was taken three years earlier,[6] nearly two years after the Indian Atomic Energy Commission had projected such tests in the ten-year profile it had given members of Parliament. In fact, India's nuclear scientists got the go-ahead from Mrs. Gandhi in 1972 after President Nixon's visit to Beijing in February.[7] India called its test the PNE (peaceful nuclear explosion), leading to Rabelaisian embellishments on the acronym.

Japan protested against the Indian test and reduced its pledge at the Aid-India Consortium meeting the next month by $10 million below its 1973 level; the U.S. pledged $75.6 million in new aid and $45 million in debt relief—amounts that were later reduced by Congress to $50 million.[8] The Indian test also presented problems for U.S. replenishment of the World Bank's soft-loan window, the International Development Agency. Official-American reaction was restrained. Assistant Secretary of State Alfred L. Atherton, Jr. testified in September 1974 that the Indian explosion had not altered the South Asian "balance."[9]

Ambassador T.N. Kaul wrote to Kissinger on July 6, 1974 to assert, "We did not use or divert Canadian material; in fact we used 100 per cent Indian material, Indian technology and Indian personnel."[10] This was to controvert the prevailing Western view that India had used fuel from a Canadian-aided reactor for the test; Canada broke off all nuclear cooperation agreements with India after the test. India's nuclear power programme was set back by at least five years and India had ultimately to turn to the Soviet Union for heavy water. An agreement for the supply of 200 tons was reached with Moscow but the Soviets insisted on India signing a tripartite agreement with the International Atomic Energy Agency on safeguards. The first supply of Soviet heavy water was made before the agreement.[11]

The U.S. chose not to contradict Kaul's assurance and during his visit to New Delhi in October Kissinger accepted India's peaceful intentions.[12] Privately, he sought, and received, Indian assurances that New Delhi would be proliferation-conscious in exports and would not pursue a nuclear weapons programme.[13] India's effort was to convince the world that despite having become a nuclear power, its intensions remained entirely peaceful in developing nuclear technology. In view of the generally critical reaction in the West, the French Atomic Energy Commission's message of congratulations to Indian scientists on the nuclear test "gladdened many hearts" in New Delhi.[14]

The Indian delegate, Brajesh Mishra, told the Committee of

Disarmament in Geneva in August 1974, "Even after exploding a nuclear device, we have, unlike others, reaffirmed our solemn declaration [on peaceful uses of atomic power]. Thus only in this respect have we broken a barrier."[15] And the chief of India's Atomic Energy Commission, H.N. Sethna, assured the eighteenth session of the International Atomic Energy Agency in September 1974, "The underground nuclear explosion formed part of this independent programme of India for peaceful uses of atomic energy." He described the Nonproliferation Treaty as "an unequal and discriminatory instrument" and said "the Nonproliferation Treaty stands or falls by its own merits and demerits."[16]

Bhutto, who, as we shall see, had activated a plan for a Pakistan bomb in 1972, reacted to the Indian test with predictable violence. He vowed that his countrymen would eat grass to match Indian capability. He broke off talks, scheduled for June 10, to discuss restoration of postal and telecommunication links and travel facilities. Pakistan contended that the test had changed the whole context of the Indo-Pakistani dialogue and revealed India's hostile intentions towards neighbours.[17]

Pakistan launched a virulent anti-Indian campaign in the press. Its declared aim was to seek security guarantees against the Indian nuclear threat. Bhutto did receive assurances of Chinese support against Indian "nuclear blackmail,"[18] but his main purpose seems to have been to extract maximum propaganda advantage out of the Indian explosion. Having done so, Pakistan suddenly decided to resume talks with India early in August; the talks were held in mid-September. Mercifully, the Indian test came after an agreement between India, Pakistan and Bangladesh on the return of the last Pakistani P.O.W.s.

The world awaited Moscow's reaction to the test with much interest because the Soviets had been exerting as much, if not greater, pressure on India to sign the NPT and shared in full measure American nonproliferation objectives. In the event, the Soviets made a major concession to New Delhi. There was no censure of India and, according to the International Institute for Strategic Studies, "The Soviet Union, far from condemning it, seemed to endorse it..."[19] *New Times* said in May 1974 that Mrs. Gandhi's Government "firmly" stood "for the use of nuclear energy for peaceful purposes."[20]

In the wake of the Indian explosion, the Soviets seemed to be justifying Mrs. Gandhi's action by lending support to the theory of

Chinese nuclear blackmail. On August 25, 1974 a United News of India report from Moscow quoted Novosti to suggest that "China already has more than two hundred atom and hydrogen bombs ready for action" and that delivery vehicles can be deployed on "open sites, in silos and caves of the Himalayas." Further, the nuclear threat "will grow immeasurably for these countries [of South and Southeast Asia] after the commissioning of another nuclear centre in Tibet." Besides, the "Chinese have built powerful radar and tracking stations" near the Indian borders, an indication of the possible direction of a Chinese nuclear rocket test into the Indian Ocean, "hurtling" over Indian territory.[21]

In September 1974, *New Times* cited a left Indian periodical about the nuclear bases in Tibet and the positioning of 300,000 People's Liberation Army troops there.[22]

The Indian test had two consequences. A nuclear suppliers' club was formed in London in 1975 following an initiative by Kissinger. It was, in effect, a cartel to tighten safeguards and export of nuclear supplies. And in 1978, the U.S. enacted the Nuclear Nonproliferation Act to impose stringent conditions on countries receiving nuclear supplies or technology. The latter would pose a major problem in Indo-American relations because it repudiated an earlier agreement on guaranteed American supplies of low enriched uranium for the Tarapur atomic power station near Bombay.

The 1971 events also had an impact on Pakistan's nuclear policy, perhaps convincing Bhutto that the bomb offered a guarantee against the threat Pakistan perceived from India and would achieve his much-cherished ambition of negotiating with India on a basis of equality. At any rate, there is evidence to suggest that Bhutto convened a secret meeting in Multan in January 1972[23] and announced his decision to start work on the bomb. The Indian test thus provided Bhutto with a stimulus and public justification to pursue his nuclear ambitions; it did not cause them.[24]

As evidence of Pakistan's nuclear programme began to proliferate, it caused much concern in the U.S. in particular. Controversy centred on France's agreement to sell Pakistan a nuclear reprocessing plant, a project that did not relate to the country's nuclear power programme. And there were multiplying revelations of Pakistan's clandestine efforts to obtain nuclear-related material.

Kissinger mounted a major effort to persuade France to abrogate the nuclear deal with Pakistan and warned Bhutto of the consequences of going ahead with the deal. During his last visit as Secretary of State, Kissinger told Bhutto that Pakistan risked losing all military and economic aid if he went ahead with the construction of the reprocessing plant. Bhutto's answer was that he would irrevocably weaken his position if he were to give in.[25]

Bhutto presented the Pakistani "bomb" as a common Islamic undertaking, which apparently helped him in obtaining Libyan financing. But the crucial question related to possible Chinese assistance in Pakistan's nuclear programme. According to experts in India and the West, Bhutto reached an agreement with the Chinese leadership in 1976 on the supply of nuclear technology, and planned to explode the first nuclear device in December 1977, six months before he was overthrown.[26]

In his last testament, Bhutto seemed to confirm the 1976 agreement. ".... My single most important achievement which I believe will dominate the portrait of my public life is an agreement which I arrived at after an assiduous and tenacious endeavour spanning over eleven years of negotiations. In the present context, the agreement of mine, concluded in June 1976, will perhaps be my greatest achievement and contribution to the survival of our people and our nation."[27] Further, he contended: "The Christian, Jewish and Hindu civilizations have this [nuclear weapon] capacity. The Communist powers also possess it. Only the Islamic civilization was without it, but that position was about to change."[28]

Reports of Chinese nuclear assistance to Pakistan were taken seriously enough in Washington to impel Secretary of State George Shultz to raise it with the Chinese during his visit to Beijing in February 1983.[29] Since a nuclear cooperation agreement was initiated in Beijing in April 1984 during President Reagan's visit to China, the Americans presumably reassured themselves that dangerous nuclear cooperation between China and Pakistan no longer existed, even if it once did exist. However, there were second thoughts on the question in Washington, as we shall see. Bhutto died convinced that America helped the army overthrow him because of his nuclear ambition.

Despite Bhutto's exploitation of the Indian nuclear test, events were taking a more hopeful turn in Indo-Pakistani relations. An agreement was signed in Islamabad on September 14, 1974 to resume postal, telecommunication and travel facilities, which had been suspended after the 1965 war and snapped in 1971. The links were restored on October 15, and on the first day 208 telephone calls to Pakistan were booked from India and 14 calls received from Pakistan.[30] Talks on resumption of overflights and restoration of civil aviation links broke down in November, but a trade protocol was signed on November 30.

In its quest for building "durable peace," India signed an agreement with Sri Lanka in June 1974 on Kachchativu island, 10.5 miles from the nearest Indian shore. Prime Minister Bandaranaike told the Sri Lanka Parliament after a visit to India in November, "Our relations with India have been very good and ... [have] never been so good."[31] But talks with Bangladesh in November on the Farakka barrage failed to produce an agreement. India's absorption of Sikkim state in August 1974 led to large-scale anti-Indian demonstrations in Kathmandu in September provoking a strong Indian protest and a hard-headed review of its policies towards Nepal.[32]

The salutary effects of the Indian explosion on Mrs. Gandhi's fortunes did not last long. The impression she gave in January 1975 was that she was facing a crisis of confidence.[33] Events were moving towards a crisis, the confrontation so desired by the CPI. It came in the form of a judgement of a high court on June 12, 1975 holding Mrs. Gandhi guilty in an election petition on two counts of election malpractices and disqualified her from holding office for six years. Although she was granted a stay to appeal to the Supreme Court, which she did to win a qualified reprieve, the judgement was a bombshell.

Buoyed by the momentum of the Jayaprakash Narayan movement, the opposition parties believed that they had nearly achieved their ambition of ousting Mrs. Gandhi and mounted a major political campaign. In the Congress party, senior leaders manoeuvred to place themselves in line for succession even as they issued statements of support for her continuing leadership.

Mrs. Gandhi faced a dilemma. Morally, she should have resigned until she could clear her name. Politically, by appointing a temporary successor, she would run the risk of fighting an uncertain intra-party battle to regain office, once she was cleared. She chose to stay in office while administering bitter medicine to the country. A state of internal emergency was declared on the night of June 25-26, 1975. Narayan, Desai and thousands of their supporters were arrested, press censorship was imposed and several constitutional provisions affecting the citizen's rights and liberties were suspended. The kind of emergency imposed took almost everyone by surprise and the country settled down to an eerie silence.

Among the opposition parties, the CPI was the lone unequivocal supporter of the Emergency. Support for Mrs. Gandhi's new regimen was forthcoming in full measure from Moscow. The Emergency, *Pravda* said on January 25, 1976, was necessitated by attempts at "internal subversion," aided by external forces, to capitalize on the difficulties posed by the 1975 economic crisis to create an atmosphere of pandemonium—"there are few who question the timeliness and expediency of the measures undertaken by the government."

The Soviet press gave enthusiastic coverage to India's new twenty-point programme for socio-economic development. "The actions taken by the Indian government against internal and external reactionaries were responded to with full understanding in the Soviet Union," wrote Y. Tsaplin in *International Affairs* of August 1976.

Tass suggested on March 17, 1976, "Contrary to popular rumours being spread, the [Indo-Soviet] treaty by no means limits the Indian nonalignment policy. On the contrary, this treaty helps frustrate all machinations and designs of big capital which always desires to see India a weak and economically backward country. For the sake of the interests of the whole of humanity, the utmost should be done ... to broaden the friendship."

The Soviet press said the Emergency had come none too soon because, as *Izvestia* wrote on March 1, 1977, the opposition planned "to undermine India's traditional friendship with the socialist world and throw open the doors to foreign private capital." "Supported by imperialism," A. Roslavlev suggested in *Pravda* on June 6, 1976, "these forces [of reaction] tried to remove the government of Indira Gandhi from power, terminate the policy of social and economic reform and change India's independent foreign policy."

On the occasion of Mrs. Gandhi's visit to Moscow in 1976, V. Skosyrev wrote in *Izvestia* on November 23: The Emergency "struck a blow against the rightist conspirators who were counting on seizing power." It instituted "long-overdue social measures"; "the Western newspapers [which] launched a noisy propaganda campaign, making the direst forecasts for the country and attempting to prove that the government would be unable to cope with the difficulties that had arisen ... prefer not to recall their hasty forecasts."[34]

The Marxists in India were outraged by the praise showered upon the Emergency; many of their leaders were in jail together with other opposition leaders and supporters. The CPI, on the other hand, basked in the dubious glory of its legitimacy in the Emergency regime. It was to have anxious moments in the latter part of the Emergency, thanks to the growing power of Mrs. Gandhi's son Sanjay.

Sanjay had received official encouragement and favours to build an ostensibly indigenous car in a factory set up on the outskirts of New Delhi. The drama of the court verdict against his mother and his contribution to the making of her decision to stay in power, rather than resign, had brought Sanjay into the centre of the power play. He found the exercise of power more exciting than tinkering with cars and set about imposing his will on the administrative machine with the help of a band of devoted young supporters who were short on scruples and long on unquestioned loyalty to their leader.

Sanjay was a man of determination and ruthlessness and one of his major contributions, which would have an important influence on his mother's fortunes, was to impose a programme of birth control on the northern states, measures which often crossed the border between persuasion and coercion. He was unabashedly for free enterprise and capitalism and had contempt for Communists.

In an interview he gave to a journalist, passed by the censors on July 27, 1975, which was subsequently withdrawn, he attacked the Communists, suggesting that "if you take all the people in the Communist Party, the big wigs—even the not-so-big wigs—I don't think you'd find a richer or more corrupt people anywhere."[35] Although the storm the interview caused among Communists and leftists in Mrs. Gandhi's party passed, Sanjay issuing a statement of contrition, he would return to Communist-baiting later in the Emergency and even win his mother's support for his attacks.[36]

The third session of the Indo-Soviet joint commission concluded its labours on April 5, 1976 with an agreement by the two countries to cooperate in building projects in other Third World countries. In July 1976, there was an agreement to open all Soviet commercial ports to Indian shipping. But the most significant developments in the field of foreign policy came in India's relations with China and Pakistan.

The Chinese had based their policy towards India since the late Fifties on hostility arising out of their concern for guarding their southern flank in a truculent, if not rebellious, Tibet and the convergence of Indian and Soviet interests against China. Long before pragmatism governed Chinese policies, Beijing sacrificed its ideological beliefs to build up a strategic relationship with the military dictatorship of India's adversary, Pakistan. China encouraged and aided the rebels in India's northeast as it also sought to promote the Maoist form of Communism in India for a time. The Chinese encouraged India's smaller neighbours to adopt anti-Indian attitudes.

Although Chinese policies made the task of the Indian leadership more difficult in taming dissidents and asserting the country's preeminence on the subcontinent, they were not successful in achieving their objectives. On the contrary, the level of Chinese hostility against New Delhi and amity with Pakistan merely served to buttress the Indo-Soviet relationship.

A reassessment of policy towards the subcontinent seems to have been in progress in Beijing in the late Sixties. It culminated in the Mao smile of May 1970. But Pakistan's problems in its eastern wing, which were to be transformed into an Indo-Pakistani imbroglio leading to a war on the subcontinent, were to stop Beijing in its tracks. Although the Chinese continued to berate India, a central fact to emerge out of Mrs. Gandhi's victory in Bangladesh in December 1971 was that India became less dependent on the Soviets. Further, the Indian nuclear test of May 1974 was an assertion of Indian independence of Moscow even as it emphasized the basic Sino-Indian rivalry in Asia.

In the mid-1970s, Chinese media described Tibet as China's "southwest outpost against imperialism, revisionism and reaction."[37] Beijing had completed its basic strategic requirements in Tibet by 1976 and a number of foreigners were allowed to visit it since October 1975. In the meantime, China had made a tactical gain in the subcontinent. Sheikh Mujibur Rahman's efforts to run his country by fiat led to an anti-Indian and pro-West young majors' coup in August 1975. Mujib and members of his family were murdered and Khondaker Mushtaque Ahmed, who had played a questionable role in contacts with the U.S. Consulate General in Calcutta in 1971, took office as the new president.[38] Mujib had been killed hardly two months after the imposition of the Emergency in India.

Pakistan had recognized Bangladesh in February 1974, but China gave no indication that it was in any hurry to follow Islamabad's example. After the coup, Beijing lost little time in establishing diplomatic relations with Dhaka. They were established in October

1975. November saw a brief, allegedly Indian-supported, coup by Brigadier Khalid Mosharraf. Mosharraf and his followers were killed, with Ziaur Rahman emerging as the new strong man.

India had sent numerous peace feelers to China since 1968. In 1976, shortly before Zhou Enlai's death, Beijing decided to accept the overtures. On April 15, 1976, it was announced in India that it was sending an ambassador to China for the first time since the 1962 border war;[39] Beijing had privately assured New Delhi that it would reciprocate. Within four days of the announcement, it was reported that Mrs. Gandhi was willing to discuss resumption of diplomatic relations with Pakistan, an offer Bhutto promptly accepted.

After three days of talks, a joint communique on May 14, 1976 said that India and Pakistan had decided to resume diplomatic relations and restore air and rail links, overflights and overland traffic between the two countries. In July 1976 the diplomatic landscape presented a striking change, with New Delhi exchanging ambassadors with Beijing and Islamabad. The Emergency was still in effect in India.

Bhutto had achieved considerable success in taking his country closer to the Muslim world of the Middle East and claimed a leadership role for himself in the Islamic world by virtue of his impending gift to it, an "Islamic bomb." His success in foreign policy, combined with his increasingly arbitrary methods of government at home, led to his downfall. The socio-economic coalition he had formed in the first years of office had come apart; dissent had grown, with people chafing at the terror often imposed by the Federal Security Force. With Pakistan rehabilitated in the world, the Army had got back the self-confidence it lost after the Bangladesh war.

Nine small disparate parties formed the Pakistan National Alliance to contest the elections, held during January-February 1977. National issues were subordinated in the elections to attacks on Bhutto's authoritarianism and the un-Islamic life he led. Bhutto won,[40] only to be greeted by an outcry against the rigging that had taken place on a considerable scale. Ironically, the People's Party would probably have won a fair election, by a small margin.

In the post-election riots that followed, Bhutto orchestrated an anti-American campaign, charging the CIA with having given the opposition alliance $25 million for the elections.[41] In Parliament on April 28, he accused the U.S. of a "colossal conspiracy" against him, chiefly because of his determination to give Pakistan a nuclear capability.[42] In June, Bhutto called for a treaty of mutual defence by all the Muslim states.⁴³ He made last-minute gestures to the Muslim constituency at home to stem the tide of protest.

But it was too late. Bhutto's opponents were also encouraged by the stunning defeat of Mrs. Gandhi in the March election and the contrast between the fairness of the Indian election and the flawed nature of Bhutto's exercise was there for all in Pakistan to see. The Army was itching to get back into the seat of power and overthrew Bhutto in a coup on July 5, 1977. Bhutto's successor was General Zia-ul-Haq, the man he had appointed the army chief over the heads of senior generals.

In India, the "gains of the Emergency" were decreasing in inverse proportion to its length. The strict regimen had initially brought about an economic improvement in the country, with discipline in offices and factories yielding results. But after a time, the country was sliding back to its old ways; dissent, despite the draconian laws, was increasing. Above all, Mrs. Gandhi wished to legitimize her power through free elections, confident in the belief that people would return her to office. In January 1977 she made the surprising announcement that elections would be held in March.

The opposition leaders were released from prison or house arrest, censorship of the press was suspended and it soon became apparent that Mrs. Gandhi had made a major miscalculation,⁴⁴ symbolized by the defection on February 2 of her veteran minister and leader of the Scheduled Castes (untouchables), Jagjivan Ram, who quickly formed his own party called Congress for Democracy. A people unused to the kind of rigour they had had to endure were raring to go to election booths to give their verdict on the Emergency. This was especially the case in the northern states; the Emergency, particularly the coercive birth control programme, had sat more lightly on the South.

Five opposition parties came together in a party the called Janata (the people) to contest the elections. It was a rout for the Congress, except in parts of the South. Mrs. Gandhi and son Sanjay also lost their individual elections. Janata, somewhat to its own surprise, was wafted to power. Congress strength in the Lok Sabha was reduced from 352 in 1971 to 153 although the number of seats in the Lower House had increased from 518 to 542. The CPI went down with Mrs. Gandhi; its strength was reduced from 23 seats to 7, all from the South.

The CPI had fought the 1977 election in cooperation with the

Congress. There was no question where Soviet sympathies lay. Moscow was avidly backing Mrs. Gandhi and berating Janata. "If the propagandist facade with which the Janata party makes its appeal to the Indian electorate is removed," intoned *Pravda* on March 12, 1977 shortly before election day, "it appears as the direct tool of extreme reaction, the defender of landlord interest, financiers, local and foreign monopolists."

The Soviets were not prepared for the defeat of the Congress party although Mrs. Gandhi's own reading of the situation was considerably less sanguine. At any rate, Moscow did not like the look or the policies of the Janata leaders. In the election campaign in February, Morarji Desai, who would soon become Prime Minister, charged Mrs. Gandhi's government with doing "whatever the Soviet Union does" and declared that if Janata came to power, the Indo-Soviet treaty might "automatically go."[45] The Soviets thus faced a major challenge to their South Asia policy.

It was too tempting an opportunity for the Chinese to pass up. In comments directed more at the Soviet Union than India, *Peking Review* exulted on April 8, 1977: "The [election] results not only declared the bankruptcy of the internal and external policies pursued by Indira Gandhi who had tailed after the Soviet Union, policies which harmed the country and brought suffering to the people; they also marked a setback to Moscow's expansionist scheme in the South Asian region. India occupies an important strategic position in Asia and the Indian Ocean. To realize their fond dream of dominating the world the new tsars curried favour with the Indira Gandhi government and tried to drag India into the orbit of their counter-revolutionary global strategy."

Immediately after the election results were announced, the tendency in Moscow was to look for the silver lining. I. Kovalev suggested in *Izvestia* of March 22, 1977: "It is indicative that Congress party candidates were most successful in places where a preelection arrangement existed between the Congress and the Communist Party of India, or where the Communist party, with no official encouragement, actively supported progressive candidates of the Congress party."

The CPI's fortunes could hardly be improved by such exercises and Kovalev was quick to signify the change in Moscow's assessment. "Mistakes and excesses in the implementation of measures grew out of laws passed after the state of emergency was declared in 1975 had an effect. The agrarian reforms proclaimed by the leaders of the Congress party were brought to a virtual standstill because of the opposition of the wealthy farmers. The Congress party leadership antagonized part of the working class by reducing wage supplements."

Even more revealing was a quotation from the CPI *Pravda* chose to publish on March 30, 1977. It said Mrs. Gandhi was not voted out of office because of her progressive policies but because of "abuses of the state of emergency directed against the common people" and promised to "judge the new government by its deeds...support its correct measures and oppose its mistaken ones."

At his first press conference after taking office, Prime Minister Morarji Desai said the Indo-Soviet treaty would lie dormant and would not be allowed to come in the way of India's relations with third countries. Further, he suggested that he was planning a shift in policy and was against nurturing particularly close relations with one superpower.[46] Both Desai and his Foreign Minister, Atal Bihari Vajpayee, subsequently declared in public statements that they would follow the path of "genuine nonalignment"[47] and "proper nonalignment," Desai declaring, "We will not have any special relations with any country."[48]

Despite the Janata government's desire to change the country's foreign policy and its leaders' public postures, it quickly came to the conclusion that given the security, arms, trade and economic linkages, any radical departure from Mrs. Gandhi's policy towards Moscow was for the long haul. The Janata leaders wished to reassure the Soviet leaders that the substance of the relationship, including the treaty, would remain unaltered. They had discovered the security implications of the treaty, particularly the nuclear protection it implicitly offered against China.

An invitation was sent to Foreign Minister Gromyko to come to New Delhi. Eager as he was to assess the changed situation, he came on April 25. The day he arrived *Pravda* carried a Tass report accusing "certain circles" of trying to "cast a shadow" on the treaty and quoted an anonymous Foreign Ministry official's denial that Janata planned to abrogate it.

From the Soviet point of view, it was a vital mission, and, after a long meeting with Desai Gromyko felt sufficiently reassured to declare that it would be "absolutely unnatural" to allow "any gaps" to develop in Indo-Soviet relations.[49] Vajpayee set the tone for Janata's policy towards the Soviet Union by telling the Soviet Foreign Minister, "We appreciate the help the Soviet Union has given us to industrialize our country and to make us self-reliant. We are also grateful for their consistent and principled support in our difficult times. We remember all this and we shall continue to value our friendship with you."[50]

Vajpayee suggested that Indo-Soviet relations could survive the defeat of an individual or party and said the treaty reflected the close ties. Three new agreements were signed and the joint communiqué made a reference to the importance of recognizing the Indian Ocean as a "zone of peace" while reiterating the need for Vietnam's admission to the United Nations.[51] Vajpayee told the Lok Sabha on June 29, 1977: "We have in fact no reason to doubt that the quality of relations between India and the socialist countries of Europe, including the Soviet Union, have in any way suffered with the change of government."[52]

Desai and Vajpayee went to Moscow in October 1977 and the Janata Prime Minister told the Soviets, "True to the principles of peaceful coexistence, we readily discovered [through the Gromyko visit] that not only was our friendship firm and our cooperation secure, but we could, with confidence, look ahead to improve our relations in the future."[53] On Soviet television, Desai went further in underlining the importance he attached to relations with Moscow: "Apart from a visit to London for a conference fixed a long time ago [of the Commonwealth] and a stop in Paris on the way back, the Soviet Union is the first country I am visiting as Prime Minister of India."[54]

A major dispute between India and the Soviet Union had erupted in the field of the rupee-rouble exchange rate. The Soviets argued that the falling price of the pound sterling, to which the rupee was linked, justified a revision from 11.39 roubles to 100 rupees to 8.66 roubles to 100 rupees in 1975. The Indians countered with the argument that the rouble was arbitrarily set in terms of gold and was not subject to market forces. The issue involved the payment of vast amounts by India in debt repayment and had led to prolonged haggling.[55]

Desai discussed the issue during his Moscow visit, but no agreement could be reached. A compromise was finally agreed to towards the end of 1978. The extent of rupee devaluation effected from its 1966 level was of the order of about 20 per cent and repayment of the enhanced amount was to be spread over a long period in the form of a virtually interest-free loan.⁵⁶

Indeed, Desai's mission to Moscow seemed to be to spell out Janata's policy as being different from Mrs. Gandhi's only in emphasis and nuances and assure the Soviet leadership that, despite ideological differences, his government was fully aware of the compulsions to cement the Indo-Soviet relationship. There was certainly a change in style and, contrary to the pattern set by Mrs. Gandhi, Desai scrupulously avoided discussing domestic Indian events, insisted that the relationship be "in the spirit of" the treaty, rather than be "based" on it, and had it recorded that the Moscow-New Delhi links did not prevent either country from cultivating cordial relations with third countries.⁵⁷

A Soviet credit of over Rs.2 billion was granted in April 1977 for new projects in ferrous metallurgy and coal and machine industry.⁵⁸ In 1979 the Soviets signed a long-term agreement on economic, trade, scientific and technical cooperation, described by official Soviet sources as "an important landmark." It envisaged cooperation in new areas, establishment and widening scientific research projects and design consultancy units, production cooperation and specialization and the designing and construction of industrial and other projects in third countries.⁵⁹

The Indo-Soviet treaty emerged unscathed from the Desai visit, the Janata Prime Minister contenting himself with reiterating his view on his return to New Delhi that "there was no question of India having special relations with any country."⁶⁰ The Soviets, however, did seem to be changing their formulations, but not their policy, on the Indian Ocean. During Desai's visit they expressed support "for the striving of the peoples of the area to make the ocean a zone of peace." The joint declaration also "urged the removal of all foreign military bases existing in the Indian Ocean and prevention and establishment of new ones."⁶¹ In June 1979, the Soviets declared that "the mutual visits of Soviet and Indian leaders and personal contacts between them [are] assuming a regular and durable nature and [have] become a good tradition." Each meeting "imparts fresh impetus" to all levels of Indo-Soviet cooperation.⁶²

The Janata government hoped to insulate the Indo-Soviet relationship from its initiatives in other fields in promoting better relations with the U.S., China and the neighbouring countries, the last being a matter of "first priority."⁶³ The outlook seemed promising, with the Carter Administration in place in Washington and the Desai government proclaiming "genuine nonalignment."

The new U.S. Administration's policy did hold out promise, with Carter's National Security Advisor, Zbigniew Brzezinski, emphasizing ties with "regional influentials."[64] President Carter, it seemed, wished to deal with India as the dominant regional power and would be mindful of its vital interests. Carter turned down the sale of A-7 aircraft to Pakistan, which pleased India, and corresponded copiously with Desai.[65] He paid a visit to New Delhi in January 1978, ostentatiously leaving out Pakistan.

At the same time, the Carter Administration had proclaimed nuclear nonproliferation as a major goal of its foreign policy. It promoted the Nuclear Nonproliferation Act, which came into collision with the U.S. contractual obligation to supply fuel for the Tarapur plant, except on conditions India found unacceptable. The nuclear question became a major point of conflict between the two countries although Desai tried to allay American concerns after his fashion.

In the event, Desai did not satisfy the Carter Administration and merely served to heighten suspicions at home. During his New Delhi visit Carter's unguarded aside to Secretary of State Cyrus Vance that he would be writing a "cold and blunt letter" to Desai on the nuclear question became a public centrepoint of his frustration. And Desai had confessed at a press conference in September 1977: "Both the Soviet Union and the United States of America wanted that we sign the Nonproliferation Treaty, and they have been applying pressure on this country for the last few years."[66]

Even as fuel supplies for Tarapur became a contentious political dispute between India and the U.S., Desai sought to give assurance to the U.S. He foreswore underground nuclear tests and suggested that India's security position would not be seriously affected even if Pakistan acquired a nuclear weapon.[67] In March 1979, he declared, "I am neither prepared for the manufacture of the nuclear bomb nor shall I sanction funds for it."[68] Further, he told the First Special Session of the U.N. General Assembly on Disarmament in 1978, "We are the only country which has pledged not to manufacture or acquire nuclear weapons even if the rest of the world did so. I solemnly reiterate that pledge before this august assembly. In fact, we have gone further and abjured nuclear explosions even for peaceful purposes."[69]

Desai's problem was that he could not, even if he had wished to, reverse India's stand that the Nonproliferation Treaty was discriminatory or accept the "full-scope safeguards" on all Indian nuclear installations demanded by the U.S. Often, Desai was caught on the wrong foot in explaining Janata's nuclear policy, leading to the charge made by one of Mrs. Gandhi's supporters, Margaret Alva, "Every statement from the government [on nuclear policy] creates a new controversy, a contradiction and more confusion."[70]

The Janata government's approach to neighbours was considerably to scale down the country's power projection and meet them more than half way to resolve contentious issues—the "logic of good neighbourliness," as Vajpayee described the policy.[71] In this Janata achieved considerable success. An agreement with Bangladesh was signed in November 1977 on the Farakka barrage, which could have been signed by Mrs. Gandhi's government in April 1977.[72] The two countries also agreed to prevent their countries from being used as hostile bases. Nepal was given the separate trade and transit treaties it wanted to emphasise its point that transit rights were governed by international conventions and laws applying to landlocked countries. But the Janata government did not accept the King of Nepal's proposal about his country being "a zone of peace," first made in 1975, to deemphasize the 1950 treaty links with India. Relations with Bhutan were upgraded to the ambassadorial level.

The army coup that overthrew the Bhutto regime in July 1977 evoked no official Indian comment. Desai accepted Pakistan's peaceful nuclear professions, and there was more than a touch of irony in the successful visit Foreign Minister Vajpayee paid to Pakistan in February 1978 since he belonged to Janata's Jana Sangh faction, identified in the public mind with a strident anti-Pakistan ideology.

Desai made other gestures to Pakistan. He adopted a line of diplomatic neutrality on Pakistan-Afghanistan differences and supported Islamabad's membership of the nonaligned movement after it left CENTO in the wake of the Iranian revolution. An agreement on Salal dam, initiated by Mrs. Gandhi's government, was signed in 1978. Vajpayee, during a visit to Kabul in September 1978, urged Afghanistan to remain nonaligned and promote trust in the region.[73] India and Pakistan pledged to quicken the pace of rapprochement within the framework of the Simla Agreement.

Desai asked Zia-ul-Haq to give a guarantee similar to India's unilateral rejection of a nuclear weapon. Zia answered by seeking agreement on the mutual or multilateral inspection of both countries' nuclear facilities or to accept South Asia as a nuclear free zone.[74] The first proposal was contrary to India's stand on the NPT, enjoying wide public support, while the second took no account of India's major problem, China's nuclear weapon capability, as Vajpayee was later to declare.[75] Despite these differences, relations between India and Pakistan, which had taken a turn for the better since 1974, were on the mend.

Indian trade agents participated in the Guangzhou (Canton) trade fair in April 1977 and Chinese interest in promoting better relations with India was heightened by the change of government in New Delhi although Desai's meeting with the Dalai Lama in April 1977 provoked an official protest from Beijing, for the record. China made friendly noises and signals came thick and fast from Beijing indicating a desire to improve relations.[76]

A concrete manifestation of the two countries' interest in promoting better relations was the visit to India in March 1978 of Wang Bingnan,[77] president of the Chinese People's Association, who invited Foreign Minister Vajpayee to Beijing. Much as Janata wanted to accelerate the pace of Sino-Indian rapprochement, the issue became enmeshed in Janata's own problems, the domestic political scene and intense Soviet anxiety.

The coming together of five parties and factions into a single Janata was a shotgun wedding provoked by Mrs. Gandhi springing a general election on the country in early 1977. Desai was made Prime Minister through a spurious consensus; the verdict would perhaps have gone in favour of Jagjivan Ram, if the issue had been put to the vote. Charan Singh had ultimately sided with Desai to keep Jagjivan Ram out and there was intense rivalry not only between them but between each of them and Desai. Superimposed on these personal animosities was the fear of all the other factions of the Jana Sangh's strength and potential.

In an astute move, the Janata leadership quickly held elections in several states to exploit the anti-Mrs. Gandhi feelings the Emergency regime had created. Desai initially had the pleasant task of dismantling the oppressive Emergency laws. But the Janata leaders became obsessively concerned with prosecuting Mrs. Gandhi and her son Sanjay for their conduct during the Emergency. An avid public lapped up the proceedings of the main commission, revealing as they did a tale of official misconduct.

But as the commission proceedings seemingly went on endlessly and the various Janata leaders and factions battled one another publicly, they began to pall. Sanjay and his loyal band of young followers, meanwhile, had mounted a campaign to make his own prosecution more difficult through wild counter-charges and, on occasion, plain hooliganism.

Mrs. Gandhi acknowledged no wrongdoing and was shrewdly building up public sympathy for herself by presenting Janata's conduct as being little short of persecution. She was given an ideal opportunity by a divided Janata government's decision to arrest her briefly.

Bhutto, now in jail in Pakistan awaiting trial on a murder charge, argued that both he and Mrs. Gandhi were being persecuted by the successor regimes.[78] But while he was to languish in prison, ultimately to be hanged, Mrs. Gandhi performed the seemingly impossible task of bouncing back to public favour, largely helped by the incompetence of a hopelessly divided government, in less than a year. To be able to fight her battles against Janata better, she engineered a second split in the Congress in January 1978, and her Congress, Mark II, was appropriately named Congress (I), for Indira.

The Janata government had been pursuing the initiatives Mrs. Gandhi had taken in exploring the China opening, building up relations with Pakistan on the basis of the Simla Agreement and trying to improve relations with the United States. Despite the predilections of many of the Janata leaders, who were more inclined towards the West, less towards Moscow, there had been no change in the substance of foreign policy.[79] India's own compulsions and those of the major external powers left little room for dramatic innovations, and the very weaknesses of the governing coalition, run by a single party only in name, created immobility.

Even in relations with neighbours, a field in which there was a striking change in the atmosphere, the Janata government found that there were limits. Nepal nursed its suspicions and Ziaur Rahman of Bangladesh felt the need for adopting anti-Indian postures. Janata had been unable to use the goodwill it had generated to greater purpose. The more concessions Janata offered, it seemed to elite Indian opinion, the greater were demands for further concessions.

The Soviets were concerned over the orientation of the Janata government in relation to both the U.S. and China, despite their public postures, and the CPI reflected this concern. Unlike Western diplomats in New Delhi, who kept in constant touch with Mrs. Gandhi, now in the opposition, the Soviets were chary of fraternizing with her, lest they offend Janata. The one significant gesture they made in maintaining their lines of communication with her led to misgivings in New Delhi. At the end of 1978, the Soviet government sent Pegov, a Central Committee member and former ambassador to New Delhi, to meet Mrs. Gandhi at Moscow airport during her stopover, keeping the Indian ambassador in the dark.[80]

A major development in the political field came with the Eleventh Congress of the Communist Party of India, held at Bhatinda from March 31 to April 7, 1978. It formalized an anti-Mrs. Gandhi line in domestic policy and sought "a left and democratic alternative" with the CPI(M). Since the Congress was attended by G.A. Aliev, then alternate member of the Politburo, it was universally assumed that the CPI's new line enjoyed Soviet support.

The Congress did criticize the Marxists by voicing Soviet views. The political resolution said, "... The CPI(M)'s position of so-called equidistance between the two [the Communist Party of the Soviet Union and the Communist Party of China] is nothing but gross opportunism and is extremely harmful to the Communist and democratic movement."[81] But the main thrust of the document was to appeal for Communist unity.

"The CPI appeals to the CPI(M)," the political resolution declared, "to end the chapter of hostile and disruptive attacks and further such unity in action on the widest scale, without putting any preconditions for such unity."[82]

Mrs. Gandhi's attack on Janata's foreign policy was part of her general offensive to gain electoral advantage. She started from the premise that the West "toppled" her because of her policy of self-reliance, the country's growing strength and the nuclear explosion. Janata, she alleged, was revising these policies, was in the West's pocket and was anti-Soviet. The Soviet Union, according to her, was India's true friend.[83]

These charges were refined by Mrs. Gandhi's spokesmen. One of them, Margaret Alva, asked the following rhetorical question in September 1978: "What is the meaning of saying that we are a large country and so we can go on making concessions?" She added: "... No country in the world, at any time in history, has ever achieved greatness with a policy of appeasement."[84]

One consequence of this propaganda barrage was that Desai began making hawkish statements on China, and Vajpayee's visit to Beijing was postponed several times, ostensibly on health grounds. The very leaders of Janata began to be classified into pro- and anti-Soviet factions.[85] Desai was placed very much on the defensive. He told a television press conference on January 1, 1979, "Our attempt with China is not made by us first. They have moved. They want to have better relations."[86]

Against the backdrop of attacks by the CPI on Janata for allegedly consorting with imperialists, Vajpayee went to Moscow in the fall of 1978 before his planned visit to Beijing. It merely served to embarrass India, with the Soviets making attacks on China in Vajpayee's presence.[87] The Chinese seemed to have come to realize that the Janata government was not strong enough to impose a realistic border settlement on the country. They were mainly interested in the symbolism of an Indian Foreign Minister's visit after sixteen years.[88] They waited patiently and Vajpayee finally made the historic trip to China in February 1979. Tass had on January 16, 1979 carried a quotation from *Izvestia* emphasizing Vajpayee's statement in Parliament that India's rapprochement with China would not be at the expense of its relations with third countries.

Despite Bhutto's proud claim that he was the architect of his country's China policy as Ayub's foreign minister, his five-year reign saw some strains in the Islamabad-Beijing relationship. In pursuit of a policy of bilateralism, Bhutto made overtures to Moscow which did not please Beijing, and he was himself wary of indications of the beginning of a Sino-Indian rapprochement. Towards the end of his rule, in the virulent anti-American atmosphere he encouraged, Bhutto reportedly came to rely increasingly on the Soviet ambassador for information, if not advice.[89]

Nor did General Zia start on the right foot with China. His efforts to coopt Wali Khan, Bhutto's adversary known for his pro-Soviet sympathies, in the formation of a national government annoyed Beijing. And Zia, who went to China towards the end of 1977 to reaffirm Pakistan's "unqualified" friendship, was snubbed during his visit.[90]

China's major arms, trade and economic relationship with Pakistan continued to proceed apace. Vice President Geng Biao went to Pakistan in June 1978 to open the Karakoram highway built by China along the ancient silk route. In December 1978, Vice Premier Li Xiannian made a hasty trip to Islamabad to reassure Pakistan of

China's unaltered support[91] against the backdrop of Vajpayee's impending visit to Beijing.

In April 1977, after the Soviets had decided that the Chinese were not willing to reorder their relations with Moscow despite Mao's death, there was a resurgence of Soviet support for Tibetans. Moscow had earlier condemned Beijing's minority policy as a violation of Marxist-Leninist principles and viewed China's role in Tibet as that of a colonial power.[92] In June 1978, the Dalai Lama stopped in Moscow en route to Mongolia.

The Sino-Japanese treaty, including the "hegemony" clause, was signed in August 1978. In December that year it was announced that the U.S. would recognize the Beijing government. Deng Xiaoping's visit to the U.S. in early 1979 highlighted the strategic alliance China was seeking with the United States. But the movement towards it in 1977 and 1978 had its inevitable fallout on Vietnam.

The Vietnam-Cambodia conflict had escalated in 1977. Although the growing U.S.-Chinese strategic convergence against the Soviet Union had its impact on Sino-Soviet rivalry in Asia, the root cause of the Vietnam-China conflict lay in Beijing's interest in frustrating Hanoi's regional ambitions. China supported the genocidal Pol Pot regime in Cambodia, and had offered Prince Sihanouk hospitality in Beijing precisely because he opposed Hanoi.

The Chinese were quick to draw a parallel between Soviet support for India in 1971 and Moscow's backing of Vietnam against the "weaker party" in its drive for global "hegemony."[93] Vietnam became the tenth full member of the Council of Mutual Economic Assistance (Comecon) in June 1978. On November 3 that year it signed a twenty-five-year friendship treaty with Moscow. Article VI of the treaty, calling for consultations if either side were attacked and for "effective measures" to remove any threat to ensure peace and security, was almost identical to Article IX of the Indo-Soviet treaty.[94] Vietnam began its full invasion of Cambodia on December 25, 1978.

During his visit to the U.S. Deng had publicly hinted at action against Hanoi and privately outlined "tentative plans to attack Vietnam."[95] China launched its attack on Vietnam in February 1979 inviting the Soviet charge of U.S.-Chinese collusion.[96] Although China announced its withdrawal on March 5, having achieved its political, but not military, objectives, Beijing's action caught Vajpayee on Chinese soil on the first visit of an Indian foreign minister in sixteen years. The Chinese leadership did not inform Vajpayee of its action nor offer him any explanation.[97] It was at the very least an embarrassment for India, in the worst case a deliberate snub, and Vajpayee cut short his visit by a day.[98]

Returning home, Vajpayee's, and other Janata leaders', problem became one of trying to rescue the historic visit from the consequences of the Chinese attack on Vietnam. Badgered by members of Parliament, the Foreign Minister finally conceded that China was an "aggressor,"[99] leading to a muted protest from Beijing.

In his report to Parliament,[100] Vajpayee declared that the boundary dispute had become "unfrozen" and the Chinese leaders had informed him that their support for Naga and Mizo rebels "was looked upon as a thing of the past." He described his talks with the Chinese leadership "frank" and "wide-ranging." He acknowledged that there were "differing assessments of the inevitability of war, the logic of disarmament and the prospects of dentente," conceding that the Chinese attitude to Kashmir was a deterrent to good relations. But he said the Dalai Lama and his supporters were free to return to Tibet.

Vajpayee's visit was a landmark. In a measure, Desai succeeded in insulating Sino-Indian relations from the fall-out of the China-Vietnam conflict. But the Chinese displayed extraordinary insensitivity to Indian opinion, Deng publicly drawing a parallel between the Chinese action in Vietnam and their foray into India in 1962. At the same time the Chinese gave every indication that they wished to pursue better relations with India, but by their action and attitude, they merely gave a handle to the CPI and other supporters of the Soviet Union to launch an anti-Chinese propaganda war.[101] There was a groundswell of opinion in favour of Vietnam in India and the China question became a domestic issue, with men like the Petroleum Minister, H.N. Bahuguna, in the forefront, attacking China.

Kosygin came to New Delhi shortly after Vajpayee's visit to China, and the Janata leaders were pleasantly surprised to discover that the Soviet mood had never been as mellow.[102] In recent years, it was not always Western reluctance to sell that was responsible for India going in for Soviet weapons. Desai vowed to bring back "genuine nonalignment" and signed the Jaguar deal with Britain in September 1978. Shortly after the Jaguar deal was finalized, India acquired eighty-five MIG-23 BN for ground attack role.[103] It was the same government that negotiated the $1.6 billion arms deal with the Soviets. Moscow had offered India MIG-25s for the first time during Janata rule.[104]

An agreement with the Soviets was signed by Mrs. Gandhi's government, which returned to power in January 1980, but it was finalized by the Charan Singh government in October the previous year. Mrs. Gandhi's contribution was to obtain an extra two years in the credit arrangement terms.[105]

The Jaguar deal had been under discussion by Mrs. Gandhi before she lost power in 1977 although she was later to attack it. One of the contenders for the Deep Penetration Strike Aircraft (DPSA) was the Swedish SAAB-37 Wiggen, which carried an American Pratt and Whitney engine. But it had ruled itself out because of U.S. refusal to authorize its sale to India on the ground that a new DPSA would be a destabilizing factor in the subcontinent.[106]

Except for brief periods, India has been perennially short of foreign currency and there is obvious attraction in paying for arms in rupees. Although Soviet arms are often not as sophisticated as their Western equivalents, they are easy to maintain.[107] After the 1965 experience in particular, reliability of spares became an important Indian consideration.[108]

Kosygin disapproved of Vajpayee's visit to Beijing and the long talk he had with Desai revealed an obsessive Soviet concern with China.[109] He did not succeed in achieving his major objectives. India resisted describing the Chinese action in Vietnam as aggression and did not accept Soviet suggestions to recognize the new Kampuchean regime. There was no reference to Cambodia in the joint communiqué. Desai's minimum terms were that Vietnam should first withdraw its troops from Cambodia; Kosygin's frank answer was that the Heng Samrin regime would, in that event, fall.[110]

In Pakistan, Bhutto was hanged in April 1979 on a split decision of the country's Supreme Court. Zia and his army colleagues had set about prosecuting him in the spirit of "us or he." Zia was perhaps fearful of his own, and the army's, fate should he reprieve Bhutto.[111] He disregarded appeals from many governments, including Saudi Arabia and China. The Janata government made no official comment on the execution, leaving the field to Mrs. Gandhi to express India's sense of outrage. China was one of the few countries frankly to express its displeasure.[112]

Despite its annoyance over the Bhutto execution, China remained supportive of Pakistan and set about building relations with Bangladesh. It welcomed Ziaur Rahman to Beijing in January 1977 and Vice Premier Li Xiannian and Foreign Minister Huang Hua went to Dhaka in March 1978. China agreed to train men of the Bangladesh air force and send "some shipments of Chinese military supplies."[113] In fact, the Chinese gave Bangladesh a squadron of MIGs and helped maintain Soviet MIGs because Moscow refused to supply spare parts after Mujib's overthrow.[114]

Before the world picture darkened in 1978, Carter was still pursuing his twin goals of nonproliferation and detente with the Soviet Union. The Nonproliferation Act was passed in 1978; so were the Glenn and Symington amendments to the Foreign Assistance Act, which called for a cutoff of economic assistance to any country which did not accept nuclear safeguards. Aid to Pakistan was terminated in August 1978 under the Glenn amendment in view of Islamabad's efforts to acquire reprocessing facilities. It was Carter's devotion to nonproliferation that led him to support Pakistan's proposal to declare South Asia as a zone of peace, opposed by India. The Soviet Union, on the other hand, had accepted India's counter-proposal, which nullified the Pakistani idea. Carter showed more enthusiasm than understanding in proposing in May 1979 that the two superpowers and China jointly declare South Asia nuclear free. To have China serve as a protector of India's security needs merely outraged the Indian elite.[115] China supported Pakistan's zone of peace proposal for South Asia as also Nepal's own zone of peace concept.[116]

Carter made a surprise announcement on March 11, 1977 that the U.S. had proposed to the Soviet Union that the "Indian Ocean be completely demilitarized."[117] He was reacting in particular to Congressional sentiments on the issue, and the proposal won New Delhi's welcome because it seemed to go some way towards India's desire to assert its own position of superiority in the Indian Ocean. The Carter Administration had earlier told India that the United States was in the ocean to counter the Soviet presence.[118] India's long-range objective was spelled out by the former Navy chief, Admiral A.K. Chatterji, who wanted a "force equal in size and competence to the naval forces of any one of the superpowers now formally operating in the area."[119]

The naval arms limitation talks stretched out into 1978, but India's enthusiasm was not shared by the other littoral countries, particularly Pakistan.[120] Although the Soviets had lately endorsed the zone of peace proposal, their sincerity came into question as the talks progressed and it became clear that the superpowers were discussing freezing force levels, not their elimination. Vajpayee openly expressed scepticism about the superpowers withdrawing from the Indian Ocean.[121]

China was plainly unhappy about the talks and launched a broadside at both the superpowers, saying that neither was interested in demilitarization of the ocean. It beleboured the Soviet Union in particular because it wished the U.S. to remain in the ocean as long as the Soviets were there. Moscow, *Peking Review* of November 4, 1977 suggested, sought to control the coastal areas of the Indian Ocean, among other areas, through "naked power politics and gunboat diplomacy." On September 9 *Peking Review* elaborated on the theme, saying that Moscow was playing a double game by declaring that there should be no bases while sending diplomats to the Maldives to seek a base on Gan island. These overtures "completely lay bare Moscow's hypocritical sympathy for setting up the Indian Ocean peace zone and show that it is the most dangerous enemy in undermining security in the region."

The naval arms limitation talks were called off in 1978 and the future of the SALT-II agreement, negotiated with the Soviet Union, became increasingly clouded.[122] Carter met Brezhnev in Vienna in June 1979. The heavy Soviet involvement in the Horn of Africa was ringing alarm bells in Washington and early in 1978 the Communists conducted a coup in Afghanistan. The Shah of Iran collapsed in the face of the burgeoning Iranian revolution. From identifying with regional influentials, the Carter Administration's focus shifted to the littoral of the western Indian Ocean, the "third strategic zone."

The U.S. Navy had already won its points on Diego Garcia and formation of a Rapid Deployment Force was being planned. Despite initial efforts to concentrate attention on India in the subcontinent, the Washington-New Delhi relationship became increasingly mired in the nuclear dispute and over economic questions. In spite of its nuclear ambitions, Pakistan began to emerge in American eyes as the more important country to check Soviet expansion in South Asia and help security in the Gulf.

The French decided to end their nuclear cooperation with Pakistan on the reprocessing project. Sanctions against Pakistan were withdrawn in October 1978, a few months after they had been imposed. Pakistan withdrew from CENTO in March 1979 and in August Zia was declaring, "Whatever the attitude of others, Pakistan, God willing, will acquire a reprocessing plant under any circumstances.[123] Zia had shrewdly adopted Bhutto's dream as his own. In April 1979 the axe fell again on aid to Pakistan, this time under the Symington amendment.

The problems in the U.S.-Pakistan relationship were compounded by the burning of the U.S. embassy in Islamabad in November 1979, involving the deaths of two Americans and two Pakistanis. The lives of many more Americans were saved in the nick of time as they were plucked out of the burning inferno. The embassy burning came in the wake of radio reports linking the U.S. with an attack on the Grand Mosque in Mecca. The tragedy did not dim Washington's revived interest in arming Pakistan in its new strategic role.

Among the decisions taken by the Carter Administration before Soviet troops moved into Afghanistan in December 1979 was the stationing of a carrier task force in the Indian Ocean on a regular basis. Washington announced the setting up of the Rapid Deployment Force and took the decision not to have SALT-II ratified. NATO decided on plans to begin deploying Euromissiles by the end of 1983 if no progress was made in negotiations with the Soviet Union.

In India, meanwhile, the Janata government collapsed in July 1978 under the weight of its own contradictions, with Mrs. Gandhi and son Sanjay giving it the final push from the sidelines. It yielded place to a conglomerate headed by peasant leader Charan Singh, who was soon to be reduced to a caretaker prime minister.[124] India's goal of building durable peace on the subcontinent and asserting its preeminence seemed to be receding each day. The Soviets had survived the biggest challenge to their South Asia policy since the mid-Fifties, despite Janata's initial assault.

Chapter Eight

Afghanistan—I

CHARAN SINGH'S interim government, interim in every sense of the word, was notable for immobility in the field of foreign policy. The new Prime Minister had little understanding of, or interest in, international affairs. But he did reverse Desai's unpopular policy on the nuclear question by declaring at an Independence Day ceremony on August 15, 1979: "I and my colleagues will have to perhaps rethink this [nuclear] issue ... if Pakistan continues with its intention [of making the bomb]."[1]

Given the circumstances, India could play only a tepid role in supporting President Tito in fighting off Castro's attempt to christen the nonaligned movement a "natural ally" of the socialist camp at the summit of the movement in Havana in the fall of 1979. Charan Singh did not attend the summit and sent his Foreign Minister, S.N. Mishra, to take his place.

In December 1979, India was in the throes of an election campaign. Mrs. Gandhi, having first helped bring Charan Singh to power by encouraging the collapse of Desai's Janata government, quickly pulled the rug from under his feet to force an election. All parties and candidates, including Mrs. Gandhi, were locked in the electoral battle. The Soviets, meanwhile, marched their troops into Afghanistan, without bothering to inform India in advance.

The first official intimation India had of the Soviet invasion was from Soviet Ambassador Yuri Vorontsov knocking on Foreign Secretary R.D. Sathe's door around midnight on December 28.[2] To add insult to injury, the ambassador drew a parallel between the Soviet action and India's military intervention in Bangladesh in 1971. The Charan Singh government temporized by issuing a statement which said:

> Consistent with the Government of India's commitment to the principles of nonalignment, it supports the right of the

Afghan people to determine their own destiny free from foreign interference.... It is also the Government of India's earnest hope that no country or external power would take steps which might aggravate the situation and that normalcy would be restored.[3]

On the advice of the External Affairs Ministry, Charan Singh called the Soviet ambassador to his home on New Year's Eve to convey "India's deep concern at the substantial involvement of Soviet military forces in Afghanistan." India, he said, valued its traditional friendship with Afghanistan and would like "its independence and nonalignment to be strengthened."[4]

While India was going through a political crisis in 1979, accentuated by the collapse of the Janata government in July, events were moving towards a tragic denouement in Afghanistan. The Communist coup in April 1978, in which Moscow did not have a direct role,[5] had brought it within the Soviet concept of the socialist camp, although Afghan governments had been traditionally friendly to the Soviet Union since the early 1920s.

Between April and December 1978 the Soviet Union concluded twenty-nine aid agreements with Afghanistan pledging $104 million; the West had committed $121 million during the period, including half by the World Bank.[6] The number of Soviet advisors jumped from 350 in April 1979 to 2,000 in June, and the first Soviet combat unit was deployed in Afghanistan in July that year.[7]

In December 1978 the Soviets signed a treaty of peace and friendship with Afghanistan, with Brezhnev declaring that it "will not only provide the foundation for the further strengthening of Soviet-Afghan friendship, but will also serve the interests of peace and security in Asia and, thereby, all over the world."[8] A singular aspect of the treaty was that, apart from its military provisions, it specifically endorsed the Soviet Asian Collective Security concept.

Despite the closer relations with Moscow foreshadowed by the coup of April 1978, the Chinese had been tactful in reporting the coup and post-coup developments. But the treaty led *Beijing Review* of December 15, 1978 to pinpoint its military aspects, in particular Articles IV and X. They said: "In the interests of the strengthening of defence capacity of the high contracting parties they shall continue to develop cooperation in the military field on the basis of appropriate agreements concluded between them" and "the high contracting parties shall facilitate the development of cooperation among Asian states and the establishment of relations of peace, good neighbourliness, and mutual confidence among them and the creation of an effective security system in Asia on the basis of joint efforts by all countries of the continent."

Predictably, the Chinese line on Afghanistan changed after the signing of the treaty. In any event, as the murderous quarrels between the two Afghan Communist factions, Khalq (masses) and Parcham (flag), were being played out in Kabul, significant rebel activity against the government surfaced in February 1979. On April 1, 1979 *Pravda* accused Pakistan of helping insurgents, and on April 12 the newspaper referred to training camps run by Pakistanis, Chinese, Egyptians and Americans.

On March 27, 1979 Xinhua suggested that Soviet accusations of complicity of Iran, Pakistan, China and others were a "smokescreen" to obscure Soviet interference in Afghanistan. Both *Pravda* and *Izvestia* had alleged that the Karakoram highway was being used for transporting arms and ammunition and propaganda material from China for subversive activities in Afghanistan and that Chinese instructors were training Afghan guerrillas. In a dispatch from Islamabad on April 21, 1979, Xinhua gave prominence to Zia's declaration that Pakistan was only giving shelter to Afghan refugees on humanitarian grounds because "it is our moral and religious duty to give shelter to those who seek our protection."[9]

Sadat revealed that the U.S., Egypt and Saudi Arabia had cooperated since early 1980 in sending arms to Afghan insurgents through Pakistan.[10] The Chinese, on their part, seem to have decided by April 1979 to give major support to Afghan guerrillas. A *Der Spiegel* report in February 1980 said that some Chinese-trained guerrillas had been arrested by government troops, suggesting that there were some 700 Beijing-trained guerrillas.[11]

As early as December 1978 a commentary in *Renmin Rinbao* had warned the West, "Today, in the face of the grave threat of war by Soviet social imperialism, the trend of appeasement similar to that of the 1930s has emerged in the West . . . "[12] The Chinese apparently saw the events in Kabul as "a new dangerous manifestation of the Soviet policy of encircling China" and had reinforced their 75-km.-long border with Afghanistan.[13]

The Soviet Union was the first country to recognize the Afghanistan regime after the 1978 coup, with India following suit, and quickly swung into action to provide support to the Parcham-Khalq coalition of Khalq's founder Taraki and Hafizullah Amin. Such support included the ruthless suppression of the insurgency. The power struggle between the two Afghan leaders was coming to a head, with Amin emerging as the strong man. He succeeded in wresting more power from Taraki and had a number of Parchamite leaders, including Babrak Karmal, banished to diplomatic posts in East Europe.

Even as Amin set about imposing textbook Marxism on a country of tribes living for the most part by their medieval traditions and codes of honour, the innovations merely served to ignite the insurgency. By the summer of 1979 the Soviets had come to the conclusion that Amin was becoming a liability and schemed with Taraki to have him removed.[14]

Taraki was asked to stop over in Moscow on his way home from the nonaligned summit in Havana in September 1979; the Afghan ambassador was excluded from Taraki's meeting with Gromyko. But Amin preempted the Soviet plan and Taraki was killed in a palace shootout on September 14 shortly after his return from Moscow.

Amin knew he was sitting on a powder keg and sent signals to the U.S. and Pakistan in a desperate attempt to buttress his position. He had the Soviet ambassador, Alexander Puzanov, recalled by Moscow in November. The U.S. charge d'affaires in New Delhi, Archer Blood, spent four weeks in Kabul after Amin's assumption of supreme power; the U.S. ambassador in Kabul, Adolph Dubs, had been killed in February 1979, leading to a drastic curtailment of U.S. aid. As President Zia-ul-Haq was to reveal later,[15] he received a "very sincere message" from Amin in mid-December asking him to come to Kabul. Zia sent his Foreign Policy Advisor Agha Shahi instead, but his plane could not land at Kabul, ostensibly because of bad weather.

Amin's exertions to buttress his position merely sealed his doom. He dismissed the five Parcham leaders he had sent to East Europe as ambassadors and asked them to return home. They did not obey Amin's orders and stayed behind, with Soviet acquiescence, if not protection. General Pavlovsky, commander-in-chief of the Soviet land forces, came to Afghanistan in the fall of 1979 and stayed in the country for two months. The new Soviet ambassador, Fikrat A. Tabeev, presented his credentials to Amin on December 1, 1979.

The stage was thus set for the massive Soviet intervention. In the first instance, 5,000 Soviet troops moved into Kabul on Christmas

Day; thousands more were to arrive by air and road over the next days and weeks. On December 27 "Kabul Radio," apparently a station on the Soviet side of the Oxus, put out a broadcast by Babrak Karmal to announce the coup: "This blood-thirsty machine is falling apart, down to its last blood-stained cog... Amin was a CIA agent."[16] Six hours later, Kabul Radio announced that Amin had been executed.

In fact, Amin was reportedly killed in a shootout with Soviet troops at Darulaman Palace. Other reports suggest Amin was dead before the staged shootout.[17] In any event, the Soviets had kept Karmal in some comfort in East Europe for precisely such an eventuality.[18] Technically, the Soviets had sent a "limited contingent" of troops "at the request of the Afghan government, a request that was first made by President Amin on 26 December 1979 and repeated by his successor on 28 December 1979..."[19] The debates in the U.N. Security Council and General Assembly merely served to confuse the vital issue of who, if anyone, had invited the Soviets in.

The United States was monitoring the unusual Soviet troop activities in Afghanistan. Assistant Secretary of State Harold H. Saunders told a Congressional committee on September 26, 1979 that the Administration had been representing to the Soviet Union "the dangers of more direct involvement in the fighting in Afghanistan."[20] On December 26 the State Department "deplored" the massive lifting of Soviet troops to Afghanistan and was making its views known directly to Moscow.[21] On December 29 President Carter used the hot line to convey to Brezhnev his strong opposition to the Soviet move and asked for the withdrawal of troops, warning of "serious consequences" on Soviet-American relations.[22]

Brzezinski explained in a television interview the next day that the Soviet intervention was "a qualitative new step involving direct invasion of a country outside the Warsaw Pact through the use of Soviet armed forces." To counter the widespread impression of a weak and indecisive Administration, Carter's National Security Advisor said that the U.S. had considerably improved its strategic capabilities in the previous three years; U.S. forces were in place in the Indian Ocean, relations with China were better and NATO was helping in strengthening Western capability.[23]

Despite the shock waves created by the Soviet invasion of Afghanistan in Washington, as in many other capitals, the truth was that neither the White House nor the State Department was focussing on Afghanistan. Washington's preoccupation was with developments in Iran. The Shah had left Teheran, for the last time, on January 16, 1979 and much before the seizure of fifty-two staff members of the U.S. embassy in Teheran as hostages on November 4, the Carter Administration was pondering over the loss of America's most important ally and surrogate in southwest Asia.

Secretary of State Cyrus Vance has recorded that through the summer and fall of 1979 a number of meetings were held to review U.S. security policy in the Persian Gulf.[24] The upshot of these meetings was a set of recommendations made to Carter in August 1979, which was approved by the President. It was decided to enhance capacity for deploying rapidly ground, naval and air forces into the area, undertaking joint exercises with friends and allies, to increase "moderately" America's permanent presence in the Indian Ocean and initiate more substantial security discussions with key states in the region. Carter also agreed to plans to gain access to local ports and airfields during a crisis, expansion of the Diego Garcia base and to preposition combat aircraft for support of American ground forces.[25]

The hostage crisis accelerated these plans. An additional task force was sent to the Indian Ocean on November 20 to buttress the task force already there. Vance worried over reports coming out of Washington suggesting the possibility of impending military action against Iran. "I felt this unwise. U.S. military presence in the area would make a collapse of the Kabul regime more dangerous for the Soviets and thus enhance the possibility of Soviet intervention."[26]

Having convinced himself that the Soviet move represented a dangerous strategic challenge, Carter sought shelter in the language of hyperbole, apart from initiating action. He described the Soviet action as the "greatest threat" to peace since World War II and confessed, "My opinion of the Russians has changed most dramatically in the last week, [more] than in the two and a half years before that."[27] On January 4, 1980 the President announced a series of punitive measures against the Soviet Union and also offered to join other nations to give military and economic aid to Pakistan "to help it defend its independence and national security against the seriously increased threat it now faces from the north."[28]

Washington announced a military and economic aid package for Pakistan of $400 million, which would be dismissed by Zia as "peanuts." Carter advanced Defence Secretary Harold Brown's planned trip to China; in Beijing, Brown was told by Defence Minister Xu Xiang Qien that "more and more countries have come to draw the same conclusion as they did that the Russians were dangerous aggressors."[29]

A. Petrov explained in *Pravda* of December 31, 1979 that "the external imperialist forces entered into a direct collusion with the internal counterrevolutionary forces" to destabilize the young Afghan regime. In an intervew with *Pravda*, published on January 13, 1980, Brezhnev said "it was no easy decision" to intervene, but that the Central Committee of the Soviet Communist Party and the government had "acted in full awareness of their responsibility and took into account all the relevant circumstances." According to him, "to act otherwise would have meant to watch passively the establishment on our southern border of a seat of serious danger to the security of the Soviet state."

The announcement of the American aid package for Pakistan led *Izvestia* to comment: "Experience shows that the arming of reactionary Pakistan military has always led to wars in the region and to an increasingly brutal suppression of the struggle of the Pakistani people themselves for freedom, democratic and social progress."[30]

In an effort to soften up Pakistan, *Pravda* said on February 13, 1980: "All this [Pakistan's actions] bears witness to the fact that Pakistan does not intend to stop its aggressive policy directed against Afghanistan and is making its territory available for the realization in the region of the aggressive plans of the U.S. and its allies."

China was quick to react to the Soviet move. In a commentary on December 29, it said: "... Afghanistan is completely under Soviet influence. Not only are Afghanistan's internal, diplomatic and military affairs under Soviet control but even the selection of government personnel and their life and death and honour and disgrace are all decided by the Kremlin."[31]

The Chinese had no hesitation in supporting a dominant strand in American thinking that the Soviet move into Afghanistan was an offensive strategy, rather than defensive in nature. The Soviet Union, a *Renmin Ribao* commentator suggested on January 21, 1980, wanted to dominate the crescent-shaped region running from the Indochina peninsula in the East to the Persian Gulf in the West. "The events that took place in Angola in 1975 and now in Afghanistan show that the Soviets are always ready to avail themselves of loopholes but are also carrying out global expansion in a planned way step by step."

People's Daily of January 1, 1980 had made it clear that "this [the Soviet intervention] indicates that the Soviet Union will make full use of the military clauses of the so-called friendship and cooperation treaties it signed with a number of countries to conduct military interference so as to further the path of expansionism." On January 16, *People's Daily* said "the Soviet Union was now one step nearer to the Indian Ocean, with opportunities for further expansion which could enable it to control oil supplies to Europe and Japan."

Moscow countered this point, *Pravda* of February 2 suggesting that the Soviet Union had no designs on Middle East oil and no intention of pushing through to the warm water ports on the Indian Ocean. America, it said, was trying "to cover up the fact that the ruling circles of the U.S. started the implementation of their unprecedented programme of militarization at least three years ago."

For India, the Soviet intervention in Afghanistan presented a series of stark and unwelcome choices. The policy-making establishment was already concerned over the turmoil in Iran and the American response it had evoked in strengthening its forces in the region and accelerating plans for an intervention force. This, it was felt in New Delhi, would inevitably invite Soviet countermoves, leading to the further militarization of the Indian Ocean and the Persian Gulf. More specifically, the strategic thinking in Washington implied the harnessing of Pakistan in American regional plans, with the prospect of a new U.S.-Pakistan arms relationship and perhaps an attempt to draw Islamabad into a regional defence arrangement. The Carter Administration had abandoned its earlier policy of buttressing American interests through regional influentials.

These concerns were enhanced manifold by the Soviet move into Afghanistan. The unkindest cut of all was that India's friend, the Soviet Union, had made the situation even more difficult for New Delhi. The Soviet action was unwelcome to India for several reasons. It had brought the Russians physically closer to India than it would have wished and had served to negate India's long-term plan for building an autonomous subsystem on the subcontinent. Indeed, for the first time since the mid-Fifties, Soviet and Indian geopolitical interests had collided in the region on a major issue close to India's heart.

There were differing perceptions in New Delhi and Moscow on the Indian Ocean, despite the rhetorical support the Soviet Union had been offering. India had learnt to live with Moscow's position, particularly because it saw no early prospect of an end to superpower competition in the ocean. Next to having the superpowers out of the ocean, it was best to have the forces of both, rather than one.

India had also successfully fought off Soviet attempts to win New Delhi's approval for the Asian Collective Security concept, even during the days of close Indo-Soviet military collaboration in 1971. New Delhi did not wish to be identified too closely with Moscow's containment of China policies and wanted to preserve as autonomous a role for itself as possible.

The Soviet move into Afghanistan had a finality about it, to the detriment of India's interests. The foreign policy establishment in New Delhi took a kinder view of Soviet motives than those held in Washington and Beijing, but it did not help resolve the Indian dilemma.[32] In the Indian view, the Soviet intervention was primarily a defensive move, accelerated by the turmoil in Iran and possible American military action against it, to ensure that Afghanistan does not harbour an anti-Soviet regime. Indians are well aware of Soviet sensitivity to events on their borders.[33]

The ideal Indian option—making up with Pakistan—to meet the new threat seemed unavailable in most Indian eyes. The two countries had fought three wars and the tangled skein of past animosities and hatreds and Mrs. Gandhi's allergy to military regimes made it unlikely that an adversarial relationship could be transformed overnight into friendship. Besides, the growing U.S.-Chinese military links and America's interest in using Pakistan for its Gulf strategy did not hold out much hope for India.

Charan Singh's diplomatic intervention in Afghan affairs ended with his sharp words to the Soviet ambassador on New Year's Eve. The election results, representing a landslide victory for Mrs. Gandhi's Congress (I), persuaded Charan Singh to opt out of making policy on a sensitive foreign policy issue. Even before Mrs. Gandhi was formally to assume the office of Prime Minister in mid-January 1980, he left the problem to her. India did not participate in the U.N. Security Council debate on Afghanistan, held two weeks after the event, but the deadline for formulating India's initial approach to Afghanistan was the General Assembly debate.

The Soviets were again wrong in predicting India's election results. They believed that Mrs. Gandhi would not get a majority, much less a convincing victory. They shared this belief with the Indian embassy in

Moscow and the Soviet assessment was duly conveyed to New Delhi.[34] But unlike in 1977, they had not publicly compromised themselves. However, the Foreign Ministry in New Delhi had noted that *Pravda* gave publicity to Zia's statement at the Havana summit in 1979, including the Kashmir issue, and during much of 1979 and 1980 Moscow had indicated its ambivalence through the Soviet press by constantly bringing up the Kashmir "dispute."[35]

Even more significant was the Soviet move implicitly to bless the new CPI line after Mrs. Gandhi's defeat in 1977, as we have seen. A Soviet Communist delegation attended the Indian Communist party's Eleventh Congress, which proclaimed the goal of Communist unity and forging a left and democratic front. The CPI confessed that its support for the Emergency was "wrong from the beginning." The party said it had "insufficiently realized that the fight against the increasingly anti-people internal policies of the Indira Gandhi government had to be given priority by our party even while supporting its anti-imperialist foreign policy as well as its progressive internal measures."[36]

Moscow's initial public reaction to Mrs. Gandhi's victory was far from enthusiastic. An early commentary suggested that the vote was not so much "for" her as "against" the discredited Janata and Lok Dal coalitions.[37] While later commentaries praised Mrs. Gandhi as an "outstanding national political leader," they also suggested that the "major successes" of the two Communist parties "stand out in especially bold relief against the background of the shattering defeat sustained by two bourgeois groups."[38]

Mrs. Gandhi's own initial reaction to the Afghan developments, while still in the opposition, came on December 31. She said, "We are against all foreign intervention. But people had been interfering in this area in one way or the other. The whole area is getting so destabilized that it is quite a danger for us."[39] On January 9 she suggested in an interview with ABC that the Soviet Union had intervened in Afghanistan because it was "deeply worried" over the developing friendship between the U.S. and China while on the same day the French Europa Radio broadcast an interview quoting her as saying that the U.S. had started the destabilization of the area but that the intervention "is a danger to us; we are against any interference from abroad."

There were thus three strands in Mrs. Gandhi's thinking: opposition to the act of Soviet intervention; an awareness of the external factors that had contributed towards it and the danger that it represented for India. Her instructions to the External Affairs team which sought her decision were that India should not join in "condemning" the Soviet action but should state its opposition to such intervention in any country. Narasimha Rao, the dark horse who would soon assume the External Affairs portfolio, was associated with the implementation of the decision. India's abstention on the General Assembly resolution condemning the Soviet action was no surprise. It was, in part, payment in kind for vital Soviet support to India at the U.N. in the past, as also to safeguard New Delhi's security concerns, in a region that had become even more dangerous, by not weakening the Soviet link.

The speech of the Indian delegate, Brajesh Mishra, as it was delivered, stunned the world. While opposing the presence of foreign troops and bases in any country, he said that the Soviet Union had assured India that it would withdraw its troops from Afghanistan when Kabul asked it to. "We have no reason to doubt the assurances, particularly from a friendly country like the Soviet Union with whom we have close ties."[40] It seemed that India was almost endorsing the Soviet action and its relations with the Soviet Union were a factor which changed the nature of the intervention.[41]

Mrs. Gandhi attempted to bring back some semblance of balance to the Indian position. At a press conference on January 16, 1980, she disapproved interference by any foreign power in the affairs of another country and said that the Soviet presence in Afghanistan had increased tension and moved danger closer to the Indian border.[42] Her Foreign Minister told the Lok Sabha: "India has close and friendly relations with the government and people of Afghanistan, and we are deeply concerned and vitally interested in the security, independence, sovereignty, and territorial integrity of this traditionally friendly neighbour of ours, and we believe that they have every right to safeguard them."[43]

Mrs. Gandhi went a step further by assuring Parliament on January 30 that India would make "every effort to ensure speedy withdrawal of Russian troops from Afghanistan."[44] This became the central theme of Mrs. Gandhi's strategy in her efforts at crisis defusion, efforts that were practically given up after Narasimha Rao's visit to Moscow in June 1980.

A January visit to New Delhi by the French President, Giscard d'Estaing, planned before the Soviet intervention and Indian elections, yielded a joint statement with Mrs. Gandhi. It said the two leaders would take "all necessary steps to defuse regional and international tension and to create a climate of mutual trust and confidence." Giscard suggested that "the intervention of the USSR [was] not necessarily programmed."[45] The joint statement, as President Carter was to suggest later, was "noncommital."[46]

Giscard had visited New Delhi as Finance Minister towards the end of 1973 and had departed with a "high esteem of India's technocrats."[47] The 1980 Giscard visit represented a change in foreign policy directions to some extent. The French had come to the conclusion that India, Algeria and Mexico represented countries of particular interest in the developing world.[48]

Later, President Mitterrand was to reiterate this policy in his own fashion. The suggestion that India, Algeria and Mexico were the pillars of the developing world for France was not a statement of government policy, he told me in an interview in November 1981. This was the impression among the general public and in the French press and "it is not a false one."[49]

Indian interest in France was to have a sympathetic Western government on its side in the broader ideological questions of the North-South dialogue as on the more immediate problem of securing armaments on favourable terms. Since 1980, Indo-French relations had been elevated to a priority level as part of a policy of buttressing relations with West Europe.[50]

President Mitterrand visited India towards the end of 1982 just as an agreement on the supply of enriched uranium for the Tarapur plant was reached.[51] At a banquet in his honour, President Zail Singh called upon France to work together with India and other nonaligned countries in building bridges between the East and the West and the North and the South.[52]

There was no joint communiqué at the end of the visit, in view of disagreements on Afghanistan and Kampuchea, and the rapport Mrs. Gandhi had built up with Giscard was missing.[53] But the two leaders were equally enthusiastic in promoting close relations between their countries, reinforced by the Indian decision to buy Mirage-2000.

Pakistan's acquiescence, if not complicity, in cross-border raids by Afghan refugees, particularly from about April 1979, was an accepted part of the turmoil in Afghanistan. Wali Khan, the opposition leader, was publicly warning the Pakistan government in

April 1979 that Zia was "playing with fire" by "organizing raids" into Afghanistan. "The Russians are not going to sit idle; they will hit back one day," he told an interviewer in Peshawar.[54] The Pakistani ambassador in Moscow, Sajjad Hyder, was warning his government that if the Taraki-Amin regime was destabilized, the Soviet Union would intervene physically and "become our neighbour."[55]

Pakistan's initial reaction to the Soviet intervention came forty-eight hours after the event, on December 29, and was couched in cautious terms. A government statement expressed "gravest concern," "all the more because the victim was an Islamic nation."[56] From April to December 1978 only 21,309 refugees had arrived in Pakistan. After Taraki was toppled by Amin, about 194,000 refugees crossed the border. In the three months of Amin's supreme power the number of refugees more than doubled. An additional 30,000 fled to Pakistan after the anti-Amin coup and by April 1980, the number of refugees had increased to 750,000.[57]

Acutely conscious as Pakistan was about its vulnerability in the face of the Soviet military presence in Afghanistan, General Zia met the crisis by keeping as many options open as possible while seeking to build a broad coalition against the Soviet Union. On the one hand, he sought to have the 1959 bilateral agreement with the U.S. transformed into a treaty (the U.S. offer was to have it affirmed by Congress[58]) and tried to build up a new major military relationship. On the other hand, Zia used the Islamic conference to gather broad support while taking care to keep the lines of communication to Moscow open. The Indian option was never seriously considered by Islamabad at the time.[59]

Although Carter had unveiled his doctrine on the Persian Gulf on January 23, 1980, making it an area of vital interest to the United States, Pakistanis "never got a clear answer to their question of whether they were included in this definition."[60] It was, however, clear that the guarantee did not extend to a Pakistani conflict with India. The $400 million aid package was a bitter disappointment to Islamabad, and Zia's response was to make an ostentatious gesture in Moscow's direction. He announced that Islamabad and Moscow would hold talks. In his words, "We want to acquire great harmony and understanding with our neighbour, the Soviet Union."[61]

Of greater significance was Pakistan's decision to host a conference of foreign ministers of Islamic nations on January 27 and 28.[62] Thirty-six foreign ministers met at Islamabad and passed a resolution condemning "the Soviet military aggression," demanding "the immediate and unconditional withdrawal of all Soviet troops" and suspended Afghanistan's membership of the conference.[63] Zia addressed the conference on January 27, 1980 declaring that an "independent Muslim country" was being made the "target of its [a superpower's] attack." "Only such a step [reversal of the course of military intervention] by the Soviet Union," he suggested, "can effectively restore the trust and cooperative relationships between it and the Islamic world."[64]

Pakistan's decision to take the Afghanistan issue to a Muslim forum was interpreted in New Delhi as an ostentatious turning back on exploring the Indian option. But Pakistan displayed remarkable diplomatic agility in keeping several balls up in the air. Zia's public rejection of the American aid package revived some hope in India of a rapprochement with Pakistan and Islamabad took pains to promote the stance of a more flexible policy.

Foreign Policy Advisor Agha Shahi told a national convention of city mayors on March 5, 1980 that the size of the American aid package "would have detracted from, rather than enhanced, our security." He said: "It is our considered view that for its security, Pakistan must depend primarily upon its national unity and strength and indigenous effort to present an iron fist in the face of any would-be intruder and, in the second place, to rely on political, moral and material support from the Islamic and nonaligned worlds as well as the time-tested friendship of China. It would not be prudent on our part to be dependent for our security on any single power."[65]

Zia sent a message to Mrs. Gandhi through U.N. Secretary General Kurt Waldheim that he would be glad to open a dialogue with India.[66] The Indian Prime Minister sent Foreign Secretary R.D. Sathe to Pakistan in early February. The message he conveyed to Zia was that Pakistan had nothing to fear from India, that great power confrontations had a logic of their own without regard to other powers' interests. Such a confrontation would undermine stability in the region and Pakistan and India must act jointly to defuse it.[67] Mrs. Gandhi sent former Foreign Minister Swaran Singh to Pakistan as her special emissary with a similar message, suggesting that Zia could withdraw his troops from the Indian border without fear.[68] Mrs. Gandhi herself met Zia at Salisbury in April 1980, but the meeting did not help bring the two countries' perspective on Afghanistan nearer.

Although Zia's rejection of the American aid package as

"peanuts" annoyed Carter,[69] Pakistan took care to keep the option of a future arms relationship with the U.S. open. Zia undertook a visit to Washington in October 1980 to secure a major concession from the Carter Administration: an agreement to supply Pakistan F-16s in operation in the U.S. and NATO air forces.[70] Zia, however, waited for the U.S. Presidential election in November, in the hope of receiving an even better deal from a new Reagan Administration. Pakistan, meanwhile, was quietly letting through arms from U.S., Chinese and other sources to the insurgents in Afghanistan.

Zia also kept up a dialogue with Moscow and took care to let India know that he was maintaining his links with the Soviet Union. In a provocative interview he gave to *The Guardian* in October 1982, Zia was to reveal that Moscow had offered him a security pact and that both Kabul and the Kremlin had indicated their willingness to recognize the Durand Line, but that he had declined to pay the price. "I will make them [Kabul and Moscow] recognize the Durand Line in my own way and, God willing, that day is not far off," he declared.[71]

As pieced together by an Indian analyst in Moscow,[72] serious negotiations between Pakistan and the Soviet Union began in September 1980 and further discussions were held at various levels subsequently, with consultations also taking place between Kabul and Moscow, and Moscow and New Delhi. A consensus was apparently reached on the acceptance of the Durand Line in exchange for Pakistan stopping arms supplies to the guerrillas. The Pakistanis did not show interest in internal political change in Kabul and the Soviets did not seek the closure of the Pakistan-Afghan border or the return of Afghan refugees.

It was tacitly recognized that Afghanistan was not in a hurry to get back refugees. The Soviet Union was also prepared to guarantee Pakistan's security and territorial integrity and the possibility of a quadrilateral undertaking by the Soviet Union, India, Pakistan and Afghanistan to guarantee the security of all was left open. A Pakistani diplomat was later to allege that the Soviets "dilly-dallied" in tying up the arrangements because Zia's position around February 1981 appeared shaky. The Russians apparently took some time to make the Karmal regime accept the Durand Line.

It seems more likely that Pakistan was probing Moscow on how far it would go and wanted to have under its belt the outline of a settlement in case it did not have any other viable option. Acceptance of such a scenario would have dramatically altered Pakistan's relations with the Soviet Union, the U.S., India and China. Zia was in no hurry to close his U.S. option, particularly with the new Reagan Administration in place.

The Soviet intervention in Afghanistan presented acute dilemmas for Pakistan. But Zia was not oblivious to the fact that the new dangers on the north had also brought him and his country a bonus. The Soviet move had helped strengthen his position at home at a time he seemed most vulnerable. And the heightened risks from the north made his country an attractive candidate for American military assistance, which would keep his dominant constituency, the army, in good humour.

In India, Mrs. Gandhi fastened on the tactic of a regional diplomatic offensive to try to defuse the crisis. Indian diplomats made forays into Sri Lanka, Nepal and Bangladesh. An emissary was sent to Kabul, the softer Afghan line leading to hopes in India on Soviet troops' withdrawal. Indeed, the linchpin of Mrs. Gandhi's strategy was a substantial Soviet gesture in moving towards the withdrawal of their troops from Afghanistan. Since India had alienated a considerable part of world, particularly nonaligned, opinion by its stand at the U.N., the expectation in New Delhi was that Moscow would help the Indian diplomatic initiative. It was no secret that the Soviets were somewhat surprised by the intensity of world reaction to their move into Afghanistan and the political cost they were continuing to pay for their action.

Gromyko's visit to New Delhi, at the Kremlin's initiative, was therefore eagerly awaited by Mrs. Gandhi. To Indian officials' dismay, the Soviet Foreign Minister brought a tough message: there would be no "give" in Moscow's position on Afghanistan. At a dinner speech, he said the U.S. was determined to "convert Pakistan into a hotbed of tension and a springboard for further escalation of aggression against Afghanistan."[73] For good measure, he also launched attacks on Pakistan, irritating India.

Mrs. Gandhi's talks with Gromyko were described as "frank" and Foreign Ministry spokesman Dixit was constrained to declare, "Mr. Gromyko reiterated the stand previously expressed by the Soviets on this issue [Afghanistan]."[74] At the end of the visit, there was no reference to Afghanistan in the joint statement, but the spokesman tried to cover up India's embarrassment by indulging in standard rhetoric. He accused the U.S. of hampering efforts for withdrawal of Soviet troops from Afghanistan, declaring, "Many things are happening in the world which impinge on the situation in Afghanistan," such as the use of Indian Ocean-Persian Gulf military facilities, Diego Garcia's strengthening, massive buildup of U.S. naval forces in the region and reports that "certain countries are openly saying" they are training Afghan rebel fighters.[75]

India decided to separate the Afghan issue from bilateral relations with Moscow,[76] a strategy the Soviet Union also avidly espoused. To assuage Indian feelings to an extent, Arkhipov was sent to New Delhi in late February bearing dividends in bilateral relations. Mrs. Gandhi had a brief meeting with Brezhnev in Belgrade in May without bringing the two sides nearer on Afghanistan. Indian newspaper accounts suggested that the Soviet leader had proposed that India call a Tashkent-style conference by getting Karmal and Zia together,[77] a non-starter, if ever there was one.

By the time the second Islamic Conference was held in May 1980, the passions of January had been replaced by moderation, with Pakistan emphasizing the need for a "comprehensive solution of the Afghan crisis," in an apparent gesture to the Soviets. Brezhnev had sent two messages to Zia in May hoping that Pakistan would hold a dialogue with the Afghan regime to find a political solution. The conference decided to form a three-man committee of Pakistan, Iran and the secretary general of the Islamic Conference "to seek ways and means, including appropriate consultations, for a comprehensive solution of the grave crisis in respect of Afghanistan." An Agha Shahi-Gromyko meeting at the United Nations in September 1980 led to hopes of a beginning of some form of negotiations with the Afghan government—hopes that proved illusory.[78]

Indian hopes of helping find a settlement of the Afghan problem had not been entirely extinguished, and Brezhnev's proposal "to negotiate a deadline for the beginning of the withdrawal of the Soviet troops from the Afghan territory" and "appropriate international guarantees of ending and nonresumption of all forms of outside interference" in Afghan affairs created a climate of optimism in India.[79] Foreign Minister Narasimha Rao went to Moscow in June and did not take long to discover that the Soviets had not softened their stand in the slightest degree, Gromyko making it clear at a luncheon for Rao, "It must be clear to all that the attempt to change the realities existing in Afghanistan is futile. Any discussions concerning this, any attempts to interfere in the internal affairs of Afghanistan are pointless."[80]

In an indication of the bitter Indian disappointment over Soviet policies, Rao made the sharpest attack on Moscow on Afghanistan ever made by an Indian spokesman in reporting to Parliament on his trip on June 17. He said:

> We are opposed to the presence of foreign troops in any country. The Soviet Union had announced that Soviet assistance to Afghanistan was limited in time, purpose, and scale and did not present a threat to security and stability in the region. However, reports coming out of Afghanistan during the past few months, even after they are discounted for the inevitable interested propaganda element, do seem to suggest that, in view of the situation there, the hope that Soviet assistance to Afghanistan could indeed remain limited in time, as originally intended, is not very strong.
>
> This is naturally a matter of concern to India as indeed to the others who seek a reduction of tension and a peaceful solution to the problems of the region. It is time to ask ourselves the question whether the Soviet troops meant for assisting in Afghanistan have not become, or are not likely to become, a pretext for those who wish to create further instability in that country. Our fear is that beyond a reasonable time-frame this could well come to pass, and this is why we urge that a stage has come when ways and means, other than military, should be devised to bring about a solution to the problem while this is still within the range of possibility.

Rao at the same time sought to separate the Afghan issue from bilateral relations, suggesting that the sharp differences had not caused "even the slightest clouding of our bilateral relations; these have indeed grown from strength to strength during the last five months." There was no reference to Afghanistan in the joint statement at the end of Rao's visit and although Indian officials went through the motions of continuing with their crisis defusion diplomacy, the realization had sunk in that Moscow had made India's task impossible.

India used a largely ceremonial visit of President Reddy to the Soviet Union in late September 1980 to seek Soviet help in the new oil crisis caused by the Iran-Iraq war. The two Middle East countries supplied 70 per cent of India's crude imports and the country was short of 3.5 million tons of crude for the remainder of the year. India asked Moscow to double its crude exports of 1.5 million tons a year; the Soviet response was positive.[81]

A major event in the Indo-Soviet calendar in 1980 was Brezhnev's visit to New Delhi in December. India had no illusion any longer about Soviet flexibility on Afghanistan and wished to buttress bilateral relations in arms and trade. For the Soviets, the symbolism of the visit was important; with the overwhelming part of the developing world ranged against them on Afghanistan, they wished to emphasize close relations with India

Just before Brezhnev's visit, Mrs. Gandhi told *The Washington Post* that the withdrawal of Soviet troops from Afghanistan was an increasingly remote possibility, but "the outcry, and the feeling that everyone was ganging up against them [the Soviets], have caused them to dig in their toes."[82] Four days before the Soviet leader arrived in New Delhi, Mrs. Gandhi and President Suharto of Indonesia called for a settlement of the Afghan issue to ensure that the Afghan people determined their own destiny "free from foreign interference and intervention."[83]

Indeed, it seemed that after Rao's visit to Moscow in June, Indian leaders had lost their inhibition in stating their differences with the Soviets on Afghanistan. President Reddy told Brezhnev at a banquet in New Delhi, "We in India remain opposed to any form of intervention, covert or overt, by outside forces in the internal affairs of the region."[84] In what appeared to be a gesture, both *Pravda* and *Izvestia* of December 10, 1980 chose to highlight India's "sincere" hope that the "independence... and nonaligned status of the states in our region will not be subjected to pressure or threats because of conflicts or interference..."

In contrast, a week earlier, on December 3, Tass had taken a swipe at Western and Pakistani reporting of Afghan events. It said: "[T]he Western reactionary circles and their mouthpieces, namely the AFP [Agence France-Presse], radio Voice of America, the voice of Germany (Deutsche Welle), radio BBC and the morally inferior mass media of Pakistan, in their desperate positions, do not have anything else to offer except the very low level of fabrications and false propaganda."

That the substance of the Soviet stand had not changed was made clear by Tass on December 9. It quoted Brezhnev as saying that the Soviet Union would discharge "to the end its duty of rendering assistance to Afghanistan." Mrs. Gandhi's talks with Brezhnev were described as "frank" and Afghanistan did not figure in the joint declaration.

Brezhnev proposed a five-point plan for achieving peace and security in the Persian Gulf, to win only a laconic response from Mrs. Gandhi. She said, "It appeared to be a constructive suggestion and was worthy of careful consideration."[85] Brezhnev did not praise Mrs. Gandhi's "farsightedness," as he did during her visit to Moscow in 1976, but restricted himself to a personal tribute. "I make no secret of the fact that we have always had a particular liking for Mrs. Indira Gandhi. She is an outstanding political and state figure of contemporary Asia."[86]

A striking illustration of how the two sides had chosen to insulate bilateral relations from the fall-out of Afghanistan was the Soviet agreement to give Rs. 40 billion for India's next plan, more MIG-25s and an additional one million tons of crude.[87] And the two leaders declared "their firm intention, in accordance with the treaty of peace, friendship and cooperation between India and the USSR, to continue strengthening and deepening Indo-Soviet friendly and mutually beneficial cooperation in the interest of the peoples of the two countries and the cause of international peace and security."[88]

Such statements, however, could not hide the chill that had crept into India's relations with Moscow after the Soviet intervention in Afghanistan.[89] On the Soviet side, there was a wariness towards Mrs. Gandhi after her return to power. Despite New Delhi's belief that it could not sacrifice Moscow's implicit nuclear protection against China and the large military and trade relationship with it in the darkening regional picture, the Soviet move into Afghanistan gave an edge to Mrs. Gandhi's efforts to enlarge the country's diplomatic options.

By the summer of 1980, India's attempts to defuse the Afghan crisis were stymied by Moscow's rigidity on the one hand and Pakistan's turning to an Islamic forum on the other. Hopes of a rapprochement with Pakistan ebbed and flowed along a seemingly preordained path until they were all but extinguished by the new American aid package Pakistan chose to accept in September 1981.

Mrs. Gandhi gave an early indication of her interest in a more balanced relationship with the U.S. in spite of her fears that the Reagan Administration would adopt hard-line policies. On China, she was keen to continue the process of reconciliation she herself had initiated in 1976, a process advanced by the Janata government.

The omens seemed propitious for building up better relations with China. The Chinese had given satisfaction to India on two points during Janata Foreign Minister Vajpayee's visit in 1979. Beijing's interference in India's northeast was "a thing of the past" and China would like countries of the subcontinent to settle problems among themselves. After the Soviet intervention in Afghanistan, China told New Delhi that it had asked Pakistan to look up to India and settle problems bilaterally and that its military aid to Pakistan was minimal.

India received many signals from China since the beginning of 1980. The Indian assumption was that the change in the Chinese attitude stemmed from their belief that Pakistan was too vulnerable and too enamoured of the Islamic option to provide a reliable shield against Soviet power, and by intervening in Afghanistan, Moscow had hurt India's geopolitical interests.[90]

In 1980, Indian officials saw "very considerable Chinese movement" in Beijing's approach to India's neighbours and some signs of it persuading Pakistan to resolve problems with India. For the Chinese, the Kashmir issue had now become a bilateral problem between India and Pakistan. The border dispute and its resolution on "a basis of equality" remained a matter of priority for India and New Delhi saw little in common with Beijing's world view, in particular on relations with the Soviet Union and Southeast Asia. Besides, Indian officials believed that the Chinese did not respect nonalignment.[91]

Indeed, signs of China wanting better relations with India were unmistakable. It was assumed in New Delhi that this Chinese interest was also determined by the fact that normal relations with India would help it in the Third World, particularly in the nations of Southeast Asia, and that a tranquil border with India would help it resolve Tibetan problems.

Mrs. Gandhi, for her own reasons, was keen to respond to China's signals. And her meeting with Chinese Foreign Minister Huang Hua in Salisbury in April 1980 was more important for its symbolism than for what was discussed. Signs of Moscow's nervousness were apparent. On February 13, 1980 *Pravda* reported that Narasimha Rao had assured Gromyko that "India...pursues a policy of normalizing and strengthening ties with its neighbours [but]...we reiterate that any improvement in these relations with any neighbouring country will not take place at the expense of the time-tested friendship with other states." During Brezhnev's visit in December, Mrs. Gandhi told him that Sino-Indian rapprochement would not affect Indo-Soviet relations.

The new momentum in Sino-Indian relations was kept up by Mrs. Gandhi's meeting with the Chinese leader Hua Guofeng in Belgrade. And in June 1980 the Chinese paramount leader Deng Xiaoping publicly unveiled the border "package," first proposed by Zhou in New Delhi in 1960, repeated to Vajpayee during his visit to Beijing in 1979, and told me by Chinese officials a few weeks later.[92] The proposal amounted to formalization of the status quo by China renouncing claims in the northeast while retaining all the territory in its possession in the west. Since several thousand square miles had been taken by China since the proposal was first made, it was unacceptable to New Delhi, but Indian officials chose to emphasize the positive elements in seeking better relations between the two countries.

A setback in the reconciliation process came with the Indian government's recognition of the Heng Samrin regime in Kampuchea. Such a step was projected in the election manifesto of Mrs. Gandhi's party, perhaps to sway pro-Communist elements to support the Indira Congress. India's emotional attachment to the Vietnamese cause was made amply clear during the Chinese invasion of Vietnam in 1979 and, on a less emotional plane, New Delhi sympathized with Vietnam's regional ambitions and favoured a counterweight to Chinese influence in Southeast Asia.

But there was no compelling necessity to recognize the Vietnamese-installed regime in mid-1980. Soviet pressures were not of a nature that could not be warded off and recognition of the Heng Samrin regime could hurt the reconciliation process with China and India's relations with a number of Southeast Asian nations. There was, indeed, no coherent official explanation for the timing of the recognition although New Delhi was disappointed that India's action was not followed by other nonaligned nations.[93]

An immediate consequence of the decision was the postponement of Foreign Minister Huang Hua's visit, scheduled for the fall of 1980. The Indian hope was that the setback would be temporary, which proved to be the case. The Chinese wanted to make a point but had no desire to negate their new policy on India. The visit was rescheduled for June 1981.

Before Huang Hua came to India, Chinese Prime Minister Zhao

Ziyang visited Pakistan, Nepal and Bangladesh to reassure traditional friends of a continuing Beijing interest in their welfare.[94] The visit was a success, with Huang claiming that it represented "a breakthrough." He had suggested that the resolution of the border dispute should also take into account national feelings and an agreement was reached to open formal border talks.[95]

A measure of wariness on the Indian side was apparent in Foreign Minister Narasimha Rao's studious allusion to Indo-Soviet relations at the banquet held in Huang's honour. Moscow had criticized the visit and quickly came to the conclusion that the Chinese foreign minister had no concrete proposals and that given the state of affairs in the Indian Ocean, the situation in Afghanistan and Kampuchea, and the twenty to twenty-five People's Liberation Army divisions along the Indian border, "these preparations do not tally with China's professions of desire for good neighbourship. Quite justified, therefore, is the cautious stand taken in Delhi in connection with the resumption of the Indian-Chinese dialogue."[96]

Although the Marxists had welcomed the Huang visit, the CPI attacked it by reviving the old cry of a Beijing-Washington-Islamabad axis against India.[97] Rao scheduled a visit to Moscow to reassure the Soviets about the abiding nature of the Indo-Soviet relationship. In fact, Huang's talks in New Delhi were comprehensive and revealed unsuspected nuances in China's world view. The Indian negotiators found the Chinese to be more critical of U.S. attitudes than they had expected and Huang showed flexibility on Afghanistan by not insisting on the immediate withdrawal of all Soviet troops. The Chinese refrain was that India and China acting together in Asia would be a force to reckon with.[98]

Undeterred by Soviet signs of nervousness, Mrs. Gandhi continued the process of reconciliation by meeting Chinese Prime Minister Zhao Ziyang at Cancun towards the end of 1981. The Chinese side did most of the talking, with Mrs. Gandhi remaining somewhat noncommunicative, perhaps because she wanted to assess Chinese intentions without giving anything away.[99] The first round of border talks was held in Beijing in December 1981, with India urging that the two countries return to the Colombo proposals as a framework for resolving the border dispute.[100] The Chinese did not accept this suggestion, but both sides were equally anxious to end it on a positive note and agreed on trade and cultural exchanges.

After her return to power in January 1980, Mrs. Gandhi said in a radio broadcast, "Come, now let us all work together." By the end of 1980 the prospect of achieving a national consensus had receded as socio-economic tensions loomed large in an era of increasing violence, inflation and bonapartism. The mood of relief that had greeted her return had given way to one of foreboding. There was, however, a noticeable bounce in industry and agriculture had proved resilient in a year of drought.[101]

The greatest tragedy to befall Mrs. Gandhi was the death of her younger son Sanjay in a plane accident in June shortly after he had been made a Congress party general secretary. During the previous five years, she had come to rely increasingly on Sanjay in making her political decisions. In elections to nine state assemblies held at the end of May, he had emerged a leader in his own right and a pulverized opposition had helplessly watched the ascendancy of Sanjay.[102]

No one had any doubt that Mrs. Gandhi was grooming Sanjay to succeed her and he seemed to demonstrate enough determination and ruthlessness to seize the prize, if frustrated. Now, in a trice, he was gone.[103] A rash of Hindu-Muslim riots in Uttar Pradesh in August 1980 presented a law and order problem and created new tensions with Pakistan. The government enacted a National Security Ordinance on preventive detention. A six-party front, including the two Communist parties, a Congress faction and Charan Singh's Lok Dal, cobbled together an agitation plan to protest against the price rise, communal troubles and the threat to civil liberties. With her subtle encouragement, Mrs. Gandhi's partymen demanded that her elder son Rajiv, an airline pilot, be brought into politics.[104]

Mrs. Gandhi, meanwhile, had evolved her own methods of getting even with the Communist Party of India and sending signals to Moscow. During Brezhnev's December 1980 visit, she had made a significant remark at a civic reception in the Soviet leader's honour. She said, "Understandably, we face onslaught from the 'right' and, not so understandably, from the 'left'."[105] Brezhnev did raise the question of CPI's support for Mrs. Gandhi during his meeting in New Delhi with a CPI delegation but his reference did not seem to be couched in terms necessitating a change in the party's policy.[106] The Marxist leaders did not have a formal meeting with Brezhnev although some of them shook hands with him at a reception.

Mrs. Gandhi launched an offensive against the ruling Communist coalitions in West Bengal and Kerala in early 1981. The CPI was facing problems of its own, the National Council expelling the party's founder member S.A. Dange, who had formed a splinter All-India Communist Party (AICP) with his daughter's help.[107] The National Council resolution was plaintive in tone, but Dange did not take away many CPI members with him. Mrs. Gandhi's aim was to take other parties away from the Communists in states ruled by them. The CPI had sacrificed the leadership of the Kerala coalition to achieve tactical unity with the CPI(M) while the latter had readjusted its sights on foreign policy—on Afghanistan and Kampuchea—for building a "left and democratic unity" strategy.[108]

Further, the Prime Minister cut a lifeline of the CPI—the many "friendship" societies linked to the Soviet Union and its allies and traditionally used by the Indian party as levers of money, influence and power in dealings with the Soviet Communist world. She set up a rival Friends of the Soviet Union (FSU) under the Congress (I) to counter the CPI-sponsored Indo-Soviet Cultural Society (ISCUS) and a parallel "world peace and solidarity" organization to the World Peace Council. It was a warning not only to the Indian Communists but also to the Soviets. She was suggesting that the local Communists could not increase the level of opposition to the Congress (I) government at the Centre while continuing to receive Moscow's support without being made to pay a price.[109]

Formally inaugurating the Friends of the Soviet Union in May 1981, Mrs. Gandhi said the need was to liberate Indo-Soviet friendship from the clutches of those who considered themselves to be "custodians" of the friendship. It was the "professional friends and foes of the Soviet Union who create problems for us," she added.[110] To their chagrin, Soviet delegates who came to attend anniversary celebrations of ISCUS also had to attend an FSU meeting. Mrs. Gandhi developed an antipathy to the Soviet ambassador, Yuri Vorontsov, since the Soviet delegation's attendance at the FSU ceremonies, if not earlier.[111]

Despite Mrs. Gandhi's hints to the Soviets about bringing the CPI into line almost since her return to power in January 1980, Moscow did not change its attitude. At the Twenty-sixth Congress of the CPSU in February 1981, Brezhnev made no mention of India's domestic situation, confining himself to foreign policy. He said: "Joint action with peaceful and independent India will continue to be one of the important areas of Soviet foreign relations."[112]

Zia was, on the other hand, employing the Soviet intervention in

Afghanistan to the hilt to buttress his own position at home. By the fall of 1980 Saudi Arabia alone had given Pakistan $7.5 billion and was committed to providing it an additional $5 billion.[113] By 1981 Pakistan had emerged as "the Third World's leading supplier of military manpower after Cuba," not counting the traditional role the Nepalese Gurkhas have played in the British and Indian armies. Pakistan had military contingents in twenty-two countries, including Saudi Arabia, the U.A.R., Kuwait, Oman, Jordan, Syria and Libya from troop training to guerrilla warfare.[114]

In October 1979, Zia had reneged for a second time to hold general elections, and in May 1980 introduced constitutional amendments to give virtually unchallenged powers of arrest and detention to military tribunals. In March 1981 he effectively abrogated the 1973 constitution, abolished national and provincial assemblies and stripped the judiciary of most of its remaining power.

Indeed, Zia displayed much political finesse in using the hijacking of a Pakistani plane to Kabul, in which an official was summarily executed, by condemning the opposition and, in particular, Bhutto's Pakistan People's Party. The hijacking was owned by the Al Zulfiqar terrorist organization linked to Bhutto's sons, who had received asylum in Afghanistan. Although both Bhutto's widow and daughter Benazir repudiated the hijacking, they had adopted a pro-Soviet approach to Moscow's intervention in Afghanistan.[115]

In the U.S., Pakistan's importance in the defence of the Persian Gulf region was well recognized after the Iranian revolution and the Soviet intervention in Afghanistan. Although Carter laid himself open to the charge of panicky overreaction to events in Iran and Afghanistan, he had initiated expanded military budgets, the buildup of naval power in the Indian Ocean and creation of the RDF.

Reagan came to power on the strength of a widespread feeling that America had been pushed around by the other superpower and had his own ideological proclivities in showing the Soviet Union its place. Indeed, the Reagan Administration had no inhibition in pursuing a clear military-oriented strategy in foreign policy. In outlining a "Strategy in the Decade of the 1980s" for the Reagan Administration, Paul H. Nitze suggested, "The principal task of the early 1980s must be to check, blunt, and as far as possible, frustrate the interrelated Soviet strategies while the energies of many nations similarly threatened have an opportunity to become mobilized and linked so as to reverse the currently adverse trends in the correlation of forces."[116]

For many American strategists, Pakistan's interest in maintaining a regional balance of power had coincided more clearly than ever before with U.S. global cold war interests. An Indian-dominated South Asian balance of power had been scuttled by the Carter Administration in the second half of his troubled term and the focus in American strategic thinking was clearly on Pakistan and the Indian Ocean and in "bleeding" the Soviets in Afghanistan.

Henry Kissinger favoured U.S. acquisition of logistical facilities or an American presence in Pakistan through a military training and support relationship.[117] U.S. Under Secretary of State for Security Affairs James L. Buckley told the Senate Foreign Relations Committee on November 12, 1981 that Pakistan was "an essential anchor of the entire southwest Asian region."

In the Reagan Administration's view, as it emerged, Pakistan's military modernization would bolster the entire southwest Asian region against Soviet pressures from Afghanistan. The transfer of arms, it claimed, would not upset the existing military balance between India and Pakistan and Pakistan would be more likely to curtail its nuclear weapons programme if its conventional forces were strengthened. The F-16s, which had in any event been promised by Carter, had enthusiastic supporters in the Pentagon precisely because of their compatibility in case of direct American participation in the region.

The point of the negotiations was not so much the quantum of arms to be given to Pakistan but the context in which the new relationship should be promoted. It was known to both sides that Carter's "peanuts" offer would be considerably augmented. But the U.S. wanted formally to draw Pakistan into its military strategy for the Persian Gulf and asked for bases on Pakistani soil.[118] At the same time American negotiators wished Pakistan to give up its nuclear weapon-oriented programme.

Zia and his advisors proved more than equal to the task of getting the best deal out of Washington. The Moscow-Islamabad dialogue was no secret, leading to American fears of "a real possibility that Pakistan might find it necessary to reach a settlement with the USSR and that would be adverse to U.S. interests."[119] Whatever the secret, or implicit, commitments Pakistani negotiators might have made, they were able to convince their American counterparts that it would be better for them not to make public declarations identifying their country with the larger American strategic objectives in the Persian

Gulf-Middle East region.[120]

The U.S. also had to remain content with assurances that Pakistan would not take the path of a nuclear military power, but it refused to stop working on its reprocessing or ancillary facilities. The American aid package was of $3.2 billion, half in economic assistance, for six years, and an agreement to sell forty F-16s worth $1.1 billion under the foreign military sales programme, most of the money to be provided by Saudi Arabia.

Soviet Deputy Foreign Minister Firyubin visited Pakistan in August 1981,[121] and although the talks did not yield any significant result, it helped Zia maintain his dialogue with Moscow. While talking to both Americans and Russians, Pakistan took a new diplomatic initiate by proposing that U.N. Secretary General Waldheim name a representative to promote a dialogue between Iran, Pakistan and the ruling party in Kabul, as distinct from the government. Karmal sent a message to Mrs. Gandhi on January 5 indicating Kabul's interest in such talks.[122]

These diplomatic moves were being made with an eye on the nonaligned foreign ministers' meeting planned for February in New Delhi. Moscow was banking on India's help in softening the inevitable criticism it would face for its action in Afghanistan.[123] New Delhi's response was to propose a bland resolution, in the full knowledge that it would be hardened by the conference participants.

In the end, India incorporated the substance of the Pakistani amendment on the withdrawal of foreign troops from Afghanistan, agreed to drop the reference to Diego Garcia in relation to the Indian Ocean at Sri Lanka's bidding and asked for the "withdrawal of all foreign forces" from Kampuchea. India, in fact, seemed to be using the foreign ministers' conference to distance itself further from Moscow on Afghanistan, leading to a measure of Soviet disappointment.[124]

Indeed, the nonaligned foreign ministers' meeting brought home to India how far off the mainstream it was on the Afghan and Kampuchean issues. The Soviet Union was in the dock in such a gathering for the first time. On February 6, Iran's representative had ruled out talks with Kabul as long as Soviet troops remained in Afghanistan. The next day the Afghan foreign minister agreed to talks without preconditions. But Pakistan's stance had hardened in the meantime. It ruled out talks in New Delhi and insisted that Iran be present at such discussions.

The proposed U.S. military aid package for Pakistan and its nuclear ambitions were engaging the attention of Indian leaders. Mrs. Gandhi addressed both these issues in a statement to Parliament in April 1981. She said the development of an atom bomb by Pakistan would have "grave and irreversible" consequences on the subcontinent. She further assured Parliament that "we shall respond in an appropriate way to any development," thus reversing the Desai stand on nuclear policy.

Mrs. Gandhi also suggested that Pakistan was using the Afghan crisis to acquire arms.[125] Going to the core of India's concern during the defence debate, she said the proposed new security relationship between the U.S. and Pakistan had introduced a "qualitative difference" in that Pakistan was once again being integrated into a strategic alliance system which would prove hostile to India's security interests.

Narasimha Rao's visit to Pakistan in June 1981 was in the nature of a last effort to persuade Islamabad to reconsider its strategy and Indian reservations on the Soviet action were made amply clear.[126] He went a considerable way towards addressing a basic Pakistani fear: "I would ... like to say categorically, on behalf of the Indian people and India's Prime Minister, that India has, and will always continue to have, full respect for the sovereignty, territorial integrity, stability and independence of Pakistan. When this is stated by Smt. [Mrs.] Indira Gandhi, I hope it will be realized that there is no voice louder and clearer and no resolve more dependable."[127]

Narasimha Rao made a good impression and at the end of his stay in Pakistan he issued a joint statement with Agha Shahi explicitly recognizing Pakistan's right to acquire arms for self-defence. The gains of the visit were, however, quickly washed away by the announcement, made almost on the heels of Rao's departure from Islamabad, that Pakistan would receive off-the-shelf deliveries of F-16s, in addition to the arms package being negotiated. One point the Pakistanis were repeatedly emphasizing in New Delhi was that the earliest U.S. arms would start arriving in Pakistan would be the fall of 1982. The Indian feeling was of being let down.[128]

A significant and, in the long-term, far-reaching consequence of the Soviet intervention in Afghanistan was a proposal by Ziaur Rahman of Bangladesh for institutionalized cooperation among the seven countries of the South Asian region—Bangladesh, Bhutan, India, Maldives, Nepal, Pakistan and Sri Lanka.[129] The reactions of both India and Pakistan were negative and cautious. Whereas India wanted to make sure it was not a ploy implying the ganging up of the other countries against it, for Pakistan it conjured up the familiar nightmare of India taking its smaller neighbours under its wing.

The Bangladesh government persevered and India and Pakistan came round to exploring the concept, New Delhi consoling itself with the thought that its enthusiasm would have been the kiss of death for it. Bilateral contentious issues were specifically kept out of SARC (South Asian Regional Cooperation). Foreign secretaries of the seven countries held four meetings before their foreign ministers met in New Delhi in August 1983, a meeting held against the background of the Sinhalese-Tamil holocaust in Sri Lanka.

Although the twelve commissions formed by SARC dealt with peripheral issues, the foreign ministers' meeting was a modest success. India dropped its earlier objections to the member countries being involved in other bilateral and multilateral arrangements with countries outside the region, particularly the superpowers.[130] SARC holds promise for the Nineties, rather than what it can achieve during the rest of this decade.

Assassinations and coups, meanwhile, were continuing to take their toll in Bangladesh. Ziaur Rahman was assassinated on May 30, 1981. Before Chittagong radio went off the air that day, it announced the installation of a "revolutionary council" and abrogation of the Indo-Bangladesh friendship treaty even while Dhaka radio was declaring that the new regime would honour all international commitments.[131] Power did not, however, go to the instigator of the coup, but to Lieutenant-General Ershad.

Chapter Nine

AFGHANISTAN—II

EVENTS in Poland and the rise of the Solidarity movement there were presenting a major problem for the Soviets in 1981 and the situation in the Middle East needed constant watching. There was a hardening of the U.S. position under the Reagan Administration. Towards China, the Soviets alternated between denunciations, threats and blandishments and Brezhnev told the Twenty-sixth Congress that "Soviet-Chinese relations remain frozen."[1]

The tone of the sixth plenum of the Chinese Communist Party, publicized in June 1981, was hardly encouraging for a Sino-Soviet rapprochement. Secretary of State Alexander Haig visited China in June and the existence of joint intelligence stations in China on monitoring Soviet missile tests was revealed.[2] Assistant Secretary of State John Holdridge let it be known that the U.S. and China were cooperating militarily, and in other ways, against the Soviets in Afghanistan, Kampuchea and elsewhere.[3]

The Soviets alleged that China had become a "junior partner" of the U.S.[4] Fecdor Burlatski said in *Literaturnaya Gazeta* of August 5, 1981 that before the "triple alliance" of the U.S., Japan and China "brings about a major change in the global correlation of forces between East and West" there would be "joint action" by the Soviet Union and other countries to forestall it. The Soviets increased their ground forces facing China from forty-six to fifty-one divisions.[5]

In Afghanistan, Russian troop strength was increased from 85,000 to 110,000, with casualities steadily mounting. But there was some hope towards the end of the year for reopening a dialogue with China. The Soviet Union proposed renewing border talks in October and in early December China said it was preparing a "constructive response."[6]

Pakistan's acceptance of the American aid package was announced in mid-September 1981. By the beginning of 1982 Mrs. Gandhi had changed her stance towards Afghanistan, reflecting India's heightened concern over the new U.S.-Pakistan military relationship. She suggested that "the recent rearming of Pakistan by the U.S. could rather be a temptation to the Soviets or the Afghans than a deterrent." "I think the Soviet Union would like to get out of Afghanistan... but I do not think the others want them to." "Pakistan had gained in every possible way—financially, militarily and in sympathy and in moral support—from the Soviet presence in Afghanistan and the U.S. would rather have the Soviets in a difficult situation as they were in Vietnam."[7]

Pakistan announced the American aid package with a footnote, offering India talks on "nonaggression" and "nonuse of force," a proposal repeatedly made by India in the past and constantly rejected by Islamabad. Mrs. Gandhi lost no time in shooting it down, convinced as she was that it was a ploy to smooth the passage of the American aid bill for Pakistan through Congress. She carried her hard line to the Canberra Commonwealth summit in the fall of 1981 and also opposed Pakistan's readmission to the Commonwealth.[8]

In the Indian view, Islamabad was very clear before it took its decision on accepting the American arms package that it would further alienate India and decided to go ahead on the assumption that it was more profitable for it to receive American arms than to chase the chimera of friendship with India.[9] But the persistence with which Pakistan promoted its new enthusiasm for a no-war pact showed up the negative Indian response as inadequate, and Islamabad was, indeed, running away with a propaganda victory.

As a consequence, India softened its stand and the two countries' foreign ministers met in New Delhi in late January 1982. These talks led Indian negotiations to assume that though the no-war proposal was initially a propaganda ploy, Islamabad had stumbled upon its potential usefulness in prompting the country's interests. The primacy of the Simla Agreement was acknowledged by both sides but there were differences on the role to assign the U.N. Charter on bilateral issues.[10]

But the major point to emerge from the meeting came in a talk Mrs. Gandhi had with Pakistani correspondents on January 30. She said that India would never attack Pakistan "war pact or no war pact" and suggested that the two countries should aim at a "friendship treaty" beyond the no-war pact. The next day she proposed to Agha Shahi that a joint commission be appointed to sort out bilateral problems, a proposal the Pakistani accepted.[11] After an initial propaganda defeat, Mrs. Gandhi had placed the ball back in the Pakistani court and Indo-Pakistani relations soon assumed the familiar form of shadow boxing.

In addition to the other signals Mrs. Gandhi had been sending Moscow, she studiously avoided visiting the Soviet Union since her return to power. The Soviets wanted to highlight the halfway mark in the Indo-Soviet treaty by organizing grand celebrations in Moscow in her presence. She did not go; nor was Foreign Minister Rao's visit to Moscow timed with the event. And the anniversary celebrations in India were downgraded.

During his visit in July 1981, Rao pointedly said that the nonaligned movement would "need to strengthen its unity and integrity," with Gromyko comforting himself with the statement: "I think our foreign policy is understood correctly by the Indian government. We are very glad."[12] Rao's basic mission was to reassure the Soviets on the Indo-Soviet relationship after Huang Hua's pathbreaking visit to New Delhi.

The Soviets adopted the posture of business as usual, taking pains to highlight the treaty and the Indo-Soviet relationship. Writing in *International Affairs* in September 1981, B. Levchenko explained: "It is...right and proper to connect the stability of Soviet-Indian relations, which are not subject to fluctuations whatever the situation, with the 1971 treaty." The "situation"—the chill in the New Delhi-Moscow relationship after the Soviet intervention in Afghanistan—did not prevent the writer from praising India's "calm, balanced approach" to the Afghanistan crisis. It was left to Brezhnev to underline the basis of the relationship at Tashkent in March 1982; he described it as "a priceless asset which strengthens in a considerable measure the feeling of security on both sides."[13]

When Mrs. Gandhi did announce plans to visit the Soviet Union, she did so in conjuction with a trip to the U.S. She promptly accepted an invitation from President Reagan and was in the U.S. towards the end of July 1982, causing some disquiet in Moscow. Tass of July 30 quoted Mrs. Gandhi as saying during the visit: "It is difficult to imagine two countries more different than the United States and India. Two states cannot have identical views but they must mutually respect them."[14]

Moscow's concern over Mrs. Gandhi's visit to the U.S. arose out of her studied efforts to balance the Indo-Soviet relationship and her recent economic policies. Many Indian economists had come to the conclusion by the early Seventies that India's credo of self-reliance was proving to be a dead end. A shift in economic policy, starting in 1975, had accelerated since Mrs. Gandhi's return to power.

The government switched from import substitution to export promotion, allowing liberal duty-free imports against exports, and adopted a more favourable approach to the import of foreign capital and technology. Signposts of the new policy included an invitation to multinationals to explore for onshore and offshore oil, an offer to Middle East investors[15] to participate in Indian industry with majority equity shares and the tapping of foreign private capital for the fertilizer and alumina industries.

India also decided to seek a loan of $5.6 billion from the International Monetary Fund to cope with balance of payments problems. Although Mrs. Gandhi took the precaution of tailoring the government's policies to IMF criteria, her move invited a political attack, particularly from the Communists and the left. In August 1982, 110 members of a fragmented opposition got together to charge Mrs. Gandhi in the Lok Sabha with abandoning self-reliance. Later, the Marxist P. Ramamurti declaimed in the Rajya Sabha, "The government has mortgaged the country's economic sovereignty, which will ultimately lead to mortgaging our political sovereignty as well."[16]

Mrs. Gandhi had her first meeting with President Reagan at Cancun towards the end of 1981 and, in spite of their very different perspectives and policies, the two leaders' talks went off rather better than anyone expected. The President's invitation to her was determined by the State Department's success in getting across to him the point that any settlement in Afghanistan could not be achieved in the long term without India's acquiescence, if not approval.[17]

The Indian Prime Minister's mission was determined by an effort to balance the country's relations with the other superpower as also to try to put across India's views on the American arming of Pakistan. There was no expectation of a change in the U.S. attitude, but a more immediate concern of India was to try to gather support for a change in the Reagan Administration's world view of the economy. Reagan and his advisors wished to graduate India out of soft loans, forcing it to borrow on the commercial market. India's view was that Washington should not penalize it for prudent money management just when it was set for the proverbial takeoff.

Neither side convinced the other, but Mrs. Gandhi's visit—her first official trip to the U.S. in eleven years—proved to be a media extravaganza. And American officials argued that the visit did help the Reagan Administration to focus attention for a while on India, a country they had tended largely to disregard in their strategic configurations. In any event, Mrs. Gandhi seemed to have succeeded to an extent in building some good will in the U.S. Administration for its neutrality, it not approval, on the multilateral loans India was seeking.

Before Mrs. Gandhi's visit to the U.S., the Soviets descended on New Delhi in March in a drove of generals led by Defence Minister Ustinov, somewhat to the embarrassment of the Indian side. Moscow's motives were to symbolize a close political relationship as also to try to dissuade India from buying the Mirage-2000, then being negotiated between Paris and New Delhi, as a counter to the F-16. At least a part of the foreign policy establishment also read the visit as a form of reassurance to Mrs. Gandhi on the eve of the Varanasi Congress of the Indian Communist Party, which would endorse an anti-Mrs. Gandhi line. Ustinov did not succeed in changing New Delhi's line on purchasing Mirage-2000.

An agreement between New Delhi and Paris was announced in October 1982. India agreed to the outright purchase of 40 Mirage-2000 and retained the option of licence-producing indigenously 110 of the modern aircraft. The first Mirage were to arrive in India in 1984.[18]

The Indian decision to go in for Mirage-2000 was an answer to an American agreement to supply India's adversary Pakistan with F-16 tactical aircraft although discussions on the purchase of the French plane were initiated by New Delhi as early as 1979. The Pakistanis had made it clear to the Reagan White House that the F-16 was a symbol of the new U.S. commitment to a "front-line" state.

For India this created both a psychological and defence problem. The F-16 would cover up to 60 per cent of Indian territory,[19] threatening defence and economic installations. The Mirage-2000 was high on the list of Indian options, apart from the opportunity it offered to diversify Indian sources of arms supplies. The Soviets, in the Indian view, did not have a matching aircraft.

The Russians had earlier lost out to the Anglo-French Jaguar Deep Penetration Strike Aircraft during the rule of the Janata coalition. Ustinov brought with him a reported offer of additional MIG-25s and licensed Indian production of the MIG-27 ground attack fighter.[20]

But the psychological need to counter the F-16, which had been propagated in India as the world's wonder plane,[21] and a deliberate attempt to buttress the Indo-French political relationship led New Delhi to resist Soviet blandishments. The successful Israeli attack on Iraqi nuclear installations in June 1981 with F-16s had heightened Indian resolve to acquire Mirage-2000.

The necessity of self-reliance in arms was brought home to India after the U.S. embargo on arms to the subcontinent during the Kashmir war in 1965 although this embargo hit Pakistan particularly hard.[22] The Russians were very sore with the Indian Mirage decision. The chiefs of the Indian Army and Navy were told by Moscow, for instance, that if their country could pay hard cash for expensive planes—a Mirage-2000 is estimated to cost between $18 million and $20 million[23]—why should it want generous Soviet credit terms of seventeen years' payment at 2.5 per cent interest?[24] Actually, India got rather good terms in the Mirage deal: 10 per cent deposit on the first forty planes and government-backed nine-year credit at 9.2 per cent interest, with the promise of uninterrupted supplies, even in a war situation.[25]

Economic factors as well as predictability and sturdiness had led India in 1980 to settle for the Soviet T-72 as the main battle tank, in preference to a Western tank which would have been three times as expensive.[26] The Indian-produced Vijayanta needed to be replaced and since an Indian MBT was not ready, at any rate with the specifications the army wanted, the choice fell on the T-72.[27] If the end result was "a Heinz Army, all 57 varieties of it," as an Indian general once called it, it was a fact of life India had to live with.[28]

Russians have been India's main arms suppliers since the mid-Sixties. Diversification is a second best option; self-reliance in arms has been a credo with India's leaders almost since independence in 1947.

For a Third World country, India's strides in arms manufacture have been impressive. It has one of the most sophisticated and advanced military-industrial bases in the developing world.[29] In 1984, India was producing under licence various versions of the Soviet supersonic MIG-21 fighters, including their power plant, and assembling MIG-23s and MIG-27s; Leander class frigates and the indigenously modified and improved Godavari; and weapons, including anti-tank and anti-aircraft guns, mortars, rockets and mines. India has also been producing the Ishapore semi-automatic rifle, its own medium tank, the Vijayanta, and the indigenously developed Marut fighter, now supersonic with a speed of 1.3 Mach.[30]

But unlike in atomic energy and space, where notable progress had been made, defence technology remained grounded in crucial areas. This was not for want of ambition. India started developing its own supersonic fighter back in the Fifties, but it was stumped for a power plant. After many experiments and an agreement with Egypt for developing a suitable engine,[31] which came to nothing, the Soviets agreed in 1962 to modify an engine to fit the airframe of the Indian HF-24.[32] India was ultimately compelled to use the British Orpheus 703 engine licence-produced domestically, but its performance was lower than specified by the Indian Air Force.

There were many reasons for Indian disappointments. There was no comparable civil structure in the field of high technology.[33] The money spent on research and development (R & D) represented about 2 per cent of the defence budget, even after increases.[34] Above all, there had been the failure to throw up a leader of stature in defence technology.

The most comprehensive statement on defence strategy in the Eighties was made by C. Subramaniam, then Defence Minister, to the National Defence College in New Delhi on October 29, 1979. He said the Indian armed forces would need to acquire greater mobility and firepower in relation to Pakistan and China. There would be a generational change of weapons, and hence their modernization and improvement.

In the early Eighties, more than 30 per cent of the defence budget went into weapons, a figure that is bound to increase.[35] The process of modernizing the forces by major weapon replacements meant larger defence spending. Defence Minister Venkataraman told Parliament in May 1983 that India planned to import $1.07 billion worth of weapons for the fiscal year ending in March 1984.[36] India was to spend $6.63 billion on defence in 1983-84, compared to $5.8 billion the previous year.[37]

Although defence expenditure had risen twice as much as the rate of growth of total government expenditure in recent years, the 1980 figures represented a $8 per capita expenditure for India, compared to $15 per capita for Pakistan and $28 for China. In 1980, India ranked 117th among 142 countries in per capita defence spending; the figures for Pakistan and China were 91st and 73rd.[38]

India had come a long way from having a "parade-ground Army," as

Defence Minister Krishna Menon used to call it in the late Fifties.[39] In 1984, India's army was the fourth largest in the world, comprising 960,000 men, and the total armed forces were 1.12 million strong. This compared with Pakistan's army of 450,000 and total forces of 478,600.[40]

Pakistan is one-eighth India's size, and, despite having lost half the country to the independent nation of Bangladesh in the 1971 war with India, it increased its budget to $1.9 billion in 1983-84.[41]

The deployment of troops along the Indo-Pakistani border remained the same with a rough numerical parity, despite the Soviet intervention in Afghanistan, although India maintained ten mountain divisions along the Sino-Indian border and had a radar screen to guard against China.[42] The China factor brought about the Indo-Soviet military relationship and remained the single most important factor in this link, but India's efforts at self-reliance in conventional weapons and acquisition of major advanced weapons were finely tuned to Pakistani capabilities.

At the Twelfth Congress at Varanasi, the Communist Party of India proclaimed that "our party is much more unified now than at the time of the Bhatinda Congress." In the presence of E.A. Shevardnadze, alternate member of the Soviet Politburo, it confirmed its 1978 anti-Mrs. Gandhi line on domestic issues while supporting her foreign policy with some reservations. Shevardnadze, on his part, said that ". . . the realistic approach of the Government of India towards events around Afghanistan . . . [is] highly appreciated in the Soviet Union."[43]

Predictably, the CPI attacked China. "The present moves of Beijing," it declaimed, "to normalize relations with India are nothing but a clever tactic to undermine and weaken Indo-Soviet friendship, to blunt our vigilance against the global Washington-Beijing conspiracies and to inveigle India into acquiescing in these."[44]

At the Twenty-sixth CPSU Congress in early 1981, CPI General Secretary Rajeswara Rao had condemned "the heinous role of the new Chinese leadership in the international arena and accused China of trying to undermine India's close friendly relations with the Soviet Union."[45] The Marxists, on the other hand, criticized Brezhnev's policy for not according priority to normalization of relations with the Chinese Communist party.[46] At the same time the CPI(M) had attacked Polish Solidarity leader Lech Walesa as an "imposter" and favoured the use of Soviet force, if found necessary.[47]

Reviewing the previous four years' developments, the Congress launched a frontal attack on Mrs. Gandhi: "It did not take much time for the unfolding of vested interests, antipeople and antidemocratic policies of the Indira Gandhi government in the internal sphere, though broadly pursuing the progressive foreign policy of our country with some vacillations."[48]

Former CPI chairman S.A. Dange won expected rebuke. "He [Dange] projected the crassest reformist line that Indira Gandhi represents nonmonopoly patriotic bourgeoisie, that Indira Gandhi would complete the national-democratic revolution within the capitalist framework and that she is pursuing socialist oriented policies."[49]

Mrs. Gandhi's visit to Moscow in September proved to be rather routine in most respects, despite efforts on both sides to drum up enthusiasm. There was no agreement on Afghanistan, and the joint communiqué took thirty-five hours to work out.[50] The truth was that Brezhnev was a very sick man and there was no private meeting between the two leaders without their delegations.[51] Rather, the visit was significant on two other counts.

At a press conference in Moscow for foreign journalists, Mrs. Gandhi said she had told the Soviet leaders that India would like to see Soviet troops leave Afghanistan because "we are against interference of any kind." Although she also gave the other side of the picture, according to the Indian formulation, Tass omitted her remarks about outside troops.[52]

More significantly, Mrs. Gandhi indulged in a calculated act of brinkmanship by twice raising the question of the Indian Communists' opposition to her during her Soviet tour. The first time she had apparently taken up the question with Brezhnev, without any immediate response from him. The second time, according to Indian press accounts, she told Gromyko of "efforts of left parties in India to weaken and destabilize her government."[53] She was holding the Soviets responsible for the conduct of the CPI and daring them to come clean.

Mrs. Gandhi also had an oblique swipe at *Pravda*, which had, on August 15, 1982, carried an article on India which had focussed on the fact that "half of the population of India—350 million people—live below the 'poverty line'." The Press Trust of India reported in a dispatch from Tallin that Mrs. Gandhi said, "Poverty remains, but many of our people have been raised above the poverty line."[54]

Mrs. Gandhi's provocative references to the Indian Communists had an interesting fallout. The well-known Soviet academic Rostislav Ulyanovsky wrote an article on India in the November-December issue of *Asia and Africa Today* to give an appearance of support for Mrs. Gandhi. He stressed that Mrs. Gandhi's party had returned to power in 1980 by winning the trust of lower strata in particular, that it was fighting against "right reactionary forces," that it was an organization of "relative historical progressiveness" and the party could boast of Mrs. Gandhi's charisma and qualities as an "outstanding stateswoman." Ulyanovsky's advice was that "disunity between the democratic movement and forces of social progress" should be ended.[55]

The Central Secretariat of the CPI was provoked to issue a statement on December 27 saying that "there is no international Communist guiding centre as in the days of the Communist International. Our party, as every other Communist party, chalks out its own political policy.... We want to reiterate that our party stands by the political line laid down at the Twelfth Party Congress held at Varanasi in April 1982 [i.e., of opposition to Mrs. Gandhi's domestic policies]."[56]

Dange scored a debating point by suggesting that to assert that the CPI leadership was "not guided by the Communist Party of the Soviet Union is a patently false statement." The CPI leadership, he said, had been meeting CPSU leaders "almost every year" to discuss the Indian situation. "The guidance of the CPSU leaders has been generally helpful."[57] Since the CPI statement was issued after Rajeswara Rao's return from Moscow, it presumably had Soviet support. In any case, the Soviets gave no indication that they wished the CPI to return to supporting Mrs. Gandhi, who had, however, achieved the purpose of causing further confusion in CPI ranks.

The Soviets were closely monitoring problems between China and the Reagan Administration, and in February 1982 renewed their invitation to China for reviving border talks. The Chinese did not immediately respond, and while waiting for a change in Beijing's attitude, Moscow kept up a campaign against China's relations with the U.S. and Japan.

For Washington, Moscow had by no means disinterested advice. "Americans, bewitched by anti-Sovietism in Beijing's foreign policy," said Moscow, "ignore the fact that China nevertheless is on the opposite side of the world social divide from the United States. So what today seems a gain may turn out for the Americans a capital failure tomorrow or the day after."[58]

The most significant Soviet overture to China came in March 1982. In a speech at Tashkent, Brezhnev called for normalization of relations based on mutual benefit and confidence-building measures along the Sino-Soviet border, accepted China's bona fides as a socialist state and disavowed any claims or threats against China. Although the Chinese responded by asking for "deeds, not words," it was clear that a new phase in the troubled Sino-Soviet relations had begun.[59]

Signs of a change in Chinese policy were appearing on the horizon since the summer of 1981 after the sixth plenum of the Eleventh Congress. Hu Yaobang was elected party chairman and a reassessment was made of Mao's role in China's revolution. The pragmatists were gaining ground and with them the idea of reviving a relationship with Moscow and East Europe, particularly for making up the economic lag. For military modernization, the Chinese wanted to go to the West for arms and technology but hoped to neutralize attacks from Moscow by building up better relations.

The degree of change was reflected in the Twelfth Party Congress in 1982. It propounded the thesis on the possibility of improving relations with Moscow and, what was music to Soviet ears, equated the U.S. with the Soviet Union as a "hegemonic" power.[60] China moderated its criticism of Third World countries close to the Soviet Union and began a dialogue with the French Communist Party. It increasingly condemned U.S. policies in Korea, the Middle East, South Africa and Central America.

There was a perceptible increase in day-to-day relations between China and the Soviet Union, with Chinese economic specialists and gymnasts coming to Moscow and Soviet athletes going to China. In April, a trade pact was signed projecting increases, and in October border talks, broken off after the Soviet military intervention in Afghanistan, were resumed at the level of the Soviet vice foreign minister, Leonid Ilichev.

The crowning of the renewed Sino-Soviet dialogue occurred during Brezhnev's funeral in November. Huang Hua, although due to retire as foreign minister shortly thereafter, was sent to Moscow to represent his country. With a world audience watching, Brezhnev's successor, Yuri Andropov, spent several moments talking to Huang.

Later, the Chinese Foreign Minister had a ninety-minute substantive meeting with Gromyko, with Xinhua reporting that he "discussed with him [Gromyko] ways of removing obstacles and promoting consultations between the vice ministers of foreign affairs of the two countries so as to achieve progress on substantive matters."[61]

During Mrs. Gandhi's visit to the Soviet Union in September 1982, it was Brezhnev's turn to assure her that any improvement in Sino-Soviet relations would not mean dilution of the quality of Indo-Soviet relations.[62] While the Sino-Soviet dialogue could pose problems for India's future policies, it enabled Mrs. Gandhi to quicken the pace of Sino-Indian rapprochement. Two further rounds of border talks were held with China and, although no substantive progress was made on the border question, both sides were keen to maintain an atmosphere of cordiality and achieve progress in other fields. After the third round of talks, Xinhua said "both sides were positive in their attitude in negotiations on the boundary question, and the air was friendly."[63]

For the first time since 1960, the annual report of the Indian Defence Ministry for 1981-82 did not list China as a principal threat to national security. The exchange of visitors between the two countries grew dramatically. Mrs. Gandhi's senior foreign policy advisor, G. Parthasarathi, met Deng Xiaoping in October 1982 under the guise of leader of a team of Indian social scientists. Deng called for better relations with India and said there was no mutual threat between the two countries despite the border dispute. He suggested that it was not difficult to settle the border issue as long as both sides took reasonable measures.[64]

Foreign Minister Narasimha Rao told an interviewer in June 1982, "It is our wish to improve relations with China and solve all outstanding problems so that relations can truly be called normal."[65] Despite the two countries' efforts to maintain the momentum for better relations, the year ended on a somewhat sour note. India had staged the Asian Games in November in New Delhi with much pride and precision and had gone out of its way to welcome and applaud the Chinese team.

At the Games' closing ceremony, a participating dance troupe from Arunachal Pradesh caused Chinese ire. Although the Chinese had said they were prepared to accept India's claims along the eastern border, it was to be part of a settlement of the whole border. A pro forma protest to the Indian External Affairs Ministry would thus have been in order, but the Chinese chose to attack India publicly through Xinhua for using the Games to assert its "discreditable" claim to territory.[66]

The Indian government described the Chinese comment as "perverse" and decided to cancel a trip to China of a three-man official delegation to participate in ceremonies honouring the memory of an Indian doctor who had helped look after Chinese Communists during their struggle for power. Although India was careful to limit the damage by reiterating its intention "to persevere in our efforts at normalization and in the settlement of the border question which is central to the development of Sino-Indian relations,"[67] the Chinese attack aroused suspicions in New Delhi.

At the very least, the manner of the Chinese protest seemed to show an utter disregard for Indian susceptibilities, and there were earlier incidents to buttress this theory. China's decision to launch an attack on Vietnam during Foreign Minister Vajpayee's visit, the parallel the Chinese sought to draw between their 1979 action against Vietnam and the Sino-Indian border war, to name two instances. Some members of India's policy-making establishment wondered whether it indicated a measure of Chinese ambivalence to the long-term policy it should adopt towards India.[68]

The Soviets made no secret of their unhappiness over India's Mirage decision. But loath to lose their biggest arms market in the developing world, they did more than complain. During Defence Minister Venkataraman's visit to Moscow in June 1983, he was shown sketches of the Soviet futuristic planes under development, the MIG-29 and the MIG-31.[69] "The Soviets told the Indian team that the new planes would be better than F-16 and F-15. They also offered updated technology for T-72 and T-80 tanks and new submarines.[70]

The MIG-31 was still in the development stage although a prototype of the MIG-29 had reportedly been tested successfully. The Russians promised to give India the planes and subsequently a production licence. Indeed, the Russians had seldom been as forthcoming. Their earlier answer to Indian queries about their future military aircraft development had been vague in the extreme.[71]

An element of exploiting the East-West competition has never been absent from India's practice of nonalignment. The tempting Soviet offer was even more attractive for economic and practical reasons. The costs of retooling India's aircraft factories for Mirage-2000 would be astronomical. Since the Soviets believed in modular development of new planes and weapons, the existing Indian production lines would merely have to be adapted for a new generation of MIGs. Besides, Russians accepted payment in rupees, essentially for the export of Indian goods.

A key element in the Indian decision to accept the Soviet offer was the realization that an Indian-produced supersonic aircraft for the Nineties would simply not be available. With much regret, the goal of self-reliance in supersonic fighter planes was put off till the next century.[72]

By the fall of 1983, New Delhi had decided to scrap production plans for Mirage-2000[73] although it had not formally given up the production option in mid-1984. The decision set off a debate among India's policy-makers and small group of defence analysts, highlighting as it did the deficiencies in the country's arms technology.[74] Indeed, the Mirage decision showed the limits of diversification plans to reduce Indian dependence on Soviet arms, representing about 70 per cent of arms imports.[75]

There was agreement on one point: the sooner Indian defence technology can build up an indigenous arms manufacturing base in sophisticated aircraft and ships and in electronics, the better it will be for the country. Prime Minister Gandhi had dismissed suggestions of Indian military dependence on the Soviet Union as "quite baseless." In a speech in Parliament in April 1981, she declared, "In the matter of supplies and spares, no country can blackmail us in times of need."[76]

India's HJT-16 was the first jet aircraft designed by an Afro-Asian country without help from the superpowers.[77] But after two decades of research the country had not been able to produce a single missile system of its own. One problem has been obsolescence and changing requirements.

Two of the country's continuing efforts are the main battle tank and a supersonic aircraft. The development of an indigenous tank had been hindered by the failure to manufacture a suitable engine.[78] In the development of a supersonic fighter aircraft, R & D efforts focussed on first making a supersonic engine; some initial successes were achieved by the engine, GTX, but it still left unresolved the problem of a suitable airframe.[79]

If these failures were a reminder of the difficulties in gaining self-sufficiency in a technological age, the other side of the coin was that India produced about two-thirds of its weapons domestically. A major new thrust was concentrated on electronics and an ambitious ship-building programme was being undertaken, including the production of Godavari class (modified Leander) frigates.

There was genuine regret in India over the passing away of Brezhnev although it had been clear for much of 1982 that his era had, in fact, ended. Brezhnev had been associated with building up the Indo-Soviet relationship during the crucial 1970s, and despite his refusal to endorse Mrs. Gandhi's domestic policies since her return to power in 1980, he had a personal rapport with her. Andropov, by contrast, was an unknown quantity.

In her tribute to Brezhnev, Mrs. Gandhi said, "Indo-Soviet friendship and cooperation grew and achieved maturity during President Brezhnev's time. He showed consistent understanding of our problems and stood by us in our moments of need."[80] She went to Moscow for Brezhnev's funeral ceremonies and had a meeting with Andropov. Andropov's answer to Mrs. Gandhi's felicitations on his taking over supreme power was unexceptionable but hardly couched in Brezhnev's traditional warm tones. He wrote in July 1983, "I express my solidarity with you that further development of Soviet-Indian friendly relations meets the interests of our people and the cause of peace on earth."[81]

In 1982, the mood in Moscow was not optimistic. While Brezhnev was slowly fading away, Soviet officials were notching up the setbacks in the face of Reagan's offensive around the globe. The Polish crisis continued to create problems for Moscow and the Middle East situation, with the defeat of the Palestine Liberation Organisation and the "steadfast" states, was bad news for the Soviets. Moscow could see only slow improvement in relations with China. India, Soviet officials believed, had arrived at the capitalist road of development and they were worried over its hospitality to multinationals. All in all, the mood was one of caution;[82] which could only have been enhanced by the military stalemate in Afghanistan despite the more aggressive tactics Soviet troops employed in 1982.

An incipient debate on Soviet commitments around the world—perhaps an overcommitment to the Third World—seems to have surfaced on Andropov's accession to power. The new regime had, in fact, acknowledged past mistakes and initiated limited economic experiments. Andropov told the Central Committee on June 15, 1983 that "the threat of a nuclear war ... causes one to reappraise the principal goals ... of the entire Communist movement." And he suggested that the future "paramount direction" of Soviet foreign policy would be to intensify cooperation with the Soviet bloc.[83]

Among the visitors to Moscow for the Brezhnev funeral was Zia-ul-Haq, who had proved himself to be an astute diplomat in the pursuit of his country's interests. He undertook a successful visit to China in October 1982, telling Chinese leaders at a banquet in Beijing on October 16 that Pakistan would do its utmost to conclude a nonaggression agreement with India. Prime Minister Zhao Ziyang assured him that the Chinese government and people would, as always, resolutely support Pakistan in its "just struggle to resist threats and interference from outside and defend national independence and state security."[84]

The Chinese also encouraged Zia to normalize relations with India, a point which had been underlined by *Beijing Review* of January 26, 1981. "The necessity does exist," it said, "for these two subcontinental nations to stand together or, in other words, to unite and cooperate, and the need today is more pressing than ever." In a signal to India, the Chinese leaders did not refer to Kashmir in their public speeches and the Chinese media ignored Zia's references to the dispute.[85]

On November 1, 1982 Zia stopped over in New Delhi for a 210-minute meeting with Mrs. Gandhi and finally accepted her joint commission proposal of the previous January. India had successfully resisted Pakistani attempts to include armed forces' representatives in the commission. The commission, at the ministerial level, was actually set up in late December. The two leaders at their November meeting also directed their officials to take up the no-war and peace treaty proposals simultaneously to get over the dispute on which should be considered first.[86]

The Delhi summit won immediate welcome from China. "Better Indo-Pakistan relations," according to *People's Daily* of November 3, 1982, "are not only desired by the two peoples but also required for developments in South Asia and the whole world." But the summit left three questions unresolved: India's insistence that neither country should offer base facilities to outside powers; a definition of Pakistan's "right" to take the Kashmir issue to the U.N. and whether the line of control across Kashmir represented an inviolable international frontier for Pakistanis.

India suspected that Pakistan was wary of making a commitment on bases because of an impending agreement to permit the U.S. to build an electronic listening station. A London report that some sixty

American electronics and listening devices experts from Egypt had been asked to be ready to go to Pakistan further fuelled Indian suspicions.[87] Nor was New Delhi reassured by Zia's remark in a television interview in New York on December 12, 1982 that "for the time being" it was not his policy to allow any bases to the U.S. in Pakistan.[88]

In Moscow in November, Andropov made a significant gesture in receiving Zia privately. The Soviets had traditionally been following a carrot and stick approach for dealing with Pakistan since their intervention in Afghanistan. Condemnation and punitive measures had alternated with offers of economic assistance and ensuring Pakistan's security concerns. After the Pakistanis turned down the Soviet package in 1981 to accept American military assistance, neither side broke off the dialogue.

The Pakistanis had lost flexibility in negotiating a political settlement with Moscow by virtue of their new arms relationship with the U.S. and an implicit role in the American Persian Gulf strategy. But Zia was careful to impose limits on the quantity and kind of arms sent to the Afghan guerrillas through Pakistan.[89] And the Pakistanis made it clear that they were keen to maintain a vigorous economic relationship with Moscow.

While keeping up the flow of rhetoric against Pakistan and punitive raids to teach Pakistan a lesson, the Soviets were actively encouraging a political settlement in Afghanistan on their terms, in view of their mounting political costs. On the military plane, there was bitter and inconclusive fighting in the Panjsher Valley in 1982, but the military losses were not such that Moscow could not bear.[90]

The United Nations was at the centre of talks to resolve the Afghan problem. Beginning in April 1981, Perez de Cuellar, and later Diego Cordovez, undertook separate visits to Islamabad and Kabul. In April 1982 Cordovez visited Teheran for the first time. There was an agreement by the end of the year to begin indirect talks in Geneva.

On an official visit to the U.S. in December, Zia displayed considerable aplomb. He said that after his talk with Andropov "I have the feeling that there now exists on the Soviet side a recognition of the need for an early resolution of the crisis." So as not to alarm his hosts, he said the indirect talks on Afghanistan were still in a preliminary phase and "we will not accept Karmal."[91]

Zia denied that his country was a conduit for arms to Afghan guerrillas as he maintained the public posture of Pakistan not being part of wider American strategic aims. He said: "I would like to acknowledge the insight evidenced by the U.S. Administration which recognized that Pakistan's ability to maintain its territorial sovereignty and national independence constituted, in itself, sufficient recompense for the assistance that would be provided by the United States."[92]

Apart from Afghanistan, the Soviets' concerns in 1983 merged to a striking degree with countering the actions of the other superpower, the U.S., on two planes: the planned deployment of missiles in West Europe and American activities in Asia. In 1979, NATO had decided to install 572 Cruise and Pershing II missiles in West Germany, Britain, Italy, Belgium and the Netherlands starting in December 1983, in the absence of an agreement with the Russians.

The Soviets launched a major propaganda offensive in West Europe to have the deployment of the missiles deferred, if not eliminated. The central Soviet objective seemed to be the Pershing IIs, whose warning time of six to eight minutes was an unacceptable risk for Moscow. Reagan had come to power promising military superiority over the Russians and the significant increases in the American defence budget and the President's rhetoric had led to growing unease in West Europe.

The battleground for the propaganda war was the West German election in early March, and both sides presented new proposals tailored to show a reasonable stance. Despite widespread opposition to the deployment of new missiles in West Europe, Reagan won the round, with the Christian Democrats headed by Helmut Kohl winning the West German election. The Soviets waited for the beginning of the actual deployment and then pulled out of both the intermediate-range and longer-range strategic arms limitation talks.

The propaganda battle had a fallout on Asia. Both China and Japan were understandably worried that a compromise agreement on intermediate-range missiles in Europe would be made at the expense of stationing more of them in Asia, especially aimed at Japan. Andropov answered this concern by declaring in late summer that any SS-20 missiles taken out of Europe would not be stationed in the East if the U.S. made no new substantial deployments.[93] Soviet officials suggested an Asian security conference to include China and Japan to allay their fears on restationing missiles in Soviet Asia.[94]

The Soviets took note of American attempts to buttress the military relationship with Japan and South Korea, underlined by the

Reagan trip to Asia. Before the Reagan foray, a meeting of Communist European and Asian vice foreign ministers was called at Ulan Bator in late October to focus attention on the "broad front directed against the socialist countries" by the U.S. and the dangers presented by the Rapid Deployment Force.[95]

With China, the Soviets maintained the momentum for better relations. Three rounds of talks were held. Sino-Soviet differences on Afghanistan, Kampuchea and troop deployments along the Mongolian border were not bridged, but the Chinese tended to leave out the Kampuchean issue in particular to promote relations in other fields. An agreement was signed to double trade levels, the Soviets promised to modernize a textile mill in Harbin and there was a significant increase in day-to-day relations.[96]

Much of Indian attention was concentrated in the early months of 1983 on the nonaligned summit whose venue had been moved at the last minute from Baghdad, at war with Iran, to New Delhi. Most members of the movement were pressing for an early summit, despite Baghdad's untenability, to prise Cuba out of the chairmanship, and India was happy to fill the breach. India had made a major contribution to the founding of the movement, but had not hosted a summit before.

The Soviets took keen interest in preparations for the summit, principally with a view to limiting the damage caused by their action in Afghanistan. Early in 1983, Leonid Zhegalov sounded the Soviet note in *New Times*. He said, "Indian politicians and diplomats are now taking an active part in drafting resolutions for the coming forum and consulting with representatives of other nonaligned countries on a wide range of questions. Some topics, like the so-called Afghan and Kampuchean questions, are tossed in from outside the movement to divert the conference from the discussion of truly burning issues, issues of paramount importance for the cause of peace and the developing countries. Delhi's stand on these questions is unambiguous."[97]

The Soviet approach won a rebuke from China, a Xinhua commentary on February 10, 1983 accusing Moscow of wanting to stifle debate on the two issues. It particularly criticized *Pravda* for suggesting that the nonaligned summit should not take up the Afghan and Kampuchean issues. In a defensive move, the Soviets had decided not to encourage their friends to raise the question of Communist countries being the "natural allies" of the nonaligned, an issue that had caused bitter debate at the Havana summit in 1979.

The Soviets were banking on India to guide the summit through the shoals of Afghanistan and Kampuchea, a goal which coincided with New Delhi's objective of bringing the summit to a successful conclusion. India's strategy was to emphasize issues of war and peace and economic development and give a global perspective to problems, instead of getting bogged down in regional issues. But there were no illusions about the contentious nature of the Afghan and Kampuchean problems.

Indian officials undertook visits to some forty countries before preparing a draft.[98] Pakistan had indicated to India before the summit, apparently in view of the progress being made in the informal talks through the U.N. mechanism, that it was not interested in histrionics, and in view of the attitude of the front-line state, there was little incentive for others to belabour the point. Kampuchea was another matter.

India was on the defensive, having recognized the Heng Samrin regime, and had to bend over backwards to give Singapore and other like-minded countries the impression that it was playing fair. But it was clear in its mind that the only solution of the problem, as far as the summit was concerned, was to follow the Havana precedent in leaving the seat vacant. India successfully resisted the ASEAN flanking move, backed by China and the U.S., to get Prince Sihanouk to address the meeting, provoking mild criticism from China, in *Beijing Review* of February 20, that the Indian decision was "irrational and incomprehensible."[99]

But the Chinese made it amply clear that they looked upon the summit and India's role in it benignly. In an interview to the Press Trust of India in Beijing, Yu Mengjia of the Foreign Ministry said China would not like the summit to be divided over immediate issues such as Cambodia and Afghanistan, but would like it to take a united stand on long-term issues such as opposition to imperialism and "hegemonism" and support for the New International Economic Order.[100]

G.L. Bondavesky arrived in Delhi at the head of a Soviet team to observe the summit, declaring in a somewhat blatant attempt at flattery: "The seventh summit will be the most crucial in the history of the movement. You now have the right lady at the right place and the right time."[101] India had earlier taken note of the withdrawal of Soviet naval units from the Indian Ocean in February followed by a sharp reduction in the number of American naval ships in those waters. The two moves were viewed in New Delhi as gestures to the summit.[102]

The twenty-three-page Indian draft, couched in moderate language, criticized the U.S. in two instances but focussed on economic and disarmament issues and dealt with most of the contentious issues tersely. The Soviets could not have been too happy with the draft; a CPI leader, Sadhan Mukherji, said it "leaves much to be desired" and criticized it for being "low key" and "liable to further dilution as a result of reactionary pressures which are already on."[103]

Singapore led the field in tying up the foreign ministers' meeting on Kampuchea for nearly three days, ultimately accepting the compromise that criteria for expelling members would be considered and reported to the foreign ministers' plenary meeting in 1985. Cambodia's seat remained vacant in New Delhi.

In the end, India's draft was stretched to ninety-two pages, with the U.S. standing condemned fifteen times while the Soviet Union was only once bracketed with the other superpower in the arms race and, in another instance, by implication in the responsibilities of the industrialized towards the developing world. The exceptional length and stridency of the declaration on regional issues, particularly the Middle East, was not entirely to India's liking, but it succeeded in saving the essence of the economic resolution which was sober and nonpolemical and called for a global economic conference. Mrs. Gandhi also took the exceptional step of publicly appealing to Iran and Iraq to seek peace.

Pravda chose to put the best face on the summit, suggesting on March 13, 1983 that "the nonaligned movement has displayed devotion to its basic principles of struggle against imperialism, colonialism, racism and war." The final declaration and the Delhi Message, it said, reflected "the deep interconnection between the struggle for full and all-around decolonization and the struggle for stronger peace and the prevention of nuclear war."[104] Later, M.F. Menashev, leader of a Soviet delegation to the Congress party's plenary session in Calcutta, praised India's "constructive ideas" and initiatives as chairman of the nonaligned movement.[105]

In July, the Soviets made a gesture to Mrs. Gandhi by inviting Rajiv Gandhi, the Prime Minister's elder son who had entered politics and was being groomed as her successor. The high-level meetings and receptions laid out for Rajiv were interpreted by one

Indian observer as his being "virtually anointed by the Soviet commissars as the unquestioned successor to Mrs. Gandhi."[106] But for Andropov, who perhaps needed to conserve his strength at that time, Rajiv met almost everyone of note, including Ustinov, Gromyko, Arkhipov, Kuznetsov, Ponomarev and Foreign Trade Minister Patolichev.

Perhaps this was a Soviet way of pleasing Mrs. Gandhi since Moscow did not wish to deliver the Indian Communist party to her. Immediately after Rajiv's return from Moscow, the pro-Communist, as distinguished from the CPI, press began lavishing praise on him. Mrs. Gandhi had, indeed, kept up pressure on Moscow and the CPI. Although what became known as the "letter episode" surfaced in the Indian press only in the fall of 1983, it was initiated by Mrs. Gandhi in June.

Mrs. Gandhi sent a letter to Andropov in June through a member of the CPI timed with the Soviet observance of the victory over Nazis. The letter made the point that the left in India—meaning the CPI—was hindering her work, rather than helping her. The bearer of the letter, Yogendra Sharma, was not received by Andropov, and the Soviets took the precaution of informing the CPI of what the letter said. Sharma was later expelled from the CPI's major policy-making body, an action that further exacerbated divisions in the party.[107]

Another major source of friction between India and the Soviet Union in the first half of 1983 was in the important field of trade. The pattern of this trade had been changing in the 1970s, with the Soviets agreeing to sell India 1.5 million tons of oil for rupees in 1973. In fact, in 1983, the Soviets became the largest supplier of oil to India, making commitments to sell 3.5 million tons of crude and 2.5 million tons of kerosene,[108] provoking an Indian economic analyst to suggest that the traditional North-South relationship had been reversed.[109] Crude and oil products constituted over 80 per cent of Soviet exports to India, and Moscow had displaced the U.S. as New Delhi's largest trading partner in 1982.[110]

The turnover in Indo-Soviet trade increased eight-and-one-half times between 1970-71 and 1981-82, showing sharp fluctuations and a dramatic increase from 1979 to 1982.[111] Short-term factors were responsible for this phenomenal increase. The spurt in oil prices gave Moscow more purchasing power and the drop in Soviet economic growth beginning in 1979 increased Moscow's demand for agricultural products and consumer goods.

The revised budget estimates for 1982-83 provided for Rs. 12,800 million in "technical credits" to meet "temporary imbalances" in India's rupee payment trade, largely with the Soviet Union. In the Soviet view this imbalance in India's favour was far from temporary; according to one estimate, India's trade surplus in 1982 was Rs. 6,680 million.[112] The trade surplus, however, cannot be equated with the balance of payments surplus because trade carries the burden of repayment of economic aid and military transactions.[113] Since payments on the last item are not made public, estimates can at best be educated guesses.

Indo-Soviet trade is conducted entirely in rupees and is based on the principle of striking a balance. Over the years, Moscow has been sufficiently concerned with the imbalance to urge India to buy more capital goods. The basic problem was that India's requirements in the 1970s and 1980s were very different from what they were in the Fifties. Self-sufficiency in capital goods industries shifted the country's demand away from capital goods to raw materials.[114]

Besides, the new liberal economic policy, partly determined by the Indian realization of the imperative need to modernize its industry, meant greater imports from the West and Japan. India thus preferred to go in for French technology for an alumina plant, Italian know-how for a Soviet-aided pharmaceuticals company, Japanese collaboration for the automobile industry and several thousand agreements with Western companies for modernizing Indian industry.

The Soviet agreement to sell India more oil was, in effect, a reluctant and short-term effort to maintain the level of trade. The Soviets were sufficiently alarmed over the long-term trend to fire a warning shot across the bow. In 1983, they suddenly withdrew from Indian markets and temporarily suspended shipment of goods. India's dependence on Soviet and East European markets in certain areas has been considerable. In percentage terms, the rupee trade area accounted for 96.8 of exports in knitwear (acrylic), 83 in cosmetics, detergents and toiletries, 76 in mica, 69 in pepper, 65 in cashews, 45 in coffee, 42 in drugs and pharmaceuticals, 41.6 in tobacco and 23 in textiles.[115]

Indian exporters were unable to find alternate markets and the Soviet move caused acute distress. In the Kandla free trade zone, fifteen out of ninety industrial units had to stop production with another twenty-five seriously affected. Many of these had been set up to meet Soviet demand. Over 120 cashew factories in Kerala were rendered idle and 200,000 workers reportedly lost their jobs.

Even before the drastic and heavy-handed method the Soviets used to make their point that India must buy more from Moscow, they were not chary of spreading their message. In sharp contrast to the euphemisms they traditionally used in relation to India, Victor P. Senin, Soviet trade representative, told an Indian journal in November 1982, "It appears that certain circles in India are against increasing purchases from the Soviet Union." The Soviet Union, he added, had "no intention of changing the pattern of payments," declaring, "Can you give an example of any country supplying you with oil and oil products and buying in exchange garments and other consumer items?"[116]

Senin was even more forthright in spelling out the basis on which the Soviets conducted their trade. "Commerce is commerce. Every businessman looks for advantages even while dealing with the most friendly partners."[117] "We too need hard currency. Our reserves are limited and we can't cope with all the orders for gold and diamonds."[118] The last point was made in response to Indian hopes of obtaining these items from the Soviet Union.

Indian officials warned the Soviets that their abrupt withdrawal from the market would have political repercussions. Large parts of the country were dependent upon Soviet trade: Punjab in hosiery, Kerala in cashews, U.P. in shoe uppers, Andhra in tobacco, apart from several enterprises set up specifically to cater to the Soviet demand. To Indian exporters, the Government sent out a message that they should diversify their markets.

During Mrs. Gandhi's visit to Moscow in September 1982, the trade issue was discussed, and the six-day visit to New Delhi of Arkhipov in May 1983 was a follow-up to the Moscow talks. Arkhipov signed a credit agreement of $140 million for the second stage of the Visakhapatnam steel plant. He also brought offers of two nuclear power plants of 440 megawatts each, four more thermal power stations of 200 megawatts each and new oil refineries.[119]

The offer of a 1,000 megawatt nuclear power plant was first made to the Janata government and repeated to Mrs. Gandhi in Moscow in 1982. India did not want to go in for such a large plant and the Arhkipov proposal was tailored to meet New Delhi's preference. India's reluctance to accept the amended offer flowed from the fact that it would mean a reorientation of its nuclear programme, based on a different technology, and posed the vexatious question of safeguards. The Soviets had proved unwilling to waive international safeguards on heavy water.

The other offers had to be declined for financial reasons. India said it could not provide the required 60 per cent of local costs during the Sixth Plan. The Soviets, on their part, were reluctant to include local costs in their aid package.[120] The trade quarrel, was, however, patched up during 1983 by India promising to try harder to import Soviet machinery and the Soviets beginning a determined effort to interest the Indian private sector in Soviet industrial products.[121]

A new trade protocol for 1984 was signed on December 9, 1983 in New Delhi in Arkhipov's presence, projecting a 24 per cent increase over the 1983 level, to rise to a record $3.84 billion. But imports from India accounted for less than 3 per cent of Soviet trade. The lopsided nature of the agreement was clear from the fact that more than 95 per cent of Soviet exports to India would be in the form of raw materials. Machinery represented only eight per cent of Soviet sales to India in 1982.[122] Having made their point, the Soviets were willing to coast along for a time, but they did not restore all items on the list they had stopped buying in early 1983.[123]

Chapter Ten

TURMOIL

THE year 1983 was a troubled one for Mrs. Gandhi and India, despite notable successes in foreign policy and in the economic field. After hosting the nonaligned summit in March, thus securing the crown of chairperson of the movement for the next three years, India played host to Commonwealth heads of government later in the year, a task performed with equal precision and aplomb.

In the economic field, the world was beginning to take note of India as "an emerging industrial power," with manufactures accounting for 60 per cent of exports.[1] Although agriculture remained a dominant part of the economy, accounting for two-thirds of the work force, a growing middle class of more than 100 million were members of an expanding modern sector.

The Indian economy rebounded from the drought year of 1979-80 and the sharp rise in oil prices and resulting inflationary pressures with two years of solid growth. The Indo-American Chamber of Commerce estimated that U.S. investment grew from $396 million in 1980 to about $500 million in 1982, with approved collaborations with the U.S. accounting for 210 out of a total of 915.

While creeping inflation was causing concern in 1983, Mrs. Gandhi's major problems lay in the domestic political field.[2] The year started badly for her, with the Congress party losing the two southern states of Andhra Pradesh and Karnataka, which Mrs. Gandhi had retained even during her otherwise disastrous performance in the 1977 elections. Although the Congress won the Delhi poll in February, its debacle in the south showed up the party's weaknesses. A shadow of its former self, the Congress was held together only by Mrs. Gandhi's strong personality.

Some steps were taken to energize the Congress and Rajiv was appointed a party general secretary. The impending general elections, which Mrs. Gandhi was obliged to hold by January 1985, cast their long shadow on the conduct of the government and political parties, but the level of ethnic and religious violence was beginning to claim equal, if not greater, attention. A long smouldering agitation in Assam in the northeast in which the Assamese demanded the deportation of about one million "foreigners" proved intractable. Assam has been subject to waves of migration from East Pakistan and later Bangladesh and militant students and an Assamese party feared that their Assamese identity would be lost by the inundation of Bengalis.

The major dispute between the Assamese agitators and the federal government lay in the cutoff point after which new arrivals would have to leave. The problem was complicated by constitutionally mandated general elections in February. The students called for a boycott, with the support of the non-Communist opposition parties. The result was an eruption of ghastly violence in rural areas. In Nellie village, the Lalung tribals killed at least a thousand Bengalis.

The Congress won, but the voter turnout was less than 33 per cent and it was a hollow victory. The killings led to inevitable recriminations between the government and the opposition parties, ultimately leading to a government commitment to build a half-billion dollar fence along the Bangladesh border.[3]

In the northern state of Punjab, in the meantime, a Sikh agitation for religious and economic demands was gathering steam. The Akali coalition had lost out to the Congress in the 1980 elections and at the heart of the agitation was the political frustration of the Sikhs' party, the Akali Dal, over losing power and a more basic fear of the Sikhs losing their identity. Sikhs were only 14 million in India's population of 700 million.

Several rounds of talks between the Sikh leaders and the government produced no compromise settlement. Mrs. Gandhi accepted their major religious demands, but insisted that they withdraw the agitation before their specific points on Chandigarh, the Le Corbusier-designed state capital shared by Punjab and Haryana, and share of irrigation water could be referred to a tribunal. The Sikh demand for greater state autonomy, also voiced by other opposition-ruled states, was met by the appointment of a commission headed by a retired Supreme Court judge, himself a Sikh.

Instead of running out of steam, the Sikh agitation was increasingly taking a violent turn. To an extent, the moderate mainstream faction of the Akali Dal had coopted the radicals, including the fundamentalist leader, Sant Jarnail Singh

Bhindranwale, to exert greater pressure on Mrs. Gandhi. The level of violence was increasing, inviting retaliation from Hindus, with a consequent feeling of insecurity in the state.

While India was experiencing bouts of ethnic violence, similar violence, between the majority Sinhalese and the Tamil minority, erupted on the neighbouring island of Sri Lanka, leading to the murder of hundreds of separatist Tamils. The explosive potential of this conflict, given the Tamils' ethnic ties to the 45 million-plus inhabitants of the Indian state of Tamil Nadu, posed problems for Mrs. Gandhi.

A news agency report from Colombo, suggesting that President Jayawardene had asked for military assistance from the U.S., Britain, Pakistan and Bangladesh because he feared Indian intervention, was hardly conducive to calm Indian fears. Mrs. Gandhi acted with restraint, and offered India's good offices to help resolve the problem while publicly accepting the integrity of the Sri Lankan state.

In the process, India formulated a South Asian doctrine, declaring that while it would not intervene in a nation's internal conflict, it would not tolerate an outside power's intervention if it was against Indian interests. If help was to be sought to resolve an internal conflict, it should be from South Asian nations, including India.[4]

Pakistan had its own crop of problems, with Zia facing his most serious challenge in the six years he had been in power. In the fall of 1983, the Movement for the Restoration of Democracy began an agitation in the Sind province which spread widely. For a time it seemed that the support it gathered in the province would end as previous agitations had, in the fall of the military ruler.

Representing about 25 per cent of Pakistan's population, Sindhis are outside the military power structure and resent the fact that the leader they contributed to the country, Bhutto, was executed by a Punjabi-dominated army. Zia rode out the storm, thanks to the army's brutality in suppressing the agitation and because it failed to ignite the Punjab masses. He had placed Bhutto's widow and daughter in varying degrees of detention for most of the period since Bhutto's ouster. After the hijacking of the Pakistani plane, the military regime again arrested Benazir, together with her mother and other opposition leaders, on March 8, 1981. She remained under detention at the end of 1983.[5]

With both Pakistan and India coping with serious domestic conflicts, the temptation was irresistible to blame the other party.

India took offence over the stridently anti-Indian campaign in the Pakistan press and charged it with encouraging the Sikhs' agitation in Punjab by supplying agitators with arms and training to fan the demand for a separate state of Khalistan, espoused by a small minority. India's compulsions were also determined by Mrs. Gandhi's electoral needs. Facing a difficult general election, it was in her interest to exaggerate the darkening regional and world environment and present herself as the only truly national leader who could handle the situation.[6]

Mrs. Gandhi laid herself open to the charge of interference by expressing her concern to party members over the happenings in Pakistan, justifying the struggle for democracy in the country. According to one newspaper account, she said while affirming India's desire to see democracy everywhere that the country could not shut its eyes to what was happening in Pakistan [the Sind agitation] because it had repercussions in India.[7] This provoked an immediate protest from Pakistan.[8]

In November 1983, Mrs. Gandhi warned her party workers about war clouds "on the Indian horizon" and threats of war "from across the border", causing something of a scare in both India and Pakistan.[9] It was suggested by an Indian commentator close to the government that the Prime Minister was reacting to Pakistani troop movements along the border from cantonments to forward positions and a provocative dinner Zia hosted for the diplomatic corps in Gilgit in disputed Kashmir.[10]

It was not long thereafter that Minister of State K.P. Singh Deo shot down this theory. He told Parliament on November 15 that it was a season for military exercises in both India and Pakistan and Pakistani forces could well be undertaking exercises and training to familiarize their ranks with new weapons acquired from the U.S.[11] The Indian Defence Ministry had suggested in its annual report, released in March, that India needed to be very vigilant, while continuing its efforts to normalize relations with Pakistan, in view of the sophisticated arms being acquired by that country, which is also "taking the path to nuclear weaponry."[12]

Pakistan had received a special six-year exemption from the provisions of the Symington and Glenn amendments, and India's concern over Zia's nuclear plans was fuelled by persistent reports in the Western press. Mrs. Gandhi told a British newspaper in February 1983 that India "had nothing to fear" if Pakistan was building its nuclear facilities for non-military use. But she added: "I don't think they are going to use it for peaceful purposes."[13] She told the London weekly *Musawaat* in April that "Pakistan's providing base facilities to the U.S. Rapid Deployment Force would certainly go against the spirit of the [nonaligned] declaration of the Indian Ocean as a zone of peace. It would also greatly complicate the situation in our part of the world."[14]

In a book released in Moscow in July 1983, two Soviet authors charged that Pakistan "is being helped by Saudi Arabia in manufacturing its own hydrogen bomb."[15] Zia countered with the suggestion that reports about a Pakistani bomb were mischievous and had been floated to create misunderstanding between Pakistan and India and several other countries.[16]

Indeed, Pakistan was sending out mixed signals. Provocative statements and actions were interspersed with suggestions that it was turning over a new leaf. In an attempt to influence the Indian elite, Foreign Minister Yakub and his officials in Islamabad gave copious interviews to an Indian political analyst in June 1983 to put forward a series of appealing theories. The Pakistanis suggested that they no longer took a "global view" of Afghanistan and had come round to the belief that they must improve relations with Moscow and New Delhi simultaneously. Further, "Pakistan now sees the Soviet Union as a South Asian power with permanent political and security interests in the region."[17]

Despite the troubled relationship, neither India nor Pakistan wished to close the door to future negotiations. India was keener to maintain a dialogue with China even as it was recognized in New Delhi that Mrs. Gandhi's domestic concerns were too pressing to permit a breakthrough. India's efforts were also spurred by moves towards a Sino-Soviet accommodation. For its part, Chinese Foreign Minister Wu Xueqian told an interviewer in March 1983, "China holds that both China and India should set store by Sino-Indian friendship and proceed from the actual conditions—the realities— and seek a just, reasonable and comprehensive settlement in a spirit of mutual understanding and accommodation through peaceful consultations. There is no other way out except this one."[18]

The Chinese had been trying to get the Dalai Lama home since 1977. The Dalai Lama sent his representatives to Tibet thrice since 1979 and himself planned a visit for 1985. But he told an interviewer in May 1984 that although "my desire is still to go there," "many

Tibetans sent verbal and written messages that, although they want to see me as early as possible, under the present circumstances I should not come." Further, he said a visit by him should be aimed at giving "some benefit to the Tibetan people," observing that arrests had followed visits by his representatives. He had given up plans for permanently going home.[19]

Mrs. Gandhi met Chinese Vice Premier Yao Yilin at Belgrade on June 9 and Yao referred to the "positive progress" made in Sino-Indian relations in the past few years. The Indian Prime Minister said she had always attached great importance to relations between the two countries.[20] Vice Premier Wan Li met two Indian members of Parliament the next month and called for joint efforts to improve relations.[21]

In April, a three-man Indian Marxist delegation had a third round of talks in Beijing to restore party to party relations. Hu Yaobang, who led the Chinese delegation, told the Marxists on April 25 that China had no territorial ambitions against any neighbouring country. "All we want is to resolve border disputes fairly, and reasonably."[22] Although the CPI(M), rather than the Chinese, had somewhat delayed the restoration of relations, the significance of this step was not lost upon India or China.

In May, the Marxist leader, E.M.S. Namboodiripad, told a press conference that while his party "could not see eye to eye with the Soviet party or the Chinese party" on the splitting of the world Communist movement, it had "always held it important that the cordial India-China relations that were established in the first half of the 1950s should be maintained and strengthened." Further, the CPI(M) had been "consistent and uncompromising" in its struggle against U.S. imperialism.[23] An immediate fallout of the restoration of relations between the Marxists and the Chinese Communist party was a slanging match between the Marxists and the CPI.[24]

But the hobgoblin in Sino-Indian relations again raised its head. An early August issue of the Chinese magazine *World Knowledge* carried a first installment of excerpts from a salacious account written by M.O. Mathai, a controversial and one-time aide of Nehru, on the first Prime Minister and Mrs. Gandhi, leading to an Indian protest. The depth of Indian feelings can be gauged by an editorial in *The Times of India* of August 30, 1983 titled "The Slandering Mandarins." The editorial made the point that it was in rank bad taste and uncharacteristic of Chinese behaviour. Beijing had not made such attacks on the Soviets even at the height of their exchanges. The Chinese did not publish the promised second installment to soothe Indian feelings.

Reports of U.S. suspension of talks on nuclear cooperation with China in September 1982, stemming from Washington's suspicions of a Sino-Pakistani collaboration in the field, had earlier caused misgivings in India.[25] And India took note of the fact that on May 16, 1983 the 4,620-meter-high Khunjerab pass at the terminus of the Chinese-built Karakoram highway in Pakistan-controlled Kashmir was open to civilian travel and trade.[26]

Indian suspicions were not allowed to stand in the way of border talks. The fourth round was held in New Delhi in October 1983, with an Indian spokesman declaring for the first time that "reasonable progress" had been made. Although there was no change in the substantive Chinese position, its delegates agreed to consider the sector-by-sector approach to the problem India had been demanding.[27]

Efforts by India and China to improve relations continued into 1984. Mrs. Gandhi met Mao Hong, a Politburo member and close aide of Deng Xiaoping, in New Delhi in January. Mao reportedly expressed China's keenness to receive Foreign Minister Narasimha Rao.[28] In February, former Foreign Minister Huang Hua led a Chinese delegation to a population conference in New Delhi. He stayed an additional three days as guest of the Indian government and met Mrs. Gandhi on February 21.[29]

Chinese nuclear capabilities, however, continued to haunt Indian policy-makers. Reports in the U.S. press in June 1984 said the nuclear sales agreement[30] initialled during President Reagan's visit to China had encountered snags in view of fresh intelligence evidence of continuing Chinese nuclear collaboration with Pakistan. The U.S. had earlier decided to rely on Prime Minister Zhao Ziyang's statement during his visit to the U.S. in January, "We do not engage in nuclear proliferation ourselves, nor do we help other nations to develop nuclear weapons." Zhao had repeated the assurance in a speech to the Chinese People's Congress.[31]

In February 1984, in an elaborate interview with a newspaper, the leading Pakistani nuclear scientist, A.Q. Khan, had announced that his country had perfected the technology of uranium enrichment through the centrifuge method, adding, "We have left India years behind." He said Pakistan could make the bomb if ordered to do so by the government.[32]

Although Pakistani official spokesmen sought to play down the interview, it appears to have been carefully timed to counter the growing tendency in Congress to make the terms of U.S. military assistance to Islamabad more stringent. In fact, the Senate Foreign Relations Committee passed an amendment on March 28, 1984 requiring the President to certify that Pakistan "is not developing a nuclear explosive device, and is not acquiring, overtly or covertly, technology, material, or equipment for the purpose of manufacturing or detonating a nuclear explosive device."[33] The amendment was deleted by the committee the next week at the suggestion of the White House. Perhaps influenced by the Khan interview, Defence Minister R. Venkataraman pitched India's security concerns on a high note. He told the Lok Sabha on March 23[34] that the situation in India's immediate neighbourhood had been changing rapidly to the country's detriment, with Pakistan becoming part of the U.S. strategic consensus and receiving arms and equipment far in excess of its legitimate defence requirements.[35]

Venkataraman said, "Such a large inventory of weapon systems in our neighbourhood cannot but cause alarm to India . . . . I have no option except to go and find matching equipment . . . . I can say with confidence that we are matching their systems with our systems."[36] Cheers greeted his declaration that India had the military edge over Pakistan.

India and the U.S., however, continued to probe areas of agreement. Interest centred for a time on New Delhi building up a new military relationship with Washington. The U.S. seemed anxious to sell India certain kinds of arms and Congressional action was taken to ease the way. A reported Indo-U.S. $1 billion arms deal, certainly an exaggeration, had been under discussion in 1982 and 1983. But negotiations, and even a preliminary agreement on artillery guns, led nowhere. The primary reason was what India considered unacceptable conditions—provisions for stoppage of arms under certain circumstances and reluctance to part with technology.[37] There was, in any event, the realization in New Delhi that the U.S. would not give India what it gave Pakistan.[38]

U.S. Under Secretary of State for Security Assistance William Schneider told the American press in April 1983 that no state-of-the-art U.S. technology would be made available to India for fear of "leakage" to Moscow.[39] There were few illusions on the Indian side.

Defence analysts believed that neither superpower would give a country defence technology unless there was a convergence of strategic interests. There was no such convergence between New Delhi and Washington.

A new development which came into play in India in recent years was the problem of kickbacks. This proved to be a further inhibiting factor in building an Indo-U.S. military relationship.[40] Besides, the Indo-Soviet military relationship imposed obvious constraints on major arms purchases from the U.S. Moscow was plainly unhappy with the projected Indo-U.S. deal. But New Delhi could have resisted such pressure if the American terms had been right.[41] Despite Secretary of State George Shultz's assertion in New Delhi on July 1, 1983 that "misunderstandings" on this score had been cleared up,[42] Indian doubts were not allayed.

The Soviets had been investing much time and effort in 1983 in the "indirect talks" on Afghanistan through the U.N. mechanism. The military stalemate on the ground continued, with the "limited contingent" of 105,000 Soviet troops remaining unaugmented. About 25,000 *mujahidin* operated in Afghanistan in loosely organized bands, and the guerrillas' supplies were bolstered, by China among other countries, by RPG-7 antitank guns, sophisticated land mines and heavy antiaircraft machine guns.[43]

The Soviets bought peace in the Panjsher valley through a deal in February 1983 with Ahmad Shah Massoud, trading safe passage for trapped Soviet garrisons for cessation of bombing raids and return of residents who had fled in 1982. The truce held for a remarkably long time.[44] The Soviets succeeded in sealing off the Wakhan corridor bordering on China and made a major effort towards the long-term Sovietization and indoctrination of youth. Russian became a compulsory language in Afghan schools and large numbers of students were sent to East Europe.

Moscow's incentive for seeking a political settlement was to reduce the inordinate political costs of the continuing military presence in Afghanistan and the fact that its objective of an acceptable regime surviving without Soviet troops was as distant as ever. A key player in the diplomatic game was Pakistan, which had remained in touch with Moscow all along, even as it continued to funnel weapons to the resistance. The Pakistanis received at least some encouragement from the Chinese to pursue the U.N. option although Beijing's attitude towards moves on Afghanistan can best be described as ambivalent.

The Soviets, on their part, had made their gestures to Pakistan by quietly removing Bhutto's sons from Kabul and imposing restraints on the Kabul-based Baluch and Pushtoon groups. There was also the implicit offer of recognition of the Durand Line. After one year of discussions, the indirect negotiations in Geneva in April 1983 produced an agreement on a comprehensive settlement but for two points: the time-frame for the withdrawal of Soviet troops and the phasing out of Pakistani help to the resistance.[45]

Pakistani Foreign Minister Yakub Khan exuded optimism, as did U.N. negotiator Cordovez. Implementation of the agreement, it was suggested, could begin early in 1984.[46] Hopes centred on the June talks in Geneva and Yakub journeyed to Washington and Moscow, among other capitals, in late May and June to prepare for the Geneva round. The optimistic mood soon turned to one of pessimism as it became clear that the Geneva talks would not achieve a settlement.

What happened? A key factor in reaching a settlement was the U.S. attitude to the talks. The mood in the State Department after the April round in Geneva was of not letting the Soviets continue the talks indefinitely to give the world an impression of reasonableness.[47] Opinion in the Reagan Administration was divided between those who wished to continue the process of "bleeding" the Soviets and others who were more inclined to look favourably on a political settlement.

For the Pakistanis, the U.S. attitude was crucial to determining their own strategy. The $3.2 billion military and economic aid package and the sale of F-16s were predicated on the Soviet military presence in Afghanistan and the convergence of U.S.-Pakistani strategic interests, to however limited an extent. The Pakistanis could not have accepted a settlement without American acquiescence, if not approval.

Even before the June talks, Harrison said that "a quiet crisis is developing between Islamabad and Washington over the desirability of pursuing the U.N. effort further."[48] The Soviets told India after the June talks that they failed because Pakistan changed its attitude at U.S. behest and became equivocal on the noninterference clause and its earlier promise to have direct contact with Kabul.[49] Pakistani officials suggested, on the other hand, that an ailing Andropov, confronted by army opposition, had put conclusion of the Afghan settlement temporarily on "hold."[50]

That Yakub's talk with Secretary of State Shultz on May 25 was an important element in the Pakistani's approach to his meeting with Gromyko in June and the failure in Geneva seems clear. According to one reliable account, Shultz told Yakub and his advisors in the presence of four other U.S. officials that the U.S. considered the U.N. agreement unworkable in the absence of some provision for the replacement of the present Kabul regime with a more representative government. The U.S. also objected to the fact that the auxiliary endorsement document, while providing for Soviet and U.S. "support" of the Afghan-Pakistani agreement in its entirety, would not directly and explicitly commit the Soviet Union to the clause governing force withdrawals in the agreement.[51]

The failure of the June 1983 round soured Pakistan's relations with the Soviet Union for a time, and superpower relations deteriorated further with the Soviet shooting down of a Korean airliner on September 1 off Sakhalin island. The Soviet action was indefensible and Moscow's subsequent reaction clumsy in the extreme. But the Reagan Administration's determination to use the incident for a full-scale propaganda offensive against the Soviets bred a mood of embittered hostility in Moscow.

The Russians, however, did not abandon their carrot and stick approach to Pakistan. According to Pakistani sources in January 1984, two Afghan air force jets bombed Pakistani territory, in apparent pursuit of an insurgent group, killing forty and wounding sixty others. It was described as the "most savage attack" since the 1978 coup and the third such attack in January.[52] The Soviets also charged Pakistan with permitting U.S. electronic intelligence sites to operate, mostly in Baluchistan and along the Makran coast, directed also against Afghanistan and India.[53]

In Afghanistan, the Soviets began a new offensive in mid-April and undertook a major action in the Panjsher valley, bringing in heavy firepower. The Soviets took heavy losses although they succeeded in making their point; the long truce in the valley was over.[54]

On the other hand, the Soviets significantly stepped up economic assistance to Pakistan even while administering warnings of joint Afghan-Soviet punitive action if Islamabad did not cease helping Afghan guerrillas. During Pakistani Finance Minister Ghulam Ishaq Khan's visit to Moscow in late December 1983, the Soviets agreed to provide $277 million on "soft terms" to build a 630 megawatt thermal power station at Multan and give credits for other facilities at the station. They also promised two deep-drilling oil rigs and help in completing the $800 million Soviet-built steel mill.

While the Soviets also reacted favourably to participating in building a $1.7 billion nuclear power plant at Chashma and a $3.7 billion dam at nearby Kalabagh, they made no firm commitments. Moscow, in fact, stepped up charges that Pakistan was on the brink of letting U.S. planes use its air bases and was approaching a strategic alliance with the U.S. in which Pakistani military installations would be used by the Rapid Deployment Force.[55]

For its part, Pakistan continued to follow its twin policy of not unduly provoking Moscow while strengthening its defence on shared threat perceptions with the U.S., hoping to resolve the dilemmas presented by this contradictory approach to the best of its ability. Pakistan's predicament seems to have fuelled a debate in the small policy-making establishment and those on its fringes on the country's longer-term strategy.

An interesting theory launched by Sajjad Hyder, former ambassador to the Soviet Union, was that Pakistan should "move towards formal and permanent neutrality" on the Austrian model. He explained "... If we are to evolve a durable *modus vivendi* with India, we are likely to pay a lesser price if this accommodation is reached on Soviet, rather than purely Indian, terms."[56] If the Pakistan government encouraged the promotion of this view, it served the useful purpose of an oblique warning to the U.S. not to push Islamabad too hard in achieving its strategic objectives in the region. At any rate, the Pakistanis continued to pursue the U.N. option on Afghanistan for what it was worth.

Benazir Bhutto was released from prison under U.S. Congressional pressure in January 1984 and allowed to go abroad. Unlike in the past, she, as also other opposition leaders, were in favour of continued U.S. military assistance to Pakistan even as they hoped that Washington would exert greater pressure on the Zia regime on human rights and holding genuine elections.[57] But Benazir also suggested that India would be doing grievous injury to democratic forces in Pakistan if it agreed to sign a no-war pact with the military regime, thus lending it respectability and legitimacy.[58]

Pakistan's relations with India took a somewhat predictable course, with expressions of peace and friendship and talks alternating with charges and counter-charges and talk of war. Pakistan accused India of major intelligence agency involvement in an incipient revolt of junior officers of the army, aimed at assassinating Zia. The plot was uncovered in January.[59] Indian charges of Pakistani involvement in the Sikhs' agitation in Punjab took on a more strident note.

Somewhat wearily, Mrs. Gandhi told Parliament on March 1, 1984 that Pakistan's complaint that India had not reconciled itself to its neighbour's existence was an old one "which we have refuted time and again. It [Pakistan] is something we agreed to, whether we liked it or not. We have accepted it and are living with it." A retired general and head of a think tank reputedly close to Zia, Lieutenant General A.I. Akram, suggested in early 1984 that no improvement in Indo-Pakistani relations could be expected as long as Mrs. Gandhi remained in power.[60]

Against this backdrop, Indian and Pakistani foreign secretaries met in the scenic setting of Udaipur in India in March to report some progress. The centrepiece of this progress was the Pakistani agreement that Kashmir could now be covered in a no-war pact between the two countries. No one expected any dramatic improvement in relations even as neither side wished to foreclose the option of a happier future.

The Soviets' problems in early 1984 went beyond Afghanistan and the frigidity in relations with the other superpower. Andropov's failing health and long public absence had already become the subject of much speculation around the world in the latter half of 1983. In February 1984 Andropov died, posing for the Soviet leadership the problem of succession for the second time in fifteen months. The selection of Konstantin Chernenko, who had lost out in the earlier power struggle, surprised the world and suggested that those who held power did not wish to make a generational change.

Both Mrs. Gandhi and General Zia journeyed to Moscow for another funeral. The Indian Prime Minister met Chernenko for twenty-five minutes on February 14, and Indian press reports said he expressed his appreciation of her "initiative, leadership and guidance in these difficult times, both as Prime Minister and as Asian statesman and chairperson of the nonaligned movement." He also wished her "every success in her endeavours for peace."[61]

Chernenko, however, administered a snub to Zia by ignoring his request for a meeting. The point Moscow seemed to be making was that it was holding Pakistan responsible for the failure of the June Geneva talks. On his return home, Zia reiterated his refusal to hold direct talks with the Karmal regime while indicating his willingness to continue "indirect" discussions.⁶²

Foreign Minister Narasimha Rao's visit to Moscow in September 1983 had revealed the pattern that had evolved in the Indo-Soviet relationship after the Soviet intervention in Afghanistan. The two sides agreed to disagree on Afghanistan and decided to concentrate on bilateral relations. The joint communiqué at the end of Rao's visit merely noted "identity or similarity of the positions of the USSR and India on the principal international issues."⁶³ Trade, as we have seen, presented problems, but the military relationship continued to yield dividends for India.

India had sought to distance itself from the Soviet Union on the political plane even while cementing the military relationship. Apart from the propaganda element involved, the situation had deteriorated considerably to India's disadvantage by developments in Iran and Afghanistan and the superpowers' reaction to them. In the fall of 1983, the Soviets were sounding out India to reactivate Article IX of the treaty, the article under which Indo-Soviet discussions were held prior to India's military operation in East Pakistan.⁶⁴ India's reaction was negative although a section of the policy-making elite was in favour of such a step.

It was in keeping with the new orientation in Indo-Soviet relations that the highest ranking Soviet visitor to New Delhi in the first half of 1984 was Defence Minister Ustinov, rather than a more politically oriented Politburo member. Ustinov's visit had to be postponed because of Andropov's impending death, and he finally came in March. During a meeting with Mrs. Gandhi, according to the Press Trust of India, the two leaders expressed shared concern over the militarization of Pakistan while underlining cooperation in defence and reaffirmed their commitment to develop friendly relations and close cooperation.⁶⁵

To no one's surprise, Ustinov reiterated the commitments made to Defence Minister Venkataraman on providing frontier military technology to India and he projected a visit by Chernenko towards the end of 1984 or early in 1985. Ustinov's talk with Mrs. Gandhi took place with only a Soviet interpreter as the third person.⁶⁶ A detailed account of the discussions, reported by an Indian analyst, was significant more for what the Soviets wished to put out for Indian and world consumption than what transpired during the talks.⁶⁷

According to this account, the Soviets took the darkest view of the Reagan Administration's policy and were prepared to face "any situation." They would not return to intermediate range or START talks in Geneva on American terms. They had merely "restored" the strategic balance by deploying their own medium-range missiles in East Europe and placing the U.S. in the range of nuclear missiles.

On China, Ustinov reportedly said that while Beijing's policies had become more sophisticated, shorn of Maoist excesses, it was still manipulating Soviet-American conflicts to advance its own interests, cooperating with the U.S. against the Soviet Union. Addressing India's concerns, Ustinov promised support in "any contingency that may arise" and said Moscow would meet India's oil requirements in case of a Gulf war.

Reagan's visit to China in late April brought home to American observers that "now, the Chinese are in the middle, able to play the Russian card against President Reagan as they please."[68] Beijing announced, on the eve of Reagan's arrival, a visit by Arkhipov in mid-May although the Soviets later postpond the trip to express their displeasure over Chinese moves in relation to Vietnam. The Chinese press omitted Reagan's censure of Russians and finally telecast a Reagan speech in full without providing translation.

The Chinese leaders ostentatiously took an independent line in foreign policy, asking the U.S. to end the "sharp confrontation" with Moscow by stopping the deployment of more missiles in Europe. Beijing also criticized U.S. policies in Central America and asked Reagan to talk to the Palestine Liberation Organization. The American assumption was that the Chinese were playing to global left while moving to the right economically and Washington's strategy was to bind China through long-term collaboration in commerce.[69]

Despite India's chairmanship of the nonaligned movement and the troubled regional picture, Mrs. Gandhi's major concerns in late 1983 and early 1984 were domestic. In December 1983, Mrs. Gandhi had organized a plenary session of the Congress in Calcutta, the first held in a decade, to refurbish the party's image. Significantly, a three-man Soviet delegation led by M.F. Menashev attended the session, declaring that the Soviet Union highly valued the positive course of the foreign policy of India and its government headed by the outstanding political leader, Mrs. Gandhi.[70] The theme of the conference was that the country's unity, integrity and security were in danger and the Congress alone could defend them. The session also took a left-leaning rhetorical stance.[71]

In early 1984 Mrs. Gandhi still had a sharp edge over the

opposition in popularity polls even while the rating of the government's performance was low.[72] The election fever had gripped the opposition parties, with sixteen opposition factions forming two fronts, the United Front and the Left Front. And seventeen opposition parties had met in Calcutta in a conclave to flex their muscles. When the government announced that it was laying aside the last tranche of the International Monetary Fund loan because the economy had recovered sufficiently, one assumption made was that it was in response to the Calcutta conclave.[73]

Punjab, meanwhile, was increasingly coming to the centre of the political stage. In the early months of 1984, its was clear that the moderate Akali leadership had little room left for manoeuvre in seeking a compromise settlement, with the radicals calling the shots under Sant Jarnail Singh Bhindranwale. The radicals, as also the moderate leaders, were ensconced in the Golden Temple at Amritsar outside the reach of law.

What lent an ominous dimension to the crisis was the violent turn it took. Enjoying safe haven in the Golden Temple and other Sikh shrines, the radicals began killing Hindu leaders as well as Sikhs who differed from them. This invited a measure of backlash in the neighbouring state of Haryana in particular, and, in Punjab, Hindu organizations held protest demonstrations leading to some violence and deaths.

The Punjab agitation, as it had evolved, was posing the greatest challenge to the government since independence.[74] Punjab was the richest state in the country, and apart from contributing to the state's prosperity, Sikhs were very much in the mainstream of the country's life, with their martial traditions ensuring a more than 10 per cent representation in the armed forces while they were only 2 per cent of the country's population.

The daily murders in Punjab were multiplying, with the beefed-up police and paramilitary forces unable to put an end to the gunmen's activities. The Hindu backlash was growing and more and more accusing fingers were being pointed at Mrs. Gandhi. The stark alternatives left to her in the end were either to see a Northern Ireland type of insurrectionary situation developing in a vital state bordering on Pakistan or to send the army in to do the unthinkable by flushing out the gunmen from the Golden Temple and other Sikh shrines and face the consequences. Some of the opposition parties were demanding that the army do precisely that.

In early June 1984, Mrs. Gandhi sent the army into Punjab and on the night of June 5-6, it stormed the Golden Temple. In bitter fighting in the temple complex, more than a thousand extremists and soldiers were killed. The army seemed surprised by the sophistication of the arms and the training of the radicals. The radical leader Bhindranwale was found killed.[75]

The government's action was welcomed by most opposition parties and was greeted by the Hindus in Punjab and people in the rest of the country with a sense of relief. The deployment of the army also won the support of both the CPI and the Marxists. The Central secretariat of the CPI welcomed it while the CPI(M) leader and West Bengal chief minister, Jyoti Basu, described it as a necessary administrative measure to save the lives of the minorities and others.[76]

The Sikhs reacted to the raiding of the Golden Temple and other Sikh shrines with a sense of shock and outrage, even though the army had taken many casualities to safeguard the *sanctum sanctorum* of the Golden Temple. Sikhs rioted in different parts of the country and called for the resignation of India's titular President, Zail Singh, a Sikh. The most serious repercussion was the mutiny of more than 1,000 Sikh troops in several army camps. Although the mutiny was quickly contained, with a number of deserters hunted down and killed, it revealed the potential explosiveness of the situation.[77]

One emotional reaction of the Sikhs was to espouse the cause of a separate Khalistan state, which had previously been supported by a microscopic minority. It was, for many, an expression of their anger, rather than a well-considered decision. For men like Jagjit Singh Chauhan, a separatist leader resident in London, it brought a windfall of support.[78] The major problem facing Mrs. Gandhi's government was the Sikhs' feeling of alienation and hurt. The basic issues which led to the agitation remained to be resolved,[79] and no credible Sikh leader was initially willing to negotiate with the government, in view of the strong feelings of the community.

The Western world's view of Mrs. Gandhi's predicament in Punjab was broadly sympathetic, despite charges of Pakistani and C.I.A. involvement emanating from New Delhi.[80] The Soviet Union expressed "full understanding of the steps taken by the Indian government to curb terrorism in Punjab."[81] *Pravda* of June 9 alleged that there were attempts by Western secret services to destabilize India by encouraging separatist elements. Soviet television, in its "World Today" programme, commented on the regret reportedly expressed by U.S. officials over the killing of Bhindranwale. "Why did they not express similar regret when Bhindrawale's terrorists were gunning down innocent people in Punjab?" it asked.[82]

The irony of the situation in mid-1984 was that while the wounds inflicted by the army action in Punjab would take long to heal, Mrs. Gandhi's electoral fortunes had turned around. The crucial Hindi heartland, which would determine the outcome of the next general election, could be expected to support her in a larger measure than before the temple raid. She had demonstrated that she was prepared to take grave risks to enforce the government's will, finally redeeming the promise that brought her to power in 1980: "the government that works."

India's foreign policy goals had, meanwhile, receded, rather than brought nearer fulfilment. Events in Iran, Afghanistan and elsewhere had provoked the U.S. to fasten on the Persian Gulf, Pakistan and the Indian Ocean to fashion a new strategy. The Soviets had positioned themselves along Pakistan's northern frontier, negating India's regional interests. The Indian Ocean had become more militarized than ever before, mocking the "zone of peace" concept.[83]

The new U.S. military relationship with Pakistan brought back to India's mind the scenario of the Fifties, with a twist. The American goal now was the containment of Soviet expansionism, with China as a friend, if not a quasi-ally. India's relations with Pakistan showed little promise of achieving the longed-for but elusive era of genuine peace.

Both India and the U.S. took deliberate steps to maintain civility in their relations, despite the wide gulf separating their strategic views and policies. Vice President Bush also took in India during his visit to the subcontinent in May—after President Reagan's publicized trip to China—to declare in New Delhi that India was a "major, pivotal power."[84]

Apart from Pakistan, a core problem of India's foreign policy, New Delhi's relations with other neighbours remained far from happy. The government's decision to build a fence along the border with Bangladesh,[85] essentially a sop to the Assamese agitators, provoked strong reaction in Dhaka. The actual erection of a small section provoked incidents, leading to the suspension of the project to cool tempers. Sinhalese-Tamil animosites revived again, causing more deaths to create problems in Sri Lanka's relations with India.

On China, the mood in New Delhi in mid-1984 tended to be

pessimistic. Elements contributing to this mood were the Chinese belief, communicated most recently by Chinese leaders to Jyoti Basu, the Chief Minister of Bengal, that an early solution to the border problem was not possible, and the contradiction implied in Beijing wanting to promote better Indo-Pakistani relations while enthusiastically supporting Pakistan's rearmament programme. In the Indian view, resolution of the Sino-Indian border problem was of primary importance and Beijing must respect India's security interest south of the Himalayan crest.[86]

Prospects of a Sino-Soviet detente seemed to be receding in mid-1984. *Bejing Review* of July 9 charged the Soviets with an "attempt to control us; we are opposed to being controlled." It said while China did not want war or strained relations with the Soviet Union, "it is unrealistic and impossible for Sino-Soviet relations to return to what they once were in history." The Chinese broadside came less than a week after China's negotiator, Qian Qichen, returned from Moscow to report that there had been no progress in improving relations.[87]

The U.S.-China relationship, particularly the agreement in principle to sell American arms, was posing problems for Washington's relations with ASEAN (Association of Southeast Asian Nations) in 1984. As Secretary of State Shultz discovered for himself during his swing through Southeast Asia in July 1984, the ASEAN nations expressed anxiety over America building up a strong China, reviving their historic fears of pressures from the North.

Shultz answered questions at press conferences in Singapore and Malaysia with some acerbity. He said: "I don't know how to allay fears people have. People had fears in the past that we didn't have a constructive relationship with China and now they fear we do. I think you have to start with the proposition that China is there. It is an important country. It has been for a long time. It will continue to be, and I don't have any doubt in my mind at all that as an economic proposition, China will develop and it seems to me that's to be expected."[88]

While the Soviet military intervention in Afghanistan tended to pull Moscow and New Delhi from each other on one plane, the consequences of Moscow's very action, together with U.S. strategic objectives in the region, brought the two countries together. India discovered that there were limits to its efforts to diversify arms purchases—limits determined by both economic and political factors. And in a worsening regional environment, the implicit security guarantees the relationship with Moscow offered tended to come to the fore.

India's success in space technology implied that it had the capability of developing an intermediate-range ballistic missile (I.R.B.M.). India had demonstrated its ability to produce nuclear weapons by detonating an underground nuclear device in 1974. In April 1983 India put a 91.5-pound satellite into earth orbit with a four-stage launch vehicle for the third time since joining the exclusive five-nation space club.[89] In 1983, the Government planned to spend $1 billion on its space projects in the next seven years.[90] In view of the costs, India has been sounding out other Third World countries on forming a consortium.[91]

Like the 1980 agreement with the Soviets, the decision in favour of MIG-29 and MIG-31 by forgoing production plans for Mirage-2000 was also a reassurance to Moscow that New Delhi would not take its diversification plans too far. India will continue to try to balance major purchases from the Soviet Union with symbolic, if not substantive, purchases from the West.[92]

The practice of this nonalignment will depend, as in the past, on the capabilities of India's defence industries and the benefits of going to Moscow or another source. India's defence planners realize that there are only three entirely self-sufficient defence-industrial societies: the superpowers and France. The U.S. is ruled out for the foreseeable future for major systems because of the divergent strategic interests of the two countries.

France, though highly desirable as a weapons supplier, is a medium power and hence unable to match the credit terms of a superpower, apart from the fact that the French tend to be high-cost producers because they do not have the economy of scale enjoyed by the U.S. and the Soviet Union. And Indian leaders have been constantly reiterating "constraint of resources," together with the goal of self-reliance.[93]

India's tentative answer to its central dilemma has been to isolate Afghanistan from the military and trade relationship with Moscow while seeking to broaden its diplomatic options. New Delhi has succeeded in a fair measure in achieving its first objective because Moscow has been equally keen to insulate the Indo-Soviet relationship from Afghanistan. But New Delhi's success in attaining its second goal has been limited and halting and leaves unanswered the broader question of the Soviet Union's direct participation in South Asia's affairs by virtue of its presence in Afghanistan.

Chapter Eleven

Prospects

THE Indo-Soviet relationship has been determined by the historic divide on the subcontinent between Hindus and Muslims, which led to the partition of British India. Indo-Pakistani enmity gave an opening to the external powers, whose presence was also needed by the two countries' requirements of economic and military assistance. Despite India's aim of keeping external powers out, it desperately needed Western, especially U.S., economic assistance even as it sought Soviet and Chinese benevolence in making nonalignment credible and in enhancing its own attractiveness for Western aid.

The U.S. alliance with Pakistan came before the flowering of Indo-Soviet amity, symbolized by the triumphal B&K tour of India in 1955. The post-Stalin policy of befriending the new nations and Indian overtures to Moscow combined with American interest in harnessing Pakistan to contain Communism to legitimize superpower interest in South Asia. With Sino-Indian friendship giving way to tensions and the border war of 1962 and Beijing's decision assiduously to cultivate India's adversary, Pakistan, the Chinese role in the subcontinent became obtrusive.

The first Indo-Pakistani war was fought over Kashmir in 1947-48; the second, again over Kashmir, in 1965. It was preceded by a mini-war in the Rann of Kutch. The third war, which led to the creation of Bangladesh in December 1971, reduced Pakistan by half.

Nehru's death in 1964 and Khrushchev's ouster later that year coincided with Soviet interest in broadening its relations with the subcontinent also to take in Pakistan. This represented the first serious political confrontation between Moscow and New Delhi since the mid-Fifties. The China factor, which had given a new dimension to Indo-Soviet relations, was also largely responsible for the Soviet attempt at balancing its relationship with India by befriending Pakistan.

Until then, Indo-Soviet interests in the region, though not

identical, had merged. Moscow's efforts to emulate the U.S. example, for its own reasons, called into question the basis of the Moscow-New Delhi relationship. Despite the restrictive element in the Soviet Union's arms assistance policy, it was the only major military power which seemed interested in helping build a self-sufficient military establishment in India. Soviet supply of arms to Pakistan, in however small a measure, created a cleavage in Indo-Soviet regional interests.

Moscow made it clear to New Delhi that it wanted to deal with it on its terms. While persevering with its policy of balancing the two major countries of the subcontinent, the Soviet Union signified its continuing primary interest in India by giving generous economic and military assistance. Tashkent represented the high point of this policy. Its failure came about as much by Pakistan's reluctance to demote ties with China and the Sino-U.S. detente as by the untenability of maintaining special and meaningful relations with both India and Pakistan.

Events in East Pakistan in 1971 precipitated a change in Moscow's policy even as it tried to cultivate Pakistan till the end. Mrs. Gandhi agreed to sign an Indo-Soviet treaty of peace and friendship in 1969 in order to detach Pakistan from the Soviet Union and buttress her own position at home. The looming third Indo-Pakistani war led to the actual signing of the treaty in August 1971 although it was not until October that year that Moscow agreed finally to support India's major political goals in East Pakistan through force.

Moscow had, meanwhile, broadened its agenda by proposing the Asian Collective Security (ACS) concept, motivated by the China factor and its desire to reorder relations in Asia in the post-Vietnam era as the superpower claiming also to be an Asian country. Reaction to the ACS was generally frosty, including, after some prevarication, in India. Moscow kept the concept pending—for the long haul.

After the 1971 war, India started on a promising note to legitimize its preeminence on the subcontinent. But Pakistan's new ruler, Bhutto, though realizing that his country was no longer in the same league as India, succeeded in being the spoiler in denying Mrs. Gandhi some of the fruits of her victory. He fashioned a new level of relations with the Middle East. Hobbled by a humbled but by no means subdued Pakistan, India could not play its full role in the region and the world.

The upheaval of the Cultural Revolution over, Beijing realized that its negative policy towards India was not achieving its goals, and the beginnings of detente were signalled by the two sides. India had been the suitor because it sought to reduce its dependence on Moscow, particularly after Soviet attempts to follow a balanced policy on the subcontinent. This process of slow rapprochement, leading to the Mao smile of May 1970, was set back by events in East Pakistan and the Indo-Pakistani war of 1971.

Efforts to improve Sino-Indian relations were postponed, not halted, and were picked up again in the mid-Seventies. They were given a fillip by Mrs. Gandhi's defeat and the coming to power of a centre-right coalition. The promise, however, remained unfulfilled, partly because of the very weaknesses of the squabbling Janata government. The Soviets displayed their anxiety over Sino-Indian moves, and retained their suspicions even after Mrs. Gandhi's return to power in 1980.

Mrs. Gandhi was certainly a known quantity for the Russians. But having burnt their fingers by backing her Emergency regimen and betting on her victory in 1977, the Soviets were more wary of her. Their wariness was accentuated by her efforts to continue the process of rapprochement with China and seek better relations with the U.S.

Events in Iran and the Soviet intervention in Afghanistan changed the whole context of the Indo-Soviet relationship. The first accelerated U.S. military moves in the region, the northwest littoral in particular, and focussed American interest on Pakistan. After the Soviet invasion of Afghanistan, American plans in the region were put into high gear and a military and economic package was offered to Pakistan.

For India, the Soviet intervention in Afghanistan represented a crisis in Indo-Soviet relations, reflecting as it did a major strategic cleavage. China accelerated its efforts in seeking rapprochement with India. Indo-Pakistani reconciliation proved unattainable. Mrs. Gandhi moved to protect India's strategic flank in the face of the Soviet presence in Afghanistan, a Pakistan likely to be rearmed and intense militarization of the Indian Ocean and the Gulf by reemphasizing New Delhi's security links with Moscow. On the political plane, she set about making overtures to the U.S. and China.

Surprised by the intensity of the world's reaction to their move into Afghanistan and India's opposition, despite its supine postures at the U.N., the Soviets were only too eager to try to insulate Afghanistan from Indo-Soviet relations. After a time, Moscow also offered an olive branch to China to begin a slow process of reconciliation.

China, for its own reasons, was interested in improving state relations with Moscow to move away from a Japan-China-U.S. alliance it had earlier proposed and take a more nonaligned posture in the world to improve its credibility.

Sino-Indian rapprochement has been halting and slower than anticipated. India, for its part, has had to recognize the limitations of its policy of diversifying arms purchases. In 1983, it accepted the Soviet offer of MIG-29s and MIG-31s under intense pressure and because of the costs involved in setting up new production facilities for the French Mirage-2000 it had ordered.

The new U.S.-Pakistan military relationship, consecrated in the first year of the Reagan Administration, meant loss of Pakistani flexibility in negotiating a deal with the Russians on Afghanistan. But it set off a debate in Pakistan on its longer-term options. The threat of Pakistan making up with Moscow was being used not only against the U.S., warning it not to push Islamabad too hard, but also against India. But the Pakistanis remained keen to complete the acquisition of all the arms under the $3.2 billion programme and the separate purchase deal on forty F-16s.

The Indo-Soviet relationship has become subject to a whole complex of factors which have made Indian goals more difficult to achieve. Superpower intervention in the subcontinent is greater today than ever before, the Indian Ocean was never more militarized and the perceived merging of Indo-Soviet strategic interests in the region has never diverged more dramatically.

There was the initial 1947-53 period of Soviet hostility followed by the 1955-64 phase of great amity. The 1965-71 period saw the Soviet attempt at following a balanced policy between India and Pakistan, introducing new strains in the Moscow-New Delhi relationship and a measure of disillusionment in India. In 1971-79, close Indo-Soviet relations were tempered by the Indian desire to distance itself somewhat from the Soviet Union to achieve its own regional ambitions. Finally, the Soviet intervention in Afghanistan in 1979 led to great misgivings in New Delhi even as India sought to protect its core relationship with Moscow.

Three external powers—the U.S., the Soviet Union and China—have interacted with the domestic compulsions of the countries of the subcontinent. U.S. policy has fluctuated from a military alignment with Pakistan to a more balanced relationship with India leading to a major economic assistance programme, to a hands-off policy on the subcontinent from the mid-Sixties, which lasted well into the Seventies, despite its approach to the 1971 events. American revival of interest was conditioned more by events in Iran and the Persian Gulf and later by the Soviet intervention in Afghanistan than by its intrinsic interest in the subcontinent. Pakistan served Washington's strategic objectives, and only for a brief while—during President Carter's first two years of office—has the U.S. accorded India the role of preeminence it desired.

The artificial nature of the *Hindi-Chini Bhai Bhai* (Indians and Chinese are brothers) phase of the early Fifties could not last. There was the basic Sino-Indian rivalry in Asia and although India had only itself to blame for the precise manner in which the relationship deteriorated, the paths of the two countries would have diverged anyway. The Chinese have traditionally suspected nonalignment and hold a different world view from India's.

The phase of unmitigated Chinese hostility to India was tempered from the late Sixties and resulted in the mid-Seventies to a reassessment in Beijing. The Soviet intervention in Afghanistan seemed to speed up this process of Chinese reassessment. But in New Delhi's view, China seemed to be in no great hurry and did not accord India a high priority in its foreign policy concerns.

The hard decision on the border problem is India's, but China has to be prepared to meet New Delhi halfway. Domestically, Mrs. Gandhi could have sold an agreement with China on the basis of peripheral Chinese concessions in the Western sector. Members of India's policy-making elite complain that though China has rebuilt its constituency in India, it is not using it to greater purpose. Perhaps, China's long-term aims in relation to India are not very clear. The changed Chinese stance is helpful to India, but Beijing has kept its options by continuing to cultivate close relations with India's neighbours, Pakistan, Nepal, Bangladesh and Sri Lanka. China's finger is very much in the South Asian pie.

The element of rivalry between India and China and the Indo-Soviet relationship serve to hinder the completion of Sino-Indian reconciliation. For India, China is not the Middle Kingdom. Unlike the Bolshevik revolution, the Chinese revolution did not excite the Indian elite. A former foreign minister has suggested that once India is sufficiently strong, the two countries can define their respective spheres of influence along Indo-China[1]. New Delhi finds Chinese condescension highly offensive.

Unlike in the Sixties, the U.S. is now interested in checkmating Soviet influence on the subcontinent and has an ally in China in this endeavour. The U.S.-China relationship in the context of the Soviet Union is inimical to Indian interests. Indeed, U.S. moves and countermoves in the region have stymied India's desire to distance itself from the Soviet Union.

Relations of a large country like India with its neighbours have built-in irritants, as the U.S.'s own experience shows. In addition, the countries of the subcontinent carry the legacy of the past and the consequences flowing from three and one-half wars India and Pakistan have fought in thirty-seven years. But it remains in India's interest to befriend neighbours, not by constantly making unilateral concessions, but by trying to meet legitimate fears through a toning down of rhetoric and resolving problems with a measure of generosity.[2]

After repeated disappointments, India's approach to Pakistan has been to leave the initiative to it to improve relations. This is at best an inadequate answer and leaves for India a passive role. Rather, the need is to follow a more activist, not belligerent, policy towards neighbours. Strange as it may appear to neighbours, Indians suffer from a fear complex—fear of isolation in a dangerous world.[3] Psychologically, the relationship with Moscow provides a crutch, signifying that India has a powerful friend.[4]

Pakistan has to begin to resolve two basic problems before it can hope to build a stable relationship with India: its security against the perceived Indian threat and its polity. Pakistan's dilemma is that it can achieve real security only with India's help, and the army is unwilling to give up political power. India can help in the process by displaying patience and understanding and by capitalizing on the Zia-ul-Haq Administration's professed desire for peace, even assuming that it is a ploy to stock up the country's armoury with American weapons. Talk of peace is better than talk of war and has its own momentum. The Indian election cycle should not be allowed to be more than a temporary hindrance to promoting peace.

The Pakistani proposal for a South Asian zone of peace might be a clever debating point to embarrass India, but it can lead the two countries nowhere because it does not take account of India's nuclear threat perceptions from China. The issue of force levels is more complex because, in view of its size and vastly greater security concerns, India does not want to parley with Pakistan on the level of its own forces.[5] But a way has to be found to define India's tolerance level of Pakistan's military capabilities. The Kashmir issue is a dead one, except for rhetorical exercises, unless the situation on the ground triggers new compulsions.

The South Asian Regional Cooperation concept is still only a faint beacon for the future.[6] There is not much difference among countries of the subcontinent on the South Asian doctrine proclaimed by New Delhi in 1983. But neighbours' suspicions of India and its power projections cloud the issue, as also the level of the Indo-Soviet relationship. The Indian option cannot be an attractive one for its neighbours if it is part of a Soviet subsystem.

Mrs. Gandhi's policy was based on the premise that the Soviets are in South Asia to stay, with their presence in Afghanistan giving them a new opportunity to control relations with Pakistan and India. She believed that she had little choice, in view of the behaviour of the other superpower and China, with Pakistan happy to frustrate India's objectives. Hence she used the Soviets to shore up support for herself at home and build up India's strength. In the process, she legitimized the Soviet role in the subcontinent.

The Janata government did not make any substantive change in foreign policy during its brief reign. But its postures in keeping domestic events out of discussions with the Soviets and questioning Soviet interference through the Indian Communist party did have a salutary effect in keeping a certain distance from Moscow.

On the other hand, through the treaty and through officially involving the Soviets in Indian Communist party affairs, Mrs. Gandhi contributed to their ability to play a more prominent role in the subcontinent than would otherwise have been possible.[7] It raises the moot question whether the level of Soviet involvement will not negate India's goal of playing an independent role in the region and the world.

India's desire to be an autonomous power centre is not in doubt; the point is the one Sir Olaf Caroe raised in 1971, whether India has a long enough spoon to sup with the devil. The Russians are gradually seeking to give India no option but to attain its power ambitions through a secondary role to serve Soviet interests in Asia. They are trying to emasculate the Indian will. The Soviet hope is that after Mrs. Gandhi, a less astute politician will walk into its parlour out of fright and lack of options.

If India must maintain "creative tension"[8] with the two

superpowers so as not to be taken for granted, it must maintain its credibility. Even some of India's friends describe the problem as one of New Delhi refusing to face facts squarely where the Russians are concerned. Mrs. Gandhi's own answer was rhetorical. She had suggested: "The attack today, the sharpest weapon used against our policy, is to allege that in effect we are following the Soviet line. Perhaps they [the critics] think that their saying so will frighten us into abandoning our friendship with the Soviet Union."[9]

It is not merely a question of scoring debating points, but one of convincing the world that India follows truly independent policies. The fact that Mrs. Gandhi kept her foreign policy critics at bay by a constellation of domestic forces and U.S. compulsions to follow policies that harm Indian interests did not offer a national solution.

The long-term Soviet aim is to build an Asian Collective Security (ACS) system in Asia, treaties with individual countries providing an underpinning. The Soviets have made no secret of either objective. The Soviet Ambassador to Pakistan, Vitaly Smirnov, declared in Islamabad in June 1983 that Moscow considered friendship treaties as the "superior form" of relationship with developing countries.[10]

India has an important role in Russia's scheme of things, unlike in the U.S.'s, but it is a restrictive one, under the Soviet wing. In the ultimate analysis, it is a junior partnership Moscow is offering India. The ACS is planned to take in not only India, but Pakistan as well, and, over the long haul, Japan.

Moscow believes that Pakistan will ultimately come to terms with the ACS. It is seeking to preempt Islamabad's choice by softening it up through Afghanistan while offering it a bait. The Soviets are, in effect, offering Pakistan their protection against India to make the Collective Security concept attractive to it.

In refusing to deliver the Indian Communist party to Mrs. Gandhi after her return to power in 1980, the Soviets were looking towards a post-Mrs. Gandhi era. So were Pakistan and, to an extent, China. The edge in Pakistanis' case was that they never quite forgave her for helping to reduce their country by half, although they themselves were largely responsible for the 1971 debacle. When they nostalgically talk about the Janata era of Morarji Desai, they perhaps fondly look back most of all to its weakness. Traditionally, weak or interim administrations in India have made special efforts to befriend neighbours though Mrs. Gandhi herself often acted with restraint in relation to neighbours.

To achieve security against India and to keep it off balance, Pakistan has traditionally done almost anything to please a protector, be it the U.S. or China, or, as it perhaps will in the future, the Soviet Union. It is being argued in Islamabad, for instance, that if Pakistan has to make up with India, it would be better to do so on Soviet, rather than purely Indian, terms.[11] Pakistan's greatest diplomatic triumph has been a negative one. Its dilemma is starker than India's, and superb Pakistani diplomacy can mitigate its problems; it cannot resolve them.

India is one of the few developing countries that remains a democracy. Over the years of independence, particularly after Nehru, the prospect of the Army taking over has often been speculated upon. This exercise has not been limited to foreign commentators. Even Jayaprakash Narayan, the father figure who inspired and brought Janata to power in 1977, was "toying with the idea of a military dictatorship in India." He suggested that in the "political instability" created by the results of the general elections in 1967, India should "summon the services of the army to fill the vacuum and set right the instability."[12]

India's diversity and multitude of problems would still seem to militate against army rule, short of a string of simultaneous major uprisings. The veracity of this thesis was underlined by the disaffection of the Sikhs following the army's storming of the Golden Temple at Amritsar in early June 1984. Sikhs are an important constituent of the army.

The domestic environment in India in mid-1984 was increasingly clouded by growing ethnic and regional tensions and violence, the bloody end of the two-year phase of the Sikhs' agitation representing the most serious political problem for Mrs. Gandhi's government. A reordering of states' relations with the federal government seems inevitable; the crucial demands relate to fiscal, rather than political, autonomy.

In the major opposition political parties, a generational change in the leadership has yet to be made. In the CPI(M) Politburo, the average age is 70 and is only a shade lower, 65, in the party's 65-member central committee. The CPI's leadership, even after Chairman Dange's expulsion, is not much younger. The non-Communist parties have also been slow in retiring their leaders, with even the younger leaders being in their late 50s.

The Marxists are now practising their own form of nonalignment between the Soviet and Chinese Communist parties while tilting towards Moscow. It remains to be determined how far they will take their militancy in the agrarian field, which has proved to be a success story in the State of West Bengal they have ruled. The CPI remains bedevilled by its ambivalence to Mrs. Gandhi, despite the opposition line General Secretary Rajeswara Rao has succeeded in giving the party, with Soviet support.

The rising middle class, around 100 million strong, is becoming a new power factor. With her political astuteness, Mrs. Gandhi was the first to recognize the new phenomenon. After the middle class had had to make do for decades with Indian-produced models of vintage gas-guzzling cars, the government offered it the Japanese Suzuki, first assembled and then to be manufactured in India. Other later model cars are also in the works.

Non-Communist parties in India tend to be insular. The stuff of politics, even more than elsewhere, is the domestic scene. Outside the evocative issues of Pakistan and China and the two Communist parties' traditional leanings, there is no real interest in foreign policy across the political spectrum.[13] Mrs. Gandhi won plaudits at home by shining abroad, but the domestic environment determined her power and popularity ratings. By the same token, she had much leeway in framing foreign policy.

The Indian civil service, which distinguished itself in many fields in the first two decades of independence, has suffered from the political upheavals of the late Sixties, the Seventies and early Eighties. In view of the domestic political climate, the independence and sturdiness of officials have eroded, resulting in less time being spent on thinking through unpalatable foreign policy options.

The Soviets do not want to see a Communist India, in view of the threat it would pose of a possible tilt towards China. Rather, they want a friendly bourgeois government, keeping away from the West, as far as major economic and military linkages are concerned, and the CPI exerting constant pressure for tailoring Indian policies to Soviet interests.

Two major decisions taken by the Soviet leadership in the last decade were motivated by its desire to retain a hold on India in the important sectors of trade and sophisticated military aircraft. Brezhnev decided to sell valuable crude for rupees and his successor Andropov offered the Soviet Union's most sophisticated aircraft to prevent New Delhi from consummating an important long-term linkage with France on the indigenous production of Mirage-2000.

The Soviets employ various methods to exercise influence in India outside official channels. They pump in money by overpaying favoured traders, inserting advertisement in obscure journals, giving cash to Communists and other politicians, including some in the Congress (I), and financing part of the CPI apparatus through advertisements in their journals, supply of modern printing presses and free medical treatment and vacations in the Soviet Union for the Indian Communist leaders.[14]

The Indian elite takes a somewhat blasé attitude to Russian money coming in. Some members of the policy-making establishment suggest that Russian money, particularly to finance parties and individuals in elections, neutralized American money[15] or money from other anti-Communist sources. However, they concede that Moscow uses the CPI for more than propaganda purposes.

The trade relationship, even more than arms, is emerging as a key factor in Moscow's efforts to expand its influence in India. The Soviet Union exercises tremendous leverage through being the major, and, in some instances, the sole importer of Indian products manufactured in large parts of the country. Although Moscow's method of making its point in 1983 was clumsy, it had government ministers scurrying around giving assurances of doing more to import Soviet machinery. In the process, the Soviets sought to coopt the citadel of Indian capitalism, the Federation of Indian Chambers of Commerce and Industry (FICCI), in their scheme by making direct approaches to it.

The level of Indo-Soviet trade has been kept artificially high through the export of crude and other raw materials because, for the Soviets, trade is an important element in a political relationship. In India's case, trade has been reinforced by agreements for Moscow to buy products of Soviet-aided industries on production sharing, joint bids for contracts in third countries and the dovetailing of the two countries' plans. The Soviets have already created vested interests among those who produce and market a whole range of goods from hosiery to tobacco, detergents to electric fans.

In India, the longed-for era of self-sufficiency in high-technology military hardware is still far away. In the meantime, India and the Soviet Union have signed long-term agreements on manufacturing new generations of MIGs, the main battle tank and a variety of other products.

Contradictions in the Indo-Soviet relationship abound. Despite the close relationship, the Indian middle class interacts with the West on the intellectual plane and derides Communist scholarship.[16] It is an indication of this contempt for Soviet thought that no major Indian newspaper maintains a full-time staff correspondent in Moscow,[17] the field being left to Communist or pro-Communist newspapers and journals, whose correspondents are, in effect, subsidized by Moscow, or the Press Trust of India (PTI) news agency which hews close to the official Indian interpretation of ties with Moscow. Dispatches like the following by PTI, patently untrue,[18] sail through the major newspapers without exciting comment:

> In the major armed clashes that India faced with its immediate neighbours in 1962, 1965 and again 1971, Mr. Brezhnev with his decisive influence in the Kremlin extended unstinted support to India.[19]

One consequence of the assiduous Indian cultivation of West Europe and the socialist trends appearing on the horizon in many of those countries is that the left in India is no longer anti-West, only anti-U.S. Even in relation to the U.S., the estimated 500,000 Indians settled in the country and the streams of relatives visiting them each year are bound to create new bonds and less prejudice on the Indian side.

Licence agreements with France, Britain, Italy and West Germany on indigenous production of arms and outright purchase of military hardware are a useful, if somewhat symbolic, demonstration of Indian nonalignment. The scale is still heavily weighted in favour of Moscow.

Above all, it is in the field of economy in which the most interesting new alignments with the West are taking shape. To great Soviet annoyance, displayed with some petulance in 1983, major Indian industries have gone to the West or Japan to update their technology. And the economic policies initiated by Mrs. Gandhi after her return to power in 1980 were more generous to the private sector and liberal in permitting imports to encourage exports. The results were encouraging enough to persuade the government to continue this policy.

Despite ritual condemnations of the "balance of power" and "sphere of influence" concepts,[20] India is employing the first to serve its needs and aspires to participate in the latter. The "zone of peace" concept in Asia has receded as an attainable objective as also India's assertion of its regional role because of heavy superpower involvement. "Bilateralism" cannot survive on the subcontinent in any meaningful sense in such an environment. India's aspirations remain global,[21] but the whole process has been set back by the more immediate compulsions to devote all attention to steering through the shoals of the Soviet presence in Afghanistan and American moves in Pakistan and the Persian Gulf.

India's gift to the developing world, nonalignment, is now espoused by all countries of the subcontinent, but the dilution it has undergone in achieving near universal acceptance in the Third World has robbed it of its glory. In India's own case, it switched from equidistance from the superpowers to maximizing relations with them. India will continue to use its balance of power strategy to try to retain leverage with the Soviet Union. Not since the late Sixties has New Delhi felt as constrained in achieving its objectives as in mid-1984. The Soviet intervention in Afghanistan has been the greatest blow to India's regional and long-term interests. Implicitly, Moscow is now claiming to be a South Asian power.

The conventional wisdom is that because of India's size and diversity and fierce nationalism, it will not be sucked into the Soviet sphere of influence. But the enmeshing of ever-increasing links in trade and the military relationship will make it harder for India to stay aloft independently. The cloying rhetoric of Indo-Soviet friendship can change and is not necessarily harmful. Politicians who can be purchased with money or flattery are.[22]

If the practice of nonalignment has reinforced Indians' basic passive nature, it represents a danger. The domestic situation in the next few years is likely to reinforce this passivity, which will make it easier for the Soviet Union to claim South Asia as its backyard. By their intervention in Afghanistan, the Soviets have not only negated India's interests but also administered a warning that the limits of India's regional role will be increasingly set by Moscow.

Nonalignment has not only served India's foreign policy objectives but also helped to harmonize different trends in the country. A further pro-Soviet orientation would create greater tensions in India, particularly with the rising middle class claiming its share of the cake. Moscow's aim is to convince Indians that they have no option but to accept Soviet terms. With U.S. strategic policies working against India, West Europe could prove to be too weak a reed for New Delhi to lean on, with China remaining a question mark as far as its long-term policies are concerned.

It is not so much a question of Soviet success in pressuring India on specific issues; there have been trade-offs on Germany,[23] on Cambodia, on arms. Rather, a country which has fought hard, and at some cost to itself, against becoming a loyalist middle power on American terms, is now in danger of being sucked into the Soviet sphere. Outside of verbal partisan warfare, there is little recognition in India of the danger of overdependence on the Soviets. Points are made in debate and forgotten. The present Indian tendency to make marginal concessions and trade-offs can lead to bigger concessions. India is not under Moscow's thumb, but the potential for Soviet ability to influence Indian policy exists.

Russia has greater stamina in Asia than America. This is determined not merely by the Soviet state structure but also by its more vital interests in South Asia in particular. South Asia is almost on the Soviet southern border, now brought closer by its intervention in Afghanistan. Since the U.S. believes that the subcontinent as such, as opposed to the northwest littoral and the Indian Ocean, is an area of peripheral interest, its policies will continue to fluctuate, depending upon regional and global considerations.

Indian assertion of its independence of Moscow will depend upon domestic stability and the policy projections of the new leadership. Other factors will impinge on this relationship. China remains the central issue of Soviet Asian policy. The Soviets want to secure the subcontinent in a special relationship on the Tashkent model better to be able to deal with Beijing and promote their long-term interests.

All indications suggest that Beijing and Moscow will not return to the relationship obtaining in the Fifties[24] even as more commerce, day-to-day contacts and civility are introduced into this relationship. China needs better relations with Moscow to pursue its own objectives. One reaction the possibility of a Sino-Soviet rapprochement has evoked is that India should make special efforts to ensure the strength of its relations with Moscow,[25] an argument that is music to Russian ears.

One factor is likely to slow down the achievement of Soviet goals in Asia. The new cold war and American power projections around the world will make the Soviet leaders more cautious in promoting their interests. Since Khrushchev's ouster, the Soviet leadership has traditionally displayed caution and deliberation in securing gains, often when opportunities have offered themselves.

India has been unable to offer an attractive alternative to the U.S. or Pakistan. The latter cannot get away from South Asia, despite the important linkage it has built up with countries of the Middle East. Once again, as in the Fifties, Indo-Pakistani problems have become coupled with the cold war. Psychologically, Pakistan wants to be in the same league as India, and India in the same league as China.

There are interesting parallels in Soviet and Chinese behaviour towards India and Pakistan respectively. After the 1971 Indo-Pakistani war, which had the effect of making India more independent of Moscow, Brezhnev came to New Delhi with the primary aim of tying India down to a series of long-range trade and economic commitments. With the major new U.S.-Pakistan arms agreement, China lost its primacy as the main arms supplier to Pakistan and began emphasizing its trade links. In both cases, trade was being used as a lever to promote and sustain close relations.

On Kashmir as well, Moscow and Beijing have been following similar policies, making their support for the positions adopted by their friends more ambiguous. The Soviet Union now takes its stand on the basis of the approach it adopted in 1964 in the U.N. Security Council.[26] In a gesture to Pakistan, Moscow had then acknowledged that there was a Kashmir dispute and had refrained from attacking Pakistan. In the newer Chinese formulations, Kashmir became a bilateral problem between India and Pakistan, and Beijing has in recent times refrained from publicizing the issue in joint statements with Pakistan.

Kashmir is the symbol of Indo-Pakistani enmity. In softening their positions, Moscow and Beijing were sending out well-understood signals, each primarily directing them at its adversary's friend. It is remarkable that Moscow should be conducting this exercise in the face of the Pakistani approach to the Afghan issue and Islamabad's arms relationship with the U.S. Its attitude is determined by its desire to coopt Pakistan and to warn India of the limits of New Delhi's freedom of action in wooing China.

The Soviet intervention in Afghanistan and its consequences have, indeed, led the two major countries of the subcontinent and the three external powers to make new approaches. Pakistan is making much of its "vigorous" dialogue with Moscow while putting out ostentatious peace feelers to India. New Delhi and Beijing have been continuing their efforts to find a basis for the border settlement. The

U.S. has indicated its interest in building a new relationship with India, especially through an arms deal.

Each of the five countries is retaining its options while probing new directions in foreign policy. For India, this has meant reiteration of the security link with Moscow even as these relations have entered their most complex and dangerous phase. The Indian perception that the treaty is an effective but limited instrument is not fully shared by the Soviets, who tend to give it the status of the central arch of Indo-Soviet relations. The treaty gave the Soviets a foothold on the subcontinent.

Indo-Soviet regional interests no longer merge, even to the extent they did, although India continues to maintain the pretence. While Mrs. Gandhi showed flexibility in her moves towards China and the U.S., much of Indian elite reaction is still mired in traditional reflexes. One assumption made by supporters of a strong relationship with Moscow is that Indian policy is determined by geopolitics. The definition offered is that combined Soviet-Chinese hostility would be more dangerous for India than only China's or that of the West.[27]

Others suggest that Russians feel hurt to hear talk of India not putting all its eggs in one basket because it calls into question Soviet friendship and reliability as arms suppliers.[28] For them, Indo-Soviet relations are a one-way street, and their argument does not apply to Moscow's attempts to coopt Pakistan or to its disruption of India's exports in 1983.

Blaming the U.S. for pushing India closer to the Soviet Union, as a large section of the Indian elite tends to do, offers no solution. Nor does the suggestion that Russia gets things on the cheap, thanks to American folly.[29] The loser in the game will primarily be India. It is not good enough to hope and pray for a more helpful U.S. policy. It is neither in U.S. nor Chinese interest for India to become a Soviet satellite, but others will not pull its chestnuts out of the fire. India is still not overdependent on the Russians, but is in danger of becoming so.

The U.S. does not offer India a viable alternative, and domestic compulsions militate against too close an alignment with Washington. Having chosen the elitist model of development, the Indian leadership must pay lip service to the socialist creed. Nehru tamed Indian Communists with his variety of socialism and Mrs. Gandhi was of the firm belief that a government, to survive, must profess to be left-leaning.[30] Communists have played a role in the making of Indian foreign policy out of proportion to their strength; they can be a catalyst for violence in large parts of the country, should they change their tack. Mrs. Gandhi's consistent efforts to have the support of at least a section of the Communists must be ascribed to the primacy she attached to refurbishing her leftist credentials to stay in power.

An instrument which could make India less dependent on the Russians would come at the cost of U.S., and Soviet, nonproliferation goals. A nagging Indian security concern, which has found little appreciation in American policy-making circles, is the perceived nuclear threat from China. The implicit Soviet guarantee is an interim and imperfect assurance for New Delhi, dependent as it is on the triangular Washington-Moscow-Beijing relationship.

India's compulsions to take the path of nuclear weaponry are clear enough to its policy-makers. But the problem has become complicated by Pakistan's progress in nuclear technology. U.S. pressures on Pakistan to desist from going ahead with its assumed nuclear weapon programme have served to delay Indian plans because New Delhi does not want to give Islamabad an easy way out of its dilemma. However, they have not negated a probable Indian decision to take the nuclear option.

Perhaps Soviet and U.S. interests will merge in India, as they once did in containing China, for preventing it from becoming a nuclear weapon power. If India does not go in for nuclear weapons before the end of the decade, it will be because of domestic turmoil or combined U.S.-Soviet pressure. The logic of the situation demands that India join the nuclear club as a full-fledged member.[31] In all likelihood, both India and Pakistan will become nuclear powers before the next decade arrives.

The Soviet Union made India's nonalignment credible; it helped build a heavy industry and arms technology base and ultimately enabled India to win the Bangladesh war. India, for its part, made the Soviet Union acceptable to the Third World and has traditionally muted its criticism of Moscow on major world issues, apart from displaying initial outright partisanship on Afghanistan, to be left out in the cold holding the baby.

Russians want to foreclose Indian options in a future setting. India will not come under the Soviet banner next year or the year after, but it is likely to become more malleable to Soviet purposes, with its fierce nationalism made progressively mellower, unless some hard decisions are taken. This is particularly true in the trade field, even more than the arms relationship, because New Delhi has to decide whether to treat trade as a means of repaying debts or to move closer to the Soviets in an area in which Moscow already enjoys alarming leverage.

Today, India is at a turning point. The future of the Indo-Soviet relationship will be determined by domestic developments, the regional and world picture and the degree of rapprochement that comes about between India and China. In more ways than one, China holds the key to unlock Indian doors to a less constrictive world. The era of Indo-Pakistani amity is for the long haul.

Indo-Soviet relations will remain close, with increasing areas of divergence between the two countries. The treaty will, in all probability, last indefinitely unless India takes the unlikely step of giving notice to end it. The best that India can hope to do is to let it stay in the background. The critical question now is to define the limits of the Indo-Soviet relationship.

Chapter Twelve

Epilogue

OCTOBER 31, 1984 was a black day in modern India's history. Indira Gandhi was gunned down by two of her Sikh bodyguards in her official residence. The wounded Sikh psyche had wreaked its vengeance through two, if not more, misguided men. Rajiv, who was campaigning for the Congress in West Bengal, returned to the capital post-haste and was sworn in Prime Minister the same evening.

Ironically, the manner of Indira's death made Rajiv's accession to power surprisingly swift and smooth, fulfilling his mother's desire in tragic circumstances. But the assassination led to large-scale rioting, looting and killing of Sikhs in New Delhi and several other northern towns. The capital, indeed, was the worst affected, and it took the authorities several days to get to grips with the situation, ultimately with the army's help.

The police proved totally ineffective, and, according to credible accounts, even incited the mobs to mayhem and murder, as did several local functionaries of the ruling Congress(I) in Delhi.[1] At the end of the carnage, thousands of Sikhs had been killed, many more were made homeless and millions of rupees worth of Sikh property was destroyed.

For a leader of exceptional qualities, Indira Gandhi's legacy to Rajiv was very mixed. She left him two major regional problems—of Punjab and Assam—unresolved. She had reduced the mother Congress party to a shadow of its former self. It was also her penchant for wanting to exercise total power that led to the demoralization of the country's civil service. Some slippage in the famed "steel frame" of India was inevitable in view of the democratization of the service and the greatly expanded tasks it had to cope with in supervising development activity. But Indira's criteria of rewarding loyalty, and not always merit, left the service confused and in low spirits.

Rajiv's coming to power was greeted with near-universal relief. He was 40, still had the "Mr. Clean" image and promised to take the country forward. He started on a cautious note, emphasizing the need to root out corruption, and gathered round him young technocrats, men the traditional politicians derisively called the "computer boys". Above all, he promised stability at a time the Sikh problem in particular was casting its long shadow. Expectation was in the air, despite the recent tragedy and carnage.

Internationally, the new Prime Minister aroused much interest, particularly in the United States.[2] He was young, unencumbered by the ideological baggage of the past, was technologically-minded and promised to take his country into the 21st Century. Washington hoped that he would, in a measure, undo his mother's pro-Soviet tilt. Despite the red-carpet treatment the Russians had given him as heir-apparent, they were nervous about his proclivities and worried that their sources of information in the Indian power structure had dried up.[3]

Notwithstanding the hopes and anxieties Rajiv aroused in the two superpower capitals, his mind was very much on domestic affairs. National elections were promptly announced for December 24 and 27, except in the troubled Punjab and Assam states. The simmering Punjab crisis, leading to the army's storming of the Golden Temple, Mrs. Gandhi's murder and the anti-Sikh killings had turned the majority Hindu mood brittle and hard.[4] The country soon discovered that the quiet, affable leader had learnt a few lessons from his mother. He fully exploited the Hindu mood to make the cause of the country's unity and integrity his central campaign theme. Far from offering balm to the Sikhs, he exacerbated their feelings, and even presented the opposition parties as being less than patriotic for allegedly colluding with Sikh extremists.[5]

The election results were a major triumph for Rajiv. The Congress(I) won 400 out of 509 seats in the Lower House, a record even Rajiv's grandfather had not achieved. The party registered a preponderant win in the northern Hindi-speaking states; even the Marxist citadel in West Bengal was breached. But Rajiv's magic was less potent in the South, in Andhra Pradesh in particular, chiefly because of local resentment over the Centre's past policies. The electorate had got Rajiv's message and the sympathy factor for Rajiv worked in his favour.

Rajiv did not make any substantive moves on Punjab because elections in a number of states were in the offing. And he mounted another major campaign. His party's performance in March was less impressive, although creditable enough. Sikkim, Andhra Pradesh and Karnataka went over to the opposition; the opposition parties, licking their wounds after the drubbing they received in the parliamentary elections, fared rather better. The electors had proved discriminating in giving Rajiv an emphatic national mandate, but showed their reservations in elections to states.

With the two sets of elections out of the way, Rajiv made his first move to tackle the Punjab problem by offering two major concessions, apart from releasing a number of Sikh leaders. He agreed to hold a judicial inquiry into the anti-Sikh riots, reversing his earlier stand, and lifted the banning orders on the All-India Sikh Students' Federation, identified with the extremist wing. As if in response, Sikh militants carried out attacks on two Congress(I) functionaries in Punjab. The events demonstrated the difficulties involved in arriving at a settlement with Sikhs, who remained alienated from the Government as a group. The Akali party, moreover, was in the throes of an internal power struggle.

Foreign policy intruded into Rajiv's major domestic concerns, particularly in relation to Sri Lanka and Pakistan. Besides, there was the commitment to host a six-nation conference of leaders from five continents in New Delhi in January. The meeting took place on schedule, with a predictable resolution crowning its labours.[6] But the Delhi scene had already been enlivened by the unearthing of a major spy scandal involving the French, the Soviets, the Poles and the East Germans. India's relations with the French, in particular, came under a cloud, and the assistant French military attaché, Alain Bolley, was sent home, as also, later, the ambassador, Serge Boidevaix. The French adopted a low profile, despite resentment in Paris over having been singled out.[7] Poland's General Wojciech Jaruzelski, however, paid a scheduled visit to New Delhi in February and answered reporters' questions about Polish complicity in the spy scandal with a promise to have the matter investigated "scrupulously".[8]

Wearing his mother's mantle as chairperson of the nonaligned movement, Rajiv sent two senior Foreign Office officials in March to Iran and Iraq to mediate in the war. It was a gesture meant more for the record than out of any conviction of achieving a breakthrough. The Indian mission met the fate of countless other missions.

The death of the ailing Konstantin Chernenko provided Rajiv with an opportunity to undertake his first, rather ceremonial, visit abroad as Prime Minister. In Moscow, he met the new Soviet leader,

Mikhail Gorbachev, as also President Zia. The Russians went out of their way to make Rajiv welcome.[9] Gorbachev also met Zia and apparently did some tough talking, specifically bringing up the question of Pakistan's support of the Afghan *mujahideen*.[10]

Perhaps Rajiv's visit to Moscow was more significant for clarifying his immediate foreign policy objectives to his senior officials. He told them that he wanted to focus on the obvious and difficult goal of improving relations with neighbours.[11] At the head of the list was Sri Lanka, in view of the vicious chain of Tamil terrorists' activities alternating with the island's undisciplined army wreaking vengeance on Tamil civilians. The issue was complicated by the Tamil extremists' hideouts in the neighbouring Indian state of Tamil Nadu and the succour they received from India.

Some embarrassment was caused to India by two incidents in March involving Russians. Igor Gueja, a 37-year-old information attaché at the Soviet embassy, defected to the U.S. after reportedly missing from a New Delhi park. It was only after a tip-off from the Russians that the U.S. owned up the defection, evoking expressions of Indian concern. In the second instance, M.V. Khitzchenko, a trade official, was shot dead in the heart of New Delhi's diplomatic area as he was being driven in his car. Despite the arrest of over 20 Afghans and a claim of a Ukrainian terrorist organization, the motive of the murder remained unresolved three months after the event.

Rajiv had two foreign calendar events to honour. The French renewed their invitation to open a year-long Festival of India, agreed to by Mrs. Gandhi. They were particularly keen on the visit to end the strained relations caused by the spy scandal. Similarly, President Reagan invited Rajiv to open a Festival of India in the U.S., flowing out of Mrs. Gandhi's visit to Washington in 1982. In the event, Rajiv decided to honour both commitments, but he took the precaution of undertaking an official visit to Moscow first. The last was a gesture to reassure the nervous Russians that India's policy of giving primacy to the Soviet Union had not changed.[12]

Rajiv's Moscow visit in May took place along somewhat predictable lines. Gorbachev was attentive, and two agreements, negotiated earlier, were signed in Moscow. The more significant of the two was a 15-year economic and commercial agreement, on the pattern of the one signed by Mrs. Gandhi, setting out cooperation between the two countries till the year 2000. True to the long-range Soviet policy of sponsoring a Moscow-supervised Asian security system, Gorbachev pointedly referred to "constructive initiatives... to ensure certain aspects of the security of the Asian continent and some of its regions", suggesting a comprehensive approach to these problems.[13] Rajiv was noncommittal and told a press conference in Moscow: "It [the issue] was discussed, but no specific proposals came up".[14]

Afghanistan did not figure in the joint communiqué. The Russians paid lip service to Indian sensitivities on the Indian Ocean as a zone of peace by jointly calling for the dismantling of all foreign bases and a ban on the creation of new ones. Moscow renewed its offer of providing atomic power plants, but Indian acceptance of the offer was withheld.[15] On the other hand, to the Soviets' satisfaction, Rajiv made clear his opposition to President Reagan's Strategic Defence Initiative. He could not have done otherwise, given his chairmanship of the nonaligned movement and the six-nation declaration signed in New Delhi in January.

With Pakistan, meanwhile, the see-saw in relations continued, belying earlier hopes. The first Zia meeting with Rajiv during Mrs. Gandhi's funeral was held in an atmosphere of some cordiality. But later Rajiv took a more strident line on Pakistan, flowing out of the compulsion of Indian elections and growing concern over Pakistani encouragement of Sikh extremists.[16] Besides, in view of his forthcoming visit to the U.S., he was loath to give up a central theme of his American tour: to make known to the Reagan Administration and the American public India's concern over U.S. arms for Pakistan and Islambad's nuclear ambitions.

Similar problems did not impinge upon Rajiv's anxiety in resolving the Tamil problem. He directed his seniormost Foreign Office official, Romesh Bhandari, to visit Colombo to convince President Jayawardene of India's bona fides. A Rajiv-Jayawardene summit in New Delhi early in June set the stage for a cessation of hostilities between the Sri Lankan army and the major Tamil extremist groups[17] and an agreement to negotiate. And in a dramatic gesture towards regional cooperation, Rajiv and the Sri Lankan President journeyed to Dhaka together to convey their personal sorrow over the devastation caused in Bangladesh by a recent cyclone. The visit followed the hopeful tone set by a decision of Foreign Ministers of the South Asian Regional Cooperation (SARC) in Thimpu, Bhutan to fix the first summit of South Asian countries in Dhaka in December.[18]

Rajiv's visit West, apart from stops in Egypt and Algeria, started in France. He had declared before coming to Paris that the repercussions of the spy scandal on Indo-French relations were "95 percent over".[19] The French authorities pulled out all the stops in welcoming the young Prime Minister. And they succeeded in moving forward the major commercial and military negotiations that had been suspended in mid-air for months.

The most important lap of Rajiv's Western tour was Washington. A U.S. agreement to provide India with high technology items, signed in New Delhi in March, had already cleared the air, and Washington anticipated the visit with hope, but few illusions. A hopeful pointer was an announcement made by the Federal Bureau of Investigation on May 13 that it had foiled a plot by Sikh militants to kill Rajiv in the U.S. New Delhi reacted with recording its deep appreciation.

Rajiv's visit to Washington achieved all that it could have been expected to. He gave the U.S. some satisfaction on Afghanistan by suggesting that India favoured a government in Kabul that the Afghan refugees in Pakistan could return to with honour.[20] But he was particularly noncommittal on a U.S. offer of arms,[21] and the differing perceptions of the two countries on world problems and on Pakistan were not narrowed. Rajiv honed in on Pakistan's efforts to build a military nuclear capability and the supply of sophisticated U.S. conventional arms to Islamabad. He was seeking to influence American public opinion, particularly on Capitol Hill.[22]

Expectedly, Rajiv expressed "deep reservations about the militarization of outer space" in his address to the U.S. Congress. But Reagan said he and Rajiv had "hit it off",[23] and the atmosphere in the relationship seemed to have improved. The liberal economic policies Rajiv had introduced through the Indian budget aroused interest in the U.S. and should encourage greater infusion of American private capital and know-how into India. The American option, for the foreseeable future, seems limited to seeking to influence Indian policy through greater interaction in trade and technology.

Rajiv's major agenda will continue to be determined by domestic events, particularly the Sikh problem and growing intercaste animosites, exemplified by months of rioting and killings in the western state of Ahmedabad over reservation of jobs and college places for the underpriviledged. A rash of terrorist bombings, ascribed to Sikh militants, in New Delhi and other cities claimed scores of lives in May. The crash of an Air-India plane, with 329 aboard, into the Atlantic in June aroused immediate suspicions in India that it was the work of Sikh militants abroad.

Predictably, Rajiv has hewn close to his mother's foreign policy during his first eight months in office. He has emphasized the primacy of India's relations with the Soviet Union even as he has sought to open a less abrasive chapter with neighbours and the U.S. Nuances are important, but it remains to be seen whether Rajiv's less effusive relations with the Russians and greater openness towards Americans are matters of style or substance.

Only in relations with China has Rajiv sounded a surprisingly pessimistic note. Not only does he seem to accord a low priority to a resolution of the border problem, but he has also coupled it with the Soviets' own efforts to improve relations with China, thus giving Moscow a form of veto.[24] In the longer term, India's opening to China and greater trade and economic interaction with the U.S. will determine how far Rajiv can move out of the Soviet orbit.

The Russians have begun to take account of the realities of the Communist movement in India by giving belated recognition to the CPI(M). For the first time, a CPI(M) delegation was invited to an official anniversary celebration in Moscow—on the 40th anniversary of victory over Fascism in May—together with the CPI. Despite ideological and personality clashes with the Marxists and divisions in the CPI, the pro-Moscow party is seeking to work in cooperation with the CPI(M).[25] The Russians, no doubt, will continue to pursue their interests in India through the CPI even as they woo Rajiv.

References

Chapter One

1. Larry Collins and Dominique Lapierre, *Mountbatten and the Partition of India*, New Delhi: Vikas, 1982, p. 15.
1. *Ibid.*, p. 47.
3. *Ibid.*, p. 74.
4. *Ibid.*, p. 70.
5. Sarvepalli Gopal, *Jawaharlal Nehru: A Biography*, Volume I, Bombay: Oxford University Press, 1976, p. 109.
6. B.R. Nanda, ed., *Indian Foreign Policy: The Nehru Years*, New Delhi: Vikas, 1976, p. 3.
7. *Mirovoe Khozyaistvo i Mirovaya Politika*, quoted in Harish Kapur, *The Soviet Union and the Emerging Nations: A Case Study of Soviet Policy Towards India*, London: Michael Joseph, 1972, p. 26.
8. W.Z. Laqueur, "The Shifting Line in Soviet Orientology," *Problems of Communism*, March-April 1956.
9. *Ibid.*
10. T.N. Kaul, *Diplomacy in Peace and War: Recollections and Reflections*, New Delhi: Vikas, 1979, p. 12.
11. *Ibid.*, p. 15.
12. Nanda, op. cit., p. 135.
13. Collins and Lapierre, op. cit., p. 47.
14. Larry Collins and Dominique Lapierre, *Freedom at Midnight*, New Delhi: Vikas, 1976, p. 354.
15. Sarvepalli Gopal, *Jawaharlal Nehru: A Biography*, Volume II, Delhi: Oxford University Press, 1979, p. 21.
16. Jawaharlal Nehru, *An Autobiography*, London: The Bodley Head, 1955, p. 366.
17. *Ibid.*, p. 608.
18. Jawaharlal Nehru, *The Discovery of India*, Calcutta: The Signet Press, 1946, p. 666.
19. Gopal, Vol. I, op. cit., p. 103.
20. Jawaharlal Nehru, *India's Foreign Policy: Selected Speeches*, September 1946-April 1961, New Delhi: Publications Division, 1961, p. 250.
21. *Ibid.*, p. 305.
22. Dedijer has explained his role in the CPI Congress thus: "All Southeast Asia was suffering from poverty and injustice; a target of imperialist advances, the people had no recourse but to defend themselves with their bare hands. It is true that we did not try to conceal our opinions. We had just emerged from the revolution, we were young and full of enthusiasm. We wanted to help all the world's oppressed

to liberate themselves as soon as possible. But all we did was to agree with the assessments that Asian Communists themselves had made." *The Battle Stalin Lost: Memoirs of Yugoslavia, 1948-1953*, New York; Grosset & Dunlap, 1972. p. 25. The Communist Party of India (CPI) was organized as an all-India party in 1933. It was placed under the tutelage of the Communist Party of Great Britain because immediately after the end of World War II Moscow had little knowledge of, or interest in, India, its preoccupations being largely European. In 1942, under British Communist Party pressure, the CPI changed its line from "imperialist war" to "people's war" after Soviet entry into it against strong Indian nationalist feelings, a stigma it bears to this day. Moscow did not formulate a clear life for the CPI between 1945 and 1949. H. Kautsky, *Moscow and the Communist Party of India*, New York: M.I.T. and John Wiley & Sons, 1956, p. 27. I have, in a large measure, relied on Kautsky in sketching out the earlier history of the CPI.
23. Laqueur, op. cit.
24. Indian Ambassador Panikkar reported to Nehru on August 5, 1951, after meeting Zhou Enlai, the Chinese Prime Minister's view, "Much depends upon India and much is expected of her by the peoples of Asia. She has won a great position of leadership by her courageous policy of independence. I hope she will maintain the leadership." Gopal, Vol. II, op. cit., p. 177.
25. *Ibid.*, p. 116.
26. On the other hand, the Soviet delegate, Andrei Vyshinsky, made his famous jibe at India during a General Assembly debate on Korea. He said: "At best you [Indians] are dreamers and idealists; at worst, you don't understand your own position and camouflage horrible American policy." J.A. Naik, *Soviet Policy Towards India: From Stalin to Brezhnev*, New Delhi: Vikas, pp. 68 and 70.
27. Nehru told the Lok Sabha (Lower House) on March 29, 1956, "In a sense, they [SEATO and the Baghdad Pact] tend to encircle us," Nehru, *Speeches*, op. cit., p. 94.
28. Collins and Lapierre, *Mountbatten*, op. cit., p. 39.
29. Nehru's statement in Parliament on March 17, 1950. Nehru, *Speeches*, op. cit., p. 456.
30. G.W. Choudhury, *India, Pakistan, Bangladesh, and the Major Powers*, New York: The Free Press, p. 13.
31. Leo E. Rose gives a clear analysis of Nehru's global policy in *India, China and the Afro-Asian Bloc*, Reprint No. 277, Center for South Asia Studies, University of California.
32. Gopal, Vol. II, op. cit., p. 241.
33. *Ibid.*, p. 243.
34. *Ibid.*, p. 105.
35. *Ibid.*, p. 107.
36. The text of the letter is in Annexure I, p. 263 in Kuldip Nayar, *Between the Lines*, Delhi: Hind Pocket Books, 1969.
37. Kaul, op. cit., p. 109.
38. Gopal, Vol. II, op. cit., p. 108.
39. *Ibid.*, p. 105.
40. *Ibid.*, p. 180. Also, Subimal Dutt, *With Nehru in the Foreign Office*, Calcutta: Minerva Associates, 1977, p. 138n.
41. Gopal, Vol. II, op. cit., p. 180.

42. Nehru told the Lok Sabha on November 20, 1950 in answer to a question, "Our maps show that the McMahon Line is our boundary—map or no map." Quoted in Neville Maxwell, *India's China War*, Bombay: Jaico, 1970, p. 75. Despite the inaccurate and sensational title, Maxwell has made a valuable contribution to literature on the border war. Perhaps because he largely swallowed the Indian line during his days as the London *Times* correspondent on the subcontinent, he has erred in giving the benefit of the doubt to the Chinese on almost every major aspect of the dispute. To his credit, Maxwell does make the point that while he had full access to Indian sources and even some secret documents, he had only the official record to go by as far as China was concerned, giving his account an "unavoidable imbalance."
43. *Ibid.*, p. 83.
44. Gopal, Vol. II, op. cit., p. 180.
45. Maxwell, op. cit., p. 73.
46. Dutt, op. cit., p. 88.
47. S. Gopal, "India, China and the Soviet Union," *The Australian Journal of Politics and History*, August 1966.
48. The *Kommunist* article said in part: "Serious mistakes have occasionally been committed in appraising the role of the national bourgeoisie of the countries of the East in the anti-imperialist movement. The progressive forces of Kemal [Ataturk] and the Kemalists in the fight against imperialism in the 1920s have been ignored. Also, in surveying the role of Gandhi in the anti-imperialist struggle, our Orientalists have not always taken as their point of departure the concrete historical circumstances in India itself." Quoted in Laqueur, op. cit.
49. Kaul, op. cit., p. 132.
50. Nanda, op. cit., p. 111.
51. Quoted in Richard B. Remnek, *Soviet Policy Towards India*, New Delhi: Oxford & I.B.H., pp. 124-25.
52. Gopal, Vol. II, op. cit., p. 248. Bhilai was later to become a symbol of Soviet propagation of the ideal relationship between Moscow and a developing country. The Soviets certainly put their best foot forward. They sent V.I. Dymshits, later elevated to the post of deputy prime minister, to Bhilai and sent their best technicians. The credit Moscow gave India for Bhilai was of $118 million. "Communist Aid Activities in Non-Communist Less Developed Countries, 1979 and 1954-79," National Foreign Assessment Center of Central Intelligence Agency, October 1980.
53. Bhabani Sen Gupta, *The Fulcrum of Asia—Relations Among China, India, Pakistan, and the U.S.S.R.*, New York: Pegasus, 1970, p. 76.
54. Gopal, Vol. II, p. 251.
55. *Ibid.*, p. 252.
56. Veljko Micunovic, *Moscow Diary*, New York: Doubleday, 1980, p. 9.
57. Bhabani Sen Gupta gives a cogent analysis of Nehru's disarmament policies in Nanda, op. cit., pp. 228-51.
58. I have relied on John Gittings' survey of Sino-Soviet differences in sketching the landmarks. *The Survey of the Sino-Soviet Dispute*, London: Oxford University Press, 1968.
59. Gopal, Vol. II, op. cit., pp. 277-90.
60. Dutt, op. cit., p. 177.

61. Gopal, Vol. II, op. cit., pp. 291-9.
62. *Ibid.*, p. 159.
63. Chester Bowles, *A View from Delhi*, Yale University Press, 1969, p. 167.
64. In the CPI, B.T. Ranadive was facing a strong attack from the Andhra faction espousing Maoism. In the early part of 1949, the process of neo-Maoism continued until it was approved by Moscow towards the end of that year. Ranadive was replaced by Rajeswara Rao of the Andhra faction in June 1950. Moscow's interference in CPI's affairs was at this time minimal and there was an inevitable time lag between what the Soviets wanted and CPI compliance. In December 1950 Palme Dutt of the British Communist Party gave a signal for a change to the Nehru government; in January 1951 the CPI discovered that "Nehru was not a lackey of imperialism after all." Kautsky, op. cit., p. 133.

In a note on foreign policy in February 1950, Nehru had written, "India does not charge the Soviet Union with responsibility for Communist activities in India, but we have little doubt that Russia has encouraged them and can certainly stop them if it so chose." During the B & K visit, Nehru had raised the CPI question with the Soviet leaders. Khrushchev told Nehru "on his 'word of honour' that the Soviet Communist Party had no connection with the Communist Party of India, and this was confirmed by the very fact that Soviet policy had placed the Indian party in an awkward position.... As for foreign subsidies to the Indian party, Khrushchev asserted that he knew nothing about such payments. Nehru then expressed the general belief that Indian nationals were employed in Communist embassies on the recommendation of the Indian Communist Party, and that the peace movement was intended to encourage Communism rather than peace." Gopal, Volume II, op. cit., pp. 64 and 253-4. Khrushchev, on the other hand, later admitted, "... We cultivated very close ties with the Communist Party of India." *Khrushchev Remembers, The Last Testament*, translated and edited by Strobe Talbott, London: Andre Deutsch, 1974, p. 306.
65. Naik, op. cit., p. 93.
66. Quoted in Rajan Menon, "India and the Soviet Union: A New Stage in Relations?", *Asian Survey*, July 1978.
67. Marshall I. Goldman, *Soviet Foreign Aid*, New York: Praeger, 1976, p. 192.
68. Myron Weiner, *Assessing the Impact of Foreign Assistance in India: A Rising Middle Power*, Colorado: Westview Press, 1979, p. 52.
69. Morarji Desai, *The Story of My Life*, Vol. II, New Delhi: S. Chand, 1974, p. 156.
70. Nanda, op. cit., p. 87.
71. Gopal, Vol. II, op. cit., pp. 46-47.
72. *Ibid.*, p. 63.
73. Sudhir Ghosh, a member of Parliament, records a talk he had with Nehru after his U.S. visit in 1961. He told Nehru, "My own impression is that you think the Americans are barbarians, in the Greek sense." *Gandhi's Emissary*, Calcutta: Rupa, 1967, p. 318. Morarji Desai, who visited Washington in 1961, was told by President Kennedy, "Whenever you consider that we are erring, you criticize us in very strong language, but when you find Soviet Russia erring in some matter, you talk to them in very polite language and hesitate to find fault with them. Do you not consider this a partial attitude?" Desai answered, "Soviet Russia is a Communist country with a dictatorial government, while you and we are

democratic countries. It is clear that Soviet Russia cannot behave like a democratic government. It is, therefore, not possible to convert them by finding fault with them or by censuring them if they do something wrong. But there is a possibility of converting them to some extent if the method of friendly persuasion is adopted." Desai suggests that Kennedy accepted "the wisdom of this stand." Desai, op. cit., pp. 171-72.

74. By stages, the CPI, under Moscow's guidance, had been made to realize first, that Nehru's foreign policy was generally good but his domestic policy bad and ultimately that there were favourable features in his domestic policy as well. Internecine quarrels in the party made these changes a painful experience for the CPI. Its victory in the Kerala elections was a shot in the arm for the rightists in the party and Khrushchev's new policy towards the developing world. Henry Gelman, *The Communist Party of India: Sino-Soviet Battleground* in A. Doak Barnett, ed., *Communist Strategies in Asia*, New York: Praeger, 1963, p. 104.
75. Quoted in S.M. Burke, *Pakistan's Foreign Policy*, London: Oxford University Press, 1973, p. 266.
76. Maxwell records that in the twelve years to mid-1959 the U.S. had given India about $1.7 billion of aid., op. cit., p. 146.
77. Arthur M. Schlesinger, Jr. gives a dramatic account of Kennedy's, and his own, great disappointment with Nehru's visit. "I had the impression of an old man, his energies depleted, who heard things as at a great distance and answered most questions with indifference.... It was, the President said later, like trying to grab something in your hand, only to have it turn out to be just fog. It was all so sad: this man had done so much for Indian independence, but he had stayed around too long, and now it was going bit by bit.... The following spring, reminiscing about the meeting, Kennedy described it to me as 'a disaster... the worst head-of-state visit I have had.'" *A Thousand Days*, London: Andre Deutsch, 1967, pp. 456-57.
78. Gopal, Vol. II, op. cit., p. 183.
79. Naik, op. cit., p. 123.
80. According to Maxwell, "that [no-war pact] was originally urged by Liaquat Ali Khan, Prime Minister of Pakistan, and turned down by Nehru." But his suggestion that the sponsorship of the proposal is determined by the country that feels vulnerable at a given moment is not borne out by facts, as later events show. Op. cit., p. 180.
81. Nehru made the statement in the Rajya Sabha (Upper House) on May 4, 1959. Quoted in Maxwell, op. cit., p. 206.

Chapter Two

1. Maxwell, op. cit., p. 98.
2. Gopal, *Australian Journal*, op. cit.
3. Dutt, op. cit., p. 133.
4. The Dalai Lama's press conference on June 20, 1959, Quoted in Gopal, *Australian Journal*, op. cit.
5. This surmise is recorded in W.R. Crocker, *Nehru*, London, 1966. Quoted in *Ibid*.
6. Maxwell says that support and direction for the rebels came from Kalimpong and

the Indian government connived at it. Op. cit, p.104.
7. Dutt, op. cit., pp. 121-2.
8. Nehru, *Speeches*, op. cit., p. 333.
9. Gittings, op. cit., Appendix J, p. 327. According to the Khrushchev account, "We knew in advance our statement [of September 9] wouldn't be well received in Peking [Beijing]." *Khrushchev Remembers*, op. cit., p. 307.
10. Nehru's statement to the Lok Sabha on September 25, 1959. Quoted in Maxwell, op. cit., p. 277.
11. Gittings, op. cit., p. 111.
12. *Ibid.*, pp. 110-1.
13. *Ibid.*, p. 105.
14. *Ibid.*, p. 111.
15. K.P.S. Menon, *The Flying Troika*, London: Oxford University Press, 1963, pp. 236-7.
16. Maxwell asserts that the Chinese suggested the officials' meeting. Op. cit., p. 163. Gopal, on the other hand, says it was an Indian suggestion. *Australian Journal*, op. cit. Nayar suggests that Krishna Menon had told Chinese Foreign Minister Chen Yi that India might accept Chinese suzerainty over the Aksai Chin area and a ten-mile strip as a buffer if Beijing accepted the McMahon Line and India's rights to the rest of Ladakh. China had reportedly accepted this and so had Krishna Menon. But Nehru's powerful Home Minister, G.B. Pant, had stood in the way. Pant met Zhou during his visit, a device Nehru used to involve other leaders in the China question as also to present a solid front to Zhou. Op. cit., pp. 174-5. K.P.S. Menon believed that "Nehru seemed personally disposed to negotiate on the frontier problem, but he gave up the idea and assumed an inflexible posture as a result of the opposition of some of his colleagues in the Cabinet and criticism in Parliament." Quoted in Karunakaran Gupta, *The Hidden History of the Sino-Indian Frontier*, Calcutta; Minerva, 1974, p. 60.
17. Gopal, *Australian Journal*, op. cit. According to Gopal, the fact that India took the initiative in publishing the officials' reports was an indication of the strength of the Indian case.
18. Gittings, op. cit., p. 120.
19. *Ibid.*, p. 124.
20. *Ibid.*, p. 131.
21. *Ibid.*, p. 146. At the Communist conference in Moscow in the summer of 1969, S.A. Dange said the CPI would continue its efforts towards "converting this area of tension [South Asia] into an area of peace and friendship" and that "the great influence and prestige of the Soviet Union" could be a "decisive force" in achieving this goal. *The Amrita Bazar Patrika*, Calcutta, June 24, 1969. A New China News Agency commentary on July 13, 1969 charged the Soviet Union with trying to use "the notorious renegade Dange" as its "agent to realize the Asian security system."
22. Gopal, *Australian Journal*, op. cit.
23. Despite the Soviet and Indian belief that China had deliberately chosen the time when Moscow was faced with a major crisis on another front, Gittings says there is no proof that China took advantage of the Cuban situation to act on the Sino-Indian border. Op. cit., p. 174.
24. Maxwell, op. cit., p. 342.

25. Nehru told a press conference in New Delhi in April 1956: "Indian forces had in the past been developed largely on the basis of British equipment and for practical reasons it was convenient, other things being equal, to continue on this basis." *The Times*, London, April 3, 1956. Ninety per cent of India's military stores and equipment in 1950 was British. Lorne J. Kavic, *India's Quest for Security: Defense Policies, 1947-1965*, Berkeley: University of California Press, 1967, p. 129.
26. Raju G.C. Thomas, *The Defense of India: A Budgetary Perspective of Strategy and Politics*, Columbia, Missouri: South Asia Books, 1978, p. 92.
27. Kavic, op. cit., pp. 85-6.
28. Minister for Defence Organization Mahavir Tyagi admitted in the Lok Sabha on March 25, 1953 that "a feeling is growing among our men that they are not paid the same attention which they had under their alien employers. It may be an unfortunate impression, but the impression is there." Quoted in Kavic, op. cit., p.137.
29. *The Hindu Weekly Review*, September 9, 1963.
30. Kavic, op. cit., Appendix X, pp. 242-3.
31. Op. cit., p. 211.
32. Wynfred Joshua and Stephen P. Gilbert, *Arms For the Third World: Soviet Military and Diplomacy*, Johns Hopkins Press, 1969, p. 58. In November 1955, the British High Commissioner, Malcolm MacDonald, conveyed his country's "grave concern" if India went in for Soviet military purchases. In March 1956 Britain's Foreign Minister Anthony Eden persuaded Nehru not to accept a Soviet offer of a squadron of Ilyushins the Indian Air Force wanted; Moscow had promised to supply the planes quickly at a reasonable price. Eden said the British would speed up deliveries of Gnats and Canberras. Gopal, Volume II, op. cit., pp. 252 and 273-4.
33. According to Joshua and Gilbert, "The Soviet Union agreed [in the summer of 1962]... to help India build two production facilities. The first would produce and assemble MIG-21s; the second would manufacture engines for a supersonic jet under development in India. The Soviet Union also pledged to deliver a number of MIG-21 jets which India claimed it needed to counter Pakistan's acquisition of F-104 fighters from the United States." Although Indonesia was the first country in the developing world to receive MIG-21s, India was the only country to obtain a licensing agreement to produce and assemble MIG-21s at home. Op. cit., pp. 59 and 73.
34. K. Subrahmanyam, Director, The Indian Institute for Defence Studies and Analyses, in a personal communication of February 10, 1984.
35. *Aviation Week*, July 23, 1962. Cited in Kavic, op. cit., p. 107. The seriousness of the Lightning offer must, however, remain open to question. Ambassador John Kenneth Galbraith, who was posted in New Delhi at the time, has suggested that President Kennedy disliked the idea. "Why should we spend $40 million to save the Indians from a foolish bargain [MIGs]?", he asked Galbraith. Although the White House later agreed on providing India fewer fighter planes and more heavy transports, "... the British went back on their Lightning offer for reasons which had mostly, I would judge, to do with cost." The U.S. offered to pay a larger share of the cost and the British "came part way back on the track," but Washington then decided to withdraw the C-130 offer. *Ambassador's Journal*, London:

Hamish Hamilton, 1969, pp. 383-6 and 399.
36. The U.S. declined to sell India Lockheed F-104s and comparable British and French aircraft were thought unsuitable or unavailable for sale. Lewis A. Frank, *The Arms Trade in International Relations*, New York: Praeger, 1969, p. 141. In early 1962, India's exploratory approach to the U.S. State Department for F-101 Voodoos and to the French for 50 Mirage-IIIs yielded no satisfactory arrangement. Kavic, op. cit., pp. 107-8.
37. Nehru later told Averell Harriman, "The Soviets had replied that they understood both the request [to the West for arms] and the need for it." Quoted in Robert H. Donaldson, *Soviet Policy toward India*, Cambridge: Harvard University Press, 1974, p. 163.
38. Among the countries that responded to India's appeal was France. Charles de Gaulle later explained that "...as upholders of the balance of power, we had every reason to wish to see India stand up to her powerful neighbour China. We gave a positive response to Pandit Nehru's appeal..." *Memoirs of Hope*, London: Weidenfeld and Nicolson, 1971, p. 262. But the terms of French military aid (hard cash) were onerous, unlike those of the U.S. and Britain, and caused resentment in Delhi. Maxwell, op. cit., p. 385.
39. K.P.S. Menon, op. cit., pp. 290-1
40. According to Maxwell, at first Russian airmen flew both the transports and the helicopters in Ladakh, training Indian copilots. There were complaints in Parliament that the Russians might report on Indian troop dispositions to the Chinese. Op. cit., p. 286.
41. Gittings, op. cit., p. 175.
42. The three-point Chinese proposal was: Pending a peaceful settlement, the armed forces of each side should withdraw 20 km. from the "line of actual control" and disengage; then China would be willing to withdraw its frontier guards in the eastern sector to north of the "line of actual control," neither side crossing this line; talks be held by the Chinese and Indian prime ministers. For Beijing, the "line of actual control" meant the line then held by the Chinese. Zhou later explained in a letter of October 27 that the line was the one "existing on November 7, 1959." In the Indian view, there was no such line and India made its stand on the September 8, 1962 line. The differences between the two lines involved territory claimed by both sides. Nayar, op. cit., pp. 180-1 and 200-1.
43. Gittings, op. cit., p. 175.
44. Nayar, op. cit., p. 222.
45. Gittings, op. cit., Appendix T, pp. 379-81. The Communist Party of India had finally called off the Telengana fighting in October 1951, and Nehru skilfully used his concept of nonalignment and friendly approach to the Soviet Union to keep the CPI from the insurrectionary path and to try to isolate it from the masses. The Indian Communists had over the years been bludgeoned by Moscow into supporting Nehru's foreign and some of his domestic policies. This had exacerbated the conflict between the right and the left, and the CPI became seriously affected by the emerging Sino-Soviet differences in 1959. By the fall of 1960 the Chinese were challenging Soviet domination of the CPI. By the end of 1961 the right wing of the CPI was openly criticizing China while the left wing was publishing statements supporting the Chinese line on Nehru. The CPI general secretary, Ajoy Ghosh, died in January 1963. Before his death, he had been

conducting a running battle with Beijing over the border question to provoke sharp Chinese attacks. Ghosh said the Chinese charges against the Indian party were an unwarranted interference in its internal affairs. Ghosh's line was opposed by the left faction, particularly in West Bengal and Andhra. In a compromise worked out in April 1962, Dange was made party chairman. In August, the CPI adopted a compromise resolution tilting towards Moscow. The Sino-Indian border war found the CPI more deeply divided than ever before. The anti-China faction won by a two to one margin in a bitter debate that preceded the adoption of a resolution by the party's National Council on November 1, 1962 appealing to all Indians to unite in defence of the motherland against aggression. Robert A. Scalapino, "Moscow, Peking and the Communist Parties of Asia," *Foreign Affairs*, January 1963.

46. Gittings, *ibid.*, p. 176.
47. *Ibid.*, p. 184.
48. Mohammad Ayub Khan, *Friends Not Masters*, Pakistan: Oxford University Press, 1967, p. 141.
49. Nayar, op. cit., p. 241.
50. Ayub, op. cit., p. 145. Pakistan's Foreign Minister told the National Assembly in November 1962, "I speak in anguish and not in anger when I have to say that one of our allies had promised us that we would be consulted before any arms assistance is given to India. I regret to observe that this has not been done." *Dawn*, Karachi, November 23, 1962. Quoted in Khurshid Hyder, "Recent Trends in the Foreign Policy of Pakistan," *The World Today*, November 1960.
51. *Ibid.*, p. 152.
52. *Ibid* Ayub's exposition of his foreign policy is contained in two chapters, pp.114-85.
53. G.W. Choudhury, "Reflections on Sino-Pakistan Relations," *Pacific Community*, January 1976.
54. Sen Gupta, *Fulcrum*, op. cit., 132-3.
55. Yaacov Vertzberger, "The Political Economy of Sino-Pakistani Relations," *Asian Survey*, May 1983.
56. Choudhury, *Reflections*, op. cit.
57. *Ibid*.
58. Quoted in Frank Moraes, *Witness to an Era*, New Delhi: Vikas, 1973, p. 233.
59. Nehru, *Speeches*, op. cit., p. 369.
60. Moraes, op. cit., pp. 220-1.
61. S.S. Khera, *India's Defence Problem*, New Delhi: Orient Longmans, 1968, p. 137.
62. Chinese Ambassador Pan Tzu-li had warned the Indian External Affairs Ministry on March 10, 1959, "It seems to us that you too cannot have two fronts." Quoted in Sen Gupta, *Fulcrum*, op. cit., p. 122.
63. Gopal, Vol. II, op. cit., p. 195.
64. According to Maxwell, the change in attitude came about because S. Gopal, then director of the Historical Division of the External Affairs Ministry, convinced Nehru that India's claim to Aksai Chin was stronger than China's. Op. cit., p. 119.
65. Indira Gandhi, "India and the World," *Foreign Affairs*, October 1972. Zhou Enlai blamed the Soviet Union for the Sino-Indian border war. According to him, the Russians had told India in 1962 that the Chinese would not fight back.

Neville Maxwell, *The Sunday Times*, London, December 5, 1971. Khrushchev, on the other hand, maintained, "I believe it was Mao himself who stirred up the trouble with India. I think he had some sick fantasy." *Khrushchev Remembers*, op. cit., p. 308.
66. Nanda, op. cit., p. 129.
67. David Floyd, *Mao Against Khrushchev: A Short History of the Sino-Soviet Conflict*, New York: Praeger, 1964, p. 366.
68. *People's Daily*, November 2, 1963. Extract in Gittings, op. cit., pp. 178-9.
69. Quoted in Nanda, op. cit., p. 113.
70. Maxwell, op. cit., p. 262. Maxwell quoted Zhou recalling Bandung ten years later to Pakistani journalists to comment on Nehru's "arrogance." p. 261.
71. A. Doak Barnett suggests the following three crucial turning points in the Sino-Soviet conflict: 1957-59: a broad divergence between China and the Soviet Union towards the U.S.; 1962-63: nuclear issues and the Soviet military build-up around China from 1965. George T. Yu (ed.), *China and the Balance of Power in Asia in Intra-Asian International Relations*, Colorado: Westview Press, 1977, pp. 34-6.
72. Gittings, op. cit., pp. 107-8.
73. Harold C. Hinton, *China's Turbulent Quest*. Quoted in Nanda, op. cit., p. 126.
74. *Motherland*, New Delhi, June 2, 1972. Quoted in Nanda, op. cit., pp. 126-7.
75. *People's Daily* and *Red Flag* of September 6, 1973 said, ".... In July [1960] the Soviet Government... provoked troubles on the Sino-Indian border...". Quoted in Gittings, op. cit., p. 161.
76. Incoming telegram, U.S. Department of State, December 19, 1963.
77. Outgoing telegram, U.S. Department of State, December 26, 1963. The State Department informed the U.S. Embassy in New Delhi that Ambassador Nehru had said, "If GOI [Government of India] had been consulted, it would have advised against IOTF [Indian Ocean Task Force] because it was not welcomed by nonaligned countries and U.S. has respect for opinion of nonaligned."
78. Gopal, *Australian Journal*, op. cit.
79. Joshua and Gilbert, op. cit., p. 59.
80. According to Indian officials, this was because the Soviets were not in a position to do so at that time. Interviews, New Delhi, October 1983.
81. Kavic, op. cit., p. 200.
82. Chester Bowles details at length how Kennedy's assassination and then Nehru's death came in the way of the final decision on arms supplies to India. The Pentagon was buttressed by a visit to the United States of Ayub, then Commander in Chief of the Pakistan army, to sabotage the long-term deal. *Promises to Keep: My Years in Public Life, 1941-1969*, New York: Harper & Row, 1971, pp. 439-84.
83. William J. Barnds makes this valid point in *India, Pakistan and the Great Powers*, New York: Praeger, 1972, p. 181.
84. I reported the Colombo meeting, as also the Djakarta preparatory conference, for *The Statesman*, Calcutta. I was the newspaper's Southeast Asia Correspondent from February 1962 till April 1967.
85. Soviet and East European assistance to Indonesia amounted to nearly 20 per cent of their assistance to the Third World through 1965. *Communist Aid Activities in Non-Communist Less Developed Countries, 1979 and 1954-79*, Central Intelligence Agency, October 1980.

86. Barnds rightly suggests that Indian leaders "probably had no very clear picture of the precise implications of the new relationship [with the Soviet Union]" and that the two countries' interest in close relations would have manifested itself in any case, despite the U.S.-Pakistan alliance immediately provoking it. Op. cit., pp. 116-7. The crucial question, however, remains: the degree of closeness in the Indo-Soviet relationship brought on by U.S. policies towards the subcontinent.
87. Nehru obviously failed in befriending Pakistan. He expressed his philosophy towards Pakistan thus in an address to the Indian Council of World Affairs in New Delhi on March 22, 1949: "We can be either rather hostile to each other or very friendly with each other. Ultimately, we can only be really very friendly, whatever period of hostility may intervene, because our interests are so closely interlinked." *Speeches*, op. cit., p. 42.

Chapter Three

1. Desai was sardonically to remark later, "Actually this [the Kamaraj plan] was the second step taken by Jawaharlalji to prevent me from succeeding him whenever such a contingency arose. Earlier he had prevented my being elected Deputy Leader of the Congress Parliamentary Party. It soon became clear that he wanted Indiraji to succeed him." ("Ji" an honorific showing respect). Op. cit., p. 204.
2. I used to meet Shastri when he was Nehru's home minister. In the way he analyzed problems, he struck me as an eminently sensible and reasonable man.
3. Kaul records Nehru telling him in February 1964, "Lal Bahadur is already acting as my Minister without Portfolio and has lightened my burden. To nominate him [as my successor] would only jeopardize his chances." *Diplomacy* op. cit. p. 154.
4. Nayar, *Between the Lines*, op. cit., pp. 17-20.
5. Indira Gandhi, *My Truth*, (Presented by Emmanuel Pouchpadass), New Delhi: Vision Books, 1981, p. 103.
6. Quoted in Sen Gupta, *Fulcrum*, p. 261.
7. Uma Vasudev, *Indira Gandhi*, New Delhi: Vikas, 1974, p. 333.
8. Krishan Bhatia, "Political Notebook," *The Hindustan Times*, January 15, 1965.
9. Kaul, *Diplomacy*, op. cit., pp. 154-5.
10. Gandhi, *My Truth*, op. cit., pp. 104-5.
11. Vasudev, op. cit., p. 324.
12. Elizabeth Krindl Walkenier gives a fascinating account of changes in Soviet economic thinking in "New Trends in Soviet Economic Relations with the Third World," *World Politics*, April 1970.
13. Kaul, *Diplomacy*, op. cit., p. 156.
14. *Link*, New Delhi, August 29, 1965.
15. Ayub, op. cit.
16. Zubeida Hasan, "Soviet Arms Aid to Pakistan and India," *Pakistan Horizon*, Fourth Quarter, 1968.
17. Choudhury, *Reflections*, op. cit.
18. Ayub, op. cit., p. 156.
19. Hasan, *Pakistan Horizon*, op. cit.
20. Kaul, by no means an enthusiastic recorder of Pakistani diplomatic successes, wrote, "He [Ayub] won the sympathy of some sections of the Soviet leadership in

the party, Government and Armed Forces." *Diplomacy*, op. cit., p. 157.
21. Choudhury, *Reflections*, op. cit.
22. Sen Gupta, "Moscow, Peking, and the Indian Political Scene," *Orbis*, Summer 1968.
23. Khera, op. cit., p. 304.
24. Interviews, New Delhi, March and October 1983. Bhabha had urged in a radio broadcast after the Chinese test that the only defence against nuclear attack "appears to be the capability and threat of retaliation." Quoted in A.G. Noorani, "India's Quest for a Nuclear Guarantee," *Asian Survey*, July 1967.
25. Bhabha had told me in an interview in New Delhi early in 1961 that it would take India eighteen months to explode a nuclear bomb, once a decision was taken by the Government.
26. Choudhury, *Reflections*, op. cit.
27. Vertzberger, op. cit.
28. Harold Wilson, *The Labour Government, 1964-1970*, London: Weidenfeld and Nicolson, 1971, p. 184.
29. Kuldip Nayar, *Distant Neighbours*, New Delhi: Vikas, p. 114.
30. Hasan, *Pakistan Horizon*, op. cit.
31. Choudhury, *Reflections*, op. cit.
32. Nayar, *Neighbours*, op. cit., p. 115. Kaul records, "Some top Soviet leaders privately assured me that it was not a shift in the Soviet policy against India, but an attempt to wean Pakistan away from the Western and Chinese influence." *Diplomacy*, op. cit., p. 159.
33. Nayar, *Neighbours*, p. 115.
34. *Ibid.*, p. 110.
35. *Ibid.*, p.112. Did China instigate Pakistan to attack India? There is no hard evidence to support this belief, widely held in India, but China's hostility to New Delhi and its efforts to complicate India's life were no secret.
36. Wilson, op. cit., pp. 133-4.
37. *Ibid.*, p. 221.
38. Address to the Pakistan Institute of International Affairs, Karachi on May 18, 1982. Extracts of the speech were obtained by me from official sources in New Delhi.
39. Choudhury, *Reflections*, op. cit.
40. Khurshid Hyder, "Recent Trends in the Foreign Policy of Pakistan," *The World Today*, November 1966.
41. Choudhury contends that the Chinese did not encourage Pakistan to go to war with India and that Bhutto and others read too much into China's assurances of support against Indian "aggression." *Reflections*, op. cit. Leo Rose has also pointed to the self-delusion of Pakistanis on the measure of Chinese support. "Pakistan's Role and Interests in South and Southwest Asia", *Asian Affairs*, December 1981.
42. Choudhury, *Reflections, ibid.*
43. Moraes, op. cit., p. 248. On the other hand, Desai says, "The Indian army had thought of attacking Lahore and taking possession of it, but did not succeed in doing so." op. cit., p. 226.
44. India's use of American weapons was, at best, marginal while Pakistan relied almost entirely on them. The Indian assumption was that by using American

armour in the Rann of Kutch, the Pakistanis were testing U.S. reaction and were reassured by the routine nature of the inquiry they received from Washington.
45. An excellent assessment of the Tashkent conference and the Soviet role is given in an unpublished paper by Thomas P. Thornton, "The Soviet Mediation between India and Pakistan: Tashkent, 1966," September 1982.
46. Desai suggests, "It was not proper, in my view, to go outside the country for negotiations, even though we had won the war." op. cit., p. 227.
47. According to Desai, "Lal Bahadurji made a declaration in the [Congress] Working Committee and also in public that we would not return to Pakistan the areas of Kashmir which we had recovered. I tried to persuade him not to make such a declaration as it would put him in a very awkward position.... Lal Bahadurji did not pay any heed to my advice and repeated his declaration." *Ibid.* But Mrs. Gandhi "was personally upset [over the terms of the Tashkent agreement] because, when I went to Haji Pir, I had told the cheering soldiers that we would not give it up." *My Truth*, op. cit., p. 107.
48. Thornton, op. cit.
49. The Soviets went to absurd lengths to indicate their impartiality. The number of Indian and Pakistani flags on the streets was precisely balanced, so were the references to the two countries and the number of times each country won first reference in Soviet statements.
50. Choudhury, *Reflections*, op. cit.
51. George Thayer, *The War Business: The International Trade in Armaments*, New York: Simon and Schuster, 1969, pp. 204-5. According to Frank, in 1967 the U.S. diplomatically forced Pakistan to return a diverted shipment of ex-West German Canadian-built F-86 Sabres to Iran, op. cit., p. 168. China made Pakistan the largest recipient of economic and military aid, with extensions totalling more than 15 per cent of its economic commitments and nearly 60 per cent of its military commitments. CIA report, October 1980, op. cit.
52. Joshua and Gilbert, op. cit., p. 59.
53. Apart from the American rejection of India's request for F-101s in early 1962, a similar fate befell approaches for Sidewinder air-to-air missiles for use in subsonic planes, made in 1960 and 1961. The U.S. State Department refused three separate requests for data on Hughes HM-55 air-to-air missile system. Kavic, op. cit., pp. 105-6.
54. *Ibid.*, p. 135.
55. Thomas, *The Defense of India*, op. cit., pp. 114 and 138.
56. Joshua and Gilbert, op. cit., p. 71.
57. Kavic, op. cit., p. 202. In November 1964, Defence Minister Chavan sought the loan of three Daring-class destroyers from Britain. He was told that India could have three mothballed weapon-class destroyers, which did not serve New Delhi's purposes. P.R. Chari, "Indo-Soviet Military Cooperation: A Review," *Asian Survey*, March 1979.
58. CPI General Secretary Ajoy Ghosh tartly observed in 1956: "The Twentieth Congress... not only ended the deification of Stalin but also demolished the belief in the infallibility of any party or any leader," *New Age*, December 10, 1956.
59. Mohan Ram, the Indian specialist on Communist affairs, has suggested that the CPSU leadership had raised the issue of a split in the CPI long before it

happened. Quoted in Sen Gupta, *Communism in Indian Politics*, New York: Columbia University Press, 1972, p. 367. John B. Wood has observed, "it is interesting to reflect that Russia, rather than China, bears more responsibility for the split, since the CPSU's developing hostility toward China, coupled with Russian state aid during the emergency [following the Sino-Indian border war], provided the preconditions for the CPI's swing to the right." "Observations on the Indian Communist Party Split," *Pacific Affairs*, Spring 1965. That the cause of the split remains a sensitive issue can be gauged by the polemics indulged in by the CPI and the CPI(M) in 1983. After the restoration of relations between the Marxists and the Communist Party of China (CPC), the CPI organ, *New Age*, suggested that the 1964 split was caused by a directive of the CPC. The response of the Marxist leader, E.M.S. Namboodiripad, was that it was a "stinking old lie." In later speeches and articles, the Marxist brought out his heavy guns to attack the CPI. His refrain was that the CPI(M) was not functioning with the "brains" of the Soviet Union or China. *The Times of India*, June 27, 1983.
60. Remnek, op. cit., p. 95.
61. Lyndon Baines Johnson, *The Vantage Point: Perspectives of the Presidency, 1963-1969*, New York: Holt, Rinehart and Winston, 1971, p. 225.
62. Vasudev, op. cit., p. 359.
63. *Ibid.*, p. 358.
64. Gandhi, *My Truth*, op. cit., p. 120.
65. *Ibid.*, p. 116.
66. Quoted in Sen Gupta, *Orbis*, op. cit.
67. Rose, *Asian Affairs*, December 1981, op. cit.
68. Gandhi, *My Truth*, op. cit., p. 120.
69. Hasan, op. cit.
70. Contained in *Peking Review* of February 18, 1966.
71. Naik, op. cit., pp. 138-9. In 1955, trade between India and the Soviet Union was only $11.7 million; it had grown to $126.6 million in 1957. James Richard Carter contends that the Soviet Union practices price discrimination in dealings with the Third World, apparently charging an average of at least 15 per cent more for Soviet goods than if purchased by the West. He makes the assumption that between 1955 and 1968, Moscow probably paid an average of 10 to 15 per cent less for imports from the Third World than if purchased at world market prices. *The Net Cost of Soviet Foreign Aid*, New York: Praeger, 1971, pp. 39 and 73. For India, the chief attractions of Soviet aid were initially to break the monopoly of private foreign investors in steel, oil, pharmaceuticals and other industries, and provide an alternate source of funds, particularly in building a heavy industry base. But Soviet assistance did not reduce Indian dependence on Western aid even as it made it a more attractive candidate for such assistance. On the obverse side of the coin, Indians were to discover "that where there is no competition, the Russians, like the Western firms before them, are capable of pricing their projects at levels that assure them an excessive return." Goldman, op. cit., p. 100. Soviet aid has been heavily concentrated on its neighbours in South Asia (over 25 per cent of commitments) and strategically located countries in North Africa and the Middle East (60 per cent). CIA report, October 1980, op. cit.
72. Quoted in Remnek, op. cit., p. 65.

73. Kaul suggests, "They knew her [Mrs. Gandhi] personally and considered her a progressive leader in her own right, apart from being Nehru's daughter." *Reminiscences, Discreet and Indiscreet*, New Delhi: Lancers, 1982, p. 251.

Chapter Four

1. Vasudev, op. cit., p. 392.
2. *The Hindustan Times*, New Delhi, September 2, 1966.
3. Vasudev, op. cit., p. 393.
4. Desai, op. cit., p. 233.
5. Quoted in Sen Gupta, *Orbis*, op. cit.
6. *Ibid.*
7. *Peking Review*, September 8, 1967.
8. Vertzberger, op. cit.
9. *Ibid.*
10. In a conversation with me in New Delhi on April 21, 1967.
11. These comments are based on personal observations. I was posted in Pakistan for *The Statesman* for six months from the spring of 1967, the first Indian correspondent permitted to be based there since the 1965 war. The state of Indo-Pakistani relations can be gauged from the fact that to get to my newspaper in Calcutta or New Delhi, I had to file to London; direct postal and telegraph communications between the two countries had been suspended in 1965. Most embassies and many Pakistan government offices still functioned in the old city of Rawalpindi and the new capital of Islamabad nearby was being built. The climate in which I functioned was brought home to me by the reluctance of even most diplomats to meet me. The deputy chief of the Canadian High Commission abruptly cancelled an appointment, suggesting that as a national of India, I was the responsibility of his country's embassy there!
12. *The Statesman*, May 20, 1967.
13. *Ibid.*, April 19, 1968. During my visit to East Pakistan in 1967 I asked a young member of the Awami League, "What do you mean by autonomy?" He smiled and hesitated just a moment before replying: "Independence. We know it and the Ayub regime knows it." Later I met a veteran member of the National Awami Party. "The word independence," he said, "might frighten some people. The ideal to propagate is two Pakistans." And he added: "Our task would be much simpler if we were sure we would not be absorbed by India."
14. *Ibid.*, "A President's Story," August 10, 11 and 12, 1967.
15. Naik, op. cit., pp. 136-7.
16. Zubeida Hasan, "Pakistan's Relations with the USSR in the 1960s," *The World Today*, January 1969.
17. Nayar, *Between the Lines*, op. cit., p. 156.
18. Hasan, *The World Today*, op. cit.
19. Joshua and Gilbert, op. cit., pp. 71-2.
20. Hasan, *The World Today*, op. cit.
21. *The Pakistan Times*, June 22, 1968.
22. I was based in Moscow for *The Statesman* from February 1968 through April 1969. The Indian mood at the time can be gleaned from a dispatch I wrote for the

newspaper, published on July 22, 1968. It opened with the following paragraph: "At one point during Dr. Zakir Husain's visit to the Soviet Union, the cry of *Hindi Rusi Bhai Bhai* [Indians and Soviets are brothers] was raised. It was just as he was about to board the train for Leningrad after completing his stay in Moscow. Nowhere else was the slogan repeated. The emotional content of the cry had become outdated, overtaken as it was by events."

23. Bimal Prasad, *Indo-Soviet Relations, 1947-1972; A Documentary Study*, New Delhi: Allied Publishers, 1973, p. 347.
24. Sen Gupta, *Orbis*, op. cit.
25. *The Times of India*, February 4, 1968.
26. This assessment was gleaned from discussions I had with Indian officials in New Delhi in January 1970.
27. A protocol was signed for 2,000 cars to be delivered to the Soviet Union in 1969 and up to 10,000 per year by 1973. The deal fell through after prolonged haggling, with the Soviets offering half of India's production costs with stipulations which would have required expensive imports from the Soviet Union. Robert H. Donaldson, *The Second World, the Third World, and the New International Economic Order* in *The Soviet Union in the Third World, Successes and Failures*, Boulders, CO: Westview Press. 1981, p. 377. An even more acrimonious controversy between India and the Soviet Union was caused by the terms the Soviets set for undertaking a large steel plant at Bokaro after the U.S. had painted itself into a corner by insisting that it be in the private sector. Moscow declined to share construction with Indian consultants, forced 300 experts on India when Indian engineers were available and proved adamant on their cost estimates. Indeed, Soviet officials made no secret of their annoyance over New Delhi's request for reexamining Bokaro's cost structure. New Delhi felt that it had no option but to accept Soviet terms and in January 1965 signed an agreement accepting Soviet credits for Bokaro of over Rs. 1,667.67 million. In a study of the Bokaro controversy, an Indian specialist on Soviet economy, Padma Desai, was constrained to observe: "Indeed, unless the Soviet Union comes to grips with the fact of a vastly increased technological competence and a growing stress on technological self-reliance in India, the future of Indo-Soviet collaboration is likely to be bleak and the Bokaro episode more than a temporary lapse in Soviet aid diplomacy." *The Bokaro Steel Plant: A Study of Soviet Economic Assistance*, New York: American Elsevier Publishing, 1972, p. 87.
28. *The Stateman*, June 21, 23 and 26, 1968 and December 21, 1968. By 1970, the Soviet Union had emerged as the second largest buyer of Indian goods; it was the main source for heavy industry and main supplier of sophisticated military equipment. In view of the heavy repayments involved for economic assistance and arms, there was a negative aid flow, estimated at $28 million for 1970-71. Robert H. Donaldson, *Soviet Policy in South Asia: Aspirations and Limitations* in *Soviet Economic and Political Relations with the Developing World*, Roger E. Kanet and Donna Bahry, eds., New York: Praeger, 1975, p. 221.
29. Inder Malhotra commented in *The Statesman* of January 24, 1969 that Skatchkov "behaved, through most of his visit, rather like a viceroy of yore on an inspection tour."
30. *The Statesman*, June 1, 1968.
31. Sen Gupta, *Fulcrum*, op. cit., p. 274.

32. Nayar quotes a Russian journalist telling him, "What did you do when the USA gave arms to Pakistan? What can you do [on Soviet arms to Pakistan]?" *Between the Lines*, op. cit., p. 138. P.N. Haksar, Mrs. Gandhi's principal advisor in the late Sixties, told me in a conversation in New Delhi on July 4, 1980: "The Russian flirtation with Pakistan in the Sixties came about because they became suspicious of us. The Russians can be deeply suspicious. They thought we were making up with the Americans."
33. *Ibid.*, p. 139.
34. This version is based on an account given to me in New Delhi on April 26, 1980 by an official who participated in the discussions on the treaty. For obvious reasons, he must remain Official "A."
35. According to Kaul, "It [the treaty] had been talked about, in a general sort of way between the two governments, for about two years. D.P. Dhar, our Ambassador in Moscow and I as Foreign Secretary, had many informal discussions with the Soviet side. I had given them a rough draft, during my official visit to Moscow in 1970. They had made some countersuggestions." *Reminiscences*, op. cit., p. 255.

  Foreign Minister Swaran Singh told Parliament on August 10, 1971 that the negotiations on the treaty had been going on for the previous two years and "secret talks had taken place at various levels." *The Statesman*, August 11, 1971.

  As we shall see, the "rough draft" Kaul is referring to is not the original draft agreed to in September 1969.
36. An extensive account of Firyubin's talk can be found in Nayar, *Between the Lines*, pp. 130-142. Girilal Jain's view of Firyubin's meeting with Bhagat was summed up in the comment that the Soviets "conducted themselves in the manner of representatives of an imperial power in their dealings with a dependency." *The Times of India*, September 26, 1968. Commenting on Kosygin's visit to India in September 1968, Kaul maintains, "He [Kosygin] virtually admitted that Pakistan was too far gone into the American and Chinese net and that their leadership could not be weaned away [from China]." *Reminiscences*, op. cit., p. 251.
37. Told me by Home Minister Y.B. Chavan in a conversation in New Delhi on May 29, 1969.
38. *Ibid.* Chavan's assessment was that the Congress would receive "a working majority." Desai, on the other hand, told me in New Delhi on June 6, 1969 that there was "a possibility the Congress will not gain a majority in 1972." Mrs. Gandhi preferred not to commit herself. In a talk in New Delhi on May 26, 1969, she replied to my query about the party's prospects in 1972 with, "Let's see."
39. In a conversation with me, quoted above.
40. Nihal Singh, Political Commentary, henceforth Polcom, *The Statesman*, July 18, 1969.
41. *Ibid.*, July 25, August 1 and 15, 1969.
42. *Ibid.*, July 25, 1969. Svetlana reports that Rikhi Jaipal, an official of the Indian Foreign Ministry, came to see her in Switzerland on March 14, 1967 after she had sought asylum in the U.S. Embassy in New Delhi. "He [Jaipal] had brought with him a draft of a letter from me to Dinesh—composed, I'm afraid, by Dinesh himself—in which this was stated very clearly. But it was true, the Indians hadn't helped me. Obviously, Dinesh needed this in order to clear himself before the Soviet Embassy. So I signed it." Dinesh was then hoping to get the Foreign

Affairs portfolio. Svetlana Alliluyeva, *Only One Year*, London: Hutchinson, 1969, p. 203.
43. Polcom, August 15, 1969.
44. *Ibid.*
45. *Ibid.*, August 22, 1969.
46. *Ibid.*, August 29, 1969.
47. *Ibid.*, October 24, 1969.
48. *Ibid.*, October 31, 1969.
49. Told me by Official "A," op. cit.
50. Polcom, op. cit., May 23, 1969.
51. *Ibid.* Not being privy to the treaty negotiations, I had then written: "It is difficult to understand why India continues to rely on Russian interpreters for such important discussions: New Delhi has a core of fluent Russian speakers."
52. *Ibid.*
53. *Ibid.*
54. Tass, condensed text in the *Current Digest of the Soviet Press*, Vol. XXI, No. 19, May 21, 1969.
55. Kaul gloats over the fact that the treaty discussions remained secret. "It was one of the few closely guarded secret negotiations that India has ever conducted. On our side, hardly half a dozen people were aware of it, including the Prime Minister and Foreign Minister. The media got no scent of it." Kaul also reveals that the Russians gave Indian officials copies of treaties they had signed with Finland and Afghanistan. Such models were rejected by the Indian side. *Reminiscences*, op. cit., p. 255.
56. Polcom, August 8, 1969.
57. According to Official "A," op. cit.
58. On September 26, 1969, I complained: "Her [Mrs. Gandhi's] last two meetings with the Soviet Prime Minister in Delhi (in May and September) took place with only Soviet interpreters present. Only the scrappiest versions of what transpired between the two are available to those in charge of making India's foreign policy." Polcom, September, 26, 1969.
59. In a conversation with me in New Delhi on May 3, 1980. This was confirmed by Y.B. Chavan, who has held several cabinet posts, including that of Foreign Minister, in a talk with me in New Delhi on July 10, 1980. He said: "It is true the treaty was more or less finalized in 1969, but there were reservations. Therefore, we did not sign it then. We signed it in 1971 when there were geopolitical compulsions."

Haksar, however, was not quite candid in telling me in New Delhi on July 4, 1980, "There was no draft [of the treaty] a year or two earlier."
60. According to Official "A," op. cit. This version was confirmed to me by Official "B," also an Indian participant in the treaty negotiations. In the words of the latter, "Dinesh took the draft, told Gromyko that India agreed to it, but said it should be put on hold for the present and Gromyko said he understood."
61. This was confirmed by Official "A," op. cit. He told me that the treaty was dropped because "it was too explosive a thing." Kaul says: "[The] Indian leadership was at first hesitant to go as far as entering into a treaty of Friendship and Peace with the USSR. Mrs. Gandhi was inclined towards it, but was not sure of the attitude of her colleagues. I had taken over as Foreign Secretary in June

1968. She sent me to Moscow to sound [out] the Soviet leaders. I exchanged drafts with them of the proposed treaty, without commitment on either side. D.P. [Dhar] followed up matters." *Diplomacy*, op. cit. p. 195.
62. Polcom, op. cit., November 28, 1969.
63. *Ibid.*, September 26, 1969.
64. *Ibid.*, October 24, 1969.
65. *Ibid.*, September 26, 1969.
66. *Ibid.*, December 12, 1969.
67. "Several U.S. officials with responsibilities relating to South Asia have expressed to this writer various degrees of displeasure at the recent rise in influence of such leftist figures as Dinesh Singh. Prime Minister Gandhi has been as acceptable to Moscow as to Washington." Richard L. Siegel, *Evaluating the Results of Foreign Policy: Soviet and American Efforts in India*, University of Denver Monograph Series, 1969, p. 21.
68. *The Hindustan Times*, August 20, 1969, quoted in Robert C. Horn, "Indo-Soviet Relations in 1969: A Watershed Year?", *Orbis*, Winter 1976.
69. George H. Quester, *Enlisting Post-1974 India to the Cause of Nonproliferation* in *India: A Rising Middle Power*, Boulder: Westview Press, 1979, p. 190.
70. *The Statesman*, September 1, 1966.
71. Sen Gupta, *Study*, op. cit., p. 78.
72. A.G. Noorani, *The Kosygin Plan* in A.P. Jain, ed., *India and the World*, Delhi: D.K. Publishing House, 1972, p. 197.
73. Justus M. van der Kroef, "Australia's Search for Collective Security," *Orbis*, Summer 1969.
74. Noorani, *Kosygin Plan*, op. cit., p. 198.
75. Marian P. Kirsch, "Soviet Security Objectives in Asia," *International Organizations*, Summer 1970.
76. *The Times of India*, June 28, 1969, and *The Indian Express*, June 30, 1969.
77. *Pravda*, June 8, 1969.
78. Quoted in Noorani, *Kosygin Plan*, op. cit., p. 193.
79. *Ibid.*, p. 195.
80. *Ibid.*
81. Gleaned from an Indian official.
82. Noorani, *Kosygin Plan*, op. cit., p. 193.
83. Lawrence L. Whetten, "Moscow's Anti-China Pact," *The World Today*, September 1969.
84. November 27, 1969.
85. Harold C. Hinton, "The Soviet Campaign for Collective Security," *Pacific Community*, January 1976.
86. Howard M. Hensel, "Asian Collective Security: The Soviet View," *Orbis*, Winter 1976. Lilita Dzirkals suggests, ".... They [the Soviets] recognize the need for a patient, long-term Soviet effort to attract the Asian states to the Soviet-focussed Collective Security System as an alternative to the dissolving U.S.-built or sponsored alliance system or their replacement with Chinese or Japanese dominance." "Perceptions of Security in East Asia: A Survey of Soviet Comment," Rand Corporation, P-6038, November 1977.
87. *Dawn*, Karachi, July 11, 1969.
88. Anwar Syed, "Sino-Pakistan Relations—An Overview," *Pakistan Horizon*,

Second Quarter, 1969.
89. *Pravda*, September 21, 1969.
90. Robert H. Donaldson, "India: The Soviet Stake in Stability," *Asian Survey*, June 1972.
91. In 1969, the Communist movement in India had split for a second time, with an extreme left faction in the CPI(M) forming a new party, the Communist Party of India (Marxist-Leninist). Its members were popularly known as Naxalites, after the peasant revolt in Naxalbari. The party formally came into being on April 22, 1969 and was launched at a rally in Calcutta on May 1.
92. Given to me in New Delhi by a senior Indian official on September 10, 1969.
93. Kissinger, op. cit., p. 850.
94. *The Statesman*, April 10, 1969.
95. Nayar, *Between the Lines*, p. 152.
96. I broke the story in *The Statesman* on June 29, 1969.
97. Sen Gupta, *Study*, op. cit., p. 123.
98. The Soviet Embassy in New Delhi told India in a note on July 7, 1971 that arms reaching Pakistan had been contracted for and shipped before March 25. *The Times of India*, July 8, 1971. Leo E. Rose quotes Pakistani sources to suggest in Chapter 7 of an excellent study of the 1971 war in a forthcoming publication that Soviet arms were being received by Pakistan in late April 1971. William J. Barnds quotes State Department figures to say that actual Soviet arms provided to Pakistan before the 1971 war were worth only $10 million. "Moscow and South Asia," *Problems of Communism*, May-June 1972.

Chapter 8 of Rose's study deals with Soviet policy and motivation. This and subsequent quotations are made from the manuscript. However, I do not agree with Rose's assessment that the tilt in American policy during the East Pakistan crisis was in favour of India, rather than Pakistan, and that differences in the U.S. Administration were over public postures, not policy.

Chapter Five

1. Choudhury, *Reflections*, op. cit.
2. Estimates of the number of refugees and the costs involved in this and later instances are based on official Indian figures which are widely accepted as being reasonably accurate.
3. Polcom., *The Statesman*, April 2, 1971. Lawrence Lifschultz quotes Bengali military commanders' assessment at the time that Pakistani military forces would be defeated within three years without Indian involvement. *Bangladesh: The Unfinished Revolution*, London: Zed Press, 1979, p. 25.
4. Rose, Chapter 7, op. cit.
5. Polcom., op. cit., April 23, 1971.
6. *Ibid.*, April 2, 1971.
7. Nayar, *Neighbours*, op. cit., p. 160.
8. Rose, Chapter 7, op. cit.
9. *Ibid.*
10. Henry Kissinger, *White House Years*, Boston: Little Brown, 1979, p. 848.
11. *Ibid.*, p. 849.

12. Choudhury, *Reflections*, op. cit.
13. Rose, Chapter 7, op. cit.
14. Told me by Official "A." At the conclusion of the visit, the Joint Statement issued on June 8, 1971 said in part, "The two sides, after a detailed discussion on the various aspects of the problems created in this context [the developments in East Pakistan], consider that it is imperative for immediate measures to be taken in East Pakistan which would ensure the stoppage of refugees from East Pakistan. Simultaneously, it is their desire to take further steps to ensure that peace is restored and all conditions of security are created for the return of the refugees to their homes in East Pakistan. Taking into account the seriousness of the situation, the two sides agreed to remain in touch with each other in order to review the situation." Bimal Prasad, op. cit., p. 390.
15. Kissinger, op. cit., p. 860.
16. *Ibid.,*
17. T.N. Kaul, *The Kissinger Years: Indo-American Relations*, New Delhi: Arnold-Heinemann, 1980, p. 22.
18. *Ibid.*, p. 48.
19. *Ibid.*, p. 54.
20. Seymour M. Hersh, *The Price of Power—Kissinger in the White House*, New York: Summit Books, 1983, p. 452. According to Kaul, "It is interesting that Kissinger later [after his return from Beijing] told our Ambassador that if China intervened in the Indo-Pak conflict, America would not be in a position to do anything about it. This is contrary to what he had said to us during his visit to Peking [Beijing]." *The Kissinger Years*, op. cit., p. 58.
21. Kaul contends, "They [the Soviets] may have been a little surprised but they did not hesitate." *Diplomacy*, op. cit., p. 196.
22. *The Hindustan Times*, September 13, 1973. It is of some significance that a treaty of such importance was signed by the two countries' Foreign Ministers, rather than executive or titular heads of state. It can be argued that the lower rank of signatories was to enable Mrs. Gandhi later to demote the treaty.
23. The text of the treaty is given in A.P. Jain, op. cit., pp. 374-377.
24. N.M. Ghatate (ed.), *Indo-Soviet Treaty—Reactions and Reflections*, New Delhi: Defence Research Institute.
25. *Ibid.*
26. Pran Chopra, *Before and After the Treaty*, New Delhi: S. Chand, 1971.
27. Ghatate, op. cit.
28. *Ibid.*
29. *Motherland*, August 23, 1971. K. Subrahmanyam, Director of the Government-supported Institute for Defence Studies and Analyses in New Delhi, suggested that the treaty would come at a price if the U.S. were to regard India as a Soviet ally. *Ibid.*, August 19, 1971.
30. *The Times of India* put the position bluntly the day after the treaty was signed. It said, "The treaty will be judged, especially in view of the circumstances, primarily by one yardstick. Whatever their reservations, the people of India will welcome it if it permits New Delhi to extend all-out support to the Mukti Bahini undeterred by fear of aggression by Pakistan, with or without China's connivance, encouragement and support. By the same token, they will be sorely disappointed if it turns out that the pact has not visibly increased the

Government's capacity to act decisively." August 10, 1971. On the other hand, as late as October and November, the Soviets were calling for a settlement based not only on the "will and interests of the East Pakistanis," but also on "respect for Pakistan's territorial integrity." The thrust of the Soviet press was an emphasis on the need to avoid war on the subcontinent. Quoted in Donaldson, *Asian Survey*, June 1972, op. cit.

31. Dinesh Singh told me in a conversation in New Delhi on May 3, 1980 that the Russians floated the Asian Collective Security idea to test reactions. Essentially, they wanted a set of "friendly countries which could, short of having Soviet bases, be activated when the need arose." According to him, an Indian interest in the treaty coincided with the Soviet interest in Asian Collective Security.
32. Desai records: "I understood that the Soviet Union, which earlier had signed a treaty of friendship with us, did not favour this recognition [of Bangladesh by India] as it did not want Pakistan to break up. We did not want to break up Pakistan either." *The Story of My Life*, Volume III, New Delhi: S. Chand, 1979, p. 17.
33. Christopher Van Hollen, "The Tilt Policy Revisited: Nixon-Kissinger Geopolitics and South Asia," *Asian Survey*, Vol. 20, No. 4.
34. Kaul, *The Kissinger Years*, op. cit., p. 60.
35. Kissinger, op. cit., p. 861.
36. Van Hollen, op. cit.
37. Kissinger, op. cit., p. 862.
38. *Ibid.*, p. 874.
39. *Ibid.*, p. 875.
40. According to Rose, the actual shipments to Pakistan from late August to March 25 totalled $3.6 million while unexpired licences for the period up to December were of less than $5 million. Chapter 8, op. cit.
41. *Ibid.*, The phrase is Rose's. Chapter 7.
42. Van Hollen, op. cit.
43. Sen Gupta, *South Asia and the Great Powers* in William E. Griffith, ed., *The World and the Great Power Triangles*, Cambridge, Massachusetts: MIT Press, 1975, p. 256.
44. *The Statesman*, October 7, 1971.
45. Zhou's message also said, "The question of East Pakistan should be settled according to the wishes of the people of East Pakistan." But this was omitted in the New China News Agency summary and by Pakistan in releasing the text. Rose, Chapter 7, op. cit.
46. *Ibid*. On the other hand, a Pakistani military spokesman declared in November 1971 that China had sent 200 military instructors to Pakistan for training troops in guerrilla warfare. *Dawn*, November 25, 1971. There were several versions of Soviet assurances to India of Soviet support, should China intervene militarily. According to Vijay Sen Budhraj, Soviet Ambassador N.M. Pegov had assured India that in case of a Chinese attack, the Soviet Union would begin diversionary action in Xinjiang. "Moscow and the Birth of Bangladesh," *Asian Survey*, May 1973.
47. Based on interviews with Indian officials. Mrs. Gandhi declared at the Moscow luncheon on September 28, 1971: "The growing agony of the people of East Bengal does not seem to have moved many governments. Our restraint has been

References

appreciated only in words. The basic issues involved and the real threat to peace and stability in Asia are being largely ignored. We are glad that the leaders of the Soviet Union have counselled Pakistan to reach a political solution which will satisfy the aspirations of the people of East Bengal. We hope these efforts will bear fruit." Bimal Prasad, op. cit., pp. 401-2.

48. Rose, op. cit.
49. *The Times of India*, October 3, 1971.
50. *The Statesman*, November 20, 1971.
51. *Ibid.*, November 4, 1971. The French writer Andre Malraux, who had offered to fight in the Bangladesh war of indpendence, met Mrs. Gandhi during her visit to Paris. He asked her whether she was willing to compromise on the independence of Bangladesh. Her reported answer was, "No." *The Statesman*, November 20, 1971.
52. Rose, op. cit.
53. Kaul, *The Kissinger Years*, op. cit., p. 63.
54. *Ibid.*, p. 43.
55. Richard Nixon, *RN—Memoirs of Richard Nixon*, New York: Grosset & Dunlap, 1978, p. 531.
56. Van Hollen, op. cit.; Hersh, op. cit., p. 460. Jha's own account is in *India Today*, New Delhi, November 1-15, 1979.
57. On the basis of conversations with Indian officials.
58. According to *The New York Times*, eight shiploads of military supplies arrived in India between August and the end of November. November 30, 1971. Rose quotes a Pakistani source to suggest that Lahore was used by Soviet aircraft as a stop on the military airlift. Chapter 8, op. cit., President Sadat of Egypt said Soviet cargo aircraft had picked up Soviet military equipment in Cairo on their way to India. *Time*, December 20, 1971. Zubeida Mustafa suggests that in early November twelve Soviet transport planes carried military equipment, mainly advanced surface-to-air missiles, to New Delhi and Bombay. "The 1971 Crisis in Pakistan: India, the Soviet Union and China," *Pacific Community*, April 1972.
59. Kissinger, op. cit., p. 892. Article I of the 1959 agreement reads: "The Government of Pakistan is determined to resist aggression. In case of aggression against Pakistan, the Government of the United States of America, in accordance with the constitution of the United States of America, will take such appropriate action, including the use of armed forces, as may be mutually agreed upon and as is envisaged in the Joint Resolution to Promote Peace and Stability in the Middle East, in order to assist the Government of Pakistan at its request." *Ibid.*, p. 1488.

According to Kissinger, "assurances were given by the Kennedy and Johnson administrations, including a letter from John F. Kennedy to Pakistani President Mohammad Ayub Khan on January 26, 1962; an aide-memoire presented by the U.S. Ambassador on November 5, 1962; a public statement by the State Department on November 17, 1962; and an oral promise by President Lyndon Johnson to Ayub Khan on December 15, 1965. *Ibid.*

The Times, London commented on December 3, 1971: "It would be wrong to put the blame on India for following this realistic policy [of military pressure on East Pakistan] and putting power to the test. For eight months the Pakistan Government has dithered almost willfully turning aside from the political realities of the eastern wing. All their political gestures have been paltry. They cannot hope now to swing international support to their side by representing themselves as innocent sufferers from unprovoked agression. And if India calculated that the cost in human suffering could be less from the limited action they have undertaken, no one can accuse them of crass misjudgement."

60. Nayar, *Critical Years*, op. cit., p. 181.
61. The debate in the Security Council was soon converted into a Sino-Soviet game of polemics. As a sample, the Soviet delegate's speech in the Council suggested, "He [Ambassador Huang Hua of China] says that the plan of the Soviet Union is to control Hindustan, and yesterday he said to control the Indian Ocean. Well, slanderers really have a limitless fantasy and imagination, and falsifiers even improve on that. The stupidity of fabrication and slander over the great friendship between the Soviet people and the people of India is one which the Soviet delegation deems beneath its dignity to reject or refer to." Bimal Prasad, op. cit., p. 441.
62. Quoted in Hersh, op. cit., p. 458.
63. Kissinger, op. cit., p. 902.
64. *Ibid.*, p. 901. The account given by writer Thomas Powers is ".... The CIA [Central Intelligence Agency] case officer handling the Indian politician in Gandhi's cabinet in New Delhi was told [within 24 hours of December 7] that a decision had just been reached to attack in the West..." *The Man Who Kept Secrets—Richard Helms and the CIA*, London: Weidenfeld & Nicolson, 1979, p. 206.
65. Kissinger, op. cit., p. 907.
66. *Ibid.*, p. 905.
67. *Ibid.*, p. 913.
68. Quoted in Hersh, op. cit., p. 460n.
69. Barry M. Blechman and Stephen S. Kaplan, *Force Without War*, Washington: The Brookings Institution, 1978, p. 200, quoted in Van Hollen, op. cit.
70. According to Leo Rose, the *Enterprise* was slightly southeast of Sri Lanka when the cease-fire was declared, on the way to the west coast of the subcontinent. It was then ordered to rejoin the 7th Fleet, rather than proceed with its mission. In a communication to me on June 30, 1983.
71. Sen Gupta, *Study*, op. cit., p. 117.
72. Collins and Lapierre quote Mountbatten telling them during one of a series of interviews conducted in the early 1970s, "Twenty-five years ago Rajagopalachari and I said it [Pakistan as one unit] would last twenty-five years." *Mountbatten*, op. cit., p. 44.
73. Kissinger, op. cit., p. 886. Van Hollen has summed up the American approach to the East Pakistan crisis best. According to him, "By attempting to resolve an essentially regional dispute through global geopolitics, the President and the National Security Advisor deemphasized and misinterpreted the political dynamics in the subcontinent and exaggerated the role and influence of the major external powers." Op. cit.
74. *Pravda*, April 22, 1972.
75. K.P.S. Menon, *Many Worlds Revisited*, Bombay: Bharatiya Vidya Bhavan, 1981, p. 339.
76. Kaul, *The Kissinger Years*, op. cit., pp. 54-55.
77. Radio Bayda, Domestic Service, December 17, 1971.

References

78. Ian Clark has suggested that the "treaty phase" of Soviet Asian policy was an aberration from the trend initiated in the 1960s. "Soviet Conceptions of Asian Security: From Balance 'Between' to Balance 'Within,'" *Pacific Community*, January 1976.
79. See Note 31 above.
80. T.N. Kaul was later propagating precisely this theme. He suggested in 1983, "They [India and other nonaligned countries] could propose sub-regional and regional agreements or treaties of peace, friendship, cooperation and nonaggression, providing for immediate consultations, should a threat arise to the sovereignty and independence of any signatory." "India Should Take a Lead in Peace and Cooperation," *Sunday*, Calcutta, March 6-12, 1983.

Chapter Six

1. Indira Gandhi, *My Truth*, op. cit., p. 157.
2. *The New York Times*, February 17, 1972.
3. *The Indian Express*, February 18, 1972.
4. Quoted by Ashok Kapur, "Indo-Soviet Treaty and the Emerging Asian Balance," *Asian Survey*, June 1972. Three years later, in April 1975, Mrs. Gandhi would tell a press conference at Kingston: "The USSR has come to our support at the right time at no cost to them, and perhaps the United States policy has given them the opportunity to do so." *Socialist India*, New Delhi, May 10, 1975.
5. Richard M. Nixon, "U.S. Foreign Policies for the 1970s: The Emerging Structure of Peace," February 9, 1972.
6. Quoted in S.M. Burke, "The Post-war Diplomacy of the Indo-Pakistani War of 1971," *Asian Survey*, November 1973.
7. *The Statesman Weekly*, March 11, 1972.
8. Nayar, *Neighbours*, op. cit., p. 208.
9. Quoted in Sheldon W. Simon, "China-Soviet Rivalry in South Asia," *Asian Survey*, July 1973.
10. *Pravda*, March 8, 1972.
11. *Izvestia*, September 9, 1972.
12. Hensel, op. cit.
13. Donaldson, *The Second Word, the Third World, and the New International Economic Order*, op. cit., p. 375.
14. A commentator in *The Hindu* argued that joining Comecon would bring benefits to India. October 13, 1972.
15. In a talk with me in New Delhi on October 26, 1983.
16. *News Digest on West Asia*, Institute for Defence Studies and Analyses, New Delhi, March 1974.
17. G.V. Matveyev, "Peking's Political Machinations on the Hindustan Peninsula," No. 4, 1972. Quoted in William J. Barnds, *Soviet Influence in the Third World*, New York: Praeger, 1975, p. 24.
18. Mira Sinha, "Into a Soviet December?", *Seminar*, New Delhi, December 1980.
19. Tass, November 27, 1973.
20. Simon. op. cit.
21. G.W. Choudhury, *India, Pakistan, Bangladesh and the Major Powers*, op. cit., p. 197.

22. New China News Agency (NCNA), August 26, 1972.
23. NCNA, November 30, 1972. Bhutto told a press conference on August 10, 1972 that Bangladesh believed it had "a kind of veto over the release of our prisoners" but "there is a veto in our hands also." Quoted in Burke, *Asian Survey*, op. cit.
24. These and subsequent quotations on the Pakistan-China economic and military links are from Vertzberger, op. cit., unless otherwise indicated.
25. *Newsweek*, November 8, 1971.
26. Choudhury, *Reflections*, op. cit.
27. *Ibid*.
28. Nayar, *Neighbours*, op. cit., p. 195. At a press conference in London, where he was flown after his release from prison in West Pakistan, Sheikh Mujib said he was condemned to die after a mock trial. He thanked India, the Soviet Union and other East European countries and Britain and France for their helpful approach to the Bangladesh crisis. *The Statesman*, January 9, 1972.
29. William E. Griffith has neatly summed up the situation: "Pakistan, like Prussia and Jordan, is an army (indeed an overwhelmingly Punjabi-Pathan army) which possesses a state, and is not likely soon to surrender it." "The USSR and Pakistan," *Problems of Communism*, January-February 1982.
30. Sen Gupta, *Study*, op. cit., p. 152.
31. Defence Minister Jagjivan Ram's statement to the All-India Congress Committee, Delhi Domestic Service, June 1, 1971.
32. "As it happened, we did recover about 400 sq. km. of our territory in Pakistan-occupied Kashmir and retained it at the Simla conference." Kaul, *Kissinger Years*, op. cit., p. 96.
33. The text of the Simla Agreement is given in Jain, op. cit., Appendix VIII B, pp. 361-363. According to P.N. Haksar, "History would record and the saner elements of Pakistan would admit that India made the largest investment in the years following the Bangladesh crisis in promoting trust and confidence." "Structuring a Durable Peace," *Seminar*, January 1979. Another Indian attitude was put forward by S.N. Antia, "In fact, recent disclosures have shown that the astute Bhutto outwitted Indira Gandhi and her advisors at Simla with outward professions of peaceful and friendly intentions, when in fact he had already set in motion the process of acquiring nuclear capability for his country at any cost much before India's Pokharan explosion of a nuclear device." "Cheer Up—Things Could Be Worse," *Mainstream*, Republic Day Number (January 26), 1981.
34. Quoted in Simon, op. cit.
35. Alexander O. Ghebhardt. "Soviet and U.S. Interests in the Indian Ocean," *Asian Survey*, August 1975.
36. Polcom, op. cit., July 4, 1969.
37. Ghebhardt, op. cit.
38. *The New York Times*, October 31, 1973 and January 25, 1974. Chester A. Crocker suggests, "It seems clear that the first regular Soviet deployments in the Indian Ocean in 1968 were related to naval arms deliveries to India and to Soviet space activities." "The African Dimension of Indian Ocean Policy." *Orbis*, Fall 1976.
39. "Naval Threat: Myths and Realities," *Mainstream*, March 7, 1981.
40. U.S. Congress, House Subcommittee on the Near East and South Asia,

References

Committee on Foreign Affairs, "Proposed Expansion of U.S. Military Facilities in the Indian Ocean," 93rd Congress, 2nd Session, 1974, pp. 82-83.

41. Indian fears were not unfounded. More than countering the Soviet threat, U.S. policy-makers were concerned with controlling the internal developments in African and Persian Gulf states in particular, supporting "friendly governments" and forestalling "local Communist coups." Memorandum prepared by Long-Range Objectives Group, "Factors Affecting Changes in the Power Position in Areas Bordering the Southern Oceans (Indian Ocean, South Atlantic), May 31, 1960" and "Study of the Feasibility and Cost of Maintaining Continuous Balanced Deployments in the Indian Ocean 1961-1965," August 25, 1960. The concept of the Fast Deployment Logistics (FDL) ships appeared in Lyndon Johnson's final (1970 fiscal year) defence budget but was given up because of Congressional opposition.
42. *The Times of India*, November 21, 1974.
43. *Ibid.*, August 17, 1974.
44. In reply to a question in the Lok Sabha on March 7, 1974. *The Christian Science Monitor* of March 5, 1974 quoted the Indian press to the effect that the Soviets had formally requested port facilities, but had been turned down. Sen Gupta suggests that the Soviet Union had sought only limited facilities for berthing and recreation. *Study*, p. 124.
45. U.S. Senate Committee on Armed Services, "Disapprove Construction Projects on the Island of Diego Garcia," Hearings, 94th Congress, 1st Session, 1975.
46. Prasad, op. cit., p. 407.
47. *Soviet Review*, June 21, 1976.
48. The first Indo-Soviet naval aid agreement had been negotiated in 1965. Only two submarines were ready and some patrol craft had arrived in India by the end of 1967. Joshua and Gilbert, op. cit., p. 74.
49. Thomas, *The Defense of India*, op. cit., p. 177.
50. Frank, op. cit., p. 90.
51. A senior minister of the Indian government, Mahavir Tyagi, made no secret of the fact that the government was pressured (by foreign parties) into getting an aircraft carrier, regarded by many as "a sort of solitary white elephant" in the Indian Navy. Khera, op. cit., p. 253.
52. Interviews, New Delhi, March and October 1983.
53. The International Institute for Strategic Studies (IISS), Strategic Survey, 1982-1983. In 1982, agreements were also reached for the purchase of eight Sea Harriers from Britain and the Franco-German Milan anti-tank missiles; production of the latter to begin in India in 1985. The Indian press reported in early 1984 that India would build an additional two Type 1500 submarines in collaboration with West Germany. *The Statesman Weekly*, February 18, 1984.
54. Interviews, New Delhi, March and October, 1983.
55. Subrahmanyam, IDSA Journal, January-March 1981.
56. Interviews, New Delhi, March and October 1983.
57. *The Times of India*, November 30, 1974, The Russians changed their mind after Washington announced in April 1975 that it was lifting the arms embargo on the subcontinent.
58. The Indian Air Force was dissatisfied with the performance of the SU-7B in the 1971 war. Thomas, "Aircraft for the Indian Air Force: The Context and

Implications of the Jaguar Decision," *Orbis*, Spring 1980. Kavic has suggested that further orders for eight An-12s and sixteen MI-4s were placed in early 1962 despite reported Indian dissatisfaction with the performance of Soviet aircraft at high Himalayan altitudes. Op. cit., p. 105. On the other hand, Frank has reported that "the SU-7 gained wide respect among Israeli pilots after observing its limited performance in the Middle East war of 1967." Op. cit., p. 98. According to Indian officials in New Delhi, the position on the supply of spares had improved considerably in 1983. Interviews, New Delhi, October 1983.

59. "USSR's Practical Response to Technical Needs," *Patriot*, December 9, 1980.
60. According to Frank, "The exposure of junior and senior officers, particularly in the ground forces, to the equipment and doctrine of the donor country creates a tradition in favour of their continued use." Op. cit. p. 32.
61. *India's Foreign Policy*, Bombay: Somaiya, 1979, p. 17.
62. Interviews, New Delhi, October 1983.
63. *Ibid*. According to DMS Market Intelligence Report, India imported approximately $2.2 billion of arms between 1975 and 1979 and exported weapons valued at $80 million. India Summary, 1982, Greenwich, CT.
64. According to an Indian Defence ministry official, "Due to financial constraints, some [old] planes have been retained. Anyhow aircraft in the IAF [Indian Air Force], like Indian politicians, don't retire gracefully." Quoted in "A Dangerous Drift," *India Today*, February 28, 1983.
65. According to Phillips Talbot, the general mood had become "surprisingly bleak, as if the air had gone out of the balloon." Asia Society Calendar, January 1973.
66. A confidential World Bank report projected the need for $12 billion foreign aid for the plan and $2 billion a year each year for the duration of the plan. "World Bank's Confidential Report on India," *Mainstream*, April 6, 1974. In a note to state chief ministers in September 1973, Dhar called for "refurbishing the progressive leftward orientation of party policy and programmes" and for "a broad framework of understanding with the CPI." Further, he suggested, "Is a policy of detente with everyone in our national interest? It would, on the other hand, appear that for years to come the U.S.A. will remain our most powerful enemy." Quoted in Sinha, op. cit.
67. In July 1973, an interviewer asked Mrs. Gandhi if 1973 had been the most difficult year for India since independence. She answered, "Yes, indeed!" Khushwant Singh, *Indira Gandhi Returns*, New Delhi: Vision Books, 1979, p. 54.
68. Thomas, *The Defense of India*, op. cit., p. 227.
69. *The Times of India*, November 15, 1972.
70. Nihal Singh, "A Year of Crisis," *The Statesman*, August 15, 1974.
71. *Ibid*., "A Year of Dissent," January 26, 1975.
72. No. 25.
73. Nihal Singh, The Political Scene, henceforth Polscene, *The Statesman*, December 5, 1974. G.L. Nanda, whose distinction had been to hold the office of Acting Prime Minister twice, hoped to persuade more than 100 members of Parliament to sign a document warning of the danger of Congress party links with the CPI. Polscene, December 27, 1974.
74. Quoted in Burke, *Asian Survey*, op. cit.
75. *The New York Times*, February 8, 1973.
76. *India News*, March 23, 1973.

References

77. Quoted In Burke, *Asian Survey*, op. cit.
78. *The New York Times*, March 16, 1973.
79. Quoted in Satish Kumar, "Major Developments in India's Foreign Policy and Relations, July-December 1974," *International Studies*, New Delhi, July-September 1975.
80. *Ibid.*
81. Paul F. Power, "The Energy Crisis and Indian Development," *Asian Survey*, April 1975.
82. Nihal Singh, "Iranian Crisis," *The Statesman*, January 23, 1979.
83. *Pakistan Affairs*, June 1, 1973.
84. *The Statesman*, July 21, 1973.
85. Power, op. cit.
86. Polscene, October 11, 1974.
87. Kumar, op. cit.
88. M. Shankar, "Pakistan's Foreign Policy," *Mainstream*, June 6, 1981.
89. Admiral Thomas H. Moorer and Alvin J. Cottrell, "The Search for U.S. Bases in the Indian Ocean: A Last Chance," *Strategic Review*, Spring 1980.
90. Kim C. Beazley and Ian Clark, *The Politics of Intrusion*, Sydney: Alternative Publishing Cooperative, 1979, p. 43. Schlesinger, in answer to a question from a senator on the matter in June 1975, replied: "It [an American naval facility in Pakistan] is undoubtedly a possibility for consideration."
91. The text of the treaty is given in Jain, op. cit., Appendix X, pp. 371-74. Sen Gupta believes that Moscow turned down an Indian suggestion that it conclude a friendship treaty with Bangladesh during the closing days of the 1971 war. *Study*, op. cit., p. 158.
92. Simon, op. cit.
93. IISS, The Military Balance 1972-73, quoted in *The Statesman*, September 8, 1972.
94. *The Asian*, Hong Kong, March 12, 1972; *Hindustan Standard*, January 24, 1972.
95. Quoted in Burke, *Asian Survey*, op. cit.
96. Based on interviews in India, March and October 1983.
97. *Dawn*, March 3, 1973.
98. *New Times*, No. 37, 1972.
99. IISS, The Military Balance 1972-73.
100. *Soviet News*, June 18, 1974.
101. Quoted in Crocker, op. cit.
102. Mohammed Ayub, "The Superpowers and Regional 'Stability': Parallel Responses to the Gulf and Horn," *The World Today*, May 1979.
103. Nihal Singh, "China Opening," *The Statesman*, September 19, 1978.
104. *Peking Review*, November 4, 1977.
105. Robert C. Horn, "China and Russia in 1977: Maoism Without Mao," *Asian Survey*, October 1977.

Chapter Seven

1. Richard K. Betts, "Incentives for Nuclear Weapons: India, Pakistan, Iran," *Asian Survey*, November 1979. The CPI denounced the Chinese test; the CPI(M)

did not do so although it refrained from sending greetings to the Chinese Communist Party. Sen Gupta, *Communism in Indian Politics,* op. cit. p. 369
2. *Ibid.*
3. Polcom, May 1, 1970.
4. This was the widespread Indian belief at the time. K. Subrahmanyam has argued that "had India possessed nuclear weapons the *Enterprise* would not have steamed into the Bay of Bengal during the Indian-Pakistan war in what appeared from New Delhi to constitute atomic gunboat diplomacy." *India: Keeping Options Open* in Robert M. Lawrence and Joel Larus, ed., *Nuclear Proliferation: Phase II,* Lawrence, KS: University of Kansas Press, 1974, p. 122.
5. Polscene, May 23, 1974.
6. *Ibid.*
7. Based on conversations with Indian officials and strategists. The research reactor Purnima, essential for testing a nuclear device, was commissioned at Trombay in 1972.
8. Power, op. cit.
9. Hearings before Subcommittee on the Near East and South Asia, Committee on Foreign Affairs, House of Representatives, 93rd Session, September 19, 1974, p. 25.
10. Quoted in A.G. Noorani, "Indo-U.S. Nuclear Relations," *Asian Survey,* April 1981. There are grounds for believing that some material was used from the Canadian-aided Cirus research reactor. The safeguards under which it functioned were, in any case, hazy.
11. The five-year estimate is based on the assessment of Indian nuclear scientists. The tripartite agreement was signed by Desai's Janata government in late 1977. Power, op. cit.
12. Polscene, November 14, 1974.
13. Power, op. cit.
14. Polscene, June 3, 1974.
15. *The Hindustan Times,* August 14, 1974.
16. *The Indian Express,* September 24, 1974.
17. "Psychologically, the Pakistanis were clearly unprepared for holding talks with India at this juncture because they felt that, in talking 'empty handed' with a nuclear India, the 'balance' would not be in their favour." Polscene, June 10, 1974.
18. Choudhury, *Reflections,* op. cit., Bhutto undertook a trip to China in 1974, his second after assuming office.
19. Ian Clark, *Australian Outlook,* op. cit.
20. No. 21.
21. Quoted in Dawa Norbu, "Strategic Development in Tibet: Implications for its Neighbors," *Asian Survey,* March 1979.
22. No. 36.
23. Steve Weissman and Herbert Krosney, *The Islamic Bomb,* New Delhi: Vision Books, 1983, quoted in "A New Weapon for Islam," *The Statesman Weekly,* October 8, 1983.
24. It can, however, be argued that Bhutto's resolve to give Pakistan nuclear capability goes back to the commissioning of a reprocessing plant at Trombay towards the end of 1964. Bhutto reportedly went to Ayub in early 1965 to seek $50 million for a reprocessing plant but was turned down.

25. Lawrence Ziring, "Pakistan and India: Politics, Personalities and Foreign Policy," *Asian Survey*, July 1978.
26. Despite the belief of many experts in India and the West that the Chinese have materially aided Pakistan's attempts to make a bomb, there would seem to be no Chinese incentive in helping Pakistan become a nuclear weapon power. It would make Pakistanis less dependent upon their relationship with China and, even worse from Beijing's point of view, would certainly invite an Indian response in kind. It is more credible to believe that China sent some heavy water shipments to Pakistan without paying too much attention to its end use. According to Dilip Mukerjee, "China admits to exporting 'a limited quantity of nuclear materials' to unspecified countries for 'peaceful purposes,' which could include the Pakistan programme ostensibly related to the development of power technology." *The Times of India*, June 9, 1983. On the other hand, no one can guarantee that Beijing did not behave aberrantly during the Cultural Revolution. But it is well to remember that Pakistan's agreement with France on a nuclear reprocessing plant was signed in 1976.
27. Zulfikar Ali Bhutto, *If I Am Assassinated . . .*, New Delhi: Bell Books, 1980, p. 203.
28. *Ibid.*, p. 118.
29. Vertzberger, op. cit.
30. *The Times of India*, October 16, 1974.
31. *The Statesman*, November 30, 1974.
32. Kumar, op. cit.
33. Polscene, January 3, 1975.
34. Mrs. Gandhi told a luncheon gathering in the Kremlin on June 8, 1976: "For our part, we especially appreciate the scope and quantum of assistance from the Soviet Union. For it has enabled us to establish heavy industries in our public sector and reinforce our independence." Brezhnev declared at the Twenty-fifth Congress, "We attach special importance to friendship with that great country [India]. In the past five years Soviet-Indian relations have risen to a new level. Our countries have concluded a treaty of peace, friendship and cooperation. And even this short period has clearly shown its tremendous significance for our bilateral ties and its role as a stabilizing factor in South Asia and the continent as a whole." Y. Tsaplin, "The Sound Foundations of Soviet-Indian Ties," *International Affairs*, August 1976. In Moscow, Brezhnev congratulated Mrs. Gandhi for "the firm and decisive steps she has taken to thwart the efforts of domestic and external reaction." *The Times of India*, October 31, 1977.
35. The text of the interview is given in Uma Vasudev, *Two Faces of Indira Gandhi*, New Delhi: Vikas, 1977, Appendix, pp. 192-208.
36. Mrs. Gandhi explained her own attack on the CPI thus, "I wanted to say that although they [CPI] do support our programme which they consider progressive, from time to time they have had entirely opposing views not only to me but to my father also. They should not be surprised. My desire was not to criticize them but also to give a perspective of how different parties reacted, especially because people asked questions about them: how is it that they were our allies more or less and are now critical? So, I wanted to put this in perspective." Indira Gandhi, *My Truth*, op. cit., p. 164.
37. Quoted in Norbu, op. cit.

38. Mushtaque hailed the "heroic overthrow" of Mujib. *The Times*, London, August 16, 1975.
39. Mohammad Habib Sidky, "Chinese World Strategy and South Asia: The China Factor in Indo-Pakistani Relations," *Asian Survey*, October 1976.
40. Moscow Radio attributed Bhutto's victory to his "sober and positive foreign policy," but the Chinese reported the result without comment. Quoted in Golam W. Choudhury, "Post-Mao Policy in Asia," *Problems of Communism*, July-August 1977.
41. *The Washington Post*, April 27, 1977.
42. Quoted in Ziring, op. cit.
43. *Ibid.*
44. Mrs. Gandhi was later to suggest, "I thought we would just get through perhaps," *My Truth*, op. cit., p. 166.
45. *The Indian Express*, February 11, 1977.
46. *The Statesman*, March 26, 1977.
47. *The Times of India*, April 8, 1977.
48. *Indian and Foreign Review*, April 1, 1977.
49. *The Hindustan Times*, April 27, 1977.
50. *The Times of India*, April 28, 1977.
51. *Pravda*, April 28, 1977.
52. *Foreign Affairs Record*, June 1977.
53. *The Hindu*, October 26, 1977.
54. *The Hindustan Times*, October 26, 1978.
55. Donaldson, *Soviet Policy in South Asia*, op. cit., p. 376. According to him, India's debt in mid-1976 stood at $450 million.
56. *Economic and Political Weekly*, December 2, 1978. It commented, "Thus on most counts the recent agreement represents a compromise in which the balance of advantage is in favour of India."
57. Quoted in Rajan Menon, "India and the Soviet Union: A New Stage in Relations?", *Asian Survey*. July 1978. During the visit Desai also raised the question of Moscow's support for the Communist Party of India by asking the Soviets: "Why do you interfere in our internal affairs?" Gujral, op. cit.
58. N. Rodionov and V. Senin, *Soviet-Indian Economic and Trade Exchanges*, New Delhi: Soviet Land Booklets, 1981, p. 23.
59. *Ibid.*, p. 18.
60. *The Statesman*, October 29, 1977.
61. *Soviet Review*, No. 23.
62. Moscow Domestic Service, June 11, 1979.
63. Vajpayee's statement in the Lok Sabha, June 29, 1977.
64. Brzezinski says, "We set for ourselves the goal of consulting on critical issues with such countries as Venezuela, Brazil, Nigeria, Saudi Arabia, Iran, India, and Indonesia." *Power and Principle*, New York: Farrar Straus Giroux, 1983, pp. 53-54.
65. It is revealing that there is not a single mention of Desai in Carter's account of his presidency, *Keeping Faith*, Bantam Books, 1982.
66. *Indian and Foreign Review*, January 1, 1978.
67. Delhi Broadcast, June 2, 1979.
68. Quoted in Sen Gupta, "A Dangerous Drift," *India Today*, October 15, 1982.

References 283

69. *Ibid.*
70. Margaret Alva, *Janata's Foreign Policy: A Critique* in K.P. Misra, ed., *Janata's Foreign Policy*, New Delhi: Vikas 1979, p. 17.
71. Atal Bihari Vajpayee, *India and the Changing International Order* in Misra, *Ibid.*, p. 8.
72. According to Jagjivan Ram, India's negotiator on the issue for both the Gandhi and Janata Governments, Mrs. Gandhi was piqued by an anti-Indian statement made by President Ziaur Rahman at that time. Nihal Singh, *My India*, New Delhi: Vikas, 1982, p. 96.
73. Quoted in Walter K. Andersen, "India in Asia: Walking on a Tightrope," *Asian Survey*, December 1979.
74. *The Hindu*, March 10, 1979.
75. Delhi Domestic Service, May 5, 1979.
76. Nihal Singh, "Options in a Dangerous World," *The Statesman*, January 9, 1979.
77. During a reception at the Chinese Embassy in New Delhi held in his honour, Wang showed much astuteness in taking Mrs. Gandhi, one of the guests, to a room for a brief private discussion.
78. Nihal Singh, "Soul Mates," *The Statesman*, October 25, 1977.
79. Desai later maintained in an interview, "There was a change [in foreign policy].... That is why Moshe Dayan [of Israel] came here to explore the possibilities of establishing full diplomatic relations with India." S.S. Bankeshwar, *The Illustrated Weekly of India*, February 27, 1983. In April 1977, Vajpayee said, "At one time we gave the impression that we were pro-American. Then we gave the impression that we were pro-Soviet. There must be change in which we are genuinely nonaligned." *The Far Eastern Economic Review*, April 15, 1977.
80. Nihal Singh, "Options in a Dangerous World," *The Statesman*, January 9, 1979.
81. "Documents of the Eleventh Congress of the Communist Party of India, 31 March to 7 April, 1978," New Delhi: Communist Party Publication, 1978, p. 38.
82. *Ibid.*, p. 39.
83. Nihal Singh, "India's Russia Complex" *The Statesman*, February 21, 1978. After news leaked out, Desai confirmed in Parliament on April 17, 1978 that Indian intelligence teams had cooperated with the CIA during Mrs. Gandhi's regime in attempting to install a nuclear-powered espionage apparatus on Nanda Devi peak in the Himalayas. *The Statesman*, April 18, 1978.
84. Alva, op. cit., pp. 15-16.
85. Nihal Singh, "China Opening," *The Statesman*, September 19, 1978.
86. Text of the press conference issued by the Press Information Bureau, Government of India.
87. "China Opening," op. cit.
88. *Ibid.*, "The Peking [Beijing] Visit," *The Statesman*, February 6, 1979.
89. Tahir-Kheli, *Asian Survey*, October 1978, op. cit.
90. *Ibid.*
91. *Dawn*, December 22, 1978.
92. Thomas J. Wersto, "Tibet in Sino-Soviet Relations," *Asian Affairs*, Fall 1983.
93. Golam W. Choudhury, "New International Patterns in Asia," *Problems of Communism*, March-April 1979.
94. Robert C. Horn, "The Soviet Challenge in East Asia," *Asian Affairs*, Spring 1983.

95. Carter, op. cit., p. 206. Recounting the Deng visit, Carter further reveals, ". . . [Deng] added that it was highly desirable for China that its arrogant neighbors know that they could not disturb it and other countries in the area with impunity." According to Brzezinski, "Citing the Chinese-Indian clash of 1962 as an example, Deng insisted that the Vietnamese must be similarly punished." *Power and Principle*, op. cit., pp. 409-10. A retort to the Chinese was given by Defence Minister C. Subramaniam in October 1979. He said: "Even the concepts of gunboat diplomacy and white man's burden are being revived with ideas of nations 'punishing' nations." Address to National Defence College, New Delhi, October 29, 1979.
96. Carter notes that Brezhnev told him, "We observed with great concern that China's first action following recognition by the United States was an attack on Vietnam." *Ibid.*, p. 258. This was a mirror image of the charge the U.S. had made on the Soviet-Vietnamese treaty preceding the Vietnamese invasion of Cambodia.
97. Vajpayee's statement to the Rajya Sabha on February 21, 1979. Text issued by the Press Information Bureau, Government of India.
98. During a visit to China early in 1979, I asked Vice Foreign Minister He Ying, "There is a feeling in India that the timing of the attack on Vietnam was not quite appropriate since Mr. Vajpayee was still in China." His answer in part was: "The timing was not of our choice. We were compelled to counter-attack at that time. It was necessary and its aim was limited." Nihal Singh, *The Gang and 900 Million: A China Diary*, New Delhi/Bombay: Oxford & IBH in association with Nachiketa, 1979, p. 41.
99. Desai later told me that Vajpayee was "emotional" in giving in to demands that China be called an aggressor, but he was eminently satisfied with his choice of Vajpayee as Foreign Minister. Nihal Singh, *My India*, op. cit., p. 96.
100. See Note 97 above.
101. The CPI organ, *New Age*, chose to attack me twice for urging India, in *The Statesman*, to exercise its China option. On October 1, 1978, it suggested, ". . . . He [Nihal Singh] has beaten all records in spouting anti-Soviet, anti-CPI slanders in the space of 36 inches." "Not Mere Anti-Sovietism, Treachery to Nation." On February 11, 1979, *New Age* wrote under the evocative heading "Statesman's Sinophilia", ". . . . He [Nihal Singh] extends his anti-Sovietism to blatant calumny against Vietnam."
102. Nihal Singh, "Kosygin visit," *The Statesman*, March 20, 1979.
103. K.R. Singh, "Fifty Years of IAF," *Mainstream*, October 24, 1981.
104. Interviews, New Delhi, March and October 1983.
105. *Ibid.*
106. Secretary of State Cyrus Vance threatened to veto the transfer to India of U.S. technology that Sweden had acquired under licence on the grounds that the Viggen might upset the military balance on the subcontinent and precipitate a new arms race. Inder Malhotra, "The Aeronautics Industry: Implications of the DPSA Deal," *The Times of India*, September 21, 1978.
107. "The Soviets, on the other hand [in contrast to the U.S.], while they are dedicated to technological improvements, have never lost sight of the fact that the best weapons are those that are inexpensive, dependable, light of weight and capable of being operated under a variety of conditions by the ordinary soldier." Thayer,

op. cit., p. 373.
108. "This [the abrupt cutoff of U.S. and other Western arms supplies in 1965] has brought home to those in charge of the country's defence, even more forcefully than the Chinese attacks of 1962, that the nation's dependence on foreign countries for defence equipment and stores must be reduced; a corollary to this being that the manufacture within the country of as many different kinds of equipment and supplies needed to equip the defence forces, must be speeded up even more than before." Khera, op. cit., p. 59.
109. "Kosygin Visit," op. cit.
110. Nihal Singh, *My India*, op. cit., p. 97.
111. Nihal Singh, "The Bhutto Drama," *The Statesman*, February 13, 1979.
112. A.K. Damodaran, "Neighbours as Strangers," *Mainstream*, June 21, 1981.
113. Choudhury, *Problems of Communism*, March-April 1979, op. cit.
114. Tahir-Kheli, op. cit.
115. Sen Gupta, "A Dangerous Drift," *India Today*, October 15, 1982.
116. Damodaran, op. cit.
117. Carter records, ". . . . I wanted to work with the Soviet leaders to establish strict limits on the permanent deployment of naval forces in the Indian Ocean, and to require prior notification if such forces had to be strengthened to protect the special interests of either nation. . . ." Op. cit., p. 217.
118. Ziring, op. cit.
119. Quoted in Andersen, op. cit.
120. A Bangladesh view, expressed by M.A. Aziz, is: "Who benefits from a zone of peace [in the Indian Ocean]? With India as the dominant power of the region and having military preponderance over its neighbors, it is natural that India will get the maximum benefit out of it. With no superpowers to deter it, India will have a free sail in the Indian Ocean, and can at times threaten the peripheral states with military muscle. It is on this presumption that Bangladesh, I believe, should support the continued presence of the superpowers in the Indian Ocean." "Bangladesh in United States Foreign Policy," *Asian Affairs*, March-April 1982.
121. Ziring, op. cit. Some Soviet spokesmen have been frank in discussing their country's position on the Indian Ocean. G.A. Aliev, Politburo member, told the CPI's Eleventh Congress at Bhatinda in early 1978: "We are also in favour of nonlittoral states reducing their military presence on a reciprocal basis [in the Indian Ocean]." *Documents*, 1978, op. cit., p. 219 E.A. Shevardnadze, Alternate Politburo member, declared at the CPI's Twelfth Congress at Varanasi in early 1982: "As for the Soviet Union, it actively supports proposals to declare the Indian Ocean a zone of peace. For a long time we have been conducting talks with the U.S.A. on limitation of military activities in this region. But the talks were interrupted by the American side. We as before are ready to solve this problem on the basis of equality and equal security." *Documents*, 1982, op. cit., p. 211. According to Thornton, "In Soviet thinking, as in American, the Indian Ocean is increasingly viewed as an extension of the Pacific, with Southeast Asia and Australia as the hinge." *Asian Survey*, op. cit., January 1983.
122. Brzezinski suggests, "By late summer of 1979, our campaign on behalf of SALT ratification was making steady progress," op. cit., p. 344.
123. Karachi Domestic Service, August 30, 1979.
124. The state of the new government can be gauged from the fact that as Prime

Minister, Charan Singh accused his Finance Minister of being a Russian agent. One of the Janata Government's last acts was to send a formal invitation to a Chinese journalists' delegation to visit India. Nihal Singh, "Bull in China Shop," *The Statesman*, August 29, 1979.

Chapter Eight

1. Delhi Domestic Service, August 15, 1979.
2. Sen Gupta, *The Afghan Syndrome: How to Live with Soviet Power*, New Delhi, Vikas, 1982, p. 13.
3. Quoted in Kuldip Nayar, *Report on Afghanistan*, New Delhi: Allied, 1981, p. 50.
4. Ibid.
5. Jimmy Carter records: "Brezhnev... asserted that the Soviets had first heard of the revolution in Afghanistan on the radio and did not instigate the change in government . . . (This was six months before the Soviet invasion of Afghanistan)." Op. cit., p. 256.
6. Sen Gupta, *Syndrome*, op. cit., p. 84.
7. *Ibid.*, p. 85.
8. *Ibid.*
9. Quoted in Gargi Dutt, *China and the Developments in Afghanistan* in K.P. Misra, ed., *Afghanistan in Crisis*, New Delhi: Vikas, 1981, p. 44.
10. NBC-TV interview in September 1980.
11. *The Times of India*, February 9, 1980.
12. "The Munich Tragedy and Contemporary Appeasement," reprinted in *Beijing Review*, January 5, 1979.
13. An Agence France-Presse dispatch from Beijing, quoted in Gargi Dutt, op. cit., p. 48.
14. The main events leading up to the coup are given in Jagat S. Mehta, "Afghanistan: A Neutral Solution," *Foreign Policy*, Summer 1982. As the civil service head of the Indian Foreign Ministry till the end of 1979, Mehta was well placed to monitor Afghan events. According to Nayar, the Indian Embassy in Kabul anticipated Soviet troops' intervention after Taraki's assassination and thought December 1979 as the outer limit. *Report*, op. cit., p. 9. The change in Soviet thinking on Amin would also seem to be corroborated by Desai's charge, made public four days before Brezhnev's visit to New Delhi in December 1980, that while he was Prime Minister the Soviets suggested that "Pakistan should be taught a lesson." The charge was denied by *Pravda* of December 7, 1980 and by Brezhnev's spokesman Leonid Zamyatin in New Delhi. But Desai sticks to his charge. In a conversation with me on Staten Island on May 19, 1984, Desai said: "In the context of Afghanistan, he [Kosygin] said [during his visit to India in 1979] that Pakistan was not behaving properly and should be punished. I told him that I would have no part in the weakening of Pakistan. I said it publicly in 1980 before Brezhnev's visit because Moscow was again encouraging India [to punish Pakistan]." According to the Fifth Report from the Foreign Affairs Committee of the House of Commons (Sessions 1979-80), the Soviet operational plan for military intervention in Afghanistan was prepared in mid/late March 1979. Quoted in Nayar, *Report*, p. 9.

15. *The Indian Express*, January 31, 1980.
16. Nayar, *Report*, op. cit., p. 7.
17. Nayar quotes Vajpayee, Foreign Minister in the Janata government, as telling him on March 23, 1980 that Amin was "poisoned by Russian cooks." *Ibid.*, p. 6.
18. Karmal, in an interview in Kabul on February 3, 1980, maintained that he had been in the Soviet Embassy in Kabul for weeks before the coup to counter the widely held view that he had been flown in by the Soviets just before the coup. *Ibid.*, p. 12.
19. The Indian delegate's assumptions, made public during the Afghanistan debate in the U.N. General Assembly on January 11, 1980, were made on the basis of Soviet assurances. Quoted in K.P. Saksena, *Afghanistan Conflict and the United Nations* in Misra, *Afghanistan*, op. cit., p. 109.
20. Hearings of the Subcommittee for Near Eastern and South Asian Affairs, Committee of Foreign Relations, September 26, 1979, p. 53.
21. *The New York Times*, December 27, 1979.
22. *Ibid.*, December 29 and 30, 1979.
23. "Issues and Answers," December 30, 1979.
24. Cyrus Vance, *Hard Choices*, New York: Simon and Schuster, 1983, p. 369.
25. *Ibid.*
26. *Ibid.*, p. 387.
27. Quoted in Sen Gupta, *Syndrome*, op. cit., p. 5
28. *The New York Times*, January 5, 1980.
29. *The Indian Express*, January 6, 1980.
30. *The Times of India*, February 9, 1980.
31. Beijing Domestic Service in Mandarin, December 29, 1979. The Yugoslav newspaper *Borba* of January 8, 1980 said the Soviet intervention in Afghanistan was a "dangerous return to the Stalinist approach of trampling underfoot the sovereignty of other countries." Iran's Ayatollah Khomeini asked the Afghan nation to learn from the Iranian nation: "They [the Afghans] should kill those who kill the people; the military should join the nation and this is the order of Islam." Quoted in Nayar, *Report*, op. cit., p. 55.
32. Interviews, New Delhi, 1980. Vance made a similar point, in terms of American interests, in March 1980. Vance told the Senate Foreign Relations Committee: "The Soviet invasion of Afghanistan increases and dramatizes the potential threat to the security of nations there and to the world's free access to natural resources and shipping routes. That is the fact whatever we may speculate about Soviet aims. For intentions cannot be known with certainty. Even if they do, intentions can change. Our response must be based upon Soviet capabilities and Soviet behavior." Statement on U.S. Foreign Policy before the Senate Foreign Relations Committee on March 27, 1980. *Hard Choices*, op. cit., Appendix V, p. 505. The Soviet Foreign Minister had warned the U.S. in early 1954 that American military aid to Pakistan "made it necessary for the Soviet Union to think about our neighbor, Afghanistan's defense, and make sure we [the Soviet Union] are safe." *The New York Times*, June 7, 1954. Shortly after the Soviet intervention in Afghanistan, T.N. Kaul called for a Monroe Doctrine for the subcontinent; so did the Jana Sangh organ, *Organiser*, Wariawalla, *Seminar*, op. cit.
33. According to Jagat Mehta, ". . . . The various Soviet comments seem to imply

that the primary Soviet objective is to prevent Afghanistan from becoming a hostile base rather than to retain the country as a strategic ally or as a model socialist state." Op. cit. Brzezinski believes that "had the Shah not fallen, it is unlikely that the Soviets would have moved so openly into Afghanistan..." Op. cit., p. 356. It is interesting to speculate whether the Soviets would have administered a snub to India, by not caring to inform New Delhi in advance of their intervention, had Mrs. Gandhi been then in power. Although India could not have prevented the Soviet action, it would have been more embarrassing for Moscow to press on with its intervention if faced with New Delhi's strong objections.

34. Interviews, New Delhi, March and October 1983. As Foreign Minister Narasimha Rao was to explain it later: "It all started on December 27, 1979, when we were in the thick of elections to Parliament. By about January 9 or 10, 1980, results came in and our party got an overwhelming majority. The Government was sworn in only on January 15. It was during this interregnum that we inherited this problem [of Afghanistan]." Address to the Pakistan Institute of International Affairs at Karachi on June 11, 1981.

35. *Ibid.*

36. Documents of the Eleventh Congress of the Communist Party of India, New Delhi: CPI Publications, 1978. I.K. Gujral, initially sent by Mrs. Gandhi as ambassador to Moscow (he stayed on in the Soviet capital to serve the two successor regimes of Desai and Charan Singh and briefly her own new government), has suggested that there has been a "sea-change" in the Soviet perception of India since their endorsement of the Emergency. CPSU functionaries, in his view, were distressed by the step-by-step denigration of the CPI during the Emergency and the 1977 results made clear to them the high price the CPI had paid for close cooperation with the Congress (I) and were now hesitant to advise the CPI to squander its "hard-earned credibility." "Affirming Indo-USSR Ties," *The Times of India*, October 8, 1982.

37. A. Usvatov, "The Return of Indira Gandhi," *New Times*, No. 2, 1980. The Congress (I), in a resolution adopted at the All-India Congress Committee meeting in New Delhi on April 21-22, 1979, had said: "It may be recalled that on Kashmir and the Bangladesh issue, the Soviet Union supported us, while the United States and the Western bloc created problems for us. To secure Soviet support in such vital issues as the 1971 war, when the U.S. sent the Seventh Fleet to intimidate us, cannot be called our tilt towards the USSR." Quoted in Partha S. Ghosh and Rajaram Pande, op. cit.

38. Boris Chekhonin, "India: Looking Into the Future," *Ibid.*, No. 4, 1980. Chekhonin wrote in *New Times* in December 1979 on "India: On the Threshold of the Election," predicting a general "fragmentation and atomization" of political forces in India, a setting in which the two Communist factions, united in action, would constitute an "important political factor." ".... The left forces," he said, "are closing their ranks on the initiative of the Communist Party of India. For the first time in the past few years the main parties of the Left—the Communist Party of India and the Communist Party of India-Marxist—have reached agreement on the distribution of constituencies between them in almost all states." The two Communist parties entered the new Lok Sabha in 1980 with 47 seats (CPI-M 35 and CPI 12), the largest contingent ever in Parliament. Sen

Gupta, "Communism and India; A New Context," *Problems of Communism*, July/August 1981.
39. Quoted in Nayar, *Report*, op. cit., p. 51.
40. *Ibid.*, p. 59.
41. Carter's comment was biting. He writes: "Even Cuba was more reticent in its praise [of the Soviet Union] than India." Op. cit., p. 479. The widespread belief in New Delhi was that the speech had been drafted by former Foreign Secretary T.N. Kaul, known for his pro-Soviet proclivities. K.P. Saksena, in Misra, *Afghanistan*, op. cit., p. 109n. It must be recorded, to Brajesh Mishra's credit, that on receiving the draft of the speech, he telephoned New Delhi to try to get it changed, without success. Interviews, New Delhi, 1980.
42. *The Indian Express*, January 17, 1980.
43. Quoted in Bimal Prasad, *India and the Afghan Crisis*, in Misra, *Afghanistan*, op. cit., p. 79.
44. *Ibid.*
45. Quoted in Nayar, *Report*, op. cit., p. 53.
46. Jimmy Carter, *Keeping Faith*, op. cit., p. 486. President Mitterrand's reaction to the Soviet action was harsher. In an interview he granted me in Paris on November 17, 1981, I asked him if France was not following a harder line towards the Soviet Union. "Yes," he answered, "perhaps I am disappointed by the Soviet invasion of Afghanistan. I cannot say I approve of it. I disapprove of it." Nihal Singh, "France Won't Re-enter NATO," *The Indian Express*, November 18, 1981.
47. Polscene, June 3, 1974.
48. According to Socialist Party functionaries in Paris in November 1981, "the French are beginning to discover India after their disappointment with China, both ideologically and commercially." Nihal Singh, "The French Way—II," *The Indian Express*, December 3, 1981.
49. *Ibid.*, November 18, 1981.
50. In 1980, Mrs. Gandhi said in a note to the External Affairs Ministry that India should cultivate closer relations in trade, commerce and technology with the emergent powers of Western Europe, Latin America and Africa. "Entente Cordiale," *India Today*, December 31, 1982. Mrs. Gandhi visited Finland, Denmark, Norway, Austria and Yugoslavia in the first half of 1983. She had earlier visited Britain, France and Italy and Prime Minister Margaret Thatcher of Britain and President Mitterrand came to India. Foreign ministers of at least seven West European countries came to New Delhi since Mrs. Gandhi's return to power, the French Foreign Minister twice. K.L. Sharma, "Indian Overtures to Europe," *The Times of India*, July 8, 1983.
51. This had been agreed to during Mrs. Gandhi's visit to the U.S. in July-August 1982. India had accepted the replacement of the U.S. by France as the supplier of uranium, thus giving up its earlier plan to use an indigenous fuel to keep the Tarapur plant running. The dispute with France centred on the terms, with India insisting that these should be the 1963 agreement between New Delhi and Washington. France initially wanted fresh safeguards but ultimately fell in line with India's views.
52. *The Times of India*, November 28, 1982.
53. *India Today*, December 31, 1982.

54. Nayar, *Report*, op. cit., p. 30.
55. Sajjad Hyder, "Cost of Refugees to Pakistan," *The Muslim*, Islamabad, reprinted in *The Times of India*, March 7, 1984.
56. *The Times of India*, January 3, 1980.
57. Syed Shabbir Hussain, Abdul Hamid Alvi and Absar Hussain Rizvi, *Afghanistan Under Soviet Occupation*, Islamabad: World Affairs Publications, April 1980, pp. 143-44.
58. Thomas Perry Thornton, "Between the Stools?: U.S. Policy Towards Pakistan During the Carter Administration," *Asian Survey*, October 1982. Thornton was on the staff of the National Security Council during the Carter days.
59. Any inclination to look at the Indian option must have been discouraged by the Indian delegate's speech at the U.N. on January 11. On February 6, 1980 Zia told Indian correspondents that Pakistan perceived Mrs. Gandhi to be "pro-Soviet." *The Statesman* and *The Indian Express*, February 7, 1980. Going by an interview Zia gave earlier to an Indian reporter, the full significance of the Soviet move into Afghanistan took some time to sink in. He told Nayar: "We thought Russian troops were being invited by Amin because he was really concerned. We expected that the poor chap wanted to stabilize his own position." *The Indian Express*, January 31, 1980.
60. Thornton, *Asian Survey*, October 1982, op. cit.
61. Quoted in Nayar, *Report*, op. cit., p. 69.
62. According to Nayar, the British Foreign Secretary, Lord Carrington, who undertook a trip of the Middle East and the subcontinent shortly after the Soviet intervention in Afghanistan, was the promoter of the Islamic Conference idea. *Ibid.*, p. 61.
63. The text of the Islamic Conference resolution can be found in Shabbir Hussain and others, op. cit., Appendix III, pp. 202-5.
64. Excerpts of Zia's speech are contained in *ibid.*, Appendix II, pp. 198-201.
65. *Ibid.*, p. 138.
66. *The Indian Express*, January 25, 1980.
67. Sen Gupta, *Syndrome*, op. cit., p. 117.
68. As Zia was to reveal later in a series of interviews with Rajendra Sareen. "... Sardar Swaran Singh said, 'General Zia, you are faced with a crisis. They have knocked on your doors at the western borders. How are you going to comply because you have your forces distributed on the east and the west? If you like to lift something from the east and put on the west, we will have no objection.'" Zia countered by proposing discussions on the two countries' force levels. He further suggested, "I said [to Swaran Singh] just shift even one-twentieth of the force, just a division or a brigade as a token that India has tried to thin out its forces facing Pakistan, then it will be an indication to me that you really mean to help me ... We have seen no reaction. Instead, it [the forces' level] has been thickened." Describing India's stand, Zia told the interviewer, "It [Afghanistan] should be resolved between India and Pakistan and not taken at the international level. It was the first response we received ... They [India] said, no, Russia has come and it is a big first power, so we should not annoy them, you are directly involved. So let India and Pakistan join. I said, all right, let us join. What should we do?" Zia elaborated, "Just, to clarify, I have no doubt about India's principal stand: the Soviet Union's forces must withdraw, the refugees must go ... We cannot go to

war [with the Soviet Union] but certainly we can pass a resolution . . ." *Sunday*, Calcutta, October 31-November 6, 1982 and November 7-13, 1982.
69. Brzezinski, op. cit., p. 448.
70. Thornton, *Asian Survey*, October 1982, op. cit.
71. Quoted in "Moscow and Gen. Zia," *The Times of India*, October 28, 1982.
72. Dev Murarka, "Pak-Soviet Relations: U.S. Concern," *Mainstream*, August 22, 1981.
73. *The Times of India*, February 13, 1980.
74. Quoted in Robert C. Horn, "Afghanistan and the Soviet-Indian Influence Relationship," *Asian Survey*, March 1983.
75. *The Los Angeles Times*, February 15, 1980. Foreign Minister Narasimha Rao told Gromyko at the banquet that "all countries of the region are members of the nonaligned movement and should be permitted to live in peace and unity without being dragged into a confrontation." Quoted in Nayar, *Report*, op. cit., p. 77.
76. According to *The Hindu* of February 29, 1980, "The Afghan question was being isolated step by step from the mainstream of Indo-Soviet relations so that the two countries can agree to disagree on this issue without impairing their wideranging cooperation . . ."
77. Quoted in Sen Gupta, *Syndrome*, op. cit., p. 133.
78. Shankar, op. cit.
79. Sen Gupta, *Syndrome*, op. cit., p. 134.
80. Reported by Tass, June 3, 1980.
81. Nihal Singh, "Gandhi Faces Winter of Discontent," *The Asian Wall Street Journal*, October 11, 1980.
82. December 8, 1980.
83. Quoted in Nayar, *Report*, op. cit., p. 174n.
84. Quoted in Horn, *Asian Survey*, March 1983.
85. *The Overseas Hindustan Times*, December 25, 1980.
86. *The Indian Express*, December 9, 1980. Brezhnev's praise for Mrs. Gandhi was criticized by Marxists who said that she would use Soviet friendship for her bourgeois government's interests. *People's Democracy*, December 21, 1980.
87. Horn, *Asian Survey*, March 1983, op. cit.
88. Quoted in Sen Gupta, *Syndrome*, pp. 139-40, op. cit.
89. Mrs. Gandhi told Parliament in December 1980 that "though India's perception of global problems did not tally with the Soviet Union's, the two countries were careful to see that these differences did not come in the way of their bilateral relations." *The Overseas Hindustan Times*, December 25, 1980. Countering criticism of the Indian stand on Afghanistan, Foreign Minister Rao had told the U.N. General Assembly on September 28, 1981, "We have unequivocally opposed the presence of foreign troops in any country and all countries. For us this includes Afghanistan, whereas presumably for some other countries, this should apply only to Afghanistan." *Mainstream*, October 24, 1981.
90. Interviews, New Delhi, 1980.
91. *Ibid*.
92. Nihal Singh, "India Meets China," *The Indian Express*, December 9, 1981.
93. Leo E. Rose believes that the Indian decision was the "result of massive confusion and indecisiveness" characteristic of the decision-making process since Mrs. Gandhi's return to power in 1980. *India's Foreign Policy in the 1980s: New*

Problems and Perspectives, in Nemai Sadhan Bose, *India in the Eighties*, Calcutta: Firma KLM, 1983, p. 49.
94. Nihal Singh, "From Beijing With Love," *The Indian Express*, July 8, 1981.
95. "Welcome Agreement," *The Indian Express*, June 30, 1981. The excitement generated among Chinese officials by the arrival of Rajiv, Mrs. Gandhi's elder son, at a reception held by the Chinese ambassador in honour of Huang was to be seen to be believed. I was present.
96. S. Irodov, *New Times*, July 1981, quoted in Wersto, op. cit.
97. "From Beijing With Love," op. cit. In July 1980 the CPI National Council supported Mrs. Gandhi's foreign policy while deploring India's withholding complete and unequivocal support for the Soviet stand on Afghanistan. It also said it was "unfortunate" that Foreign Minister Rao had criticized the prolonged Soviet troops' presence in Afghanistan. Quoted in Sen Gupta, "Communism and India: A New Context," *Problem of Communism*, July-August 1981. The CPI(M) Politburo, on the other hand, criticized China's attitude to the Soviet Union and the U.S. but qualified it significantly: ". . . . Despite our sharp delineation of Chinese policies, we refuse to join the Indian revisionists who . . . seek to run down China. They act as storm troopers of the CPSU." *The Times of India*, June 27, 1980. While the CPI had expectedly supported the Soviet military intervention in Afghanistan, the Marxists' support was something of a surprise. The latter was given after a meeting of the Politburo in New Delhi with only three members present—Harkishan Singh Surjeet, E.M.S. Namboodiripad and P. Ramamurti—and was resented by West Bengal Chief Minister Jyoti Basu, among others, at the time. Interviews, Calcutta, October 1983. General V. Tatarnikov quoted Brezhnev in *Izvestia* of July 22, 1981 as saying: "It is time those who are encroaching on the DRA [Democratic Republic of Afghanistan] realize that their adventurist plans are bound to fail. The revolutionary process in Afghanistan is irreversible. The Afghan people and their government have the support and solidarity of the Soviet Union and the other socialist states and progressive forces all over the world."
98. "From Beijing With Love," *Ibid.*
99. Nihal Singh, "India Meets China," *The Indian Express*, December 9, 1981.
100. Inder Malhotra, "Delhi-Beijing Dialogue," *The Times of India*, November 3, 1983.
101. Nihal Singh, "State of the Nation," *India Today*, January 1-15, 1981.
102. *Ibid* "The State of India after Sanjay," *The Asian Wall Street Journal*, July 8, 1980.
103. Sanjay was given a state funeral in all but name although he was a mere member of Parliament and one of the party general secretaries. Many of the Congress (I)-ruled state governments declared the funeral day a holiday. "Those who were pleading for some time that Mrs. Gandhi should govern the country without her son are now discovering that in his death she has lost her main emotional and political support." Nihal Singh, "The Royal Family," *India Today*, July 16-31, 1980.
104. "Gandhi Faces Winter of Discontent," op. cit.
105. Quoted in Kewal Varma, "Will Moscow Influence CPI Policies Again?", *Sunday*, October 31-November 6, 1982.

References

106. Interviews, New Delhi, March and October 6, 1983.
107. Gujral reveals that during his term as ambassador in Moscow, when Dange sought to promote Indian Communists' cooperation with Mrs. Gandhi and the Congress (I), his status was downgraded from Octobrskaya hotel to Sputnik, from a Zil car to Chaika. Later, Moscow did not condone his "sin of breaking the party." Op. cit.
108. Nihal Singh, "Bashing the Reds," *The Indian Express*, April 21, 1981.
109. *Ibid.* N.V. Goldin, Soviet Minister of Heavy Industry, reportedly pleaded with some Congress (I) members not to leave the World Peace Council, telling them: "It has an Indian [Ramesh Chandra] as its chairman." *Sunday*, March 23-April 3, 1982.
110. *The Times of India*, May 28, 1981.
111. Interviews, New Delhi, March and October 1983.
112. Supplement to *New Times*, No. 9, February 1981.
113. *The Economist*, London, September 13, 1980. Brzezinski makes it clear that "... the Saudis, who did undertake to facilitate Pakistani arms purchases, in return for a Pakistani military input into Saudi security" and an agreement in principle had been reached on additional Saudi arms purchases in return for Saudi help for Afghans and Pakistanis. Op. cit., pp. 449-50. Zia told an interviewer in September 1981, "All we have provided Saudi Arabia is a number of instructors, some technicians, in the three services." *U.S. News and World Report*, September 21, 1981. According to Colin Legum, an additional estimated 6,000 Pakistani troops were brought into Saudi Arabia to guard Tabuk and Riyadh. *The Times of India*, October 14, 1983.
114. Devlet Khalid, "Pakistan's Relations with Iran and the Arab States," *Journal of South Asian and Middle East Studies*, quoted in Robert G. Wirsing and James M. Roherty, "The United States and Pakistan," *International Affairs*, Autumn 1982. According to Colin Legum, Pakistan had an estimated 15,000 troops in Saudi Arabia at the end of 1982. *The Times of India*, May 13, 1983. Lt.-Gen. E.A. Vas (retd.) quotes reliable sources to suggest that Pakistani pilots man two Mirage-V squadrons of Abu Dhabi (U.A.E.) and one Pakistani artillery unit is located in Dhofar. Besides, Pakistan is reported to have earmarked a division as a standby Rapid Deployment Force for use in Saudi Arabia in the event of external or internal threat. "Pakistan's Role in the Gulf Region," *Sunday*, June 6-12, 1982.
115. Begum Nusrut Bhutto said that her party would recognize the Afghan government and not permit Afghan rebels to operate from Pakistani soil. Shankar, *Mainstream*, op. cit.
116. Quoted in Richard P. Cronin, "The U.S. and Pakistan: Security and Nuclear Proliferation," Issue Brief No. IB81122, Library of Congress, Washington, D.C., updated 8/18/81.
117. *Ibid.*
118. Zia disclosed in April 1982 that he rejected an American proposal to station troops and arms in Pakistan made at the time the aid package was being negotiated. *The New York Times*, April 4, 1982.
119. Cronin, op. cit.
120. Defence Secretary Weinberger was involved in an interesting exchange on the subject with members of the House Foreign Affairs Committee in March 1982.
    Secretary Weinberger:.... We have a feeling that we enhance our own

defense at considerably less cost both in manpower and weapons and from an economic point of view if we can help with a forward defense of the United States by arming and equipping to the extent we can a number of other countries.

....

.... Pakistan has requested more [in military supplies] than we have been able to give them.

Mr. Gejdenson: So you feel that, for instance, if American troops or American interests were endangered in the Middle East, that we could count on the Pakistanis or the Jordanians or the Saudis to help us out with troops, equipment, or what have you?

....

Secretary Weinberger: We think in one way or another that because we have relationships with them in a number of ways, some of which include the furnishing of supplies that they want, that they will add to our security interests. Obviously, there have been disappointments in the past, but we would not make the requests if we did not feel that they were very much in our interests.

Later, President Reagan's conventional arms transfer policy of July 8, 1981 was explained thus: "The United States . . . views the transfer of conventional arms and other defense articles and services as an essential element of its global defense posture and an indispensable component in its foreign policy." Hearing before the Committee on Foreign Affairs, House of Representatives, Ninety-seventh Congress, Second Session, March 10, 1982. Assistant Secretary of State Veliotes told a press conference in Washington early in December 1982: "One of the top priorities in February 1981 was to review our relations with Pakistan with a view to developing a renewed close relationship. There were a number of factors involved in this, but the most important, of course, was the Soviet invasion of Afghanistan. Pakistan is not only a country of considerable importance to the U.S. but we have friends in the Gulf who are quite concerned about the well-being of Pakistan. This was one of the top priorities of the Reagan Administration when it came in." *The Times of India*, December 5, 1982.

121. Firyubin made an unexpected detour to New Delhi after his Pakistan visit, to be urged by India to "take some meaningful initiative on Afghanistan." *The Far Eastern Economic Review*, September 4, 1981.
122. *The Statesman*, January 5 and 6, 1981.
123. "We Rejoice at Your Achievements," *New Times*, No. 4, January 1981.
124. S. Irodov, "The Delhi Conference," *New Times*, No. 8, February 1981. Zia, in the interview with Sareen, gave himself a pat on the back. He said: "It was Pakistan which saved the situation [at the nonaligned foreign ministers' conference] and a lot of embarrassment to the Indian government and the Indian delegation . . . India was not prepared to say anything against the Russians." Op. cit.
125. *The Statesman*, April 10, 1981. Moscow eagerly took up Mrs. Gandhi's

References 295

argument. *Izvestia* of May 7, 1981 said: "Neither Washington nor Islamabad now conceals the fact that this generous flow of American arms is meant to transform the Pakistani army into a real threat to Afghanistan and India, suppress internal opposition to Zia-ul-Haq's regime and provide a continuous supply of arms for the Afghan counterrevolution, which entrenched itself in Pakistan . . . Pakistan will be part of a world-wide defence chain."

126. Nihal Singh, "Coping With Pakistan," *The Indian Express*, November 11, 1981.
127. Address at Karachi, op. cit.
128. Nihal Singh, "An Important Visitor," *The Indian Express*, June 24, 1981.
129. As Bangladesh's Foreign Minister, A.R. Shams-ud-Doha, put it in an address to the Asia Society in New York on January 26, 1984, "The stability of our region has been eroded by the induction of external pressures. This has constituted both a constraint and an impetus to regional cooperation."
130. "A Step Forward," *The Times of India*, August 5, 1983.
131. Nihal Singh, "A Double Tragedy," *The Sunday Standard*, May 31, 1981.

Chapter Nine

1. Quoted in Thomas W. Robinson, "The Soviet Union and Asia in 1981," *Asian Survey*, January 1982.
2. Foreign Information Broadcast Service—Soviet Union (FBIS-SU), June 19, 1981.
3. *Ibid.*, July 17, 1981.
4. *Ibid.*, June 16, 1981.
5. U.S. Senate Foreign Relations Committee on Sino-American Military Relations, October 27-28, 1981.
6. United Press International report from Beijing, December 8, 1981.
7. *The Overseas Hindustan Times*, January 7, 1982. Quoted in Horn, *Asian Survey*, March 1983.
8. Nihal Singh, "Coping With Pakistan," *The Indian Express*, November 11, 1981.
9. *Ibid.*
10. *Ibid.*, "Making Peace With Pakistan," *The Indian Express*, February 10, 1982.
11. *The Statesman*, January 31, and February 1, 1982.
12. *The Overseas Hindustan Times*, July 30, 1981.
13. *Soviet Review*, April 1982. *Izvestia* said on October 1, 1982, "In glancing back over the past decades we rejoice that both our countries are marching firmly along the path of the lasting consolidation of bilateral relations."
14. During Mrs. Gandhi's U.S. visit, the Soviet press had warned her to beware of an "arsenal of Hollywood smiles" and said "sweet words can turn into a stab in the back." *The Far Eastern Economic Review*, October 1, 1982. Senator Daniel Patrick Moynihan has suggested: "Their [Russian] armor is now in the Khyber Pass. Of necessity, the ruler of India is in Washington." *The Washington Post*, July 29, 1982.
15. Mrs. Gandhi undertook a visit to Saudi Arabia in April 1982. A joint communiqué at the end of the visit declared that the security of the Gulf was linked with that of the subcontinent and that, in this context, India sought to normalize relations with Pakistan. *The Far Eastern Economic Review*, June 11, 1982.

16. Nihal Singh, "India's Halting Steps Toward Economic Liberalization," *The Wall Street Journal*, December 27, 1982.
17. Interviews, Washington, D.C. 1983. According to Thomas P. Thornton, "The United States and India need each other badly. India is the only effective barrier to Soviet expansion in the subcontinent." *The New York Times*, July 16, 1982.
18. *The Times of India*, October 19, 1982.
19. Richard P. Cronin and Douglas D. Mitchell, "Issues Concerning Pakistan's Acquisition of the U.S. F-16 Fighter Bomber Aircraft," Congressional Research Service, Report No. 81-225F, October 5, 1981, p. 28.
20. IISS Strategic Survey, India, 1982-83.
21. The mystique of the F-16 casts a spell on both sides of the border. Peter Galbraith has reported: "Imaginative drawings of the aircraft or the words 'F-16' appear on buses, trishaws, and trucks throughout the province [Punjab in Pakistan]. The nationalistic pride inspired by the aircraft is presumably a plus for the military regime". "United States Security Interests in South Asia," a Staff Report prepared by Peter W. Galbraith for the Committee on Foreign Relations, United States Senate, U.S. Government Printing Office, Washington, D.C., 1984, p. 7.
22. See note 108 in Chapter Seven.
23. Cronin and Mitchell, op. cit., p. 31.
24. Interviews, New Delhi, October 1983.
25. IISS, 1982-83, op. cit.
26. *The Times of India*, June 27, 1983.
27. *India Today*, October 15, 1982.
28. Quoted in Khera, op. cit., p. 54.
29. According to the IISS Strategic Survey, 1982-83, in conjunction with successes in the space technology programme and the sophisticated nature of India's military-industrial base, India is "clearly now one of the most advanced in the Third World". DMS Market Intelligence report for 1981 observed, "India is one of the few developing countries to achieve remarkable successes in arms manufacture." DMS, Greenwich, CT.
30. Frank, op. cit., p. 37; interviews, New Delhi, March and October 1983; and K. Subrahmanyam's communication to me of February 10, 1984. According to *The Times of India* of December 8, 1983, Maruts were still flying with the subsonic Orpheus engine of British design at the end of 1983.
31. An agreement with the U.A.R. was signed on September 28, 1964 for suitable power plant for HF-24. Thomas, *Defense of India*, op. cit., p. 110.
32. An agreement was concluded in July 1962 for the licensed manufacture of the Mach 1.4 engine. Kavic, op. cit., p. 134.
33. According to Subrahmanyam, India's decision to launch the country on a design for a supersonic aircraft in the 1950s and early 1960s "was perhaps overly ambitious." IDSA Journal, January-March 1981. Kavic has highlighted the fact that India was one of only four or five countries to proceed with the development of a supersonic fighter aircraft. He also pointed out the irony of a country dependent on U.S. grain and massive foreign economic assistance being committed to two supersonic plane projects. Op. cit., pp. 136-37.
34. The Scientific Advisor to the Defence Ministry, V.S. Arunachalam, lamented in January 1984 that R & D should be pegged at the 2 per cent level. *The Times of India*, January 6, 1984.

References

35. Subrahmanyam, IDSA Journal, January-March 1981.
36. Reuters dispatch in *The Overseas Times*, May 13, 1983.
37. *Ibid.*
38. Ruth Leger Sivard, "World Military and Social Expenditures, 1983," *World Priorities*, Washington, D.C., p. 38.
39. Khera, op. cit., p. 54.
40. IISS, 1983-84.
41. Reuters dispatch in *The Overseas Times*, June 17, 1983.
42. Cronin and Mitchell, op. cit., p. 5.
43. Documents of the Twelfth Congress of the Communist Party of India, 22 to 28 March 1982, New Delhi: Communist Party Publication, 1982, p. 210.
44. *Ibid.*, p. 44.
45. FBIS-SU, February 26, 1981.
46. *People's Democracy*, March 22, 1981. The Marxists were not invited to the CPSU Twenty-sixth Congress.
47. *Ibid.*, February 15, 1981.
48. Documents of the Twelfth Congress, op. cit., p. 88.
49. *Ibid.*, p. 106.
50. *The Statesman Weekly*, September 28, 1982.
51. This was hardly a surprise for the Indian negotiators. During Brezhnev's 1980 visit to New Delhi, at a meeting of the two delegations, he persistently enquired about the stranger who was talking. The "stranger" was no other than the Soviet ambassador to India. Interviews, New Delhi, March and October 1983.
52. Mary Wisniewski, "Indira on the High Wire," *The Far Eastern Economic Review*, October 1, 1982. Girilal Jain quotes a Soviet diplomat to suggest that the Gandhi-Brezhnev meeting was in effect two seats of monologues. "Limits to Indo-U.S. Ties," *The Times of India*, July 6, 1983.
53. United News of India dispatch from Tallin, *The Times of India* September 25, 1982.
54. *Ibid.*
55. Quoted in Sen Gupta, "Ivan, Indira and India," *India Today*, January 31, 1983.
56. *Ibid.*
57. *The Times of India*, January 2, 1983.
58. "PRC-USA: Some Results and Problems of Rapprochement," *Far Eastern Affairs*, Moscow, No. 1, 1982.
59. Quoted in Thomas Perry Thornton, "The USSR and Asia in 1982: The End of the Brezhnev Era," *Asian Survey*, January 1983.
60. *Ibid.*
61. Quoted in Sen Gupta, "Straws in the Wind," *India Today*, December 15, 1982.
62. Gujral, op. cit.
63. *The Times of India*, February 3, 1983.
64. *Ibid.*, October 24, 1982.
65. Nayan Chanda, *The Far Eastern Economic Review*, July 2, 1982.
66. *The Times of India*, December 14, 1982.
67. *Ibid.*
68. A *Times of India* commentator suggested, "This incident seems to indicate that the Chinese long-term policy towards India is either uncertain or they prefer to have scant respect for the Indian susceptibilities." December 10, 1982.

69. Jane's *All The World's Aircraft* 1983-84 distinguishes between MIG-31, known as Foxhound by NATO, and MIG-29, known as Fulcrum, probably for a dual role as an air superiority fighter and a ground attack aircraft. Quoted in Drew Middleton, *The New York Times*, December 16, 1983.
70. Interviews, New Delhi, October 1983.
71. *Ibid.*
72. *Ibid.*
73. *Ibid.*
74. Defence Minister Venkataraman told Parliament on April 12, 1983 that a good deal of defence equipment was still being imported in view of the ever-widening technology gap between the advanced and developing countries. *The Times of India*, April 13, 1983.
75. In an interview with me in New Delhi on October 21, 1981, Subrahmanyam made the point that with the country having to rely on the Soviets for the main battle tank and the main fighter aircraft, diversification was of peripheral importance. "We should pick and choose," he added. He questioned the wisdom of the Mirage-2000 and West German submarine deals. He said that even the MIG-21s India was building required about 30 per cent Soviet parts because it was uneconomic to produce some equipment in very small quantities. Besides, the Vijayanta tanks produced in India still required 3 to 5 per cent British parts for the same reason. Subrahmanyam conceded that the Indo-Soviet military relationship limited India's options but it was not one of subservience. In his view, the way to reduce dependence on the Soviets was to begin a major effort in defence technology now so that in ten to fifteen years India could produce its own equipment in most fields. He believed that India's relations with the Soviet Union would remain stable as long as the Soviets were kept in their place and were not employed as advisors in the Indian Defence Ministry and were not asked to prepare Indian plans. These assumptions were based on the premise that India and the Soviet Union would not share a common border.

    Others were not equally sanguine and were all for going to the West to try to balance the Indo-Soviet relationship. "If the U.S. won't play ball with us," a former senior foreign service officer told me in New Delhi on October 10, 1983, "we have to go to West Europe." France, though rated by many as mercenary, was particularly favoured because of the level of its military technology and its sympathetic views on problems of the Third World and India's importance in the scheme of things.
76. Mrs. Gandhi's reply to the Defence Debate in Parliament on April 9, 1981. Text issued by the Press Information Bureau, Government of India, New Delhi.
77. Kavic, op. cit., p. 136.
78. Delays over the development of an Indian MBT have drawn persistent criticism in Parliament and outside it. The main writer on military affairs for *The Times of India*, Inder Malhotra, bemoaned the long delay in developing the MBT in "Defence Debate Pradox," April 7, 1983. The MBT project was sanctioned in 1974, and eight years later, Rs.160 million had been spent on it. Work on the engine was undertaken in 1976. It was initially hoped to have the first Indian MBT by the end of the 1980s. *The Times of India*, October 22, 1982.
79. *The Times of India* of December 8, 1983 commented on a somewhat pessimistic note that "GTX may not fly at all."

References   299

80. *The Times of India*, November 12, 1982.
81. *Ibid.*, July 13, 1983.
82. Sen Gupta, "The View from Moscow," *India Today*, August 15, 1982.
83. Quoted in Stephen Sestanovich, "Do the Soviets Feel Pinched by Third World Adventures?" *The Washington Post*, May 20, 1984.
84. *The Times of India*, October 19, 1982.
85. Sen Gupta, *Syndrome*, op. cit., p. 170.
86. Inder Malhotra, "Beyond the Delhi Summit," *The Times of India*, November 4, 1982. The Pakistanis, however, continued to follow a discriminatory policy towards India in trade. The private sector was barred from trading with India. India's exports to Pakistan fell from a peak of Rs.471 million in 1977 to Rs.219 million in 1980-81. Imports from Pakistan rose from Rs.347 million to Rs.962 million during the period. *The Times of India*, November 25, 1982.
87. *The Times of India*, December 24, 1982.
88. *Ibid.*, December 14, 1982.
89. According to Carl Bernstein, the limits imposed by Zia were about two planeloads of arms a week. "Arms for Afghanistan," *The New Republic*, Washington, D.C. July 18, 1981.
90. In the understatement of the year, *Komsomolskaya Pravda* of June 3, 1982 declared: "It is too soon to say that absolutely all the population of Afghanistan have resolutely gone over to defending democractic power."
91. Address and answers to questions at a luncheon in his honour by the Foreign Policy Association in New York on December 9, 1982. I was present. According to Pakistani diplomats, Andropov had told Zia that if Pakistan stopped interfering in Afghanistan's affairs, the Soviet Union would put forward a timetable for a phased, complete withdrawal of Soviet troops. *The Far Eastern Economic Review*, December 10, 1982.
92. *Ibid.*
93. Quoted in Thomas Perry Thornton, "The USSR and Asia in 1983," *Asian Survey*, January 1984.
94. *The Times*, London, April 14, 1983.
95. Thornton, *Asian Survey*, January 1984, op. cit.
96. *Ibid.* Foreign Minister Wu Xueqian told an interviewer on March 2, 1983, "So far, I have not seen any signs of a possible Soviet troop withdrawal." He was pointedly referring to Soviet troops along the Sino-Mongolian border, which, he said, were deployed after the Khrushchev era. *The Far Eastern Economic Review*, March 31, 1983.
97. Quoted in "Charting a New Course," *India Today*, March 31, 1983.
98. Nihal Singh, "What Really Happened at NAM," *The Illustrated Weekly of India*, May 8, 1983.
99. Prince Sihanouk was rather more undiplomatic. He told a press conference in Beijing: "If you accept Castro to be the dictator, if you accept Indira Gandhi to be a dictator, if you accept Vietnam to be a dictator, then you let others become slaves to the person people call 'the No. 1 man in India'—Indira Gandhi." Associated Press dispatch in *The Times of India*, February 6, 1983.
100. Quoted in *The Far Eastern Economic Review*, March 17, 1983.
101. Quoted in "India Takes Charge," *India Today*, March 31, 1983. On the eve of the nonaligned summit, the Soviets were also indulging in their own propaganda

warfare. The pro-Soviet section of the Indian press, with *Patriot* in the lead, launched an anti-U.S. campaign based on a forged document in which the American representative in the U.N., Jeane J. Kirkpatrick, spelled out the blueprint for U.S. operations to balkanize India and foster divisions in the Third World. The Indian government's reaction was cautious, but Tass picked up the *Patriot* report, which was played back in India. William Claiborne, *The Washington Post*, February 17, 1983.

102. *Ibid.*, March 15, 1983.
103. *Ibid.*
104. The official U.S. reaction was that the final declaration of the summit was "in many respects an imbalanced and political document." *The Times of India*, March 16, 1983.
105. *The Times of India*, December 30, 1983. Commenting on the summit, *Izvestia* of March 13, 1983 said: "No doubt the most significant feature of the Delhi summit was that its participants have resolutely come out against the nuclear threat and the wasteful and dangerous arms race, for real measures in the field of disarmament."
106. Janardhan Thakur, "Mr. Clean's Soviet Baptism," *The Overseas Times*, New Jersey, July 29, 1983.
107. Nihal Singh, "Indira Gandhi's Troublesome Ties with Soviet Union," *The Christian Science Monitor*, November 29, 1983. Unabashed. Sharma later told an interviewer, "As far as I am concerned, Mrs. Gandhi is the only leader who can keep the country safe . . . Mrs. Gandhi is the best bourgeois . . . They [the Soviets] too think that Mrs. Gandhi should be supported. They have a soft corner for her because she has proved to be an exceptional leader of Indians and is doing all she can to prevent a large-scale nuclear war that threatens the world." Sankaran Thakur, " 'Mrs. Gandhi is the Best Bourgeois' says CPI Leader Yogendra Sharma." *The Overseas Times*, October 28, 1983.
108. Jayashekhar, *The Economic Times*, Calcutta, January 12, 1984.
109. Swaminathan S. Aiyar, "Indo-Soviet Trade-I", *The Indian Express*, October 3, 1983. The Chinese alleged, in *Peking Review*, No.30, 1969, that "predatory" Soviet aid to and "unequal" trade with India were turning the latter into a "raw material processing plant for Soviet revisionism."
110. In 1983, the U.S. regained the position of being India's largest trading partner, with India achieving a favourable balance of nearly $400 million, largely through the export of Bombay High oil. The total trade turnover was of $8 billion in 1983. India exported heavy crude because it did not have the facility to refine it, Indian refineries being geared to light crude. *The Overseas Times*, February 3, 1984 and *The Christian Science Monitor*, May 16, 1984. Crude production in India had risen from 10.5 million tons in 1980-81 to an estimated 26 million tons in 1983-84. *Economic and Political Weekly*, March 10, 1984. According to B. Chekhonin, "economic cooperation is becoming an increasingly important factor for both countries [India and the Soviet Union]." Some 4,500 Indian specialists have received or undergone training in Soviet educational establishments and enterprises and hundreds of Indian students have graduated from Soviet institutions. *International Affairs*, May 1982.
111. Jayashekhar, "India's Trade with the Soviet Bloc: Growing Dependency and Commodity Inconvertibility," *Problems of Nonalignment*, New Delhi, June-

August 1983. According to the Director General, Commercial Intelligence and Statistics, Calcutta, India's surplus balance with the rupee trade area (the Soviet Union and East Europe) in 1981-82 was Rs. 3,485.3 million. Going by Soviet figures, India's surplus in early 1983 was 1,145 million roubles. The scope of Indo-Soviet trade and economic relations can be gauged from a 1982 diary compiled by the Soviets. In 1982, sixteen ministers and senior Soviet officials visited India. They included Arkhipov, Skatchkov and ministers or deputy ministers of non-ferrous metallurgy, construction of heavy industry enterprises, land reclamation and aircraft and oil, power, coal and agriculture industries. Protocols signed in 1982 covered the following fields, among others: non-ferrous metallurgy, science and technology, book publishing and printing, implementation of the long-term agreement signed in March 1979, oil technology, scientific and technical cooperation in agriculture, power, coal and a trade protocol for 1983. "Diary of Soviet-Indian Friendship 1982," *Soviet Review*, January 20, 1983. Over fifty industrial plants have been set up with Soviet collaboration and thirty more projects are being implemented with Soviet help. "Trade: The Soviet Connection," *India Today*, October 15, 1982. Aid from the Soviet bloc is tied to projects and is offered only in goods and services. It is generally in the form of medium-term credits of ten to fifteen years after completion of deliveries. Repayment is made through the export of goods by India. Sumitra Chisti, "Nonaligned India's Economic Relations with the Socialist Bloc," *The Nonaligned World*, January-March 1983. There is a great difference between the trade plan and the actual plan, the former being notional. The Soviet Union's imports of manufactured goods are far below the projected figures. The Russians are hard negotiators. Agreements to double trade periodically fit into the Russian bureaucratic exercises and make them feel good. They are seldom implemented to the letter. Interviews, New Delhi, October 1983. Soviet-aided projects provide 35 per cent of Indian steel, nearly 80 per cent of metallurgical and other heavy equipment, 50 per cent of oil extraction, 30 per cent of oil refining, over 11 per cent of total electricity generated and a sizable portion of the coal output and production of medicines and instruments. Arkhipov's statement in Moscow before his May 1983 visit to India. *Soviet Review*, May 19, 1983.

112. *Ibid*. According to K.K. Sharma, the Soviet deficit in 1982 stood at $668 million. "Mutual Re-evaluation for India and USSR," *The Financial Times*, London, May 11, 1983. *The Far Eastern Economic Review* of June 2, 1983 quotes independent sources to place India's accumulated surplus at about $2 billion. In 1982, India exported $1.9 billion worth of goods to the Soviet Union and bought from it $1.2 billion of goods. *The Overseas Times*, May 13, 1983.

113. Chisti, *Nonaligned World*, op. cit. Commerce Minister V.P. Singh told Parliament in May 1983 that arms purchases from the Soviet bloc were paid for over twenty to thirty years through Indian export of "special goods" that did not appear in annual official statistics. The Soviets supply capital goods to India under special rouble credits distinct from the barter-trade agreement. Hence the surplus cannot be used for paying outstanding credits, but only for importing goods. *The Far Eastern Economic Review*, June 2, 1983. One suggestion made by the well-known Indian analyst on Soviet economy, Jayashekhar, was that the Soviets should pay interest on unutilized trade surpluses at the rate they charge on their credits for various projects. He would also like India to have two

categories of trade, one maintained in hard currency. Quoted in above. According to one estimate, the current rate of arms payment by India is roughly Rs. 3 billion a year, which would imply Soviet credits worth Rs. 40 billion on this account. Aiyar, *The Indian Express*, October 4, 1983. *Economic and Political Weekly* has suggested that "India's persistent trade surplus with the Soviet Union has definitely given a fillip to arms purchases from that country." July 9, 1983.

114. Another factor inhibiting Soviet exports to India has been the poor capacity utilization and crippling cost overruns in public sector projects. In 30 selected industries, representing 51 per cent weight in the index of industrial production, capacity utilization declined from 74.5 per cent in 1972 to 69.8 per cent in 1982; in capital goods the decline was from 80.6 per cent to 66.7 per cent. During the same period overall capacity in these 30 industries was increased by 47 per cent. The steel industry in 1983 had a surfeit of problems: low capacity utilization, high inventories in plants and imports to meet particular demands. The omnibus Steel Authority of India (SAIL) was losing Rs. 10 million a day, according to an official statement in Parliament. In 1982, cost overruns in the power sector ranged from 80 per cent to 600 per cent; time overruns from 18 months to 96 months. *The Times of India*, December 16 and 27, 1983.

115. Jayshekhar, *Problems of Nonalignment*, op. cit.

116. *Indo-European Affairs*, New Delhi, November 1982.

117. Indian experts admit that there was some evidence of switch trade in India's exports to the Soviet bloc in the late Sixties. But they maintained in 1983 that the magnitude of depression in prices was not very high and probably affected a few traditional products like cashew kernels, mica and oil cakes. Chisti, *Nonaligned World*, op. cit.

118. *Indo-European Affairs*, op. cit. India's exports of precious stones were valued at Rs. 8.2 billion in 1982-83, but their import requirements were as high as Rs. 6.7 billion yielding net export earnings of only about 20 per cent. *Economic and Political Weekly*, March 10, 1984.

119. *The Overseas Times*, May 20, 1983. According to a new British study, the Soviet Union's net aid/GNP ratio stood at 0.19 per cent in 1980 and suggested that its net aid disbursements were $2.8 billion in 1982, of which $2.4 billion were from the Soviet Union. By 1981 the non-Communist developing countries classified as Group 2 were making larger repayments of outstanding Comecon aid loans than they received as disbursements from Comecon. The net aid was thus negative in 1981 and 1982. "Soviet, East European and Western Development Aid 1976-82," Foreign Policy Document No. 85. Figures in a U.S. State Department study show that during 1954-81 the Soviet Union's economic aid to India was $3,080 million and from East Europe $455 million. For Pakistan, the figures were: $920 million from the Soviet Union and $150 million from East Europe. In 1981, 1,625 Soviet economic technicians were in India (for one month or longer, rounded to the nearest five) and 1,130 Indian technicians were being trained in the Soviet Union and East Europe. U.S. Department of State, February 1983, op. cit.

120. Interviews, New Delhi, October 1983. The Soviet terms of economic assistance have become increasingly onerous, compared to Western aid. In the mid-1970s, it was estimated that Soviet credits were repayable for 10 to 12 years with a 2.5 to 3 per cent rate of interest. On the other hand, Western loans were, on an average, repayable over 29.9 years at 2.8 per cent interest a year, with a grace period of 7.4

years. *The Economic Times*, May 9, 1976.
121. An Indian government view of the trade problem was given by the senior Commerce Ministry official, Abid Hussain, in New Delhi in January 1983 to writers on financial affairs. He said: "The idea that the Soviet Union is absolutely backward is certainly not correct. Maybe the socialist countries are not advanced so much [as some of the Western nations], but they have areas of excellence from which we can make our purchases." Further, he suggested, "If we can get crude oil and fertilizers from the Soviet bloc, then the rouble is as good as the dollar." "Trade Policy with Soviet Bloc Stays," *The Times of India*, January 11, 1983.
122. *The Statesman Weekly*, December 17, 1983 and *The Indian Express*, October 3, 1983.
123. The Soviets had told their Indian counterparts that they had to stop buying cashew because they had to buy almonds from Afghanistan to support that country. Nobody in New Delhi took this argument at face value. Nihal Singh, *Monitor*, op. cit. It can only be speculated upon whether Khrushchev's weakness for cashewnuts was responsible for the large quantities the Russians bought in earlier years. According to M.O. Mathai, the powerful and controversial assistant of Nehru, "Khrushchev had a weakness for cashewnuts. Mangoes and cashewnuts were sent to him in Moscow every year by the Prime Minister as was done to some other foreign dignitaries." *My Days With Nehru*, New Delhi: Vikas, 1979, p. 191.

Chapter Ten

1. According to U.S. Department of Commerce. *The Times of India*, February 5, 1983.
2. Commenting on the annual reports of the External Affairs and Home Ministries for 1982-83, an Indian columnist, A.S. Abraham, wrote, "The Government may have done a splendid job abroad, but it has done a shabby one at home." "Reports on Home and Abroad," *The Times of India*, April 15, 1983.
3. Nihal Singh, "Roots of Assam Violence Run Deep in India's History," *The Christian Science Monitor*, February 24, 1983. Also, Robert L. Hardgrave, Jr., "India in 1983: New Challenges. Lost Opportunities," *Asian Survey*, February 1984.
4. Nihal Singh, "A Lesson from Sri Lanka," *Newsweek International*, October 10, 1983. Also Hardgrave, *Ibid.*
5. Staff Report, op. cit.
6. Nihal Singh, "'Imperial' Prime Minister May Face New Test in India," *The Asian Wall Street Journal*, January 27-28, 1984.
7. *The Times of India*, August, 27, 1983.
8. *Ibid.*, August 28, 1983.
9. Inder Malhotra, "Gen. Zia, MRD and India," *The Times of India*, November 17, 1983.
10. G.K. Reddy, *The Hindu*, November 11, 1983.
11. *The Times of India*, November 16, 1983.
12. *Ibid.*, March 26, 1983.
13. John Elliott, *The Financial Times*, February 25, 1983.

14. *The Times of India*, April 29, 1983.
15. I.B. Redko and N.B. Shastokolsky, *Indian Ocean: Zone of Tension and Peace*, quoted in *ibid.*, July 17, 1983.
16. Interview with *Asahi Shimbun*, quoted in *ibid.*, July 17, 1983.
17. Sen Gupta, "Thinking Anew," *India Today*, June 30, 1983.
18. V.G. Kulkarni, *The Far Eastern Economic Review*, March 31, 1983.
19. Clyde Haberman, "Dalai Lama Unsure About Tibet Visit," *The New York Times*, May 14, 1984. According to John F. Avedon, in the latest round of arrests in the fall of 1983, 3,000 dissidents were interned and 35 publicly executed. "China's Tibet Problem," *The New York Times*, June 23, 1984.
20. *The Times of India*, June 11, 1983.
21. *Ibid.*, July 11, 1983.
22. *Ibid.*, April 27, 1983.
23. *Ibid.*, May 22, 1983.
24. *Ibid.*, June 27, 1983.
25. "Disturbing Questions," *Ibid.*, September 24, 1982.
26. *Ibid.*, May 17, 1983.
27. Inder Malhotra, "Delhi-Beijing Dialogue," *ibid.*, November 3, 1983.
28. Subhash Chakravarti, "PM-Deng Aide Talks Significant," *ibid.*, January 21, 1984.
29. *Ibid.*, February 21, 1984.
30. Defence Minister Venkataraman had told reporters on April 29 that India was "naturally worried" about the U.S.-Chinese nuclear agreement. The Government, he said, would have to take necessary measures to safeguard India's interests. *The Statesman Weekly*, May 5, 1984.
31. Dan Oberdorfer, "Arms Issue Snags Pact With China," *The Washington Post*, June 15, 1984 and Richard Halloran, "U.S.-China Nuclear Pact Hits Snags," *The New York Times*, June 16, 1984.
32. Interview with *Nawa-i-Waqt*, Lahore, quoted in Inder Malhotra, "More About Pakistan's Bomb," *The Times of India*, April 5, 1984.
33. Galbraith, Staff Report, op. cit., p. 30.
34. "Pak Position Unacceptable," *The Statesman Weekly*, March 31, 1984.
35. In an interview published by *The Far Eastern Economic Review* on July 2, 1982, Foreign Minister Narasimha Rao said, "Pakistan, like any other sovereign country, has the right to acquire arms for her legitimate self-defence. However, when Pakistan goes in for a massive acquisition of highly sophisticated armaments, it becomes a matter of legitimate concern for India."
36. The chain reaction of an accelerated U.S. arms assistance programme for Pakistan was hardly a surprise to Washington. According to Richard P. Cronin, "Given its demonstrated proclivity for clear military superiority against Pakistan, few if any analysts doubt that India will seek to counter any significant accretion of Pakistani air power. This could well result in an increase in Indian arms purchases from the Soviet Union." "The U.S. and Pakistan," op. cit.
37. Richard Halloran, "$1 billion Sale of Artillery Appears Likely" and Bernard Weinraub, "India Said To Be On Verge Of $1 billion Arms Deal with U.S." *The New York Times*, July 30, 1982 and May 20, 1983 respectively. India, for instance, found U.S. conditions for the sale of TOW anti-tank missiles unacceptable, particularly Washington's insistence on its right to suspend sales

during periods of tension in South Asia and its refusal to transfer technology for manufacture. India needed TOW badly and subsequently went in for Milan anti-tank missiles, which were twice as expensive as TOW. Interviews, New Delhi, October 1983. Reuters quoted a Defence Ministry official, Brigadier Ramamohan Rao, as saying in May 1983: "We have shown interest in U.S. equipment but we have to ensure 1) that it is suitable for India, 2) that we get guaranteed supplies of spares and 3) that we can secure a transfer of technology, with the possibility of manufacture here. Right now, I don't think they [Americans] are able to adjust to this kind of market. They are reluctant to agree to a transfer of technology." *The Overseas Times*, May 27, 1983. But American interest in forging an arms relationship with India was clear from a statement of John Hughes, U.S. State Department spokesman: "We want to help India meet its legitimate security requirements and believe military sales would make a positive contribution to U.S.-Indian relations." Quoted in "Time for Reagan to Play India Card," *The Statesman*, May 1, 1983.

38. Foreign Minister Narasimha Rao voiced this opinion in a conversation with me in New Delhi on October 24, 1983. I was told by State Department officials that India would be unlikely to get F-16s even if it asked for the plane because the deal with Pakistan flowed from a special military relationship. One non-government American expert said, on the other hand, "Indians complain about not getting what they want from us, but why don't they test us? Probably they won't get F-16s if they asked, but they haven't. It would have been a good Indian decision to acquire F-20 [on offer], but I knew from the beginning that the Russians would not tolerate it. F-20 is a relatively dated airframe with a simple but good engine, and India could have developed a market for it abroad. Actually, it would have been a good deal for India in order to get more from the Russians, but people in South Block [home of India's External Affairs Ministry] don't see it that way." Interviews, Washington, D.C., 1983.

39. According to Schneider, the fear of "leakage" arose out of the size of the Soviet military mission in New Delhi. Schneider also announced that the U.S. was going to sell "several hundred" 155 mm. artillery pieces to India worth $900 million. *The Washington Post* report cited in *The Times of India*, April 7, 1983. The Indian press had reported in December 1981 of a crash of a MIG-25 flown by a Soviet pilot. The pilot bailed out at an Indian Air Force base in Uttar Pradesh, was met by Soviet advisors on the ground and promptly sent back to Moscow without giving evidence to an inquiry commission announced later. *India Today*, February 15, 1982. The official Indian position is reflected by the following assertion of Subrahmanyam: "We have pursued a policy of not permitting any other country which may supply equipment to us to send training teams or large contingents of maintenance and technical personnel to this country. Our effort has always been to get a few of our best people trained in the supplier country and thereafter to set up our own training facilities." "Indian Defence Problems," *The Times of India*, March 29, 1983. According to a U.S. State Department publication, there were 150 Soviet military technicians in India in 1981. These personnel were in India for one month or longer, the figures rounded to the nearest five. "Soviet and East European Aid to the Third World, 1981," U.S. Department of State, February 1983.

40. An Indian foreign policy analyst put it to me in New Delhi in October 1983 thus:

"The American manufacturers will give kickbacks. But who knows whether the deal will not make the front page of *The New York Times* three months later?"

41. According to Senator Orrin Hatch, "I have information that the Soviet Union has warned the government of India not to go ahead with the proposed visit of the U.S. naval ship to Bombay port and Moscow has also warned Delhi against the purchases of American arms in general." *The Times of India*, July 3, 1983. Actually, a U.S. naval vessel did visit an Indian port. Defence Minister R. Venkataraman confirmed in Parliament that USS Whipple of the U.S. Seventh Fleet visited Cochin port on February 17-18, 1984. *The Times of India*, March 24, 1984.
42. Shultz told a press conference in New Delhi on July 1 that his talks had made "headway" in clearing misunderstandings about the sale of arms to India by the U.S. *Ibid.*, July 3, 1983.
43. Selig S. Harrison, "A Breakthrough in Afghanistan," *Foreign Policy*, Summer 1983.
44. Malhotra, "Afghan Issue Four Years On," *The Times of India*, February 16, 1984.
45. Harrison, op. cit.
46. *Ibid.*
47. Interviews, Washington, D.C., Summer 1983.
48. Harrison, op. cit. He further suggested that Yakub's strategy was to probe "definitive signs of Soviet intentions before opening up a potentially explosive dialogue with Washington" since Pakistan did not want to lose U.S. military aid. He also quotes Zia telling *U.S. News and World Report*, "We agree in principle...that the Soviet Union could even have a very pro-Soviet Afghanistan."
49. Interviews, New Delhi, October 1983. Also, Malhotra, "Afghanistan Issue Four Years On," op. cit.
50. Harrison, "Soviet Policy in South Asia," Testimony before the Subcommittee on Asian and Pacific Affairs, Committee on Foreign Affairs, U.S. House of Representatives, July 28, 1983.
51. *Ibid.*
52. "Pakistan Reports Cross-Border Raid," *The Washington Post*, January 29, 1984.
53. Thornton, *Asian Survey*, January 1984, op. cit. The U.S. Administration's decision to seek Congressional approval to station military personnel in Pakistan "on a regular assignment" to "enable Pakistan to make effective use of U.S. arms" caused anxiety in New Delhi. *The Times of India*, March 2, 1984.
54. Drew Middleton, "Afghan Drive: A Costly Gain for Russians," *The New York Times*, May 27, 1984. Middleton quotes a British estimate to suggest that Russians lost 500 men in the Panjsher operation, with an additional 2,000 men killed throughout the country since mid-April. Earlier, the Soviets were believed to have lost only 5,000 men since 1979.
55. William Claiborne, "Soviets Increase Aid to Pakistan; New Tactic Seen," *The Washington Post*, January 27, 1984. Claiborne also quotes a Pakistani official as saying that it was in both countries' interest to expand bilateral relations "to keep the fallout from the contention over Afghanistan to a minimum."
56. "Towards Formal Neutrality," *The Times of India*. March 10, 1984. Reprinted from *The Muslim*, Islamabad. In December 1983, former Foreign Minister Agha

Shahi warned his countrymen that their acquiescence in attempts to link the Afghanistan issue with the wider U.S.-Soviet cold war and hostility would imperil Pakistan because Russians might even station nuclear missiles in Afghanistan and Americans might insist on taking countermeasures. He suggested that it would be wiser to adhere strictly to the nonaligned movement, rather than make Pakistan part of "any strategic consensus directed against the Soviet Union." *The Times of India*, February 23, 1984.

57. Galbraith, Staff Report, op. cit., pp. 11-12. Benazir's mother had been released earlier and allowed to proceed abroad for medical treatment; Mrs. Gandhi had publicly appealed for her release.
58. Quoted in Malhotra, "India-Pakistan Dialogue," *The Times of India*, March 8, 1984.
59. Mary Ann Weaver, "Failed Coup Against Leader May Have Involved India," *The Christian Science Monitor*, March 19, 1984.
60. Quoted in *The Times of India*, March 8, 1984.
61. "Indo-Soviet Peace Bid Urged," Press Trust of India dispatch in *ibid*., February 15, 1984. Chernenko also assured Mrs. Gandhi that there would be no change in the Soviet Union's policies towards India. Sen Gupta, "For Better or Worse," *India Today*, March 31, 1984.
62. Malhotra, "Moscow, Islamabad and Kabul," *ibid*., February 23, 1984.
63. Quoted in Thornton, *Asian Survey*, January 1984, op. cit.
64. Interviews, New Delhi, October 1983. At the same time, the Soviets were not chary of attacking organizations they considered reactionary. In September 1983, the Soviet weekly, *Novoye Vremya*, launched a full-scale attack on the Rashtriya Swayamsevak Sangh (RSS), the paramilitary associate of the Bharatiya Janata Party. Under the heading, Blackshirts from the Ganges, the weekly attacked the RSS, calling it a spokesman of the "interests of the upper stratum of Hindu bourgeois, whose social basis is made up of small and middle bracket tradesmen, reactionary-minded intellectuals, ruined bourgeois and Hindu lumpens, pressed down by the capitalist machine." According to the weekly, the reactionaries exploited, not without success, the inability of left forces and the ruling Congress (I) to agree on joint action to avert the danger from the rightists. Quoted in *The Times of India*, September 21, 1983.
65. "Indo-Soviet Concern Over Pak Arming," *The Times of India*, March 6, 1984. Ustinov declared at the March banquet held in his honour: "We also worry about the United States' militarization of the states of South Asia, including those next to peaceful India." *Economic and Political Weekly*, March 17, 1984.
66. *Ibid*.
67. Sen Gupta, *India Today*, March 31, 1984. In fact, the account reads like a Soviet handout.
68. Hendrick Smith, "This Time Around, Peking Holds Some Cards of its Own," *The New York Times*, April 29, 1984.
69. *Ibid*. Christopher S. Wren reported from Beijing that August First Radio, believed to be in the Soviet Union, was providing a running commentary on the Reagan visit to China. It said the Reagan visit was like "the weasel going to pay his respects to the hen" (synonymous with treachery). The next day the radio warned that "a smiling tiger [Reagan] is the most treacherous.'" "Peking Finds the Airwaves Filled With Unkind Remarks," *The New York Times*, May 7, 1984.

70. *The Times of India*, December 30, 1983.
71. *The Times of India* commented, "It looks as if we are back in the late Sixties when a number of self-proclaimed radicals and Marxists strode the corridors of power in New Delhi." "Shades of Castro," December 31, 1983. The Marxists seemed somewhat relieved that the attack on them during the Congress plenary session "exploded the myth of its [CPI (M)'s] having come to an understanding with the Congress." The West Bengal chief minister, Jyoti Basu, told an interviewer, "We are not and never have been one with the Congress, despite what some people might say about CPM [CPI (M)] hobnobbing with that party." *The Times of India*, December 31, 1983. Even some members of the CPI (M) believed that Basu had come to develop a cozy relationship with Mrs. Gandhi. They were disillusioned enough about the lack of revolutionary fervour of the CPI(M) government in West Bengal, particularly after it returned to power in the state. Interviews, Calcutta, October 1983.
72. Sen Gupta, "Davids and Goliath," *India Today*, February 29, 1984.
73. *Ibid.*
74. At the end of July 1983, the retiring army chief, General K.V. Krishna Rao, had given a diplomatic but clear warning on Punjab. He said he hoped a political solution to the Punjab problem would soon be found. *The Times of India*, August 1, 1983.
75. A detailed account of the army action can be found in "Operation Bluestar," *India Today*, June 30, 1984.
76. *The Times of India*, June 5, 1981.
77. *India Today*, June 30, 1984.
78. It was the same Chauhan who had declared in London in December 1971 after a visit he had paid to Pakistan just before the start of the Indo-Pakistani war that President Yahya Khan would permit Sikhs to open a broadcasting station at Nankana Sahib and an airline in Lahore and Rawalpindi if the Sikhs would create a "Sikhistan" (separate state for Sikhs). Nihal Singh, "New Western Approach to Indian Army Action," *The Statesman*, December 5, 1971.
79. In an interview with the British Broadcasting Corporation, Mrs. Gandhi said on June 18 that concessions offered to the Akali Dal before the temple raid were still "broadly on the table." *The New York Times*, June 20, 1984.
80. Rajiv Gandhi, shortly after his return from Moscow, had said that there was "definite interference from the USA in the Punjab situation." *The Statesman*, September 16, 1983. India had earlier protested to the U.S. over a visa granted to Jagjit Singh Chauhan, the separatist Khalistan leader. After the temple raid, Chauhan claimed that he had established a Khalistan House in London. About 100 demonstrators marched to the U.S. Embassy in New Delhi on June 30, 1984 to protest at alleged CIA involvement with Sikh extremists. The U.S. Embassy and the State Department have strongly denied the allegation. *The New York Times*, July 1, 1984.
81. United News of India Moscow dispatch in *The Times of India*, June 11, 1984.
82. *Ibid.*
83. India's approach to the Indian Ocean was expressed in forthright terms by Foreign Minsiter Narashimha Rao in his address to the U.N. General Assembly in September 1981. He said: ".... It needs to be reiterated that great power presences in the Indian Ocean are unacceptable not only in the context of their

rivalry, but under any circumstances whatsoever. Were they to agree among themselves to stay put in this ocean, they would still be equally unwelcome. Together or separately, we want them out." *Mainstream*, October 24, 1981, op. cit.
84. *The Times of India* took exception to Bush's description, declaring, ".... While recognition of India's status as a major power is only a statement of fact, the use of the term pivotal must raise the question: pivotal to what and for whom?.... America does not regard India as a pivotal power in this part of the world." "No False Promises," May 16, 1984.
85. In December 1983, the Soviet Union was asked to cut its embassy staff in Bangladesh by 50 per cent. Thornton, *Asian Survey*, January 1984.
86. Malhotra, "Delhi-Beijing Dialogue," *The Times of India*, June 7, 1984.
87. Cited in Christopher Wren, "China, After Talks in Soviet, Says Halcyon Days Are Gone," *The New York Times*, July 10, 1984.
88. Bernard Gwertzman, "China-U.S. Ties Make Southeast Asia Squirm," *The New York Times*, July 15, 1984. Gwertzman suggested that the public reactions of ASEAN governments, Malaysia and Indonesia in particular, were somewhat different from what they told Shultz privately. But the American dilemma remains to be resolved.
89. The other members of the space club are: the U.S., the Soviet Union, France, China and Japan.
90. Nihal Singh, "The Sky is the Limit," *Newsweek International*, April 23, 1984.
91. *The Times of India*, June 14, 1983.
92. Foreign Minister Narasimha Rao told me in New Delhi in October, "I have told the Russians we will continue to buy [arms] from others. We are nonaligned."
93. Mrs. Gandhi's reply to the defence debate in Parliament, April 9, 1981.

Chapter Eleven

1. Interview, New Delhi, March 1983.
2. Mrs. Gandhi, however, suggested: "With Mr. Bhutto and Pakistan our fault has always been overgenerosity." *My Truth*, op. cit., p. 190.
3. I had commented in 1978: "A distressing aspect of the Indian scene is the defeatist mood to be found among a section of South Block [the home of India's External Affairs Ministry]. If global strategies flow from the power equations between the two superpowers, countries like India can merely react to their changing postures in the different regions. In the rivalry between the two, the U.S.A. views China as a potential ally against the Soviet Union in containing the latter's 'expansionism.' Hence the U.S.A. would not hurt Chinese susceptibilities in its own relations with India. Therefore, runs the argument, India has no choice but to remain on the side of the Russians." Nihal Singh, "India's Russia Complex," *The Statesman*, February 21, 1978.
4. Mrs. Gandhi declared after the signing of the treaty in August 1971: The treaty has "gained India a powerful friend." *The Times of India*, August 20, 1971.
5. In this context, an Indian defence analyst asked the rhetorical question: "Would China talk to Vietnam about its own force levels?" Interview, New Delhi, October 1983.
6. Mrs. Gandhi's cautious comment while inaugurating the first SARC foreign

ministers' meeting in New Delhi was: "We are at the beginning of what promises to be a useful journey." *The Times of India*, August 2, 1983.

7. In an exchange in Parliament in March 1984, Mrs. Gandhi said: "We have our own system. I don't think they [the Soviets] interfere."
   Dr. Swamy (Janata): You think so?
   Mrs. Gandhi: Yes.
   Vajpayee interjected to say that the Prime Minister had, in fact, invited the Soviet President to "interfere in India's internal affairs" [a reference to Mrs. Gandhi's letter to Andropov complaining about the left's opposition to her policies]. *The Times of India*, March 2, 1984.
8. The phrase is used in Cohen and Park, *India: Emergent Power?*, op. cit., p. 68.
9. Gandhi, *My Truth*, p. 134.
10. *The Times of India*, June 30, 1983.
11. Sajjad Hyder, *The Times of India*, March 10, 1984, op. cit.
12. *The Indian Express*, May 8, 1967.
13. *Economic and Political Weekly* lamented on April 2, 1983 that, outside predictable left views, there was "total indifference towards questions of foreign policy on the part of all the other opposition parties" in the parliamentary debates on the nonaligned summit and the External Affairs Ministry.
14. According to Janardhan Thakur, of over thirty companies exporting rice, tobacco and other commodities to the Soviet Union and East Europe, many are owned by members of the Congress (I). He says that "the party [Congress (I)] bristles with functionaries at various levels who have been engaged in a highly profitable business with the Soviet Union and East European countries." *The Overseas Times*, July 29, 1983. Jyoti Basu, the CPI(M) leader, undertook a medical trip to the Soviet Union in the summer of 1983, but the West Bengal Marxist Party boss, Promode Das Gupta, was reluctant to go to Moscow for treatment of chronic asthma. *The Times of India*, August 8, 1983 and August 9, 1982. Promode died in China at the end of November 1982.
15. According to Daniel Patrick Moynihan, "We had twice, but only twice, interfered in Indian politics to the extent of providing money to a political party. Both times this was done in the face of a prospective Communist victory in a state election, once in Kerala and once in West Bengal, where Calcutta is located. Both times the money was given to the Congress party, which had asked for it. Once it was given to Mrs. Gandhi herself, who was then a party official." *A Dangerous Place*, New Delhi: Allied, 1979, p. 41. Leo Rose, quoting knowledgeable sources, says the Soviets normally donate 2 to 3 per cent of their returns from trade with India—a very large amount—to friendly Indian organizations "with little or no hindrance from the Indian government." "The Superpowers in South Asia: A Geostrategic Analysis," *Orbis*, Summer 1978. An interesting exchange took place in the Rajya Sabha on May 5, 1983. Commerce Minister V.P. Singh told the House that the Government had no proof that funds generated by Soviet transactions with private traders were being used to finance Indian political parties. An opposition Congress member had charged that in a rice deal with the Soviet Union, an under-the-table transaction of Rs.400 million rupees was made by substituting coarse rice for quality rice.

A.G. Kulkarni: Some of it went to the party of the gentleman sitting next to me [Yogendra Sharma of the CPI]. But the major share went to the party of Mr.

Vishwanath Pratap Singh [Congress (I)].
Yogendra Sharma: No, no. I deny it.
V.P. Singh: Mr. Kulkarni has passed on benefits to me. I would have to find out where they are.
The Minister said the agency involved in the deal had been fined Rs.30,000 and a fraudulent licence, submitted by it, had been passed on to the Central Bureau of Investigation. Hence, he maintained, there was no government connivance in the deal. *The Times of India*, May 6, 1983.

16. In a study, Stephen Clarkson has suggested, "This coexistence of great friendliness [with the Soviets] with an underlying distrust is one part of the double contradiction on which the dynamic of India's nonalignment is based." "The Low Impact of Soviet Writing and Aid on Indian Thinking and Policy," *Survey*, Winter 1974.

17. *The Statesman* has been the only exception. I opened The Statesman bureau in Moscow in February 1968 and closed it in April 1969. This decision was influenced by costs, which tend to be prohibitive for independent foreign correspondents, and the fact that I was required to return home for a senior appointment.

18. In the 1962 Sino-Indian border war, the Soviets initially supported China to adopt a neutral attitude to signal tacit support for India. During the 1965 Indo-Pakistani war, Moscow shocked India by the stance of studious neutrality it took between New Delhi and Islamabad. In 1971, the Soviets finally fell in with India's objectives with great reluctance and after much persuasion.

19. "Brezhnev Was a Warm Friend of India," *The Times of India*, November 12, 1982.

20. According to former Foreign Minister Vajpayee, "the theory of balance of power is at best medieval." *Janata's Foreign Policy*, op. cit., p. 10. Another former Foreign Minister, Y.B. Chavan, has suggested: ".... The doctrine of 'spheres of influence' is an anachronism and should not be allowed to influence or distort international relations." Op. cit., p. 27.

21. Foreign Minister Narasimha Rao declared in Parliament in December 1983 that India had "no global aspirations but had aspirations for the globe." *The Times of India*, December 8, 1983.

22. In an indication of continuing Soviet efforts to support its friends, the victory of H.N. Bahuguna, who won an important by-election against Mrs. Gandhi's party, was duly recorded in *Pravda*. Interviews, New Delhi, October 1983.

23. A joint communiqué at the end of the West German Foreign Minister's visit to New Delhi in March 1957 expressed Indians' sympathy with the German people's desire for unity. During Nehru's Moscow visit in 1961, the communiqué spoke of "German states." When Shastri went to Moscow in 1965, he and Kosygin referred to "two German states." Naik, op. cit., pp. 123-24.

24. Kaul has reported: "During Khrushchev's visit to Peking [Beijing] after Camp David, Mao told him, 'You can take the leadership of Europe, but leave Asia to us.' Khrushchev replied: 'No one has asked us to take over the leadership of Europe. Who in Asia has asked you to take over the leadership of Asia?' Obviously, Mao did not like this reply and is reported to have turned strongly against Khrushchev personally ever since." *Diplomacy*, op. cit., p. 46. According to a Soviet diplomat who defected to the West from the embassy in Rangoon in

1959, a gentleman's agreement in 1955-56, which recognized Southeast Asia as a "Chinese sphere" and India, Afghanistan and points west as a "Soviet sphere," had ended in 1958 by Chinese "intervention" in India. Donaldson, *Soviet Policy Towards India*, op. cit., p. 152.

25. Sen Gupta believes: "If China begins to care for Soviet friendship, India must be all the more careful to maintain and strengthen its friendship with the Soviet Union." "China's Second Long March," *India Today*, April 30, 1983.
26. The Soviet ambassador to Pakistan, asked in an interview with the Karachi weekly *Mag* whether Khrushchev's line on Kashmir held good, said the Soviet attitude to Kashmir was what the Soviet representative had said at the U.N. Security Council in February 1964. *The Times of India*, July 12, 1983.
27. Kaul, *Diplomacy*, op. cit., p. 96.
28. Gujral, op. cit.
29. This view was expressed to me by P.N. Haksar, Mrs. Gandhi's former principal aide. Interview, New Delhi, July 4, 1980.
30. Mrs. Gandhi wrote in *Foreign Affairs*: "I do not doubt that if we had followed the advice of the Western bloc, conditions in India would have deteriorated and the extremists would have been strengthened." Op. cit.
31. As Defence Minister C. Subramaniam had declared in October 1979: ".... Nuclear weapons are becoming the twentieth century symbol of white man's burden as the gunboat was in the nineteenth century." Speech to National Defence College, op. cit.

Chapter Twelve

1. A dispassionate account of the Delhi carnage was jointly published in a booklet, *Who are the Guilty?*, by People's Union for Democratic Rights and People's Union for Civil Liberties, New Delhi, Second Edition, December 1984.
2. *The Statesman* commented that "the expectation at home and abroad seems to be that conventional non-alignment is likely to undergo some shift". *The Statesman Weekly*, January 12, 1985.
3. Interviews, New Delhi, December 1984 and January 1985. Typically, Soviet press reports implied that Washington was involved in Indira Gandhi's murder. U.S. Secretary of State Schultz protested against these reports to Soviet Prime Minister Nikolai Tikhonov in New Delhi; both had journeyed to the Indian capital for Mrs. Gandhi's funeral. Tikhonov denied the charge, but the Soviet press and Tass continued publishing reports strongly suggesting that the U.S. had at least an indirect hand in the assassination. *The Statesman* commented in November: "Friendship with the Soviet Union is now accepted almost by national consensus as the cornerstone of India's foreign policy". *The Statesman Weekly*, November 10, 1984.
4. "The assertion of identity by the Hindu majority is unabashed, even abrasive. It is a heady wine and the mood in India is upbeat.... Millions of Indians clearly want to believe that Rajiv is a messiah divinely sent to lead the country to greatness. And these hopes seem to rise in inverse proportion to the nature and intensity of the problems facing the country". Nihal Singh, "Honeymoon Days in New Delhi", *Newsweek International*, January 28, 1985.

5. *The Statesman* admonished Rajiv: "... By constantly harping on the assassination and blaming it on 'foreign agents' with whom the opposition parties are said to be in league, Mr. Gandhi only fans sectarian prejudice and may even contribute to the destabilization against which he repeatedly warns". *The Statesman Weekly*, December 15, 1984.
6. The Delhi Declaration, signed by leaders of six nations on January 28, strongly urged prohibition of the development, testing, production, deployment and use of all nuclear weapons. The accent was on preventing an arms race in space and on a comprehensive test ban treaty. Apart from Rajiv, the other signatories were: Tanzania's Julius Nyerere, President Raoul Alfonsin of Argentina, President Miguel de la Madrid of Mexico, Prime Minister Olaf Palme of Sweden and Greece's Andreas Papandreou. *The Statesman Weekly*, February 2, 1985.
7. According to a charge sheet filed in a Delhi court, the Soviet Union, apart from France, Poland and East Germany, was implicated in the spy scandal, which involved junior government officials passing on secret documents to Indian businessmen who had connections with diplomats from the four countries. Three Soviet diplomats who had received intelligence reports on India's relations with neighbours left New Delhi shortly after the spy ring was busted on January 17. The Soviet diplomats were identified as Rudnev, Portonov and Krilov. *The Statesman Weekly*, April 20, 1985. An informed Indian source told me in June 1985 in Paris that the severity of Indian reaction to French complicity was due to the French Ambassador being summoned by the Foreign Office in New Delhi and asked to help with detailing the sensitive documents passed on to Bolley, the assistant military attache. The Ambassador feigned total ignorance. Rajiv himself told *Le Monde* on the recall of the French Ambassador, in an interview published on June 4, 1985: "The decision which we took was not based only on the spy affair. There have been other preceding incidents". French pique was best expressed by *Le Monde* of February 3-4, 1985. It wrote: "If the new Prime Minister of India succeeds in 'controlling' the crisis, without placing Paris in an impossible situation, it will show that he has foiled a scheme whose aim was to discredit France in particular and the West in general. A contrary outcome would indicate, on the other hand, that Indira Gandhi's successor does not want to, or cannot, impose his policy". According to the weekly *L'Express*, the "Bolley affair" was aimed at securing information on Soviet arms supplies to India and the uncovering of the operation probably amounted to the "delayed vengeance" by the Soviet KGB. *The Statesman Weekly*, February 16, 1985.
8. During talks, Rajiv raised the involvement of a Polish diplomat in the spy scandal with Jaruzelski. *The Statesman Weekly*, February 16, 1985.
9. Rajiv met Gorbachev on March 13. Indian press reports said the Soviet leader reaffirmed his country's desire to enlarge and strengthen political, economic and cultural relations. Rajiv expressed India's firm commitment to nuclear disarmament and international peace. Both leaders affirmed the policy of "mutual friendship of their countries". *The Statesman Weekly*, March 16, 1985.

An agreement was signed with the Soviet Union in February for the import of 5.5 million tons of crude and petroleum products in 1985, the crude component being 3 million tons. In 1984, India had imported about 6 million tons of crude and petroleum products from the Soviet Union. Out of India's total imports, 50 per cent of petroleum products and 25 per cent of crude come from the Soviet

Union. *The Statesman Weekly*, February 9, 1985. A protocol with the Soviet Union was signed on February 9, including new areas of cooperation in medical sciences and public health. *Ibid.*, February 16, 1985.
10. *India Today*, April 30, 1985.
11. Rajiv had made a brief and pointed reference in his national broadcast on January 5 to his government's determination to resolve India's problems with neighbours. *The Statesman Weekly*, January 12, 1985.
12. Rajiv defined the contours of his forthcoming visit to Moscow at a party meeting on May 4, declaring that it was "to renew our bonds of friendship and I look forward to increasing cooperation with the Soviet Union, to make personal contact with the new Soviet leaders and establishing a long friendship for the future". He said India's relations with the Soviet Union had always been strong, warm and friendly and "we want to make them even stronger". *The Statesman Weekly*, May 11, 1985. A nine-point joint communiqué at the end of the Rajiv visit suggested that Indo-Soviet friendship and cooperation were developing "dynamically" on a planned basis and were being "constantly enriched with new form and content". *Ibid.*, June 1, 1985. More soberly, *Pravda* of May 26 described Rajiv's visit as "a considerable event in the international life of these days." Rajiv himself said on his return to New Delhi that the visit had been "very successful". *The Statesman Weekly*, June 1, 1985.

Narasimha Rao, now Defence Minister in the Rajiv Government, concluded a twice postponed visit to Moscow in April. At a luncheon given by Defence Minister Marshal Sergei Sokolov, Rao expressed appreciation of Soviet understanding of India's efforts to bring about greater cooperation in the South Asian region even as it built its defences to meet legitimate needs. *Ibid.*, April 6, 1985. The discussions apparently centred on the acquisition and manufacture of T-80 main battle tanks, three configurations of MIGs—27, 29, and 31—and MI-24 helicopter gunships as well as long-range surface-to-surface missiles and a fleet of 21 naval vessels. India was said to have been offered "exceptionally cheap credit terms, with rupee payments staggered over two decades". *Ibid.*, May 25, 1985.
13. *The Statesman Weekly*, June 1, 1985.
14. *Ibid.*, May 25, 1985.
15. On his return from Moscow on May 26, Rajiv said there were certain problems regarding safeguards on the offer of nuclear power plants. *Ibid.*, June 1, 1985.
16. President Zia, who came to New Delhi in November, said later that he was "more than satisfied" with his recent meeting with Rajiv, declaring: "I am very optimistic about Indo-Pak relations now that there is a much younger leadership". Zia's optimism was belied by Rajiv's address to Air Force commanders in New Delhi in November expressing fears about U.S. weapons for Pakistan being used against India. At the same time Indian press reports were suggesting that New Delhi was undertaking an in-depth review of relations with Pakistan in the context of foolproof evidence of Islamabad's "direct involvement and connivance" in permitting Sikhs from Western countries to indulge in anti-Indian activities on Pakistani soil. *The Statesman Weekly*, November 24, 1984. Union Home Secretary M.M.K. Vali made the first specific official accusation in Srinagar on October 4 that the Government had evidence of Pakistan's involvement in the Punjab trouble. Later, Indian officials were declaring that

there was enough evidence to suggest that Sikh terrorists were being trained at specific locations across the border; absconders trying to sneak into Pakistan had been apprehended on the border. *India Today*, November 15, 1984. In January, Rajiv was repeating his mother's line: "Since the arms that Pakistan was acquiring were not the sort that could be trained on Afghanistan, who else but India was the target?" *The Statesman Weekly*, January 12, 1985. In March, Zia was injecting his interpretation of Indo-U.S. relations. He told *Jang* newspaper that the U.S. admitted that India was wholly going towards the Soviet Union. This was deplorable for the Americans because they had interest in India because of its huge position in the subcontinent. The Americans, the President said, suggested at the same time that it was not an easy thing to turn India away from Russia. *Ibid.*, March 16, 1985. In an interview with *The Financial Times*, published on April 4, Rajiv said the U.S. had let down India a number of times and was now arming Pakistan and allowing it to develop a nuclear bomb. He underlined India's "strong friendship" with the Soviet Union, which had "stood by us in times of need". In the Upper House on May 3, Rajiv said India was taking fresh initiatives to improve relations with neighbours, but "Pakistan is still a problem". On Rajiv's change of tone on Pakistan, *The Statesman* commented: "The prospect of stabilizing relations, which seemed relatively bright recently, has again receded into the distance". *The Statesman Weekly*, May 11, 1985.

17. On June 18 Sri Lankan National Security Minister Lalith Athulathumudali announced cessation of hostilities in agreement with the five main opposition Tamil groups. *The Statesman Weekly*, June 22, 1985.

18. A two-day meeting of South Asian Foreign Ministers ended in Thimpu on May 14 after unanimous adoption of a charter on the future institutional set-up for SARC, to be launched at the first summit to be held in Dhaka on December 7 and 8. Sri Lanka had earlier expressed reservations, but now agreed in principle to converting SARC into a South Asian Association for Regional Cooperation and establishment of a Council of Foreign Ministers to meet once a year. At Sri Lanka's instance, it was agreed that the Council's functions and modalities required further consultations. The charter authorizes the Council of Ministers to consider, at an appropriate time, the question of setting up a secretariat. Official sources said the charter pledges the SARC countries to abjuration of force, non-interference and strict adherence to the principles of the U.N. Charter and nonalignment. In a joint communiqué, the Foreign Ministers reiterated their firm commitment to the process of regional cooperation and expressed optimism about the Dhaka summit. *The Statesman Weekly*, May 18, 1985.

19. Rajiv said in answer to a question: "It is difficult to forget and forgive one hundred percent. Let us say that it is 95 percent forgotten and forgiven..." *Le Monde*, June 4, 1985. Indian newspapers reported the delivery of the first batch of Mirage-2000 in February. *The Statesman Weekly*, February 9, 1985.

20. Rajiv told the joint session of Congress to prolonged applause: "We stand for a political settlement in Afghanistan that ensures sovereignty, integrity, independence and nonaligned status, and enables the refugees to return to their homes in safety and honour". *The Statesman Weekly*, June 25, 1985.

21. U.S. Deputy Assistant Secretary for Defence, Major-General Kenneth D. Burns, told the House of Representatives subcommittee on South Asia on February 28, 1985: "India has a major arms supply relationship with the Soviet Union, has

sealed some prominent transactions in Europe and benefits from the productions of its extensive defence industries. In this regard, I wish to stress that we are prepared to give serious consideration to requests which India may wish to make for U.S. military and dual-use equipment". *The Statesman Weekly*, March 9, 1985. Discussions Rajiv had with U.S. officials in Washington, including Defence Secretary Caspar Weinberger, concerned possible U.S. arms sales to India. He told reporters that India had "certain reservations" about an arms relationship with the U.S., which would require further discussions. It was not acceptable to India that the U.S. could change its rules retrospectively in respect of defence deals. *Ibid.*, June 25, 1985.

22. Rajiv told a party meeting on May 4 that the Government was considering "action to be taken" by India in view of Pakistan developing nuclear weapons. "We are looking into various aspects of this development and what action we should take". Defence Minister Narasimha Rao told Parliament the same day that the Prime Minister's remarks should not be interpreted to mean that there would be a review of India's nuclear policy. *The Statesman Weekly*, May 11, 1985. According to the Indian Defence Ministry's report for 1984-85, "Pakistan's relentless pursuit of nuclear weapons capability, with the assistance and connivance of certain countries, had added a new dimension to our security environment". *Ibid.*, May 18, 1985. In August 1984, Mrs. Gandhi had declared: "India will not deviate from its peaceful nuclear policy no matter what Pakistan does", adding that the nuclear issue could not be "viewed at the micro level". *India Today*, May 31, 1985. In an interview with *The Los Angeles Times*, published on February 22, 1985, Rajiv volunteered that "...at the moment I don't see a situation arising when we would start up again making the bomb. Just the fact that Pakistan made a bomb would not make us change our policy".

A major Indian concern has been the possibility of Pakistan acquiring the Hawkeye airborne early-warning radar surveillance plane. According to Stuart Auerbach of *The Washington Post*, "the Reagan Administration told New Delhi that the best way to keep Hawkeyes out of Pakistan's hands was to persuade the Soviet Union to ease its troops' pressure on the Pakistan-Afghan border and to stop its jets from attacking Pakistani border villages". *International Herald Tribune*, June 17, 1985.

23. *Newsweek International*, June 24, 1985. Henry Kissinger placed his finger on a central area of Indo-U.S. discord. In an interview with *India Today* during a visit to New Delhi in February, he said in answer to a question: "I attempted to treat India as a leading country and a central point of South Asian policies.... Then the question is, what does one mean by central role and how does one articulate it, and does that mean one can do nothing without the permission of India? I would say we should do nothing without discussing with India, but I don't think we should give any country the veto power over our foreign policy in any part of the world". *India Today*, February 28, 1985.

24. Xinhua had praised Rajiv after he had taken over, noting that he had expressed the hope that Sino-Indian relations would be restored to the level of the early 1950's. *The Statesman Weekly*, November 17, 1984. Addressing his parliamentary party on the eve of the new Parliament's session in January, Rajiv said he was happy some headway had been made in talks with China, "but the way is long". *The Statesman Weekly*, January 19, 1985. Addressing army

commanders in New Delhi on April 24, Rajiv disclosed that efforts to resolve the border issue with China had yet to make substantial progress. He honed in on the border problem yet again by telling the Upper House on May 3: "We want to improve our relations to earlier levels. But the resolution of the boundary question was central to India's relations with China and this problem cannot be forgotten." *Ibid.*, May 11, 1985. After Rajiv's three-hour summit talks with Gorbachev in Moscow on May 21, the Indian press reported that the two leaders agreed that it was important to improve relations with China and that it was necessary to keep on trying. *Ibid.*, May 25, 1985.

25. According to *The Statesman*, "Until 1977, the Kremlin's foreign policy appeared totally to determine the CPI's stand. But that has not been the case since, and the CPI and CPI(M) have been working together on many fronts despite Moscow's enthusiastic approval of the regime in New Delhi. The invitation to Moscow, therefore, marks a substantial victory for the CPI(M) which has always been critical of effective Soviet support for Mrs. Gandhi". *The Statesman Weekly*, May 11, 1985. After the Congress(I)'s record-breaking victory in the parliamentary elections, CPI General Secretary Rajeswara Rao said in a statement on December 31, 1984 that his party would support every positive step of the new Government in the interest of the unity and integrity of the country as also measures towards the welfare of the people. But he added that the CPI would play the role of the Left opposition and fight against the "anti-people, pro-vested interests and anti-democratic policies of the Government". *Ibid.*, January 5, 1985.

INDEX

Abdullah, Sheikh, 5, 13
Adhikari, G., 45
Afghanistan,
  coup, 148
  Soviet invasion, 150
  treaty with S.U., 151
  refugees, 162
  and U.N., 196, 213
AICP, 174
Aid India Consortium, 18, 124
Akali Dal, 206-7
Akram, A.I., 217
Aksai Chin, 12-13, 23-24, 27, 34
Al Zulfiqar, 175
Albania, 27, 31
Alliluyeva, Svetlana, 267-68n
Alva, Margaret, 139, 142
Amel'ko, Admiral, 107
Amin, Hafizullah, 153-54, 162
Andropov, Yuri, 190, 194-95, 197, 217, 234-35
Arkhipov, 166, 201, 203-4, 219
Asian Collective Security, 76-79, 98, 100-101, 151, 158, 226, 232, 246-47
Assam agitation, 206
Azad, A.K., 16

Bahuguna, H.N., 145
Bajpai, G.S., 12
Bandaranaike, Sirimavo, 31
Bandung Conference, 10
Bangladesh, 96-97
  China's veto, 100
  agreement on POW's, 117
  Soviet assistance, 119
  Chinese recognition, 131
Basu, Jyoti, 221, 223

Bhabha, Homi, 48
Bhagat, B.R., 68
Bhandari, Romesh, 247
Bhilai, 14
Bhindranwale, Jarnail Singh, 206-7, 220-21
Bhutto, Benazir, 175, 207, 216
Bhutto, Nusrut, 175, 207
Bhutto, Z.A., 46, 49, 76-77, 92, 105, 132, 139, 141, 146
  and Tashkent, 52-53
  and East Pakistan, 81
  as President, 100
  and POWs, 106
  and Mrs. Gandhi, 106
  and Kashmir, 107
  and SEATO, 117
  and Bangladesh's recognition, 118
  and nuclear bomb, 125-26
  coup against, 133
Blood, Archer, 153
Boidevaix, Serge, 245
Bolley, Alain, 245
Bowles, Chester, 38
Brandt, Willy, 120
Brezhnev, Leonid, 31, 59, 76-78, 97, 173-74, 190-91, 194
  visits to India, 101-2, 168-69
  and nonalignment, 121
Brown, Harold, 155-56
Brzezinski, Zbigniew, 138, 154
Bulganin, Nikolai, 14
Bush, George, 95, 222

Caroe, Olaf, 97
Carrington, Lord, 290n
Carter, Jimmy, 138, 147, 162

and Brezhnev, 148
and Afghanistan, 154-55
and Zia-ul-Haq, 164
CENTO, 9, 109, 139, 149
Chatterjee, A.K., 147
Chaudhuri, J.N., 49, 51
Chauhan, Jagjit Singh, 221
Chavan, Y.B., 112
Chen Yi, 50
Chernenko, Konstantin, 217, 245
China,
  and India, 10
  change, 23
  and Tibet, 23-24
  border incidents, 27
  three-point proposal, 30
  and Pakistan, 32-33
  nuclear bomb, 42
  attack on Shastri, 47
  and 1965 war, 51
  arms to Pakistan, 53
  border subversion, 58
  support to Pakistan, 92
  and Bangladesh, 102-3
  and Japan, 144
  and Vietnam, 144
  and Afghanistan, 152
  and Asian Games, 191-92
Clifford, Clark, 109
Cominform, 3, 15
Commonwealth, British, 4
Congress Party, 1, 6
  Avadi session, 17
  Kamaraj plan, 42
  Bangalore session, 69
  and CPI, 70
  split, 70, 141
  Calcutta plenary, 219
Cordovez, Diego, 196, 214
CPI, 142, 145, 173, 187-88, 249
  split, 55
  and Mrs. Gandhi, 57
  support for Emergency, 129
  loss in 1977 elections, 134
CPI(M), 55, 60, 84, 142, 187, 249
  and China, 6, 210
  fall of government, 70
Cuban crisis, 27

Dalai Lama, 23-24, 144, 209-10
  and Morarji Desai, 140
Dange, S.A., 60, 188-89
  and AICP, 174
Daoud, Mohammad, 122
Dayan, Moshe, 283n
De Cuellar, Perez, 196
De Gaulle, Charles, 258n
Delhi riots, 243
Deng Xiaoping, 122, 144-45, 191
Desai, Morarji, 18, 42-43, 56, 61, 143
  as Prime Minister, 135-36
  and Carter, 138
  nuclear policy, 138-39
  and Pakistan, 139
  and Zia-ul-Haq, 139-40
  and China, 140
  and Dalai Lama, 140
D'Estaing, Giscard, 160-61
Dhar, D.P., 67, 71-72, 88, 94, 101, 113, 115
Diego Garcia, 109, 148, 155, 166
DMK, 89
Dobrynin, A.F., 90
Dubs, Adolph, 153
Dulles, John Foster, 9, 18, 20
Durand Line, 164
Dutt, S., 23, 29

East Pakistan, 83
  refugees, 90-91
Egypt, 95
Eisenhower, Dwight, D., 9
Ershad, F.M., 179

F-16s, 164, 176-78, 184-85
Farakka barrage, 22, 128, 139
FICCI, 235
Firyubin, Nikolai, 68, 94, 177
Ford, Gerald R., 115
FSU, 174

Gandhi, Indira, 43, 142, 149, 163, 169-70, 173-74, 194-95, 210-11, 217, 243
  first visit to Soviet Union, 8
  and Kosygin, 45
  as Prime Minister, 56
  and World Bank, 57

Index

and Vietnam, 58, 115
and China, 62
and CPI, 70, 114, 188-89, 201
and East Pakistan, 84-86
in Moscow, 93, 191
and Nixon, 93
and Z.A. Bhutto, 106
and Shah of Iran, 116-17
prosecution against, 140-41
and Afghanistan, 158, 181
and Reagan, 183-84
Gandhi, Mahatma, 1
Soviet view of, 4
Gandhi, Rajiv, 173, 200-201, 243-44
election triumph, 244
and Punjab problem, 245
in Moscow, 245-47
and Zia-ul-Haq, 247
and Sri Lanka, 247
and France, 248
and Reagan, 248
and Afghanistan, 248
and China, 249
Gandhi, Sanjay, 130, 133
prosecution against, 140-41, 149, 173
Ghosh, Ajoy, 258-59n, 263n
Ghosh, Atulya, 60-61
Giri, V.V., 70, 82
Gorbachev, Mikhail, 246-47
Gorshkov, Sergei, 108
Grechko, Andrei, 82
Gromyko, Andrei, 73, 78, 88, 90, 135-36, 153, 165-66, 182, 191
Gwadar, 82, 118

Haig, Alexander, 180
Haksar, P.N., 72
Harriman, Everell, 258n
Heng Samrin, 146
Indian recognition, 171
Ho Chi Minh, 19, 72
Hu Yaobang, 190, 210
Hua Guofeng, 171
Huang Hua, 170-71, 190, 211
Hungary, 16
Husain, Zakir, 65, 67
Hyder, Sajjad, 216

IMF, 183, 220
India
and Chinese maps, 12-13
incidents with China, 27
debacle, 27-28
army, 28-29
superpower guarantee, 48-49
1965 war, 51
defence build-up, 54
anti-Soviet feelings, 67
NPT, 75
and Vietnam, 89
and *Enterprise*, 96
recognition of Hanoi, 100
new weapons, 111-12
nuclear explosion, 123
thaw with China, 132, 170-71
rouble rate, 136
and Afghanistan, 150-52
border talks, 172
trade with Soviet Union, 201-4
and U.S. arms, 212-13
and space, 224
Indian Ocean, 38, 96, 107-8, 110, 137, 147, 148-49, 157-58, 199-200, 222, 228
Indo-Soviet Treaty, 67, 71-72, 87-89, 97-98, 135, 137, 182
Indonesia,
and nuclear bomb, 39
coup attempt, 39
ISCUS, 174
Islamic Conference, 162-63, 166

Jaguar deal, 146
Janata, 140, 149
Jana Sangh, 60, 66, 114
Japanese Peace Treaty, 10
Jaruzelski, Wojciech, 245
Jayawardene, J.R., 207, 247
Jha, L.K., 88, 94
Jinnah, M.A., 1, 9
Johnson, Lyndon, B., 48, 56

Kachchativu island, 128
Kalimpong, 24
Kamaraj, K., 43, 55, 60-61
and Kamaraj Plan, 42

Index

Karmal, Babrak, 154, 177
Kashmir,
  tribal invasion, 5
  and U.N., 7
  early Soviet attitude, 13-14
  talks with Pakistan, 32
  Shanghai communiqué, 99
Kaul, T.N., 4, 13, 44-45, 67, 70, 87, 90, 97-98, 124
Kennedy, J.F.,
  and India, 21
  and Pakistan, 32
Kerala,
  Communist victory, 20
Khan, A.Q., 211-12
Khan, Ayub, 48-49, 67, 80-81
  overture to Moscow, 46-47
  and 1965 war, 52
  and foreign policy, 63-64
Khan, Liaquat Ali, 9, 22
Khan, Nur, 64, 78
Khan, Tikka, 105
Khan, Wali, 143, 161-62
Khan, Yahya, 77, 81-82, 85, 88, 91, 94, 105
Khan, Yakub, 214-15
Khomeini, Ayatollah, 287n
Khrushchev, Nikita, 13
  and Kashmir, 14
  and Goa, 14
  Twentieth Congress, 15
  Camp David, 26
  fall, 42
Kissinger, Henry, 86-87, 90, 93-95, 121, 176
  secret visit to China, 88
  visit to India, 115
  and Pakistan bomb, 126-27
Kohl, Helmut, 197
Kollantai, Madame, 4
Korea, 8
Kosygin, Alexei, 44-45, 57, 66-67, 70-71, 145-46
  and 1965 war, 53
  in Pakistan, 65
  in India, 65
  and regional economic plan, 76

Lall, K.B., 101
Lee Kuan Yew, 75
Li Xiannian, 143-44
Lin Biao, 92
Liu Shaoqi, 53
Longju incident, 24

Macmillan, Harold, 29
Malenkov, Georgi, 8
Mao Hong, 211
Mao Zedong, 10, 122
  Hundred Flowers, 26, 37
  "Mao smile", 80
Massoud, Ahmad, Shah, 213
McMahon Line, 26, 30
McNamara, Robert, 109
MEDO, 9
Mendes-France, Pierre, 19
Menon, K.P.S., 4, 97
  and Khrushchev, 26
Menon, Krishna, 16, 19, 187
  and Moscow, 29-30
  and debacle, 30
Mikoyan, Anastas, 39
Mirage-2000, 161, 184-85, 192-93
Mishra, Brajesh, 124-25, 160
Mishra, S.N., 150
Mitterrand, Francois, 161
Mizos, 80
Moutbatten, Lord, 2, 4, 5
Mustaque Ahmed, Khondakar, 91, 131

Nagas, 79
Namboodiripad, E.M.S., 62, 210
Nanda, Gulzari Lal, 46
Narayan, Jayaprakash, 13, 114, 128
Nasser, President, 14
  and Suez, 15
Naxalbari, 61
Naxalites, 79
Nehru, B.K., 38
Nehru, Jawaharlal,
  interim government, 2-3
  Pan-Asianism, 6
  first visit to S.U., 6
  and West, 7
  1955 visit to S.U., 13

Index

and disarmament, 15
and Suez, 16
and Hungary, 16
and planning, 17
visit to Hanoi, 19
and U.S., 20
and Pakistan, 21
and Zhou Enlai, 26
and Parliament, 33, 35
achievements, 40-41
Nehru, Motilal,
Soviet view of, 4
Nepal,
"zone of peace", 139
and Janata, 139
Nitze, Paul H., 175
Nixon, Richard, 72
and East Pakistan, 86
and Gromyko, 90
and India, 99
and China, 99
Nonalignment,
first summit, 15
Colombo proposals, 31
"genuine nonalignment", 135
Havana summit, 150
New Delhi Foreign Ministers' meeting, 177
New Delhi summit, 199-200
No-War Pact, 21-22
and "friendship treaty", 181
NPT, 125, 139

Pakistan,
and U.S. arms, 9
attitude to India, 10
and Zhou, 11
enmity towards India, 63
and Asian Collective Security, 78
crackdown on East Pakistan, 83
and China, 104
and arms deal, 177
and MRD, 207
and Sikhs' agitation, 208
and nuclear bomb, 208-9, 211-12
Pandit, Vijayalakshmi, 4
Panikkar, K.M., 11

Pant, G.B., 256n
Parthasarathi, G., 88, 191
Patel, Vallabh Bhai, 11
Patil, S.K., 61, 66
Pavlovsky, Gen., 153
P'eng Teh-huai, 37
Punjab agitation, 206-7, 220
Army operation, 221, 248-49

Radcliffe, Cyril, 2, 48
Radhakrishnan, S., 13, 33
Rahman, Mujibur, 81, 102, 105, 131
and POWs, 106
visit to Pakistan, 117
Rajagopalachari, C., 89
Ramamurti, P., 183
Ram, Jagjivan, 116, 123, 133, 140
Ranadive, B.T., 7, 55
Rann of Kutch, 48
Rao, Narasimha, 160, 166-67, 178, 182, 191, 211, 218
Rao, Rajeswara, 187, 189, 234
Rau, B.N., 13
RCD, 46
Reagan, Ronald, 175, 197-98
in China, 219
Reddy, Sanjiva, 69-70, 167-68
Roosevelt, Franklin D., 5
Roy, M.N., 8

Sadat, President, 121
SARC, 178-79, 247
Sathe, R.D., 150, 163
SEATO, 33, 46, 109
Sethna, H.N., 125
Shahi, Agha, 153, 163, 166, 178, 181
Shastri, Lal Bahadur, 42
as Prime Minister, 43-44
visit to Moscow, 49
and Kashmir, 52
and Tashkent, 53-55
Shevardnadze, E.A., 187
Shultz, George, 127, 213, 223
Sihanouk, Norodom, 199
Sikkim, 51, 128
Simla Agreement, 106-07
Singh, Charan, 89

as Prime Minister, 150
and nuclear policy, 150-51
Singh, Dinesh, 69, 72-74, 79, 98
Singh, Kewal, 66
Singh, Swaran, 73-74, 82, 87, 114-15, 163
Singh, Zail, 161, 221
Soekarno, President, 15
  loss of power, 39
Soviet Union,
  and Kashmir, 16
  aid to India, 17-18
  and China, 25
  arms to India, 29
  polemics with China, 36
  attack on Morarji Desai, 45-46
  shift on Kashmir, 46
  and Rann of Kutch, 49
  and 1965 war, 50
  verbal attacks on India, 57
  aid to Pakistan, 64
  trade with India, 65-66
  arms to Pakistan, 66
  and maps, 71, 102
  and radio broadcasts on India, 71
  and East Pakistan, 85
  and Bangladesh, 102
  and Mrs. Gandhi's defeat, 134
  and Punjab agitation, 221
Spy scandal, 245, 248
Sri Lanka,
  and Tamil problem, 207, 246-47
Stalin, 15
Subramaniam, C., 186

Tabeev, Fikrat A., 153
Taraki, Noor Mohammed, 153
Tarapur, 138, 161
Tashkent conference, 52-53
Thant, U, 91
Tibet, 10-11, 131
Tito, President, 14, 150

United Nations,
  and Kashmir, 5, 21
  and 1965 war, 51
  and 1971 war, 95
U.S.A.,
  and Indus Waters, 18
  and PL 480, 18
  aid to India, 19
  arms to Pakistan, 20
  arms to India, 30
  and East Pakistan, 86
  nuclear cooperation with China, 211
Ussuri clashes, 83
Ustinov, Dmitri, 218

Vajpayee, A.B., 89, 135
  as Foreign Minister, 135-36, 140, 143
  in Kabul, 139
  in China, 144-45
Vance, Cyrus, 138, 155
Venkataraman, R., 112, 192, 212
Vietnam, 56
  and China, 144
  in Comecon, 144
  treaty with Moscow, 144
Vorontsov, Yuri, 150, 174

Waldheim, Kurt, 163, 177
Warsaw Treaty, 27
Wilson, Harold, 48
  and Kashmir, 50
Wu Xueqian, 209

Xu Xiang Qien, 156

Yao Yilin, 210
Yugoslavia, 31, 95

Zhao Ziyang, 171-72, 195
Zhdanov, Andrei, 3
Zhou Enlai, 8
  and Bandung, 11
  and Nehru, 26, 36
  and Kashmir, 90
  and Mrs. Gandhi, 91
Zhukov, E., 3
Zia-ul-Haq, 133, 163, 195-96, 217
  and Morarji Desai, 139-40
  and China, 143
  nuclear policy, 149
  and Afghan refugees, 152
  and Carter, 162
  in the U.S., 164
  and Rajiv, 247
Ziaur Rahman, 141, 178-79
  in China, 147
Zumwalt, Elmo, 96
Zuyenko, Sergei, 119

LIBRARY OF DAVIDSON COLLEGE

Books on regular loan may be checked out for **two weeks**. Books must be presented at the Circulation Desk in order to be renewed.

A fine is charged after date due.

Special books are subject to special regulations at the discretion of the library staff.

OCT 1 9 '90				
JAN 0 8 1992				